Multilingual FrameNets in Computational Lexicography

Trends in Linguistics
Studies and Monographs 200

Editors

Walter Bisang
(main editor for this volume)
Hans Henrich Hock
Werner Winter

Mouton de Gruyter
Berlin · New York

Multilingual FrameNets in Computational Lexicography

Methods and Applications

edited by

Hans C. Boas

Mouton de Gruyter
Berlin · New York

Mouton de Gruyter (formerly Mouton, The Hague)
is a Division of Walter de Gruyter GmbH & Co. KG, Berlin.

♾ Printed on acid-free paper which falls within the guidelines
of the ANSI to ensure permanence and durability.

Library of Congress Cataloging-in-Publication Data

Multilingual FrameNets in computational lexicography : methods and applications / edited by Hans C. Boas.
p. cm. – (Trends in linguistics. Studies and monographs ; 200)
Includes bibliographical references and index.
ISBN 978-3-11-021296-9 (hardcover : alk. paper)
1. Lexicography – Data processing. 2. Semantics, Comparative.
I. Boas, Hans Christian, 1971–
P327.5.D37M856 2009
413'.0285–dc22
2009020625

ISBN 978-3-11-021296-9

ISSN 1861-4302

Bibliographic information published by the Deutsche Nationalbibliothek

The Deutsche Nationalbibliothek lists this publication in the Deutsche Nationalbibliografie; detailed bibliographic data are available in the Internet at http://dnb.d-nb.de.

Cover design: Christopher Schneider, Laufen.
Typesetting: RoyalStandard, Hong Kong.
Printed in Germany.

For Chuck Fillmore,
whose keen insight and dedication
continue to inspire developers of FrameNet lexical resources
for languages around the world

Acknowledgments

I am indebted to a number of people without whom this volume would not exist. Charles Fillmore, Collin Baker, Miriam Petruck, Josef Ruppenhofer, Michael Ellsworth, and the many other colleagues and friends at FrameNet and at the International Computer Science Institute (ICSI) in Berkeley were a great inspiration. Their advice, recommendations, and suggestions have been much appreciated. An enormous debt is owed to Charles Fillmore for his wisdom, enthusiasm, patience, and constant encouragement. His insights have influenced my thinking about language in innumerable ways. Thank you Chuck!

I am grateful to the *Deutscher Akademischer Austauschdienst (DAAD)* ('German Academic Exchange Service') which awarded me a one-year long postdoctoral fellowship to work with the FrameNet project at ICSI from 2000–2001. During this year I became interested in applying English FrameNet frames to the description and analysis of other languages, specifically German and Spanish. Over the past ten years, FrameNet received most of its funding from the National Science Foundation through a number of grants (most notably IRI #9618838, March 1997–February 2000, "Tools for lexicon-building"; then under grant ITR/HCI #0086132, September 2000–August 2003, entitled "FrameNet++: An On-Line Lexical Semantic Resource and its Application to Speech and Language Technology"). I want to thank the National Science Foundation for supporting FrameNet over the years and hope that the funding will continue in years to come.

I want to thank Birgit Sievert and Wolfgang Konwitschny for their guidance at Mouton de Gruyter and for seeing this volume through to publication. I also want to thank the authors and the publishers who allowed me to reuse their papers. Specifically, I would like to thank Oxford University Press for allowing me to re-use the papers by Fontenelle (2000) and Boas (2005), which originally appeared in the *International Journal of Lexicography*. A special thanks goes to the people who provided feedback on the manuscript: The series editors of TiLSM (Trends in Linguistics. Studies and Monographs) Walter Bisang, Hans Henrich Hock, and Werner Winter; My colleagues and friends Sue Atkins, Collin Baker, Jason Baldridge, Hans Ulrich Boas, Inge De Bleecker, Michael Ellsworth, Katrin Erk, Raphael Feider, Charles Fillmore, Thierry Fontenelle, Seizi

Iwata, Russell Lee-Goldman, Alexis Palmer, Miriam Petruck, Marc Pierce, Elias Ponvert, Josef Ruppenhofer, Louise Swanepoel, and Jana Thompson.

Finally, I want to thank my wife Claire and our daughter Lena for their love, patience, and support. My parents Hans Ulrich and Ursula Boas have also been a constant source of support.

Austin, Texas; May 2009
HCB

Contents

1. Recent trends in multilingual computational lexicography

Hans C. Boas

1. Introduction

Computational lexicography encompasses the computational methods and tools designed to assist in various lexicographical tasks, including the preparation of lexicographical evidence from many sources, the recording in database form of the relevant linguistic information, the editing of lexicographical entries, and the dissemination of lexicographical products (see Atkins and Zampolli 1994).[1] One of the results of computational lexicography is a dramatic enhancement of Natural Language Processing (NLP) systems through richer machine-readable dictionaries (Boguraev and Briscoe 1989). One early example is the machine-readable version of the Longman Dictionary of Contemporary English (henceforth: LDOCE; Procter 1978), which turned out to be particularly useful for NLP research because it offered detailed subcategorizations of major word classes (see Amsler 1980, Michiels 1982, Ooi 1998, and Fontenelle 2008).

While the emergence of machine-readable dictionaries (MRDs) also facilitated the conception, compilation, and updating of dictionaries for human consumption (Makkai 1980, McNaught 1988), many of the traditional problems of lexicography remained. For example, Atkins (1993: 38) points out that "most machine-readable dictionaries were person-readable dictionaries first." As such, MRDs are often troubled by a variety of problems: omission of explicit statements of essential linguistic facts (Atkins, Kegl, and Levin 1986), unsystematic compiling of one single dictionary, ambiguities within entries, and incompatible compiling across dictionaries (Atkins and Levin 1991). Such problems – as well as new insights – lead lexicographers to revise and restructure MRDs, as, for example, has been

1. For an overview of theoretical and practical aspects of lexicography, see Zgusta (1971), Landau (1989), Béjoint (1994/2001), Svensen (1993), Green (1996), Hartmann and James (1998), Benson (2001), and Fontenelle (2008).

done with the second edition of the LDOCE (Summers 1987) to facilitate its access and use. Despite these issues, MRDs became more widespread during the 1980s, both for human consumption and for machine use. Among the dictionaries made available in machine-readable form were the Collins English Dictionary (1986), the Webster's New World Dictionary (1988), the Oxford Advanced Learner's Dictionary (1989), and the Collins Cobuild English Language Dictionary (1987). Moreover, machine-readable versions of bilingual dictionaries were developed by several publishers, such as the Collins-Robert English-French dictionary (Atkins and Duval 1978). In subsequent years, computational linguists became increasingly interested in developing multilingual lexical resources for a variety of NLP applications, such as machine translation and information extraction.

In this chapter I trace the development of multilingual computational lexicography by covering the period that stretches from the early years to the start of the 21st century. First, I offer a brief account of early machine-readable multilingual lexical resources. In providing this outline, I do not address the many issues raised by theoretical linguistics about the design of mono- and multilingual computational lexical resources (for an overview, see, among others, Atkins and Zampolli 1994, Fontenelle 1997, Heid 1997/2006, Ooi 1998, Calzolari et al. 2001, and Altenberg and Granger 2002). Then, I briefly discuss a number of research initiatives of the 1980s and 1990s that aimed at developing more comprehensive multilingual lexical databases with more semantic information. In this connection, I touch on the increased use of electronic corpora and different theoretical approaches underlying the design of these resources. I next provide an overview of the workflow and design of the FrameNet project, whose outcome, the FrameNet lexical resource for English, forms the basis for the multilingual FrameNets discussed in this volume. Finally, I discuss the development of FrameNets for other languages and compare their design, methods, workflow, tools, and resources used to develop them.

2. The emergence of multilingual lexical databases

The first systematic efforts to produce multilingual MRDs date back to the beginnings of machine translation (MT) in the 1940s when words were organized in lists according to alphabetical order. The source language words were encoded on one side and the target language words on the other side of the lists (see Papegaaij et al. 1986, Ooi 1998). However, this approach proved to be unsuccessful because the translation of words in combination with word-order rules of the target language could not effectively deal with lexical ambiguity. The ensuing range of translations of each potential interpretation of each word resulted in what Ramsay (1991: 30) characterizes as "the generation of text which contained so many options that it was virtually meaningless."

These early exercises in developing MRDs for MT demonstrated the prevalence of the "lexical acquisition bottleneck." To develop large-scale lexical resources for multilingual NLP applications, there were in principle two different approaches: (1) re-using existing resources, or (2) building MRDs from scratch with the help of teams of trained lexicographers. Over the next decades, several efforts were aimed at creating more sophisticated MRDs using these two methodologies. In what follows, I present a brief overview of a select number of these efforts to set up the context for our discussion of the design of multi-lingual FrameNets in sections 4–5.

During the 1950s and 1960s, MRDs became more structured, partially due to the development of more sophisticated syntactic parsing techniques and the newly emerging designs of MT systems that made principled distinctions between linguistic rules, the grammar, and the lexicon (Lehmann 1998). One system that employed such a design was the METAL translation system developed by the Linguistics Research Center at the University of Texas at Austin beginning in the 1960s, whose development continued (with various modifications) until the 1990s (see Slocum 2006). To produce German-to-English translations, the system relied on monolingual dictionaries for English and German that were largely created from scratch, each containing about 10,000 entries. The entries in the METAL dictionary were indexed by canonical form (the usual spelling one finds in a printed dictionary) (Bennett and Slocum 1985). For the input of lexical entries, a lexical default program was developed that allowed the lexicographers to specify only minimal information about a particular entry such as root form and lexical category. The program then heuristically encoded most of the remaining necessary features and values. The METAL lexicon included detailed morpho-syntactic information about part of speech, inflectional class, gender, number, mass vs. count noun, and gradation. With respect to syntax, the lexicon specified the subcategorization frame and the types of auxiliaries. On the semantic side, the METAL lexicon provided only minimal information, namely about the semantic type and the domain (Calzolari et al. 2001: 108–109). The resulting MRD was somewhat limited in scope – it was originally developed for technical translations from German to English – but its minimal entry structure was consistent and provided the types of information needed for the task at hand.

Starting in the early 1980s, the European Community funded a number of multi-lingual NLP projects that relied on MRDs. For instance, the EUROTRA project (Johnson et al. 1985) was aimed at developing a state-of-the-art transfer based MT system for the seven, later nine, official languages of the European Community in order to reduce the amount of time and money spent on the manual translation of documents. In contrast to the older SYSTRAN MT system, which relied heavily on lexical information and only involved minor support for rearranging word order (Gerber and Yang 1997), dictionaries generally played a secondary role in EUROTRA, while grammatical modules were accorded primacy (Alberto and Bennett 1995, Johnson et al. 2003). To keep transfer between languages as simple as possible, operations were reduced to a minimum. In the lexicon, this meant that sense distinctions were identified during the monolingual analysis, while the bilingual resources made use of sense distinctions to relate two lexical entries as translational equivalents. To distinguish different senses, EUROTRA primarily relied on information about argument structure differences, semantic typing of heads, and semantic typing of arguments (see Calzolari et al. 2001: 93). In the following section I discuss various projects that incorporated significantly more semantic information in their multilingual lexical databases than those reviewed above.

3. The focus on semantic information in multilingual lexical databases

During the 1990s, the European Commission explored ways to construct multilingual lexical knowledge bases from machine-readable versions of conventional dictionaries to increase the amount of lexical detail available for multilingual NLP applications at a reasonable cost. To this end, the Research Programs formulated by the Commission made funds available for the ACQUILEX project (Calzolari and Briscoe 1995), which extracted lexical information from multiple MRDs in a multilingual context for English, Dutch, Italian, and Spanish. The goal was the creation of a unique integrated multilingual lexical knowledge base that was maximally re-usable and that was rooted in a common conceptual/semantic structure (Calzolari 1991). This structure was then linked to individual word senses of the languages and was intended to be rich enough to allow for a deep processing model of language (Zampolli 1994). In addition, for each word sense the lexical knowledge base (LKB) contained phonological, morphological, syntactic, and semantic/pragmatic information capable of deployment in the lexical components of a wide variety of practical NLP systems. Figure 1 illustrates the structure of an entry in the LKB.

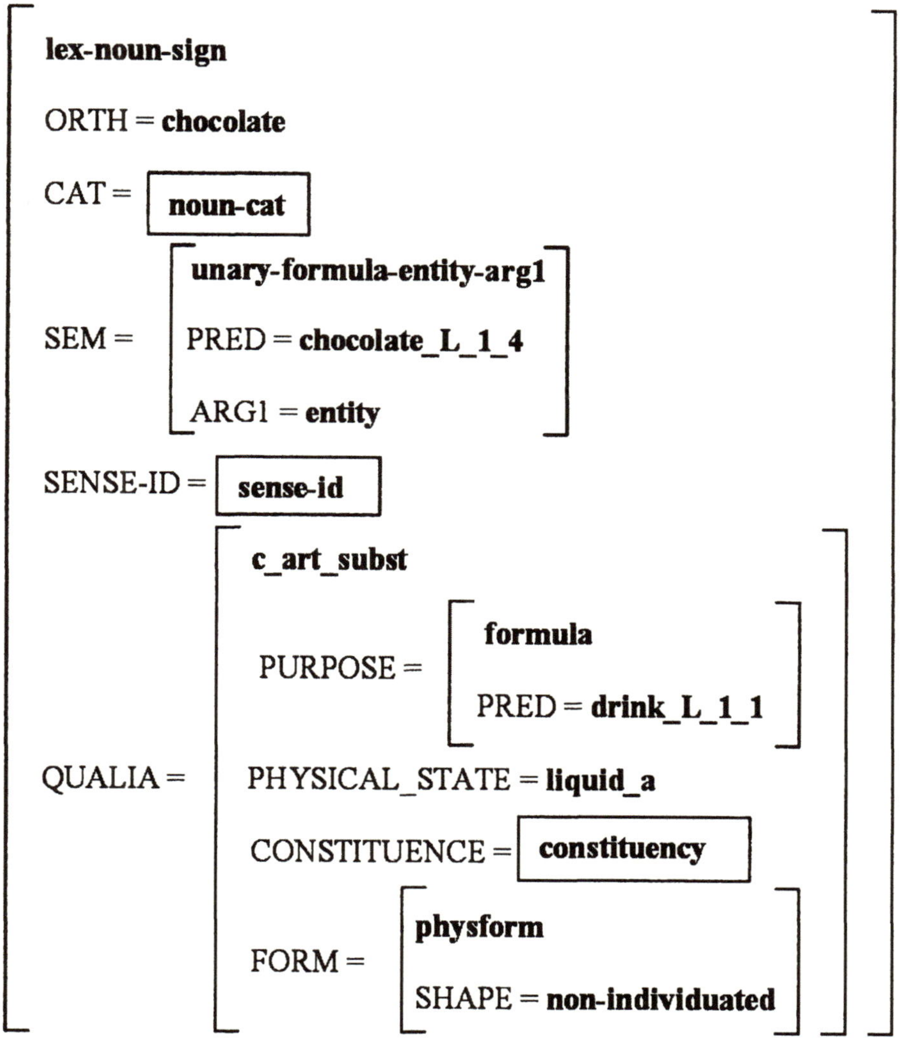

Figure 1. The LKB entry for *chocolate* (Copestake 1992)

Figure 1 shows that more detailed semantic information played an important role in ACQUILEX. Pustejovsky's (1995) concept of "qualia structure" (labeled QUALIA in Fig. 1) served as a theoretical backbone for capturing semantic information and for compiling lexical entries for the project. More specifically, ACQUILEX lexicographers relied on general conceptual templates whose argument slots contain attributes such as agent, set_of, location, used_for, cause_of, color, etc. (for details, see Fontenelle 1997: 13).[2]

Another project funded by the European Commission was EUROTRA-7 (Heid and McNaught 1991), which studied the feasibility of creating large scale shareable and reusable lexical and terminological resources. The project followed up on a 1986 workshop on *Automating the Lexicon: Research and Practice in a Multilingual Environment* (known as the *Grosseto Workshop*), which showed that there was a growing need for standardized and reusable lexical descriptions that could be employed independently of the theoretical framework used for grammatical description (see also Zampolli 1991 and Walker et al. 1995). Focusing on the standards for orthography, phonology, phonetics, morphology, collocation, syntax, semantics, and pragmatics, EUROTRA-7 investigated a broad range of diverse sources of lexical materials as well as different applications relying on lexical components. At the same time the project studied how different theoretical frameworks required various types of information, as well as depth and coverage of descriptions. This investigation resulted in a detailed list of diverging and converging needs, which led to a methodological recommendation for future actions towards developing specifications for reusable linguistic resources. More specifically, the project found that although different theoretical approaches basically described the same facts, they made different generalizations using varying descriptive devices (see Heid et al. 1991).

To provide the various frameworks with reusable lexical and terminological data, EUROTRA-7 recommended going back to the most fine-grained observable differences and phenomena.[3] This methodology would provide extremely detailed linguistic descriptions that would allow the statement of explicit and reproducible criteria for each observable difference. Representing the data in a problem-oriented high-level formalism such as typed feature structures would thus create a common data pool that could form the center of a model consisting of three main areas: acquisition, representation, and application. The recommendations pro-

2. For details on the LKB, see Copestake (1992) and Copestake and Sanfilippo (1993).
3. Other projects building on the recommendations of EUROTRA-7 were MULTILEX (MULTILEX 1993), and GENELEX (Antoni-Lay et al. 1994).

duced by EUROTRA-7 were significant for the development of future multilingual lexical resources because they explicitly described (1) the initial specifications needed for a model of a reusable lexicon, and (2) the need for standardized formats allowing researchers from academia and industry to use the same lexical resources for a variety of applications, regardless of their theoretical backgrounds.[4]

One of the follow-up projects to EUROTRA-7 was EAGLES (*Expert Advisory Group on Language Engineering Standards*), which started in 1993 with the specific aim to define standards and prepare the ground for future standard provisions. From the outset, EAGLES was not only concerned with standardization of multilingual computational lexicons, but also grammar formalisms, evaluation and assessment, and spoken language. The EAGLES working group on computational lexicons resulted in a series of recommendations for devising standardized architectures for multilingual lexicons.[5] These recommendations were instrumental in the design of the PAROLE-SIMPLE lexicons for twelve European languages (Calzolari et al. 2001: 83), including the semantic lexicons with about 10,000 word meanings. To capture the various dimensions of word meaning, the semantic representation relied on an extension of Pustejovsky's (1995) "qualia structure", which was used as a representational device for expressing the multi-dimensional aspect of word meaning. The semantic layer (SIMPLE) provided a common library of language independent templates, which represented blueprints for any given type to reflect the conditions of well-formedness and to provide constraints for lexical items belonging to that type (Calzolari et al. 2001: 83). The SIMPLE model integrated three types of formal entities, as shown in Figure 2.

The central formal entity was the SemU (semantic unit). It was used to encode word senses as semantic units and could be identified as a semantic type in the ontology, in combination with other types of information that helped to identify a word sense (in addition to distinguish it from other senses of the same lexical item). While SemUs were language specific, those which identified the same sense in different languages were assigned the same semantic type (Calzolari et al. 2001: 83). The second formal entity in the SIMPLE model was the (Semantic) Type, which represented the semantic type assigned to SemUs. The four semantic types were organized

4. See http://www.ilc.cnr.it/EAGLES96/edintro/node11.html.
5. See http://www.ilc.cnr.it/EAGLES96/browse.html#wg2 and http://www.ilc.cnr.it/EAGLES96/EAGLESLE.PDF for details on the recommendations created by EAGLES.

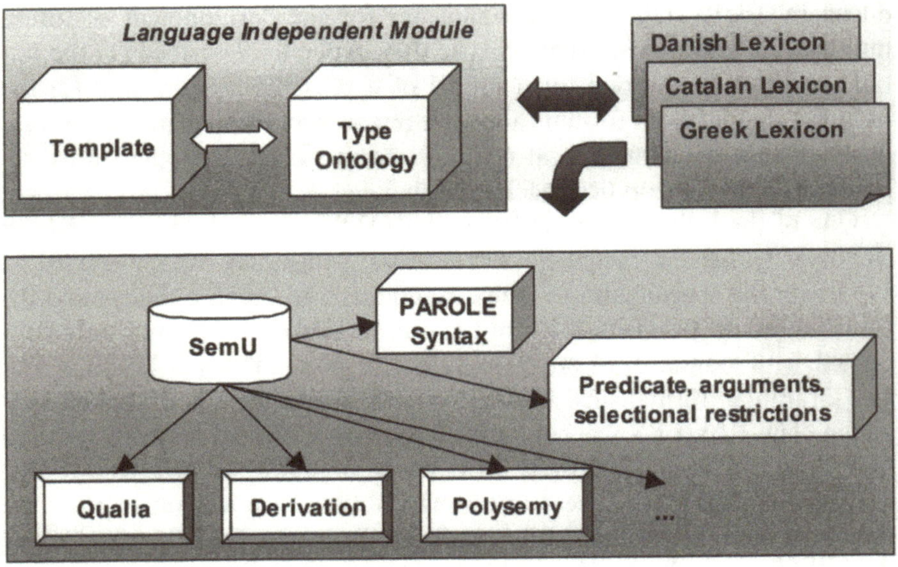

Figure 2. Structure of SIMPLE (Calzolari et al. 2001: 85)

in terms of Pustejovsky's (1995) qualia structures, which in turn were characterized in terms of type-defining information and additional information. The third formal entity was the Template, a schematic structure used by lexicographers to guide, harmonize, and facilitate the encoding of lexical items. The Template stated the semantic type in combination with additional information such as domain, semantic class, gloss, predicative representation, argument structure, polysemous classes, etc. (Calzolari et al. 2001: 83).

The EAGLES initiative and the PAROLE-SIMPLE projects laid much of the groundwork for another initiative for standardizing multilingual lexical resources, namely ISLE (*International Standards for Language Engineering*). One of the outcomes of the ISLE project was a list of detailed suggestions for best practices in the creation and structuring of multilingual lexical entries. At the center of this effort was the MILE (the Multilingual ISLE Lexical Entry), which was envisaged as highly modular and layered. The modularity concept is important in two respects. First, the horizontal level allows independent but linked modules to target different dimensions of lexical entries. Second, the vertical level presumes a layered organization that allows for different degrees of granularity of lexical descriptions, so that both "shallow" and "deep" representations of lexical

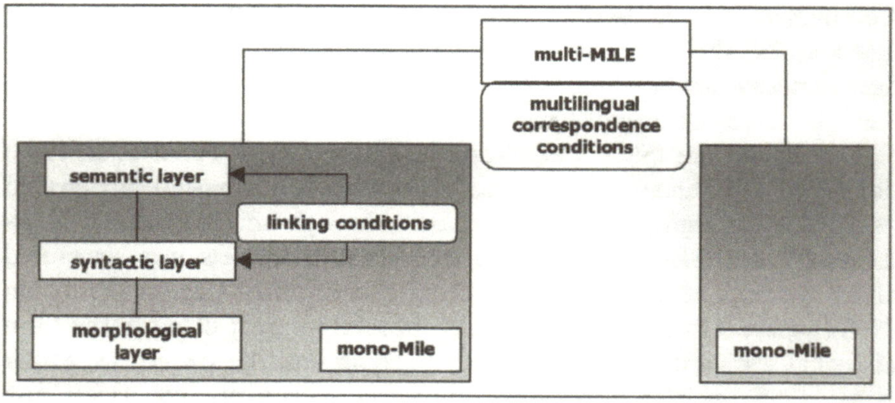

Figure 3. Organization of multi-MILE (Calzolari et al. 2003: 74)

items can be captured. According to the MILE specifications, this feature makes the adoption of different styles and approaches to the lexicon used by existing multilingual systems possible (Calzolari et al. 2003: 8). The organization of MILE, shown in Figure 3, consisted of two modules at the top level, namely mono-MILE, which specified monolingual lexical representations, and multi-MILE, which defined multilingual correspondences. Since space does not permit a full discussion of the MILE (see Calzolari et al. 2003 for full details), consider Figure 3 as an illustration of how each monolingual entry consisted of independent modules providing morphological, syntactic, and semantic information. According to Calzolari et al. (2003: 74), the advantage of this architecture was that it allowed multilingual resource development through the integration of monolingual computational lexicons. This meant that "source and target lexical entries can be linked by exploiting (possibly combined) aspects of their monolingual descriptions."

While the multi-MILE architecture also allowed for the enrichment of syntactic and semantic information that may be lacking in original monolingual lexicons, the authors pointed to a few issues that remained problematic, especially the proper characterization of collocational information and of multi-word expressions. Another important point is the authors' observation that semantic information have "often remained outside standardization initiatives, and nevertheless have a crucial role at the multilingual level" (Calzolari et al. 2003: 74). To lay out the relevant issues surrounding the integration of semantic information in multilingual lexical resources, I now turn to two projects funded by the European

Commission that focused on this important task, namely EuroWordNet and DELIS. This overview sets the stage for the discussion in section 3 of how semantic information is encoded in FrameNet, which serves as the basis for the multi-lingual FrameNets discussed in this volume.

During the late 1990s, EuroWordNet (Vossen 1997, Peters et al. 1998) developed a multilingual lexical database connecting independently created WordNets for eight European languages through an unstructured Inter-Lingual-Index (ILI). Each of the individual WordNets was structured along the lines of the original Princeton WordNet for English (Fellbaum 1998), where semantic information is encoded in great detail in the form of lexical semantic relations between synonym sets (the *synsets*, see Miller et al., 1990) such as hyponymy, antonymy, meronymy, etc. (see Cruse 1986). In EuroWordNet, each language-specific WordNet is an autonomous language-specific ontology where each language has its own set of concepts and lexical-semantic relations based on the lexicalization patterns of that language (Vossen 2004).[6] As such, EuroWordNet differentiates between language-specific and language-independent modules. Figure 4 illustrates how a language-independent module, in this case the lexicon of ItalWordNet, is linked to an unstructured ILI and a top concept ontology.

The ILI provides mapping across individual language WordNet structures and consists of a condensed universal index of meaning (1024 fundamental concepts) (Vossen 2001, 2004).[7] Each ILI record consists of a synset and an English gloss specifying its meaning. Although most concepts in each WordNet are ideally related to the closest concepts in the ILI, there are four so-called equivalence relations that map between individual WordNets and the ILI (cf. Vossen 2004: 165–167). Identifying equivalents across languages with EuroWordNet requires a number of steps. One first identifies the correct synset to which the sense of a word belongs in the source language. When there is a one-to-one mapping between synsets and ILI-records, the equivalence relation EQ_SYNONYMY holds

6. In EuroWordNet, there are no concepts for which there are no words or expressions in a language. In contrast, GermaNet (Hamp and Feldweg 1997, Kunze and Lemnitzer 2002), which is a spin-off from the German EuroWordNet consortium, uses non-lexicalized, so-called artificial concepts for creating well-balanced taxonomies.
7. The reason for leaving the ILI unstructured is explained in Vossen et al. (1997: 1) as follows: "A language-independent conceptual system or structure may be represented in an efficient and accurate way but the challenge and difficulty is to achieve such a meta-lexicon, capable of supplying a satisfactory conceptual backbone to all the languages."

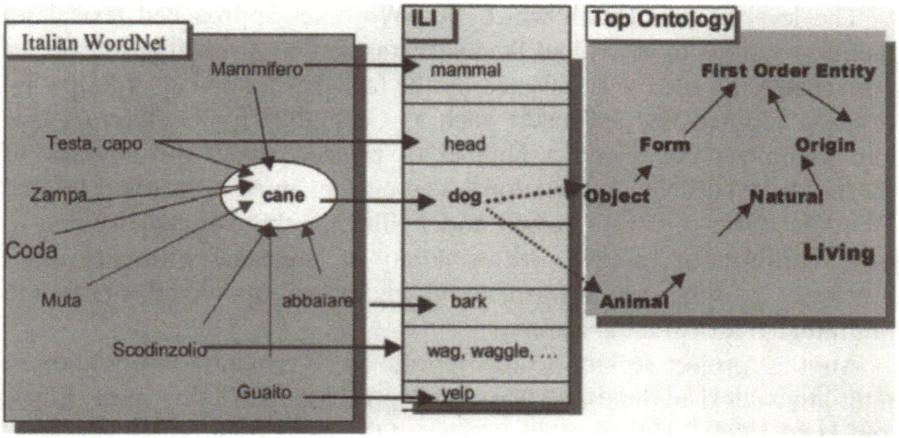

Figure 4. Portion of the ItalWordNet Lexicon for the synset {cane 1} (Calzolari et al. 2003: 23)

and the synset meaning is mapped to the ILI (which is linked to a top-level ontology).

Finally, the corresponding counterpart is identified in the target language by mapping from the ILI to a synset in the target language. The idea behind this mapping relation is described by Vossen et al. (1997: 2) as follows:

> Each synset in the monolingual wordnets will have at least one equivalence relation with a record in this ILI [. . .] Language-specific synsets linked to the same ILI-record should thus be equivalent across languages. The ILI starts off as an unstructured list of WordNet 1.5 synsets, and will grow when new concepts will be added which are not present in WordNet 1.5.

Whenever there is no exact one-to-one mapping that is represented by EQ_SYNONYMY, the mapping is captured by three other mapping relations, which I address only briefly. The first is EQ_NEAR_SYNONYM. It holds when a meaning matches multiple ILI-records simultaneously, when multiple synsets match with the same ILI-record, or when there is some doubt about the precise mapping. The second relation, EQ_HAS_HYPERONYM, holds when a meaning is more specific than any available ILI-record. The third relation is EQ_HAS-HYPONYM. It holds when a meaning can only be linked to more specific ILI-records (for details see Vossen (2004: 165)).

The level of detail with which EuroWordNet approached lexical semantic relations in individual languages (as well as cross-linguistically) is remarkable. Its success is reflected by the fact that a number of follow-up projects adopted this approach, such as GermaNet for German (Kunze and Lemnitzer 2002) and a number of projects under the auspices of the Global WordNet Association.[8] The current move towards a Global WordNet Grid (GWG) (Vossen and Fellbaum, this volume) seeking to link WordNets of an even greater variety of languages with each other represents a further step towards providing more semantic information in multilingual lexical databases.

Another project seeking to incorporate more semantic information in multilingual lexical databases was the corpus-based DELIS project (Emele and Heid 1994).[9] Unlike other projects, DELIS focused on the problems of lexicographic relevance and worked towards developing tools that allowed lexicographers to efficiently access corpus materials for specific descriptive tasks (see Heid 1996b). To determine the feasibility of such a corpus-based approach, DELIS developed a set of parallel monolingual lexicon fragments for English, French, Italian, Danish, and Dutch. The lexicon fragments were parallel in that (1) they covered the same fragment (the most general verbs of sensory perception and of speech), and (2) they were based on the same theoretical approaches and on comparable classifications and descriptive devices (Heid 1996a). Using a typed feature structure system (Emele 1993), DELIS also aimed at systematically comparing and describing the interaction between syntax and semantics in the five languages. On the syntactic side, DELIS adopted a syntactic description close to that of Head-Driven Phrase Structure Grammar (Pollard and Sag 1994). On the semantic side, DELIS described lexical items in terms of Frame Semantics (see Fillmore (1985) and section 3). The dictionary architecture in DELIS exhibited three distinct characteristics. The first was that the DELIS architecture was modular. There were separate hierarchical modules for each of the descriptive levels encoded, i.e. Morphosyntax, Syntax, and Semantics (see Heid 1996a: 296).

As Table 1 illustrates, the levels included predicate-argument structures with semantic roles, a description of subcategorized elements in terms of

8. See http://www.globalwordnet.org/gwa/wordnet_table.htm for a list of language-specific WordNet projects.
9. DELIS (Descriptive Lexical Specifications and Tools for Corpus-based Lexicon building) was funded in part by the European Union and operated from February 1993 through April 1995.

grammatical functions, and a description of the phrase structural constructs through which the arguments are realized. One advantage of this approach was that the interaction between the levels could be expressed by means of relational statements, effectively implementing linking rules. This was possible because for each level-specific module there was an inventory of descriptive devices such as a role inventory, an inventory of grammatical functions, and an inventory of phrase types. Another advantage was that individual monolingual lexicons were modules which could be combined to form a multilingual lexicon (Heid 1996b).

Table 1. Summary of components and classes (Heid 1996b)

Construct → Level ↓	Descriptive Devices	Constellations (Classes)
lexical semantics	ROLES	ROLE CONSTELLATIONS
functional syntax	GRAMM. FUNCTIONS	TOPMOST SYNTACTIC CLASSES
categorial syntax	SYNTACTIC CATEGORIES, PHRASE TYPES	SPECIFIC SYNTACTIC CLASSES

The second defining characteristic was that DELIS dictionaries were classificatory in that the description of each level was organized in monotonic multiple inheritance hierarchies of types, each type defining a class of linguistic objects from a particular point of view. This approach allowed DELIS lexicographers to define for a lexical semantic field the combinations of semantic roles, in combination with a syntactic subcategorization hierarchy (Heid 1996a).

The third central feature of DELIS was that there was neutral access to different types of lexical information. This meant that for a given lexical entry, information was flowing together from different descriptive levels without privileging any single level, thereby guaranteeing access neutrality (Heid 1996a). As Figure 5 illustrates, each descriptive level is a separate, usually hierarchical component of the lexical specifications. This means that single readings (indicated by a black dot in Figure 5) inherit from the relevant classes of each component (Heid 1996b).

To illustrate the structure of a DELIS entry, consider Figure 6, which represents the schema of a verb entry in the DELIS dictionary. The top section of the entry ("LEMMA") specifies the head form of the lemma. The mid-section of the entry encodes Frame Element Groups (FEGs), which combine the description of the participants (in terms of semantic

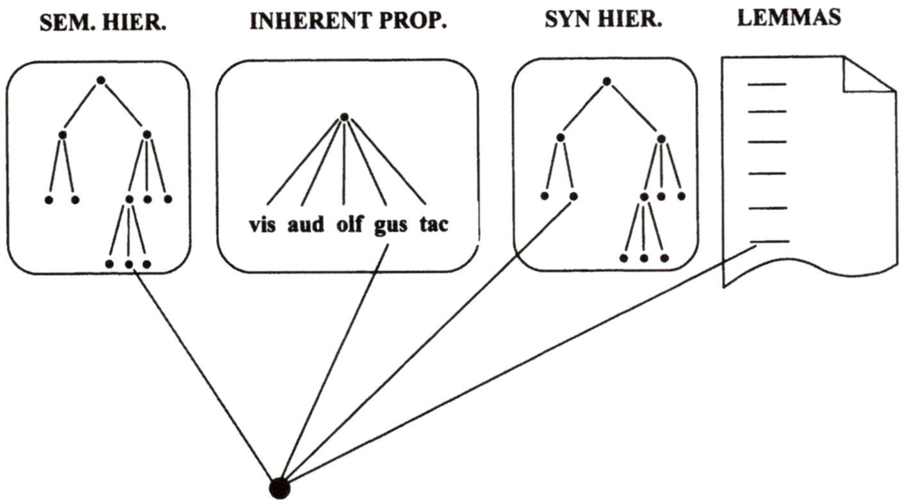

Figure 5. Access-neutrality: information from different levels flowing together, no single level privileged (Heid 1996a)

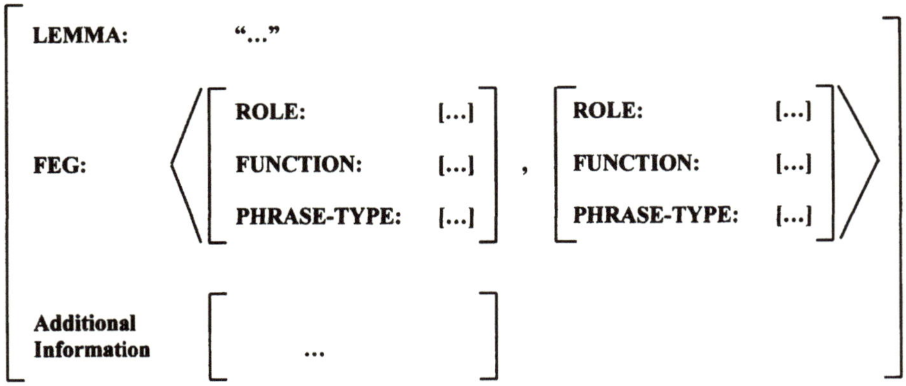

Figure 6. Schema of a verb entry in the DELIS dictionary (Heid 1996a)

roles, cf. Fillmore 1985) with a syntactic description in terms of grammatical functions (subject, direct object, etc.) and syntactic categories (Heid 1996b).

As I will show in the remainder of this chapter, the DELIS architecture is of particular interest because it implemented a number of design features that later became important for the English FrameNet project, which began its work two years after DELIS came to an end. More importantly, however, is the fact that DELIS laid much of the conceptual groundwork for the design of multilingual FrameNets (see also Heid 1997), which are the topics of the papers in this volume.

4. The emergence of multilingual lexical databases

The FrameNet project builds on Frame Semantics, a theory developed by Charles Fillmore and his associates over the past three decades. It differs from other theories of lexical meaning in that it builds on common backgrounds of knowledge (semantic "frames") against which the meanings of words are interpreted.[10] A "frame is a cognitive structuring device, parts of which are indexed by words associated with it and used in the service of understanding" (Petruck 1996: 2). The central concepts underlying Frame Semantics are characterized by Fillmore and Atkins (1992: 76–77) as follows.

> A word's meaning can be understood only with reference to a structured background of experiences, beliefs, or practices, constituting a kind of conceptual prerequisite for understanding the meaning. Speakers can be said to know the meaning of the word only by first understanding the background frames that motivate the concept that the word encodes. Within such an approach, words or word senses are not related to each other directly, word to word, but only by way of their links to common background frames and indications of the manner in which their meanings highlight particular elements of such frames.

Consider, for instance, the `Compliance` frame, which is evoked by several semantically related words such as *adhere*, *adherence*, *comply*, *compliant*, and *violate*, among others (Johnson et al. 2003). The `Compliance` frame represents a kind of situation in which different types of relationships hold between "Frame Elements" (FEs), which are defined as situation-specific semantic roles.[11] This frame concerns ACTS and STATES_

10. For an overview of Frame Semantics, see Fillmore (1970, 1975, 1976, 1977a, 1977b, 1982, 1985), and Fillmore and Atkins (1992, 1994, 2000), among others. Furthermore, the September 2003 issue of the *International Journal of Lexicography* was devoted exclusively to FrameNet.
11. Names of Frame Elements (FEs) are capitalized. Frame Elements differ from traditional universal semantic (or thematic) roles such as Agent or Patient in that they are specific to the frame in which they are used to describe participants in certain types of scenarios. "Tgt" stands for target word, which is the word that evokes the semantic frame.

OF_AFFAIRS for which PROTAGONISTS are responsible and which violate some NORM(S). The FE ACT identifies the act that is judged to be in or out of compliance with the norms. The FE NORM identifies the rules or norms that ought to guide a person's behavior. The FE PROTAGONIST refers to the person whose behavior is in or out of compliance with norms. Finally, the FE STATE_OF_AFFAIRS refers to the situation that may violate a law or rule (see Boas 2005a).

Applying the principles of Frame Semantics to the description and analysis of the English lexicon, the FrameNet project (Lowe et al. 1997, Baker et al. 1998) at the International Computer Science Institute in Berkeley, California, is in the process of creating a database of lexical entries for several thousand words taken from a variety of semantic domains. Based on data from the British National Corpus and other corpora, FrameNet identifies and describes semantic frames and analyzes the meanings of words by appealing directly to the frames that underlie their meaning. In addition, it studies the syntactic properties of words by asking how their semantic properties are given syntactic form (Fillmore et al. 2003a: 235). Between 1997 and 2008, FrameNet defined close to 7,000 lexical units (LUs) (a word in one of its senses) in more than 900 frames.

The workflow of FrameNet begins by defining frame descriptions (based on corpus evidence) for the words to be analyzed. Then, the following steps are taken: "(1) characterizing schematically the kind of entity or situation represented by the frame, (2) choosing mnemonics for labeling the entities or components of the frame, and (3) constructing a working list of words that appear to belong to the frame, where membership in the same frame will mean that the phrases that contain the LUs will all permit comparable semantic analyses" (Fillmore et al. 2003b: 297). The next step focuses on finding corpus sentences in the British National Corpus that illustrate typical uses of the target words in specific frames. Then, these corpus sentences are extracted mechanically and annotated manually by tagging the FEs realized in them. At last, lexical entries are automatically prepared and stored in the database (for more details, see Fillmore and Atkins 1998 and Fillmore 2003b).

Users accessing the FrameNet data on-line may use different types of search interfaces that allow searches by lexical unit (LU) or by semantic frames.[12] Lexical entries in FrameNet are structured as follows: They offer

12. This section is based on Boas (2005a). The FrameNet data can be accessed online at [http://framenet.icsi.berkeley.edu].

a link to the definition of the frame to which the LU belongs, including FE definitions, and example sentences exemplifying prototypical instances of FEs. In addition, the FrameNet database includes a list of all LUs that evoke the frame, and provides for each frame-specific information about various frame-to-frame relations (e.g., child-parent relation and sub-frame relation (see Fillmore et al. 2003b)).

The central component of a lexical entry of a LU in FrameNet consists of three parts. The first provides the Frame Element Table (a list of all FEs found within the frame) and corresponding annotated corpus sentences demonstrating how FEs are realized syntactically. Note that FrameNet uses different colors to highlight each FE, making it easier to identify individual FEs. Due to formatting restrictions, FE names are not color-coded in Figures 7–9.

Figure 7 illustrates how FEs in the FE table and the corresponding annotated corpus sentences are displayed for the LU *comply*. In this part, words or phrases instantiating certain FEs in the annotated corpus sentences are annotated with the same FE name as in the FE table above them. This type of display allows users to identify the variety of different FE instantiations across a broad spectrum of words and phrases.

Notice the split of annotated corpus sentences into different groups according to different types of combinations of FEs. Numbers in the table represent the total number of annotated example sentences in FrameNet. Numbers at the beginning of each annotated example sentence represent their location in the British National Corpus. For example, in the first annotated example sentence in Figure 7 *comply*, which is the target ("Tgt") evoking the `Compliance` frame, occurs with the FEs Act, Degree, and Norm, while in the second example sentence it occurs only with Act and Norm. The numbers at the beginning of sentences show where each sentence occurs in the British National Corpus. FE names are displayed in terms of subscript notations following the first square bracket.

Next, consider Figure 8, which illustrates the second part of a lexical entry in FrameNet, namely the Realization Table of the Lexical Entry Report. Besides providing a dictionary definition of the relevant LU, in this case *comply*, it summarizes the different syntactic realizations of the frame elements. In the left column we find the names of different core FEs (Act, Norm, Protagonist, and State_of_Affairs), in the middle column we see the number of annotated example sentences in FrameNet, and in the right column we find the different types of syntactic realizations of the respective FEs. Consider the FE Norm, which appears 23 times, 21 of those times as a prepositional phrase headed by *with*, once as a definite null in-

Num	**FE/LUset** (sort = FE; Compliance, comply, V,)
01	Act + Degree + **comply.V** + Norm
02	Act + **comply.V** + Norm
01	Norm + **comply.V** + (Protagonist)
03	Protagonist + **comply.V** + Degree + Norm
01	Protagonist + **comply.V** + Manner + Norm
10	Protagonist + **comply.V** + Norm
01	Protagonist + **comply.V** + Norm + Time
01	State_of_Affairs + **comply.V** + Norm
01	State_of_Affairs + **comply.V** + (Norm)
02	**comply.V** + Norm + (Protagonist)
23	

01. : Act + Degree + **comply.V** + Norm

1. 123614: [<Act> The last minute addition of the recommendation] did not [<Degree> in any way] *comply*^{Tgt} [<Norm> with the law] and the recommendation would be quashed.

02. : Act + **comply.V** + Norm

1. 123626: The court was told that [<Act> her appearance before the registrar] was solely to *comply*^{Tgt} [<Norm> with the formalities of Scots law].
2. 123758: [<Act> Spending by public sector organisations] has to *comply*^{Tgt} [<Norm> with complex and changing legal regulations], and is exposed to scrutiny at a number of levels.

01. : Norm + **comply.V** + (Protagonist)

1. 123932: If [<Norm> this rule] is not *complied*^{Tgt} [<Norm> with], the issuer is guilty of an offence, any subsequent contract etc entered into may be unenforceable and the issuer of the advertisement may face criminal charges and/or fines. [<Protagonist> CNI]

Figure 7. First part of FrameNet entry for *comply*

Comply.v

Frame: Compliance

Definition: COD: act in accordance with a wish or command

The Frame elements for this word sense are (with realizations):

Frame Element	**Number Annotated**	**Realizations(s)**
Act	(3)	NP.Ext (3)
Norm	(23)	PP[with].Dep (21) DNI.–(1) NP.Ext (1) PP[to].Dep (1)
Protagonist	(18)	CNI.–(3) NP.Ext (15)
State of Affairs	(2)	NP.Ext (2)

Figure 8. FrameNet entry for *comply*, Realization Table

stantiation (DNI), once as an external noun phrase argument, and once as a prepositional phrase headed by *to* (for details see Boas 2005b).

The third part of the Lexical Entry Report summarizes the valence patterns found with a LU, that is, "the various combinations of frame elements and their syntactic realizations which might be present in a given sentence" (Fillmore et al. 2003a: 330). The third column from the left in the valence table for *comply* in Figure 9 illustrates how the FE NORM may be realized in terms of two different types of external arguments: either as an external noun phrase argument, or as an external prepositional phrase headed by *with*. Clicking on the link (in this case "3" or "1") in the column to the left of the valence patterns leads the user to a display of annotated examples sentences illustrating the valence pattern (see Figure 7 above).[13]

13. FEs which are conceptually salient but do not occur as overt lexical or phrasal material are marked as null instantiations. There are three different types of null instantiation: Constructional Null Instantiation (CNI), Definite Null Instantiation (DNI), and Indefinite Null Instantiation (INI). See Fillmore et al. (2003b: 320–321) for more details.

Valence Patterns

These frame elements occur in the following syntactic patterns:

Number Annotated	Patterns		
3 TOTAL	**Act**	**Norm**	
(3)	NP Ext	PP[with] Dep	
1 TOTAL	**Norm**	**Norm**	**Protagonist**
(1)	NP Ext	PP[with] Dep	CNI –
16 TOTAL	**Norm**	**Protagonist**	
(2)	PP[with] Dep	CNI –	
(14)	PP[with] Dep	NP Ext	
1 TOTAL	**Norm**	**Protagonist**	**Protagonist**
(1)	PP[with] Dep	NP Ext	NP Ext
2 TOTAL	**Norm**	**State_of_Affairs**	
(1)	DNI –	NP Ext	
(1)	PP[to] Dep	NP Ext	

Figure 9. Partial FrameNet entry for *comply*, Valence Table

FrameNet differs from other approaches to lexical description such as WordNet (Fellbaum 1998) in that it makes use of independent organizational units that are larger than words, i.e., semantic frames (see also Atkins 2002, Ohara et al. 2003, Boas 2005b, Atkins and Rundell 2008). As such, FrameNet facilitates a comparison of the comprehensive lexical descriptions and their manually annotated corpus-based example sentences with those of other LUs (also of other parts of speech) belonging to the same frame. Another advantage of the FrameNet architecture lies in the way lexical descriptions are related to each other. Using detailed semantic frames which capture the full background knowledge evoked by all LUs of the same frame makes it possible to systematically compare and contrast their numerous syntactic valence patterns (see Atkins 2002, Boas 2005a).

5. The structure and development of multilingual FrameNets

I now turn to an outline of the individual chapters in this volume. The main chapters provide a state-of-the-art implementation of the FrameNet methodology for the description and analysis of languages other than English. The FrameNets for other languages described in this volume vary from the original Berkeley FrameNet in the following points:

(1) Projects such as SALSA (see Burchardt et al., this volume) are interested in full-text annotation of an entire corpus instead of finding isolated corpus sentences to identify lexicographically relevant information as is the case with the Berkeley project, Spanish FrameNet (see Subirats, this volume), or the Romance FrameNet initiative;[14]
(2) FrameNets use different types of resources as data pools. That is, besides exploiting a mono-lingual corpus as is the case with Japanese FrameNet (see Ohara, this volume), projects such as French FrameNet (Pitel, this volume) also employ multi-lingual corpora and other existing lexical resources (see Fontenelle, this volume);
(3) FrameNets for other languages differ in the tools for corpus searches and annotation. While the Japanese and Spanish FrameNets choose to adopt the Berkeley FrameNet software (Baker et al. 2003) with slight modifications, others such as SALSA develop their own to conduct semi-automatic annotation on top of existing syntactic annotations found in the TIGER corpus, or they integrate off-the shelf software packages as is the case with French FrameNet or Hebrew FrameNet (Petruck, this volume);
(4) FrameNets focus on different semantic domains. While the majority of non-English FrameNets aim to create databases with broad coverage, other projects such as the *Kicktionary* (Schmidt, this volume) focus on specific lexical domains such as football language or terminology from bio-technology (see Dolbey et al. 2006);
(5) To produce parallel lexicon fragments for other languages, projects utilize different methodologies. While German FrameNet (Boas 2001, 2002) and Japanese FrameNet (Ohara, this volume) rely on manual

14. See http://www.icsi.berkeley.edu/~vincenzo/rfn/index.html.

annotations, French FrameNet and BiFrameNet (Fung and Chen 2004) use semi-automatic and automatic approaches to create parallel lexicon fragments for French and Chinese.

To highlight the similarities and differences between the Berkeley FrameNet and other FrameNets, this volume is divided into four thematic sections. Chapters 1–3 offer an introduction to the basic concepts underlying the development of FrameNets for other languages, further expanding the initial proposals emerging from the DELIS project discussed in the previous section (Heid 1996a). Fontenelle's chapter *A bilingual lexical database for Frame Semantics* (a reprint of his 2000 *International Journal of Lexicography* paper) demonstrates how a FrameNet-type lexical database can be derived from an existing bilingual English-French dictionary. This contribution is significant, because it is the first to suggest (1) using the collocational information contained in the Collins-Robert bilingual machine readable dictionary to derive parallel lexicon fragments, and (2) combining Fillmore's Frame Semantics (Fillmore 1985) with Mel'čuk's lexical functions (Mel'čuk et al. 1988) in order to identify core frame elements, together with their syntax (see Alonso-Ramos 2003 and Bouveret and Fillmore 2008 for similar approaches). Fontenelle also shows how the database organization of the computational database makes it possible to readily access combinatorial information that is implicit and relevant to translation.

Boas' chapter *Semantic frames as interlingual representations for multilingual lexical databases* (a reprint of his 2005 *International Journal of Lexicography* paper) first discusses some of the key problems in the construction of multi-lingual lexical databases, such as polysemy, differences in syntactic and semantic valence patterns, differences in lexicalization patterns, and measuring paraphrase relations and translation equivalents. Based on the architecture of the English FrameNet database (Fillmore et al. 2003), it then suggests how FrameNet tools can be re-used to construct FrameNets for Spanish, German, and Japanese. Comparing some parallel Spanish lexicon fragments that result from this workflow, Boas' chapter demonstrates how parallel FrameNet entries differ from those of other multilingual lexical databases: (1) they provide for each entry an exhaustive account of the semantic and syntactic combinatorial possibilities of each lexical unit; (2) they offer for each entry semantically annotated example sentences from large electronic corpora, and (3) by employing semantic frames as interlingual representation, the parallel FrameNets make use of independently existing concepts that can be empirically verified.

Schmidt's *The Kicktionary – a multilingual lexical resource of football language* directly implements the ideas proposed by Boas in the previous chapter. Schmidt describes the creation of an experimental tri-lingual FrameNet database (English-German-French) for a specific lexical domain, namely soccer (football) words. This FrameNet-type approach is different from other FrameNets in that it utilizes publicly available corpora from the world soccer organization (FIFA), which are available for a number of different languages. This contribution first shows how soccer texts in different languages are prepared for cross-linguistic comparison using a keyword-in-context program for parallel corpora. Then, it discusses how different lexicalization patterns found in the three languages influence the creation of parallel lexicon-fragments for soccer words, using FrameNet tools. Finally, this chapter addresses the question of polysemy and coverage of specific word senses (technical vocabulary) when dealing with domain-specific words in the creation of multi-lingual FrameNets.

Chapters 4–6 describe the different methods used for creating broad-coverage FrameNets for typologically diverse languages. While the Spanish, Japanese, and Hebrew FrameNet projects adopted the design and workflow of the original Berkeley FrameNet, they each differ with respect to the types of resources and tools used. They also vary in that each project has to address language-specific issues such as lexicalization patterns or frame composition. The discussion of a variety of language-specific phenomena demonstrates that it is not always possible to straightforwardly create parallel lexicon fragments on the basis of English FrameNet frames and lexical entries alone.

Subirats' chapter *Spanish FrameNet: A frame semantic analysis of the Spanish lexicon* demonstrates the re-usability of the English FrameNet tools for the creation of a lexical database for Spanish verbs, nouns, and adjectives. It first discusses the compilation of a 300-million word corpus (including both New World and European Spanish texts) for annotation purposes and the tagging of the corpus. It then describes the output of a tagger, which is a set of deterministic automata, one per corpus sentence, whose transitions are tagged with the lexical and morphological information of the word form in the electronic dictionary. Finally, it explains the extraction and subcorpora creation processes which provide annotators with examples of each possible syntactic configuration in which a lexical item can occur. Part two of Subirats' chapter shows how the English-based FrameNet tools (annotation software and database structure) are re-used for the creation of Spanish lexical entries, and how parallel lexical entries can be linked to each other. Finally, part three analyzes differences in lexicalization patterns in the communication and motion domains in order to show how such linguistic differences influence the design of the Spanish FrameNet database.

Ohara's *Frame-based contrastive lexical semantics in Japanese FrameNet: The case of 'risk' and 'kakeru'* explains the tools, resources, and workflow of the Japanese FrameNet project, which aims at creating a Japanese lexicon based on Frame Semantics. It first discusses in detail a number of technical issues that arise when re-using English FrameNet tools for the description of a non-Indo-European language: compilation of a Japanese corpus suitable for annotation purposes, assignment of morphological and sentence boundaries, and development of an annotation tool for Japanese. Then, the chapter addresses some of the linguistic problems with applying frame-semantic categories to the description of Japanese: (1) how to identify and capture multiple senses and uses associated with a single form, (2) how to deal with recognized differences in senses and conditions of use among verbs related in meaning, and (3) how to create Japanese-specific frames for cases in which English-based frames are not fine-grained enough to capture some of the relevant semantic distinctions made in Japanese. Finally, the paper shows how Japanese lexicon fragments can be systematically linked to their English counterparts.

Petruck's chapter *Typological considerations in constructing a Hebrew FrameNet* illustrates the challenges faced when creating a FrameNet resource for a Semitic language. It first discusses how Hebrew FrameNet is aimed at documenting the range of semantic and syntactic combinatorial possibilities (*valences*) of each word in each of its senses by annotating example sentences and compiling the results for display. It then examines how full-text annotation of frame evoking elements (FEEs) for an existing newspaper corpus are created in order (1) to develop the infrastructure for using the FrameNet Desktop for the analysis of Hebrew texts and (2) to investigate at what level of linguistic description and computational representation the lexicon of contemporary Hebrew can be characterized in the same terms as the lexicon of English, thereby necessarily considering the matter of transferability of FrameNet machinery to a language other than English. The investigation of how events and scenarios are expressed through the same or different frames illustrate the different lexicalization patterns of Hebrew and English (Talmy 2000), thus contributing to cross-linguistic studies as well.

Chapters 7–8 address the question of how parts of the FrameNet workflow can be automated when creating FrameNets for other languages. This is an important issue because the current workflow of the Berkeley project is time and labor intensive due to its reliance on the manual creation of frames as well as the manual annotation of corpus examples.[15] The chapter *Using FrameNet for the semantic analysis of German: annotation, representation, and automation* by Burchardt et al. discusses the tools, workflow, annotation practices, and goals of the *Saarbrücken Lexical Semantics Acquisition* (SALSA) Project, which creates a FrameNet-type lexical database for German. One of the significant outcomes of SALSA is that the English frames and FEs developed by the Berkeley project for English can be re-used fortuitously to describe German predicate-argument structures. SALSA differs from the English FrameNet design and workflow in that it annotates all frame-evoking words in an entire corpus (the German TIGER corpus) thereby maximizing both annotation consistency and coverage. This is in contrast to the Berkeley FrameNet, which focuses on lexicographically relevant examples from the BNC. The chapter details the treatment and annotation of limited compositionality phenomena such as support verb constructions, idioms, and metaphors. This chapter also demonstrates how SALSA investigates several options for acquiring a semantic lexicon semi-automatically, including shallow semantic parsing. Finally, this chapter addresses some typological differences (vagueness, ambiguity, verb class membership, cross-linguistic paraphrase modeling, etc.) that arise when applying English-based semantic frames to the description of German words.

Pitel's chapter on *Cross-lingual labeling of semantic predicates and roles: A low-resource method based on bilingual l(atent) s(emantic) a(nalysis)* examines how existing FrameNet tools (annotation software and database) can be adapted for the creation of a French FrameNet. Besides discussing linguistic-typological and technical issues that arise during this process, this chapter focuses on the question of how the modified tools and resulting lexical entries for French can be re-used for other Romance languages such as Italian, Romanian, Portuguese, and Catalan, which are currently being analyzed by the Romance FrameNet consortium (inspired by MultiSemCor). The goal of this effort is to (1) create a consistent aligned and frame-annotated multi-lingual corpus; (2) highlight cross-language regularities, and structural intra- and extra-typological idiosyncrasies; (3) create a semantically indexed translation memory and an inverse multi-lingual dictionary; (4) create one of the first freely available resources that contains cross-

15. Note that some proposals have been put forward for automatically inducing frame semantic verb classes in English (see Green and Dorr 2004, Green et al. 2004).

languages sub-categorization and collocational mappings; (5) reuse the work done on automatic role assignment and semantic parsing.

The last two chapters offer different perspectives on multilingual computational lexicography that go beyond the methodology underlying the various FrameNet-like projects. Farwell et al.'s *Interlingual annotation of multilingual text corpora and FrameNet* offers a fresh look at the usability of multilingual annotated corpora for inducing FrameNet-type lexicon fragments for a variety of languages. The chapter describes the annotation process being used in a multi-site project to create six sizable bilingual parallel corpora annotated with a consistent interlingua representation. The authors examine the multilingual corpora (as well as the three stages of interlingual representation being developed), the annotation process, and the methodology for evaluation the interlingual representations. The resulting interlingual representations are then compared with the semantic frames and lexical entries of the FrameNet database in order to discuss the differences and their implications for natural language processing tasks, such as machine translation, question answering, and information extraction.

The final chapter *Universals and idiosyncrasies in multilingual WordNets* by Vossen and Fellbaum addresses design issues surrounding the use of an interlingual index for mapping between lexical databases for different languages as opposed to semantic frames. Building on prior results, the authors propose an extension of the EuroWordNet model (Vossen 1998) to cover a large number of languages (including lesser-known ones), in the "Global WordNet Grid" (GWG). Vossen and Fellbaum envision that the GWG will include an ontology as the basis for a universal concept index and that it will allow the large-scale empirical investigation of fundamental theoretical questions. This enterprise will eventually reveal which lexicalizations are universal or idiosyncratic and how they can be linked to the universal concept index. Finally, the authors offer a comparison of the linguistic-typological differences between multilingual WordNets and multilingual FrameNets, thereby highlighting the different goals of the two approaches.

References

Alberto, P. and P. Bennett (eds.)
1995 *Lexical issues in machine translation*. Studies in Machine Translation and Natural Language Processing, Vol. 8. Luxembourg: European Commission.

Alonso-Ramos, M.
2003 Éléments du frame vs. Actants de l'unité lexicale. In: *MTT 2003 – Proceedings of the First International Conference on Meaning-Text Theory*, 77–88. Paris: École Normale Supérieure.

Altenberg, B. and S. Granger (eds.)
2002 *Lexis in contrast.* Amsterdam/Philadelphia: John Benjamins.

Amsler, R.A.
1980 *The structure of the Merriam-Webster Pocket Dictionary*. Ph.D. dissertation, The University of Texas at Austin.

Antoni-Lay, M.-H., G. Francopoulo and L. Zaysser
1994 A generic model for reusable lexicons: The GENELEX project. *Literary and Linguistic Computing* 9(1), 47–54.

Atkins, B.T.S.
1993 The contribution of lexicography. In: Bates, M. and R.M. Weischedel (eds.), *Challenges in Natural Language Processing*, 37–75. Cambridge: Cambridge University Press.

Atkins, B.T.S.
2002 Then and now: competence and performance in 35 years of lexicography. In: *EURALEX 2002 Proceedings*. Reprinted in Fontenelle, T. (ed.), *Practical Lexicography – A Reader*. Oxford: Oxford University Press (2008).

Atkins, B.T.S. and A. Duval
1978 *Robert and Collins Dictionnaire Français-Anglais, Anglais-Français*. Paris: Le Robert/Glasgow: Collins.

Atkins, B.T.S., J. Kegl and B. Levin
1986 Explicit and implicit information in dictionaries. In: *Lexicon Project Working Papers 12*, Center for Cognitive Science, MIT, Cambridge, MA.

Atkins, B.T.S. and B. Levin
1991 Admitting impediments. In: U. Zernik, (ed.), *Lexical Acquisition Using Online Resources to Build a Lexicon*, 233–262. Hillsdale: Lawrence Erlbaum Associates.

Atkins, B.T.S and M. Rundell
2008 *Oxford Guide to Practical Lexicography*. Oxford: Oxford University Press.

Atkins, B.T.S. and A. Zampolli (eds.)
1994 *Computational Approaches to the Lexicon*. Oxford: Oxford University Press.

Baker, C.F., C.J. Fillmore and J.B. Lowe
1998 The Berkeley FrameNet Project. In: *COLING-ACL '98: Proceedings of the Conference*, 86–90.

Baker, C.F., C.J. Fillmore and B. Cronin
2003 The structure of the FrameNet database. *International Journal of Lexicography* 16, 281–296.

Béjoint, Henri
1994 *Tradition and Innovation in Modern English Dictionaries*. Oxford: Clarendon Press.

Béjoint, Henri
2001 *Modern Lexicography*. Oxford: Oxford University Press.

Bennet, W.S. and J. Slocum
1985 The LRC machine translation system. *Computational Linguistics* 11(2–3), 111–121.

Benson, P.
2001 *Ethnocentrism and the English Dictionary*. London: Routledge.

Boas, Hans C.
2001 Frame Semantics as a framework for describing polysemy and syntactic structures of English and German motion verbs in contrastive computational lexicography. In: P. Rayson, A. Wilson, T. McEnery, A. Hardie and S. Khoja (eds.), *Proceedings of Corpus Linguistics 2001*, 64–73.

Boas, Hans C.
2002 Bilingual FrameNet dictionaries for machine translation. In: M. González Rodríguez and C. Paz Suárez Araujo (eds.), *Proceedings of the Third International Conference on Language Resources and Evaluation*, Vol. IV, 1364–1371. Las Palmas, Spain.

Boas, Hans C.
2005a Semantic frames as interlingual representations for multilingual lexical databases. *International Journal of Lexicography* 18(4), 445–478.

Boas, Hans C.
2005b From theory to practice: Frame Semantics and the design of FrameNet. In: S. Langer and D. Schnorbusch (eds.), *Semantik im Lexikon*, 129–160. Tübingen: Narr.

Boguraev, B. and T. Briscoe
1989 *Computational Lexicography for Natural Language Processing*. London and New York: Longman.

Bouveret, M. and C.J. Fillmore
2008 Matching verbo-nominal constructions in FrameNet with lexical functions in MTT. In: E. Bernal and J. De Cesaris (eds.) *Euralex 2008 Proceedings*, 297–308. Barcelona.

Calzolari, N.
1991 Lexical databases and textual corpora: perspectives of integration of a lexical knowledge base. In: U. Zernik (ed.), *Lexical acquisition: exploiting on-line resources to build a lexicon*, 191–208. Hillsdale: Lawrence Erlbaum.

Calzolari, N. and T. Briscoe
1995 ACQUILEX-I and –II: Acquisition of lexical knowledge from machine readable dictionaries and text corpora. *Cahiers Lexicologique* 67(2), 95–114.

Calzolari, N., R, Grishman, M. Palmer, B.T.S. Atkins, N. Bel, F. Bertagna, P. Bouillon, B. Dorr, C. Fellbaum, D. Gibbon, N. Habash, E. Lange, S. Lehmann, A. Lenci, S. McCormick, J. McNaught, A. Ogonowski, J. Pentheroudakis, S. Richardson, G. Thurmair, L. Vanderwende, M. Villegas, P. Vossen and A. Zampolli.
2001 *Survey of major approaches towards bilingual/multilingual lexicons*. ISLE Computational Lexicons Working Group Deliverable D2.1–D3.1. Online: http://www.ilc.cnr.it/EAGLES96/isle/ISLE_Home_Page.htm.

Calzolari, N., F. Bertagna, A. Lenci and M. Monachini, with S. Atkins, N. Bel, P. Bouillon, T. Charoenporn, D. Gibbon, R. Grishman, C.-R. Huang, A. Kawtrakul, N. Ide, H-Y.Lee, P.J.K. Li, J. McNaught, J. Odijk, M. Palmer, V. Quochi, R. Reeves, D.M. Sharma, V. Sornlertlamvanich, T. Tokunaga, G. Thurmair, M. Villegas, A. Zampolli and El Zeiton.
2003 *Standards and best practice for multilingual computational lexicons and MILE (the multilingual ISLE lexical entry)*. Deliverable D2.2–D3.2, ISLE Computational Lexicon Working Group. Online at http://www.ilc.cnr.it/EAGLES96/isle/ISLE_Home_Page.htm.

Copestake, A.
1992 *The Representation of Lexical Semantic Information*. Ph.D. dissertation, University of Sussex.

Copestake, A. and A. Sanfilippo
1993 Multilingual Lexical Representation. Paper presented at the *AAAI Spring Colloquium on Building Lexicons for Machine Translation*. Stanford, CA. *ACQUILEX II Working Papers No. 3*.

Cruse, A.
1986 *Lexical Semantics*. Cambridge: Cambridge University Press.

Dolbey, A., M. Ellsworth, and J. Scheffczyk
2006 BioFrameNet: A domain-specific FrameNet extension with links to biomedical ontologies. Paper presented at the *International Workshop Biomedical Ontology in Action*, November 8, 2006, Baltimore, MD.

Durand, J., P. Bennett, V. Allegranza, F. Van Eynde, L. Humphreys, P. Schmidt, and E. Steiner
1991 The Eurotra Linguistic Specifications: an overview. In: *Machine Translation 6*, 103–147. Dordrecht: Kluwer.

Emele, M.
1993 TFS – The typed feature structure representation formalism. In: H. Uszkoreit (ed.), *Proceedings of the EAGLES workshop on implemented formalisms*. Saarbrücken: DFKI-Report.

Emele, M. and U. Heid
1994 *Delis*: tools for corpus based lexicon building. In: *Proceedings of Konvens-94*, (Heidelberg: Springer) 1994, [=Informatik Xpress 6].

Fellbaum, C.
1998 *WordNet: An Electronic Lexical Database*. Cambridge, MA: MIT Press.

Fillmore, C.J.
1982 Frame Semantics. In: Linguistic Society of Korea (ed.), *Linguistics in the Morning Calm*, 111–138. Seoul: Hanshin.

Fillmore, C.J.
1985 Frames and the Semantics of Understanding. *Quadernie di Semantica* 6(2), 222–254.

Fillmore, C.J. and B.T.S. Atkins
1992 Towards a frame-based lexicon: The semantics of RISK and its neighbors. In: A. Lehrer and E. Kittay (eds.), *Frames, Fields, and Contrasts: New Essays in Semantic and Lexical Organization*, 75–102. Hillsdale: Erlbaum,

Fillmore, C.J. and B.T.S. Atkins
1994 Starting where the dictionaries stop: The challenge for computational lexicography. In: B.T.S. Atkins. and A. Zampolli (eds.), *Computational Approaches to the Lexicon*, 349–393. Oxford: Oxford University Press.

Fillmore, C.J. and B.T.S. Atkins
1998 FrameNet and lexicographic relevance. In: *Proceedings of the First International Conference on Language Resources and Evaluation*. Granada, Spain.

Fillmore, C.J. and B.T.S. Atkins
2000 Describing polysemy: The case of *crawl*. In: Y. Ravin and C. Leacock (eds.), *Polysemy*, 91–110. Oxford: Oxford University Press.

Fillmore, C.J. and M. Petruck
2003 FrameNet Glossary. *International Journal of Lexicography* 16(3), 359–361.

Fillmore, C.J., C.R. Johnson and M. Petruck
2003a Background to FrameNet. *International Journal of Lexicography* 16(3), 235–250.

Fillmore, C.J., M. Petruck, J. Ruppenhofer and A. Wright
2003b FrameNet in action: The case of attaching. *International Journal of Lexicography* 16(3), 297–332.

Fontenelle, T.
1997 *Turning a Bilingual Dictionary into a Lexical Semantic Database*. Tübingen: Niemeyer.

Fontenelle, T.
2008 Linguistic research and learners' dictionaries: the Longman Dictionary of Contemporary English. In: A.P. Cowie (ed.), *Oxford History of English Lexicography*, 412–435. Oxford: Oxford University Press.

Fung, P. and B. Chen
2004 BiFrameNet: Bilingual frame semantics resource construction by cross-lingual induction. In *Proceedings of COLING 2004*. Geneva, Switzerland.

Gerber, L. and J. Young
1997 SYSTRAN MT Dictionary Development. Paper presented at the *MT Summit*, San Diego.

Green, J.
1996 *Chasing the Sun: Dictionary-makers and the Dictionaries they made*. London: Pimlico.

Green, R. and B. Dorr
2004 Inducing a Semantic Frame Lexicon from WordNet Data. In: *Proceedings of the Workshop on Text Meaning and Interpretation, Association for Computational Linguistics*, Barcelona, Spain, 2004.

Green, R., B. Dorr and P. Resnik
2004 Inducing Frame Semantic Verb Classes from WordNet and LDOCE. In: *Proceedings of the 42nd Annual Meeting of the Association of Computational Linguistics.*

Hamp, B. and H. Feldweg
1997 GermaNet: a lexical-semantic net for German. In: P. Vossen, N. Calzolari, G. Adriaens, A. Sanfilippo and Y. Wilks (eds.), *Proceedings of the ACL/EACL-97 Workshop on automatic information extraction and building of lexical semantic resources for NLP applications,* Madrid, 9–15.

Hartmann, R.R.K. and G. James
1998 *Dictionary of Lexicography*. London/New York: Routledge.

Heid, U.
1996a On the verification of lexical descriptions in text corpora. In: N. Weber (ed.): *Semantik, Lexikographie und Computeranwendungen*, 289–306. Tübingen: Niemeyer.

Heid, U.
1996b Creating Multilingual Data Collection for Bilingual Lexicography from Parallel Monolingual Lexicons. In: *Proceedings of Euralex 1996*, Göteburg University.

Heid, U.
1997 *Zur Strukturierung von einsprachigen und mehrsprachigen kontrastiven elektronischen Wörterbüchern*. Tübingen: Niemeyer.

Heid, U.
2006 Valenzwörterbücher im Netz. In: P. Steiner, H.C. Boas and S. Schierholz (eds.), *Contrastive Studies and Valency*, 69–89. *Studies in Honor of Hans Ulrich Boas.* Frankfurt/New York: Peter Lang.

Heid, U., W. Martin and I. Posch
1991 *Feasibility and standards for the collocational description of lexi-*

cal items. Stuttgart and Amsterdam, EUROTRA-7 Study, Document DOC-9/4.

Heid, U. and J. McNaught
1991 *EUROTRA – Feasibility and Project Definition Study on the Reusability of lexical and terminological resources in Computerized Applications – Final Report* Stuttgart/Luxembourg: IMS-CL/ Kommission der europäischen Gemeinschaften.

Johnson, R., M. King and L. des Tombe
1985 EUROTRA: A multilingual system under development. *Computational Linguistics* 11(2–3): 155–169.

Johnson, R., M. King and L. des Tombe
2003 EUROTRA: Computational techniques. In: S. Nirenburg, H. Somers, and Y. Wilks (eds.), *Readings in Machine Translation*, 345–350. Cambridge, MA: MIT Press.

Kunze, C. and L. Lemnitzer
2002 GermaNet – representation, visualization, application. In: *LREC 2002 Proceedings* Vol. V.: 1465–1491.

Landau, S.I.
1989 *Dictionaries: The Art and Craft of Lexicography*. Cambridge: Cambridge University Press.

Lehmann, W.P.
1998 Machine Translation at Texas: The Early Years. Online at http://www.utexas.edu/cola/centers/lrc/mt/earlymt.html.

Lowe, J.B., C.F. Baker and C.J. Fillmore
1997 A frame-semantic approach to semantic annotation. In: *Proceedings of the SIGLEX Workshop on Tagging Text with Lexical Semantics: Why, What, and How?* held April 4–5, in Washington, D.C., USA in conjunction with ANLP–97.

Makkai, A.
1980 Theoretical and Practical Aspects of an Associative Lexicon for 20th Century English. In: L. Zgusta, L. (ed.), *Theory and Method in Lexicography: Western and Non-Western Perspectives*, 125–46. Columbia, SC: Hornbeam Press.

McNaught, J.
1988 Computational Lexicography and Computational Linguistics. *Lexicographica* 4, 19–33.

Mel'čuk, I., N. Arbatchewsky-Jumarie, L. Dagenais, L. Elnitsky, L. Iordanskaja, M.-N. Lefebvre and S. Mantha.
1988 *Dictionnaire Explicatif et Combinatoire du Français Contemporain. Recherches Lexico-sémantiques*. Montréal: Les Presses de l'Université de Montréal.

Michiels, A.
1982 *Exploiting a Large Dictionary Database*. Ph.D. dissertation, University of Liège.

Miller, G., et al.
1990 Five Papers about WordNet. In: *CSL-Report* 43. Cognitive Science Laboratory, Princeton University.

MULTILEX (ed.)
1993 *Standards for a Multifunctional Lexicon*, CAP GEMINI INNOVATION for the MULTILEX Consortium, Paris.

Ooi, Vincent
1998 *Computer Corpus Lexicography*. Edinburgh: Edinburgh University Press.

Papegaaij, B.C., V. Sadler and A.P.M. Witkam (eds.)
1986 *Word Expert Semantics: An Interlingual Knowledge-based Approach*. Dordrecht: Foris.

Peters, W., I. Peters and P. Vossen
1998 The reduction of semantic ambiguity in linguistic resources. In: A. Rubio, N. Gallardo, R. Catro, and A. Tejada (eds.), *Proceedings of the First International Conference on Language Resources and Evaluation*, 409–416. Granada.

Petruck, M.R.L.
1996 Frame Semantics. In: J. Verschueren, J.-O. Östman, J. Blommaert and C. Bulcaen (eds.), *Handbook of Pragmatics*, 1–13. Amsterdam/Philadelphia: Benjamins.

Pollard, C. and I. Sag
1994 *Head-Driven Phrase Structure Grammar*. Chicago: University of Chicago Press.

Procter, P. (ed.)
1978 *Longman Dictionary of Contemporary English* (1st edition). Harlow: Longman.

Pustejovsky, J.
1995 *The Generative Lexicon*. Cambridge, MA: MIT Press.

Ohara, K., S.K. Fujii, H. Saito, S. Ishizaki, T. Ohori and R. Suzuki
2003 The Japanese FrameNet Project: A preliminary report. In: *Proceedings of the Pacific Association for Computational Linguistics* (PACLING03), 249–254.

Ramsay, A.M.
1991 Artificial Intelligence. In: K. Malmkjær (ed.), *The Linguistics Encyclopedia*, 28–38. London: Routledge.

Slocum, J.
2006 *Machine translation at Texas: The later years*. Online at http://www.utexas.edu/cola/centers/lrc/mt/latermt.html.

Summers, D.
1987 *Longman Dictionary of Contemporary English* (2nd edition). Harlow: Longman.

Svensen, B.
1993 *Practical Lexicography*. Oxford: Oxford University Press.

Talmy, L.
2000 *Toward a Cognitive Semantics*. Cambridge, MA: MIT Press.

Vossen, P.
1997 EuroWordNet: a multilingual database for information retrieval. In: *Proceedings of the DELOS workshop on Cross-language Information Retrieval*, March 5–7, 1997, Zurich.

Vossen, P.
1998 (ed.) *EuroWordNet: A Multilingual Database with Lexical Semantic Networks for European Languages*. Dordrecht: Kluwer.

Vossen, P.
2001 Condensed meaning in EuroWordNet. In: P. Bouillon and F. Busa (eds.), *The language of word meaning*, 363–383. Cambridge: Cambridge University Press.

Vossen, P.
2004 EuroWordNet: A multilingual database of autonomous and language-specific wordnets connected via an inter-lingual-index. *International Journal of Lexicography* 17(2), 161–173.

Vossen, P., W. Peters and P. Díez-Orzaz
1997 The Multilingual design of the EuroWordNet Database. In: K. Mahesh (ed.), *Ontologies and multilingual NLP, Proceedings of workshop at IJCAI-97*, Nagoya, Japan, August 23–29.

Walker, D., A. Zampolli and N. Calzolari (eds.)
1995 *Automating the Lexicon: Research and Practice in a Multilingual Environment*. Oxford: Oxford University Press.

Zampolli, A.
1991 Technology and linguistic resources. In: M. Katzen (ed.), *Scholarship and Technology in the Humanities*. London: British Library Research.

Zampolli, A.
1994 Introduction. In: B.T.S. Atkins and Z. Zampolli (eds.), *Computational Approaches to the Lexicon*, 3–16. Oxford: Oxford University Press.

Zgusta, L.
1971 *Manual of Lexicography*. The Hague: Mouton.

Part I. Principles of constructing multilingual FrameNets

2. A bilingual lexical database for Frame Semantics

Thierry Fontenelle

1. Introduction

For nearly twenty years now, researchers have tried to tap the contents of machine-readable dictionaries with a view to extracting, formalizing and representing the linguistic information they contain and turning it into formats usable in machine translation, information retrieval, automatic dictionary look-up, question answering, etc. More recently, especially as a result of advances in dictionary-making in the Anglo-Saxon world, corpora have become one of the main sources of information for populating the large computational lexica required by any NLP system. Indeed, some researchers claim that pure dictionary research has run its course and that the time has come to envisage applications only, yet it is far from clear whether all the information contained in MRDs has really been tapped and whether the electronic versions of large commercial dictionaries have yielded all their secrets, making them intellectually less interesting and scientifically less worthy of attention. This is far from certain, since the new generation of dictionaries are the result of scores of person-years of close scrutiny of corpus-based evidence, which has had to be dissected, digested, interpreted, condensed and regurgitated by teams of highly skilled lexicographers. Neglecting this data would be tantamount to reinventing the wheel with imperfect tools. Indeed, in this author's view, these findings argue for a combination of linguistic resources, viz. existing dictionaries and textual corpora, rather than the exclusion of one resource in favor of the other.

2. Frame Semantics

Though it is by no means new, frame semantics has been attracting a good deal of attention recently in computational lexicography circles.[1] The

1. This paper was first published in the *International Journal of Lexicography* in 2000, Vol. 13.4: 232–248. Frame semantics can be seen as a sophisticated

theory is indeed at the heart of an ambitious project run by the University of Berkeley in the field of semantic tagging and corpus-based dictionary construction, viz. the FrameNet project (Fillmore and Atkins 1998, Baker et al. 1998, Lowe et al. 1997, Gahl 1998). The aim of this project is to describe word senses by using corpus evidence. At first glance, such a venture may not appear particularly original: ever since the publication of Cobuild, the first corpus-based English learners' dictionary (Sinclair et al. 1987), many English-based dictionary projects have attempted to do just that. The originality of the FrameNet project is that it aims at including in the resulting lexical database a description of all possible constellations of so-called 'frame elements', a description which complements the 'traditional' morpho-syntactic information one is used to finding in such lexicons. An additional feature of FrameNet is that each word sense is linked to a set of corpus-derived sentences that have been annotated with frame-semantic information. In a way, this can be seen as a form of semantic tagging (see also Fillmore and Atkins 1998).

2.1. What are frames?

The 'frame' in frame semantics represents a sort of situation, an aspect of reality in which various keywords, e.g. *see, behold, spot,* in the case of the 'perception frame', are contrasted with one another and can be classified as a function of the relationships which hold between the various actants or frame elements (here, 'Experiences' and 'Percepts'). A frame-based lexicon aims at describing the combinatory potential of a given lexical item, which boils down to explicitly indicating how each frame element can be realized, syntactically as well as lexically, at the surface level. One of the early examples described by Fillmore is the so-called commercial transaction scene, which involves four frame elements: a SELLER (S), GOODS (G), a BUYER (B) and the PRICE/MONEY (P). A speaker who wishes to describe a commercial transaction may resort to a series of verbs such as *sell, buy,*

---

development of case grammar (Fillmore 1968). The derived theory is not as recent as some might think, however, since Fillmore had already laid the foundations nearly 20 years ago, in what might be considered a seminal paper in which the main concepts were introduced (Fillmore 1982). A decade later, thanks to subsequent advances in the field of corpus linguistics and the development of corpus query tools, the DELIS European LRE project was to produce the very first fragments of corpus-based lexical descriptions using frame semantics (in the field of perception and speech act vocabulary – see Heid 1994, 1996).

pay, charge or *cost.* The choice of one of these verbs means that the speaker imposes a point of view from which he or she considers the situation as a whole. All these verbs can be contrasted as a function of the ways in which they enable the various frame elements to be realized syntactically. Consider the following sentences, which can be considered as paraphrases insofar as they describe the same frame:

(1) John sold the car to Peter for $2,000.

(2) Peter bought the car from John for $2,000.

(3) Peter paid John $2,000 for the car.

(4) John charged Peter $2,000 for the car.

(5) The car cost Peter $2,000.

The sentences above clearly show that the various frame elements – say, BUYER and SELLER – can occupy different positions. In terms of syntactic functions, they can be realized differently, which has strong implications for the lexical description of the verbs. For each lexical entry, the number and nature of the frame elements need to be specified, together with information on how a given element is to be realized at surface level. Such a description will, for instance, indicate that the verb *buy* takes a BUYER (B) as first syntactic actant (subject), GOODS (G) as second syntactic actant (direct object), and optionally a SELLER (S), appearing in a prepositional phrase introduced by *from,* and MONEY (M), appearing in a prepositional phrase introduced by *for.* Similarly, the verb *charge* takes a SELLER (S) as first syntactic actant (subject), MONEY (M) as second syntactic actant (direct object), and optionally a BUYER (B), appearing as indirect object, and GOODS (G), appearing as an optional prepositional phrase introduced by *for.* It should be pointed out that, unlike case grammar, frame semantics does not postulate the existence of 'universal' frame elements. Rather, they should be seen as heavily dependent on the frame or scenario in which they are to be found. Very much as in plays or movies, where an actor may play entirely different parts, a given lexical item may be assigned different semantic functions, depending on which frame is activated. Consider the following sentences:

(6) Her doctor bought a superb BMW for £25,000.

(7) Her doctor drove his BMW at lightning speed around the city.

(8) Her doctor was able to cure her cancer.

While (6) can undoubtedly be interpreted in terms of the commercial transaction scene described above (the noun *doctor* being an exponent of the BUYER frame element), (7) illustrates the DRIVING frame (see Baker et al. 1998). In this latter frame, the noun *doctor* plays the part of a DRIVER (a primary mover), which appears here as a subject, while the BMW is a VEHICLE and appears as a direct object. Other relevant elements for this frame have been identified by the FrameNet researchers, i.e. a CARGO, a RIDER or a PATH, the last of which surfaces in (7) as an oblique complement *(around the city)*. The last sentence above, (8), illustrates yet another frame, viz. the HEALTH frame, which is described at length in Lowe et al. (1997). In this frame, the noun *doctor* plays the part of a HEALER, i.e. an individual who tries to restore the health of a PATIENT. In (8), the HEALER frame element appears as the subject of the verb *cure,* but this verb can also appear with a different constellation of frame elements (a so-called Frame Element Group, or FEG), as is shown in the following examples excerpted from the Cobuild dictionary (Sinclair et al. 1987):

(9) It was used as a folk-medicine to cure snake-bite.

In (9), *cure* occurs with a MEDICINE frame element appearing in subject position and a WOUND surfacing as a direct object. Other possible frame elements in the HEALTH frame are PATIENT, DISEASE (see *cancer* in (8)), BODY PART, SYMPTOM or TREATMENT.

2.2. Frame semantic tagging

Semantic tagging is currently a live issue in computational lexical semantics. The aim here is to move beyond traditional part-of-speech or syntactic tagging and try to assign word senses to lexical items in a corpus. The assignment process can be manual, which is both tedious and time-consuming, and requires special lexicographical skills. It can also be automated, and several projects now attempt to use large-scale lexical resources as 'gold standards', whether these are commercial dictionaries, such as the *Cambridge International Dictionary of English* (CIDE) (Procter 1995; see Harley and Glennon 1997) or research-oriented lexical databases such as WordNet (Fellbaum 1998).

The FrameNet researchers have developed a number of corpus tools which enable them to browse quickly through corpus data and assign the appropriate frame element tags to the sentences they are examining. Different colors are used for the various frame elements, which make the structure of the concordances more explicit. This approach enables the linguists to retrieve from the corpus, say, all sentences featuring a given frame element group (e.g. a verb surrounded by a given constellation of frame elements). The frame semantic annotation itself is purely manual, however, and relies heavily on the expertise of the coder, who has to become a skilled lexicologist well-versed in the linguistic theory which underlies the project. In the following sections, we would like to show how a separate resource, which was not primarily built with this perspective in mind, could be used to partially identify some frame elements and the combinatory potential of a number of lexical items.

3. A bilingual lexical-semantic database

After realizing that the collocational potential of bilingual commercial dictionaries had never been fully exploited, we embarked on the construction of a lexical-semantic database based on the machine-readable version of the Collins-Robert English-French dictionary (first edition, Atkins and Duval 1978). The original idea was to create a multi-access database in which the very rich and sophisticated collocational and thesauric material of the dictionary would be made readily accessible. In addition to the creation of access programs, designed to enable users (linguists, lexicographers, NLP designers, translators...) to surf on the dictionary in a highly opportunistic mode, in order to discover implicit information, we also decided to add a semantic layer to the original data. This spurred us to enrich the dictionary with information on the lexical-semantic relationship linking headwords and a series of 'indicators' appearing at word sense level. For space reasons, we cannot go into the details here and will limit ourselves to a general presentation of this database. Fontenelle (1997a, 1997b) provides detailed explanations of the rationale of this project and of its possible applications.

3.1. The Collins-Robert bilingual dictionary

Good bilingual dictionaries such as the Collins-Robert dictionary (henceforth CR) provide users with information about contextual restrictions and the conditions which have to be met for a given translation to apply in a given context. They do not simply list possible translations in a row, but use a whole gamut of indicators – synonyms, collocations, semantic restrictions, subject field codes, etc. – to guide the translation process. The following system was applied by the CR lexicographers:

- Typical subjects of a verb headword appearing in italics and between square brackets;
- Typical direct objects of a verb, or typical noun modified by an adjective, appearing in italics (unbracketed);
- Typical noun complements of a noun headword appearing in italics between square brackets;
- Synonyms, paraphrases, micro-definitions appearing in italics between parentheses;
- Subject fields appearing in italics, between parentheses and with an initial capital letter.

The following examples illustrate these conventions, which are applied consistently throughout the dictionary:

grunt *vi [pig, person]* grogner...
fluff *vt* **a** *(also ~* **out***) feathers* ébouriffer; *pillows, hair* faire bouffer. **b** *(* do badly) audition, lines in play, exam* rater, louper*
sty *n [pigs]* porcherie
platoon *n (Mil)* section; *[policemen, firemen etc]* peloton; *(US Mil)* ~ **sergeant** adjudant

The information above shows that the dictionary contains a lot of crucial information which can be put to good use in a word-sense disambiguation perspective, and more specifically in a translation selection perspective. It shows, for example, that the verb *fluff* should be translated as *rater* or *louper* in French if it applies to an exam, and that the translation *ébouriffer* is unacceptable in this particular context, since the latter normally applies to cases where *feathers* appears in direct object position.[2] The avail-

2. One immediately sees the limitations of this approach: in order to save space, the lexicographers have indeed not been able to list all collocates and have selected the most salient or the most frequent ones. The problem is to match a sentence such as 'The student fluffed his test' with the second sense of *fluff*, even though *test* is not listed as a possible collocate of the verb. This problem is addressed by the members of the DEFI team in Liège, who use the CR database in addition to a number of other bilingual and monolingual machine-readable dictionaries to automatically select the 'best' translation in context, which, in the present case, forces them, inter alia, to compute the semantic similarity between *test* (the disambiguating context) and *exam* (the information provided in one of the dictionaries). See Michiels (1998) and Dufour (1998) for more details of the DEFI project on word sense disambiguation and translation selection, and Michiels (2000) for recent results.

ability of the dictionary in machine-readable form, and more specifically in database format[3], makes it possible to access the data via access keys other than the traditional alphabetical ordering of the headwords, which is the only access path a user of the paper version can resort to. More specifically, the user can, for instance, focus on the occurrence of a given item appearing in italics somewhere in the micro-structure of an entry and ask the computer to list all headwords under which this italicized indicator appears.

A quick glance at the four examples above shows that *pig* is used under *grunt* and *sty,* but the complete list of occurrences of *pig* in italics is quite informative. This item in fact appears under *boar, dig, food, geld, grunt, keep, mash, nuzzle, root, root up, rout, slop, snout, sow, sty,* and *swill.*

3.2. Lexical functions and Meaning-Text Theory

The data above is undoubtedly interesting insofar as it includes a variety of collocations and semantically-related words which bear some resemblance to what can be extracted when one computes statistics such as Mutual Information scores to discover significant co-occurrence relations (Church and Hanks 1990). The relationships between the various elements differ widely, however, and there is no explicit way of specifying that *boar* and *sow* refer to male and female pigs respectively and are therefore closer to each other than, say, *grunt* or *sty.* In order to make such distinctions explicit and add a semantic layer to the original dictionary, we decided to label the 70,000-odd pairs of semantically-related items with lexical relations. The mechanism we opted for was based upon the lexical function paradigm developed by Mel'čuk in the framework of his Meaning-Text Theory (Mel'čuk *et al.* 1984). The list of lexical functions used in our database and the rationale which underlies the choice of additional relations can be found in Fontenelle (1997a). To illustrate the theory of lexical functions with data borrowed from the CR dictionary, it is sufficient at this stage to understand that a lexical function is a meaning relation between a keyword and other words or phraseological combinations of words. The general form of such a function is f(X) = Y, where X is the keyword and Y is the related item (usually, though not necessarily, a collocate) which has to be selected to express the meaning denoted by f(X). In the

3. The structure of the database and the work which was necessary to transform the data from the typesetting tape into a database are described in Fontenelle (1997a).

data above, the relationship between *pig* (the italicized item corresponds to the keyword X) and *grunt* can be represented in terms of the lexical function Son (typical verb for the sound of X), which is written as follows:

Son (pig) = grunt

Similarly, the relationship between *pig* and *sty* was coded in terms of the S_{loc} lexical function (typical location/place):

S_{loc} (pig) = sty

We have extended the original Meaning-Text Theory to cater for a number of additional links, such as part-whole relations[4], or male/female relations. Focusing on the occurrences of *pig,* we are then able to retrieve the data below from the dictionary database. The order applied to display the information here is: dictionary headword, part of speech of the headword, italicized item, French translation of the headword, French translation of the italicized item, lexical function, if any.

boar (n): ~ pig ~ ⇨ verrat < m > (porc, male)
dig (vi): ~ pig ~ ⇨ fouiller (porc,)
food (n): ~ pig ~ ⇨ pâtée < f > (porc,)
geld (vt): ~ pig ~ ⇨ châtrer (porc,)
grunt (vi): ~ pig ~ ⇨ grogner (porc, son)
keep (vt): ~ pig ~ ⇨ élever (porc,)
mash (n): ~ pig ~ ⇨ pâtée < f > (porc,)
nuzzle (vi): ~ pig ~ ⇨ fouiller du groin (porc,)
root (vi): ~ pig ~ ⇨ fouiller (avec le groin) (porc,)
root up (vt sep): ~ pig ~ ⇨ déterrer (porc,)
rout (vi): ~ pig ~ ⇨ fouiller (porc,)
slop (n): ~ pig ~ ⇨ pâtée < f > (porc,)
snout (n): ~ pig ~ ⇨ museau (porc, part)
sow (n): ~ pig ~ ⇨ truie < f > (porc, female)
sty (n): ~ pig ~ ⇨ porcherie < f > (porc, sloc)
swill (n): ~ pig ~ ⇨ pâtée < f > (porc,)

---

4. Mel'čuk does not consider part-whole relations as lexical functions because they are not one-to-one relations. For information retrieval or language teaching purposes, however, such knowledge is undoubtedly essential and can provide crucial clues when disambiguating word senses. We therefore made use of the Lexical Function mechanism to formalize these relations whenever they were present in the dictionary.

As can be seen above, the lexical function mechanism is not always rich enough to cope with some basic relations. A number of nouns are not assigned any lexical function because the list of 60-odd lexical functions normally includes standard relations, which occur with a large number of keywords and a large number of arguments. It is clear that, from a semantic perspective, some mechanism could be devised to capture the strong similarity between *food, mash, slop,* and *swill,* which all refer to the typical food of pigs. In terms of frame semantics, these four nouns could be seen as the exponents of a given frame element applying to pigs, which could be called Food, for instance.

The data above could also be represented diagrammatically, since the lexical function mechanism makes it possible to group together collocates which share a common meaning component with respect to the node (the keyword). In this way, the bilingual dictionary can be seen as a resource for constructing partial semantic networks, as is shown in Figure 1 (see also Fontenelle 1997b).

The retrieval program associated with the database makes it possible to access the data via any element of the dictionary entry, including the lexical functions which were added subsequently. All these elements can be queried in isolation or in combination with each other. This makes it possible to ask, say, whether there are any verbs expressing the typical sound made by a pig, or to list transitive verbs (part of speech = vt) which can take the word *pig* as direct object, whatever the lexical function associated with it, if any.

4. Acquiring data for frame semantic descriptions

In this section, we would like to show how the CR database can be used to produce a partial description and fragments of dictionary entries in a frame semantic perspective. It should be pointed out that the Mel'čukian approach normally focuses on standard lexical functions, i.e. relations which are pervasive in general language. Therefore, lexical functions can be seen as a type of "universal" relation with often unpredictable realizations. In comparison, frame elements are more likely to be highly specific and often apply only to a microscopic world which the frame semanticist tries to describe as minutely as possible.

However, one may safely argue that a number of frame elements will probably recur repeatedly across a large number of frames. Frame elements referring to locatives or instruments, for instance, are cases in

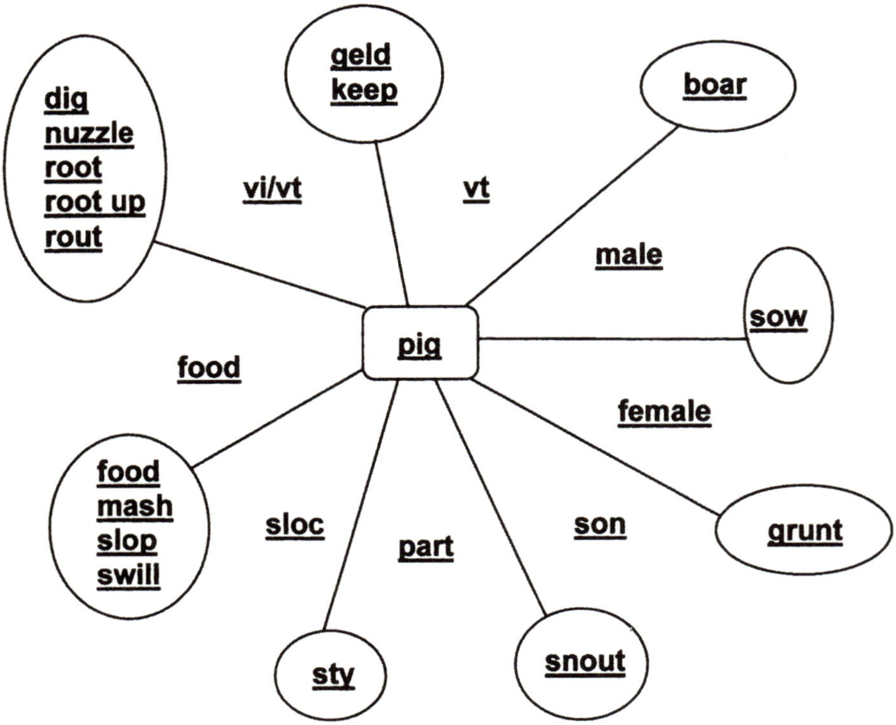

Figure 1. Semantic network of *pig*

point. This is just an area where the CR database provides interesting data. Since the query programs also make it possible to concentrate on the realization of a given lexical function, without starting from a given keyword, it is possible to extract from the dictionary the list of all triples featuring the lexical functions S_{loc} or S_{instr}, which denote typical locations or typical instruments associated with a keyword respectively. Such a query will generate hundreds of bilingual records, such as the following combinations:

S_{instr} (conjurer) = wand (baguette magique)
S_{instr} (cowboy) = noose (lasso)
S_{instr} (hangman) = noose (corde)

S_{loc} (fox) = earth, hole, kennel (repaire, terrier)
S_{loc} (bishop) = see (siège épiscopal)
S_{loc} (sentry) = shelter (guérite)

As will become obvious below, however, the dictionary database is also useful in identifying the following linguistic elements when describing a given frame:

- The vocabulary used when activating a frame, i.e. the central verbs around which frame elements are going to revolve;
- The frame elements themselves;
- The semantico-syntactic relationship between predicates and frame elements.

As is argued below, all this information may cater for a preliminary and non-exhaustive description of a frame. The idea is then to have this data complemented with corpus data.

5. The `Examination` frame

We would like to focus on the `Examination` frame, which describes a situation in a school or academic environment in which someone goes in for an exam and has to satisfy a number of requirements in order to pass it. At this stage, it is important to realize that a verb such as *examine* has at least two different senses, one the 'school' sense (= "test", as in *The professor examined 10 students yesterday*), the other, the 'medical' sense (*The doctor examined his patient*). Similarly, the deverbal noun *examination* exhibits the same polysemy and will probably only occur with different restricted sets of collocates (*prepare (for), sit, take, fail, pass ... an examination* for the 'school' meaning vs. *carry out, fail a medical examination,* but not **sit/take/fluff a medical examination* for the 'medical' sense). Interestingly, it seems that the nouns *examination/exam* are likely to be preceded by the adjective *medical* when they are used in the second sense defined above. In this paper, we are only concerned with the 'school examination' frame. Needless to say, the 'medical examination' frame will involve a different set of frame elements and phraseological combinations.

In order to identify the central predicates, i.e. the main vocabulary used to talk about this frame, the starting point can consist in retrieving the information contained in the database for the noun *examination.* Since it is impossible to predict that only *examination* has been used as a metalinguistic indicator in the microstructure of the dictionary entries, it is preferable to cast the net somewhat wider and query the database against occurrences of related terms such as *exam* or *test.* The list of items associated with these nouns includes the following verbs (see below): *be in process, fail, fluff, go in for, hold, pass, prepare, set, sit, supervise, superintend, take, undergo...*

Such a list obviously raises the question of the scope one gives to the examination frame. Criteria for 'framehood' still need to be defined and one immediately sees that some verbs, such as *fail* or *pass*, are more central (core) to this frame and belong to it, while other verbs, such as *supervise* or *superintend*, are much more peripheral and have more general meanings. However, it seems that we need to consider phraseological and collocational combinations and various types of multi-word units, instead of taking single words only into account. If one adopts the former perspective, it is clear that restricted collocations such as *sit an examination* or *supervise/hold an examination* do belong to the `Examination` frame, while the isolated verbs *sit*, *supervise* or *hold* might not (Fillmore, personal communication). In any case, it is clear that statistical data such as provided by mutual information scores is of no use in helping us decide which words belong to a given frame and which do not. Purely syntactic criteria do not seem to be helpful either. In fact, one possible solution may be provided by the encoding point of view, since what we are interested in when describing a frame eventually comes down to identifying how speakers of a language talk about the participants in this frame and which idiosyncratic conventions they use in this context. It is just this type of onomasiological perspective that the lexical database used in this experiment allows us to adopt.

A second task is to identify the frame elements themselves which play a part in this frame. Apart from the nouns *examination*, *exam* and *test* themselves, which can be described as a type of central Event in this frame, the presence of at least two other frame elements can be identified on the basis of subscripts associated with the main actors ('actants' in the terminology used by Mel'čuk).

The database contains the following records, which point to possible denominations for the first (S_1) and second (S_2) actants of the nouns *exam* and *examination*:

entrant (n): ~ exam ~ ⇒ candidat(e) (examen,s_2)
jury (n): ~ examination ~ ⇒ jury <m> (examen,s_1)

We suggest using the terms EXAMINER for the first actant and EXAMINEE for the second actant. Obviously, the information contained in the dictionary is very limited here and indeed unsatisfactory since it does not cater for numerous other possibilities which only a corpus analysis would reveal (see below).[5]

In Meaning-Text Theory, subscripts also appear in the lexical functions associated with some of the verbs collocating with these nouns. Consider the following examples, excerpted from the database:

fail (vt): ~ examination ~ ⇒ échouer à (examen,antireal2)
fluff (vt): ~ exam ~ ⇒ rater (examen,antireal2)
go in for (vt fus): ~ examination ~ ⇒ se présenter à (examen,oper2)
pass (vt): ~ exam ~ ⇒ être reçu à (examen,real2)
prepare (vi) {TO PREPARE FOR}: ~ examination ~ ⇒ préparer (examen,preparoper2)
sit (vt): ~ exam ~ ⇒ passer (examen,oper2)
take (vt): ~ exam ~ ⇒ passer (examen,oper2)
take (vt): ~ test ~ ⇒ passer (test,oper2)
undergo (vt): ~ test ~ ⇒ subir (test,oper2)

All the verbs above can be used when describing the frame from the perspective of the second actant, in MTT parlance. This means that the second actant, viz. the person who is being examined or tested, is the subject of the verbs above. In stating this, one clearly sees that there are a number of semantically nearly 'empty' verbs (which some linguists call 'support verbs'), which appear as the exponents of the Oper lexical function. Saying that somebody *sits, takes, undergoes* or *goes in for* a test or an exam is tantamount to saying that he or she is being examined or tested. The outcome of the test can be described in terms of the Real function, which indicates that the requirements have been met and that the

5. It would be interesting to resort to thesauri to expand the list of possible realizations for some of the frame elements identified here. It is clear that nouns such as *student*, *applicant*, *candidate*, *pupil*, etc. would fall within this category. Nouns such as *professor*, *teacher*, *examiner*, *president*, *jury*, *evaluator*, etc. would be the exponents of the EXAMINER frame element. Finally, it ought to be stressed that the Event frame element need not necessarily be realized by the nouns *exam* or *test*. A sentence such as *I failed my Maths A level* (CIDE, s.v. **A level**) reveals that terms like *A level*, *B level*, *competition* and other very specific items such as *International Baccalaureate* or *IB* can be considered hyponyms of *examination*, which should be captured in a thesaurus (consider the authentic sentence: 'Evans is to allow some pupils to take the International Baccalaureate instead of A-levels', *Financial Times*, 12 February 2000, p. xii).

outcome of the test is successful (X *passed the exam*), while AntiReal denotes a failure to comply with these requirements (X *fluffed/failed the exam*).

Note that the lexical functions can be used to account for a different meaning in a cross-linguistic perspective. Consider the following famous false friends in English and in French (*pass an exam ≠ passer un examen*). These collocations can be represented as follows:

FR: $Oper_2$ (examen) = passer

EN: $Real_2$ (exam) = pass

The data retrieved from the CR database can be represented as in Table 1 below. This table shows the main predicates (verbs) used when activating the examination frame and the frame element groups (FEG) which can be identified on the basis of the information provided by the lexical functions contained in the database. Since three frame elements at least are possible, the figures indicate whether these frames occupy the position of subject (1) or direct object (2) of the verb in question. If the frame element appears in the form of a prepositional phrase, the preposition heading this PP is indicated. Finally, the first column on the left is used to capture a very broad semantic category inferred from the lexical functions. These categories can be seen in the form of a process, with a beginning (the preparation), a middle (the examination itself and the set of semantically impoverished verbs which can be used to support the noun bases), and an end (the outcome, whether a success or a failure).

As can be seen below, Table 1 also includes a number of frame element groups which do not necessarily involve an Event (i.e. a hyponym of *exam* or *test*). The verb *fail*, for instance, can appear with different constellations of frame elements, as the following sentences clearly show:

(10) Many $students_{[EXAMINEE]}$ failed the driving $test_{[EVENT]}$.

(11) The $examiners_{[EXAMINER]}$ failed $him_{[EXAMINEE]}$ because he had not answered all the questions.

In order to discover patterns involving Examiners or Examinees, we queried the CR database against the occurrences of a set of prototypical nouns standing for these frame elements, viz. *pupil*, *candidate*, *student* or *professor*, *teacher*. Some of the triples contained in the database are listed below. The semantic-syntactic behavior of the verbs in question is formalized in Table 1 below, specifying for instance that the intransitive verb

Table 1. Frame Element Groups in the `Examination` frame

	Verb	*Examiner*	*Examinee*	*Event*
PREPARE (Prepar)	Set	1		2
	Prepare		1	for
MAKE/DO Oper/Func	Examine	1	2	
	Sit		1	2/for
	Take		1	2
	Be in process			1
	Go in for		1	2
	Undergo		1	2
[+Control]	Supervise	1		2
	Superintend	1		2
	Hold	1		2
SUCCEED (Real,Fact)	Get through		1	
	Pass	1	2	
	Pass		1	(2)
FAIL (AntiReal, Liqu)	Carve up	1	1	
	Eliminate	1	2	
	Fail		1	(2)
	Fail	1	2	
	Fluff		1	2
	Plough	1	2	
	Refuse	1	2	
	Reject	1	2	
	Turn down	1	2	
	Weed out	1	2	

get through takes an EXAMINEE as a subject to express success or that an EXAMINEE can appear as the direct object (second actant) of a series of verbs expressing failure caused by an EXAMINER. In the latter case, an EXAMINER can *carve up/eliminate/fail/plough/refuse/reject/turn down/weed out* an EXAMINEE.

carve up (vt sep): ~ candidate ~ ⇒ massacrer [informal] (candidat,liqu)
eliminate (vt): ~ candidate ~ ⇒ éliminer (candidat,liqu)
examine (vt): ~ candidate ~ ⇒ examiner (< in > en) (candidat,real2)

fail (vt): ~ candidate ~ ⇒ refuser (candidat,liqu)
fail (vi): ~ candidate ~ ⇒ échouer (candidat,antifactO)
get through (vi): ~ candidate ~ ⇒ être reçu (candidat,factO)
pass (vt): ~ candidate ~ ⇒ recevoir (candidat,real2)
plough (vt): ~ candidate ~ ⇒ recaler [informal] (candidat,liqu)
refuse (vt): ~ candidate ~ ⇒ refuser (candidat,liqu)
reject (vt): ~ candidate ~ ⇒ refuser (candidat,liqu)
turn down (vt sep): ~ candidate ~ ⇒ refuser (candidat,liq)
weed out (vt sep): ~ candidate ~ ⇒ éliminer (<from>de) (candidat,liqu)

6. Refining the descriptions with corpus data

The data provided by the CR database should not be considered as the be-all and end-all of the exercise. Clearly, the dictionary database can only offer a starting point leading to a fragmentary description of the behavior of a number of items participating in a given frame. Fragmentary though they may be, however, the frame element groups outlined in Table 1 above provide an interesting insight into the general structure of the `Examination` frame. The combinatory potential of its components receives a preliminary description and the lexical functions prove to be interesting clues leading to the discovery of a number of frame elements and to the identification of basic semantic relations holding between them. The notion of subscripts used in Mel'čuk's Meaning-Text Theory to indicate the deep actants of a keyword (see the functions S_1, S_2, $Oper_1$, $Oper_2$, $Real_1$, etc. above) is particularly interesting insofar as it helps identify the perspective from which the frame is seen when one selects a given predicate to activate it. Such functions are very general, however, and the proper labeling and identification of the frame elements can only be arrived at after a careful, in-depth intellectual analysis. The predigested material contained in the database can be used to carry out this type of analysis, without forgetting that corpus data should then be used to complement the descriptions. Corpus evidence would for instance show that at least two additional frame elements should be added to those we had already identified. Sentences such as the following (excerpted from the corpus-based CIDE, which is used here for illustrative purposes only and cannot provide all or only the appropriate collocates) are cases in point since they illustrate the use of other frame elements, which could be called SUBJECT, as in (12) and (13) or RESULT, as in (14):

(12) I passed *in history* but failed *in chemistry*. (Note that *I passed history but failed chemistry* is also possible, though CIDE does not indicate this.)

(13) She is taking *Physics* and *Maths* at A-level.

(14) John got three *passes* and four *fails* in his exams.

In (12), the SUBJECT frame element is introduced by the preposition *in*, while it appears as the direct object of *take* in (13). It is usually realized as a noun corresponding to a traditional discipline studied at school (*English*, *maths*, *geography*...). In (14), the EXAMINEE sits an exam and gets a result which reflects his/her performance in terms of pass/fail, marks or grades, and levels of distinction, thus: *passes*, *fails*, *As*, *Bs*, *Cs*, *distinction*, *honors*, etc.

7. Casting the net wider: using the dictionary as a thesaurus

We saw above that one of the primary tasks the frame semanticist is faced with is to identify core elements which can be considered as central predicates belonging to a specific frame. If we adopt an encoding perspective as a criterion for 'framehood', we are interested in retrieving items which native speakers use when talking about a given situation. In Section 5, above, we argued that verbs such as *fail* or *pass* are clearly more central to the examination frame than *supervise*, *superintend* or *plough* or *weed out*. In our search for central predicates, we can also use the possibilities offered by the thesaurus-like organization of the bilingual database. A bilingual entry indeed frequently offers what might be considered as a type of reassuring information (see also Michiels 2000), which can appear as a synonym or a hyperonym, normally in parentheses, especially when the entry is ambiguous and the user needs to be guided to the correct meaning before the appropriate translation can be selected. In the Collins-Robert database, such information is accessible through the Syn and Spec functions, which are used to indicate relations of synonymy and hyponymy (specific term) respectively. Starting from a central predicate such as *fail*, one may then query the database against synonyms of the verb *fail*, which amounts to retrieving verbal entries containing some italicized and parenthetical reference to *fail*. The list of potential candidates includes verbs such as *break down*, *fall down*, *flop*, *flunk*, *fold*, *go down*, *go under*, *let down*, *pip*, or *plough*. Not all these verbs belong to the `Examination` frame, however. *Flunk* definitely does, as the entry from the printed dictionary shows:

flunk (*esp US*) **1** *vi* (= *fail*) être recalé* or collé*; (= *shirk*) se dégonfler* **2** *vt* (**a**) (= *fail*) **to flunk French/an exam** être recalé* *or* être collé* en français/à un examen; **they flunked ten candidates** ils ont recalé* *or* collé dix candidats (**b**) (= *give up*) laisser tomber

Although the entry is divided into two main senses on the basis of transitivity patterns, it is clear that 'senses' **1** and **2(a)** are more closely related than are **2(a)** and **2(b)**. But the entry tells us more than the fact that *fail* can be used transitively or intransitively. Prototypical frame elements are mentioned in the form of examples. We can infer from the above entry that the following constellations of Frame Element Groups are possible, bearing in mind that a lot of this information is implicit, since nothing tells us explicitly that the subject of *to flunk French* corresponds to an EXAMINEE:

{Examinee} (vi reading: He flunked.)
{Examinee, Subject} (to flunk French)
{Examinee, Event} (to flunk an exam)
{Examiner, Examinee} (they flunked ten candidates)

On the basis of the additional information extracted along the lines outlined above, a revised frame-semantic lexical entry for the verbs *fail*, *flunk*, *get*, *pass*, and *take* would then appear as follows (see Table 2). The analy-

Table 2. Fail/Flunk/Get/Pass/Take: Frame Element Groups

	EXAMINER	EXAMINEE	EVENT	SUBJECT	RESULT
Fail	1	2			
Fail		1	(2)	(in)	
Fail		1		(2)	
Flunk	1	2			
Flunk		1	(2)		
Flunk		1		(2)	
Get		1	(in)	(in)	2
Take		1	2	(in)	
Take		1		2	
Pass	1	2			
Pass		1	(2)	(in)	(with)
Pass		1		(2)	(with)

sis of the semantic valence of these verbs provides ample evidence that we need a much more refined description than can be achieved with traditional semantic features such as [+Human], [+Abstract], etc.

8. Conclusion

The idea of using a lexical-semantic database incorporating Mel'čukian lexical functions in a frame semantic perspective is only at its preliminary stage. Results are encouraging, however, given the emphasis laid by both theories upon a deep semantic description of the actants playing a part in a 'linguistic' scenario and of their combinatory potential. Standard lexical functions are obviously too general in some cases to capture fine-grained meaning distinctions. They can be used to identify core frame elements, together with their syntax, however, and the collocational database provided by the Collins-Robert bilingual MRD houses data upon which fragments of frame-semantic lexical entries can be based.

Acknowledgements

The original development of the Collins-Robert lexical-semantic database took place at the University of Liège. Thanks are due to the publishers for granting us access to the tapes of the dictionary and for allowing us to go on using it for research purposes. A similar vote of thanks goes to Sue Atkins, Charles Fillmore and Tony Cowie, who read a preliminary version of this paper and provided me with interesting and stimulating comments.

References

A. Dictionaries and thesauri

Atkins, B.T.S. and A. Duval
1978 *Robert-Collins Dictionnaire Français-Anglais, Anglais-Français.* (First edition; third edition edited by Sinclair, L. and Duval, A.) Paris: Le Robert and Glasgow: Collins. (CR)

Fellbaum, C. (ed.)
1998 *WordNet: An Electronic Lexical Database.* Cambridge, Mass. and London: MIT Press.

Mel'čuk, I. et al.
1984 *Dictionnaire Explicatif et Combinatoire du Français Contemporain.* Montréal: Presses de Université de Montréal.

Procter, P. (ed.)
1995 *Cambridge International Dictionary of English.* Cambridge University Press. (CIDE)

Sinclair, J. et al. (eds.)
1987 *Collins COBUILD English Language Dictionary.* (First edition.) Glasgow: HarperCollins. (Cobuild)

B. Other references

Baker, C, C.J. Fillmore and J.B. Lowe
1998 The Berkeley FrameNet Project. In: *Proceedings of ACL/COLING 1998.*

Church, K. and P. Hanks
1990 Word association norms, mutual information and lexicography. *Computational Linguistics* 16.3: 22–29.

Dufour, N.
1998 Recognizing collocational constraints for translation selection: DEFI's combined approach. In: T. Fontenelle, P. Hiligsmann, A. Michiels, A. Moulin and S. Theissen (eds.), *EURALEX '98 Proceedings*, 109–118. 8th International Congress of the European Association for Lexicography. Liège: Université de Liège.

Fillmore, C.J.
1968 The case for case. In E. Bach and R.T. Harms (eds.), *Universals in Linguistic Theory*, 1–88. New York: Holt, Rinehart and Winston.

Fillmore, C.J.
1982 Frame Semantics. In: The Linguistic Society of Korea (ed.), *Linguistics in the Morning Calm*, 111–137. Seoul: Hanshin.

Fillmore, C.J. and B.T.S. Atkins
1992 Towards a frame-based lexicon: the case of RISK. In: A. Lehrer and E. F. Kittay (eds.), *Frames, Fields and Contrasts*, 75–102. Hillsdale NJ: Lawrence Erlbaum Associates.

Fillmore, C.J. and B.T.S. Atkins
1994 Starting where the dictionaries stop: the challenge for computational lexicography. In: B.T.S. Atkins and A. Zampolli (eds.), *Computational Approaches to the Lexicon*, 349–393. Oxford: Oxford University Press.

Fillmore, C.J. and B.T.S. Atkins
1998 FrameNet and lexicographic relevance. *Proceedings of the Granada Conference on Linguistic Resources*, 417–23.

Fontenelle, T.
1997a *Turning a bilingual dictionary into a lexical-semantic database.* Tübingen: Max Niemeyer Verlag.

Fontenelle, T.
1997b Using a bilingual dictionary to create semantic networks. *International Journal of Lexicography* 10.4: 275–303.

Gahl, S.
1998 Automatic extraction of subcategorization frames for corpus-based dictionary making. In: T. Fontenelle, P. Hiligsmann, A. Michiels, A. Moulin, and S. Theissen (eds.), *Euralex '98 Proceedings*, 445–452. 8th International Congress of the European Association for Lexicography. Liège: Université de Liège.

Harley, A. and D. Glennon
1997 Sense tagging in action. In: *ACL 1997 Conference on Tagging Text with Lexical Semantics: Why, What and How? Proceedings of the Workshop. Special Interest Group on the Lexicon.* Association for Computational Linguistics.

Heid, U.
1994 Relating lexicon and corpus: computational support for corpus-based lexicon building in DELIS. In: W. Martin, W. Meijs, M. Moerland, E. ten Pas, P. van Sterkenburg, and P. Vossen (eds.), *Euralex '94 Proceedings*, 459–471. 6th International Congress of the European Association for Lexicography. Amsterdam: Free University.

Heid, U.
1996 Creating a multilingual data collection for bilingual lexicography from parallel monolingual lexicons. In: M. Gellerstam, J. Järborg, S.-G. Malmgren, K. Norén, L. Rogström, and C.R. Papmehl (eds.), *Euralex '96 Proceedings*, 573–590. 7th International Congress of the European Association for Lexicography. Göteborg: University of Göteborg.

Lowe, J. B., C. Baker, and C.J. Fillmore
1997 A frame-semantic approach to semantic annotation. In: *Tagging Text with Lexical Semantics: Why, What, and How? Proceedings of the Workshop. Special Interest Group on the Lexicon, Association for Computational Linguistics*, 8–24.

Michiels, A.
1998 The DEFI matcher. In: T. Fontenelle, P. Hiligsmann, A. Michiels, A. Moulin, and S. Theissen (eds.), *Euralex '98 Proceedings*, 203–211. 8th International Congress of the European Association for Lexicography. Liège: Université de Liège.

Michiels, A.
2000 New developments in the DEFI matcher. *International Journal of Lexicography* 13.3: 151–67.

3. Semantic frames as interlingual representations for multilingual lexical databases

Hans C. Boas

1. Introduction[1]

Globalization and its effects on many areas of life requires a previously unforeseen level of detail of cross-linguistic information without which it is difficult, if not impossible, to provide accurate resources for efficient communication across language boundaries. Over the past decade, research in computational lexicography has thus focused on streamlining the creation of multilingual lexical databases in order to meet the ever-increasing demand for tools supporting human and machine translation, information retrieval, and foreign language education. However, creating multilingual lexical databases poses a number of problems that are more numerous and more complicated than those encountered in the creation of monolingual lexical databases.

One of the main problems that arises in the creation of multilingual lexical databases (henceforth MLLDs) is the development of an architecture capable of handling a wide spectrum of linguistic issues such as diverging polysemy structures (cf. Boas 2001, Viberg 2002), detailed valence information (cf. Fillmore and Atkins 2000), differences in lexicalization patterns (cf. Talmy 2000), and translation equivalents (cf. Sinclair 1996, Salkie 2002). A closely related question is whether MLLDs should employ an interlingua to map between different languages. If one decides in favor of an interlingua for mapping purposes, a choice needs to be made between using an unstructured interlingua as in EuroWordNet (Vossen

1. This paper was first published in 2005 in the *International Journal of Lexicography* Vol. 18.4: 445–478. I am grateful to Charles Fillmore, Collin Baker, Carlos Subirats, Kyoko Hirose Ohara, Hans U. Boas, Jonathan Slocum, Inge De Bleecker, Jana Thompson, and three anonymous referees for very helpful comments on the material discussed in the article.

1998, 2004), or a structured interlingua as in ULTRA (Farwell et al. 1993) or SIMuLLDA (Janssen 2004).

Another problem underlying the creation of adequate MLLDs concerns the sources of information used for constructing them. Whereas most MLLDs primarily rely on machine-readable versions of existing print dictionaries, very few take advantage of the multitude of information contained in electronic corpora that have become available for increasing numbers of languages over the past decade.[2]

This paper addresses these important issues by demonstrating how the English FrameNet database (Fillmore et al. 2003a) provides a solid basis for conducting cross-linguistic research, thereby facilitating the creation of MLLDs capable of overcoming a number of important linguistic problems.

As we will see, semantic frames as well as the underlying framework of Frame Semantics (Fillmore 1982, Fillmore and Atkins 1994) have been successfully employed by a number of FrameNet-type projects for languages other than English. In these projects, semantic frames play a central role in the building and connection of lexicon fragments across languages such as English, German, Spanish, and Japanese.

The remainder of the paper is structured as follows. Section 2 describes in detail some of the cross-linguistic problems that the architecture of any MLLD needs to address. Section 3 provides a brief survey of Frame Semantics. Section 4 discusses the architecture of FrameNet, which forms the basis for the creation of parallel lexicon fragments described in Section 5. This architecture, which employs semantic frames as an interlingual representation for connecting the various lexicon fragments differs in important ways from other types of interlingua approaches. Instead of using traditional lexical-semantic concepts such as synonymy, antonymy, and meronymy in combination with conceptual ontological information, the complementary approach proposed in this paper aims at linking parallel lexicon fragments by means of semantic frames. Section 6 compares the structure of MLLDs created on frame semantic principles with the architecture of other MLLDs. Finally, Section 7 provides a summary and gives an overview of open research questions.

2. See Atkins et al. (2002) for a recent approach to the design of multilingual lexical entries within the ISLE framework.

2. Linguistic problems for multilingual lexical databases

2.1. Polysemy

Whereas polysemy is seldom a serious problem in human communication, lexicographers have traditionally been concerned with how to best account for the fact that one word can carry several different meanings (cf. Leacock and Ravin 2000). Over time, lexicographic procedures have been established that have resulted in the listing of multiple dictionary senses for polysemous words where sub-senses are grouped together with their respective definitions (cf. Béjoint 2000: 227–234). However, dictionaries often vary in their organization of word senses, which makes it difficult to compare definitions across different dictionaries (cf. Atkins 1994, Goddard 2000). For example, in their discussion of the verb *risk*, Fillmore and Atkins (1994) compare the definitions found in ten different print dictionaries and come to the conclusion that "all the dictionaries agree on the clear stand-alone existence of Sense 1 (*risk your life*), but cannot agree on Sense 2 (*risk falling/a fall*) and Sense 3 (*risk climbing the cliff*)" (Fillmore and Atkins 1994: 353).

Looking beyond the well-known issues surrounding the treatment of polysemy in a single language, we find even greater problems when it comes to accounting for polysemy across languages. Overcoming these problems is not only important for the design of traditional lexicons, but also crucial for the successful implementation of MLLDs. In other words, without a satisfactory account of cross-linguistic polysemy, it is difficult, if not impossible, to construct adequate MLLDs. For example, Altenberg and Granger (2002) distinguish between three different types of cross-linguistic polysemy patterns that can be located along a continuum, where complete overlap of word senses is on one end of the continuum, and no correspondence among word senses across languages is found at the other end of the continuum. On one end of the continuum we find "overlapping polysemy" which refers to cases in which items in two languages have roughly the same meaning extensions (Altenberg and Granger 2002: 22). An example of overlapping polysemy is provided by Alsina and DeCesaris' (2002) comparison of the adjective *cold* with its Spanish and Catalan counterparts *frío* and *fred.* The authors discuss the varying degrees of polysemy exhibited by the three adjectives and come to the conclusion that the three adjectives exhibit "almost complete" overlapping polysemy patterns. Overlapping polysemy poses relatively few problems for multilingual dictionaries, but it is unfortunately very rare.

In contrast, diverging polysemy structures are very common. In their contrastive study of English *to crawl* and French *ramper*, Fillmore and Atkins (2000) demonstrate that the two verbs exhibit semantic overlap when it comes to the basic senses describing "the primary motion of insects and invertebrates, and the deliberate crouching movement of humans" (2000: 104). However, they differ widely in their meaning extensions when it comes to more specialized senses. For example, whereas English *crawl* can be used to describe slow-moving vehicles, French requires *rouler au pas* (literally: move at walking pace, or slowly) instead of *ramper*. Similarly, whereas *crawl* exhibits a meaning extension describing "creatures teeming" (*You got little brown insects crawling about all over you.* (2000: 96)), French requires *grouiller* instead of *ramper* to express the same concept (Fillmore and Atkins 2000: 107). Examples such as these show that adequate MLLDs must not only take into consideration the multitude of different senses of words across languages, but also have to include effective mechanisms that allow for the linking of extended word senses in diverging polysemy patterns.[3]

The third type of cross-linguistic phenomenon posing problems for MLLDs are cases in which there are no clear equivalents in the target language. As Altenberg and Granger (2002: 25) point out, these cases may lead to two types of problems: "either the lack of a clear translation equivalent in the target language results in a large number of zero translations, indicating that the translators have great difficulties finding a suitable target item, or in a wide range of translations, indicating that the translators find it necessary to render the source item in some way but, in the absence of a single prototypical equivalent, vary their renderings according to context." However problematic it may be to find proper equivalences for "difficult" lexical items cross-linguistically, it is necessary to account for them within MLLDs. Without their inclusion, neither humans nor machines will be able to successfully employ MLLDs for translation purposes. With this brief overview of problems surrounding cross-linguistic polysemy patterns, we now turn to another linguistic issue that needs to be accounted for when designing MLLDs, namely the accuracy of syntactic and semantic valence patterns.

3. For examples of diverging polysemy patterns among nouns, see Svensen (1993) on *wood* and *forest* and their French and German equivalents. See Chodkiewicz et al. (2002: 264) on the various meanings of *proceedings* and their French equivalents.

2.2. Syntactic and semantic valence patterns

Besides providing information about a word's different senses, any MLLD should provide detailed syntactic information illustrating the various ways in which meanings can be realized. To illustrate, consider the following examples.

(1) a. The mother cured the child.
    b. The mother cured the measles.
    c. The mother cured {the child/the measles} with pills.

(2) a. The mother cured the ham.
    b. The mother cured the ham with hickory smoke.

(3) a. [NP, V, NP]
    b. [NP, V, NP, PP_with]

The sentences in (1) exemplify some of the syntactic valence patterns associated with one sense of *to cure*, namely the healing sense. In contrast, the examples in (2) illustrate some of the syntactic valence patterns found with the preserving food sense of *cure*. The syntactic frames in (3) summarize the syntactic commonalities among the two different senses of *cure*. That is, whereas the syntactic frame in (3a) represents the valence pattern exhibited by (1a), (1b), and (2a), the syntactic frame in (3b) summarizes the valence patterns of (1c) and (2b). From the perspective of a human user the information in (1)–(3) is readily interpretable because humans have already stored the representation that makes the link between the underlying meaning of the senses and their different syntactic realizations.

However, NLP-applications face a much harder task when trying to identify the different meanings of *cure* because they are typically trying to establish the meanings based on syntactic information of the type in (3) alone. That is, without having access to information about the different semantic types of Noun Phrases or Prepositional Phrases that may occur with the different senses in postverbal position, it is difficult to decide what sense of *cure* is expressed. This example illustrates that lexical databases should contain adequate information not only about a word's different senses, but also how a single sense of a word may be realized in different ways at the syntactic level.[4]

---

4. Note that resources such as WordNet (cf. Fellbaum 1998) provide important information that can be used to determine the semantic type of complements.

Similar issues arise in multilingual environments. Discussing the various Swedish counterparts for *get*, Viberg (2002: 139) reviews the "large number of senses which are both lexical and grammatical." As Table 1 shows, the multitude of syntactic frames associated with *get* are relevant for the identification of the appropriate sense.

Table 1. The major meanings of *get* (cf. Viberg 2002: 140)

Meaning	*Frame*	*Example*
Possession	get + NP have + got + NP	Peter got a book Peter has got a book
Modal: Obligation	have got to + $VP_{infinitive}$ gotta + $VP_{infinitive}$	Peter has got to come Peter has gotta come
Inchoative	get + ADJ/Participle	Peter got angry
Passive	get + PastPart (by NP)	Peter got killed (by a gunman)
Causative Motion:	get + NP + to $VP_{infinitive}$	Peter got Harry to leave
Subject-centered	get + Particle get + PP	Peter got up/in/out ... Peter got to Berlin
Object-centered	get + NP + PP	Peter got the buns out of the oven

Similar to our discussion of *cure* above, it is clear that any lexical database must contain fine-grained valence information of the kind contained in Table 1 in order to successfully identify the different senses of *get*. At the next step, MLLDs should also provide information about translation equivalents in other languages. Table 2 lists the most frequent Swedish equivalents of *get*.

Table 2. The most frequent Swedish equivalents of English *get* (cf. Viberg 2002: 141)

Possession		*Motion*		*Inchoative*	
få	'get'	komma	'come'	bli	'become'
ha	'have'	gå	'go'		
ta	'take'	stiga	'step'		
ge	'give'	kliva	'stride'		
skaffa	'acquire'	resa sig	'rise'		
hämta	'fetch'				

The Swedish data demonstrate that the identification of Swedish equivalents of *get* require detailed information about the specific sense of *get* in English source texts. Any MLLD aimed at providing useful information for humans and machines will therefore have to include detailed syntactic and semantic valence information showing how to map specific sub-senses of a word from one language into another language. The following section discusses a related problem, namely different types of lexicalization patterns across languages.

2.3. Differences in lexicalization patterns

As Talmy (1985, 2000) points out, languages show strong preferences as to what kinds of semantic components they lexicalize. This property, in turn, has a number of important implications for the design of MLLDs. For example, Japanese motion verbs differ from English motion verbs in how they realize various types of paths (Ohara et al. 2004). The verbs *wataru* ('go across') and *koeru* ('go beyond, go over') "describe motion in terms of the shape of the path traversed by the theme that moves" (Ohara et al. 2004: 10). As examples (4a) and (4b) show, *wataru* ('go across') is used with an accusative-marked direct object NP describing a path. Ohara et al. point out that *kawa* ('river') in (4a) "denotes an area that lies between two points in space", whereas *hasi* ('bridge') "refers to a medium or a passage that is constructed between the two points."

(4) a. nanminga kawa o watatta
refugees NOM river ACC went.across
'The refugees went across (crossed, traversed) the river.'

b. nanminga hasi o watatta
refugees NOM bridge ACC went.across
'The refugees crossed the bridge.' (Ohara et al. 2004: 10)

Differences arise when we look at semantically related verbs such as *koeru* ('go beyond') which takes an accusative marked direct object NP such as *kawa* ('river') in (5a). However, *koeru* does not allow *hasi* ('bridge') as its direct object as is illustrated by (5b).

(5) a. nanminga kawa o koeta
refugees NOM river ACC went.beyond
'The refugees went beyond (passed) the river.'

b. *nanminga hasi o koeta
refugees NOM bridge ACC went.beyond
(Intended meaning) 'The refugees passed the bridge.'
(Ohara et al. 2004: 10)

According to Ohara et al. (2004), the differences between these verbs illustrate the necessity to identify and include in lexical descriptions the subcategories of different types of paths that can occur with motion verbs in Japanese. They point out that *wataru* ('go across') may be described as taking an accusative-marked route, while *koeru* ('go beyond') may be characterized as taking an accusative-marked boundary as the direct object (2004: 10).[5] These examples demonstrate that Japanese makes a more fine-grained distinction between different types of path expressions than English. In other words, whereas in English the type of path is typically unimportant in terms of lexical selection, Japanese verbs exhibit a larger variety of lexicalization patterns with respect to path expressions.

While these systematic differences in lexicalization patterns pose relatively few problems to bilingual speakers, it is far from clear as to how these differences between languages should be encoded in MLLDs. That is, in order to successfully "mirror the expertise of bilingual humans" (Sinclair 1996: 174), it is first necessary to determine how to systematically account for differences in lexicalization patterns in the design of MLLDs. We return to this issue in Section 5.

2.4. Measuring paraphrase relations and translation equivalents

Another linguistic problem requiring attention in the design of MLLDs concerns two related issues, namely dealing with paraphrase relations and measuring translation equivalents across languages. When accounting for paraphrase relations, lexical databases should include information about the fact that certain words and multi word expressions are paraphrases of each other, i.e., they may be substituted for each other and still express the same meaning. Compare the following examples.

(6) Jana argued with Inge about the theory.

(7) Jana had an argument with Inge about the theory.

---

5. For a discussion of different lexicalization patterns posing similar types of problems, see Talmy (1985) for motion verbs in English and Atsugewi, and Subirats & Petruck (2003) for emotion verbs in English and Spanish.

Both sentences express the same type of situation. However, the two examples differ in how the situation is expressed syntactically. In (6) it is the verb *argue* which takes *Jana* as a subject, and *with Inge* and *about the theory* as prepositional complements. In (7), it is the multi word expression *to have an argument*, which occurs with *Jana* as its subject, and *with Inge* and *about the theory* as its prepositional complements. This example shows that the number of words evoking a given meaning may differ across sentences. Any lexical database that is used for translation purposes must not only take into account paraphrase relations within a single language, but it should also include a description of how to map such paraphrases cross-linguistically.

In other words, when it comes to translation equivalents, the question is not only how to "measure" them cross-linguistically, but also how to match them from different paraphrases in the source language to different types of paraphrases in the target language. Consider the following examples from German, which are translation equivalents of (6) and (7).

(8) a. Jana stritt mit Inge über die Theorie.
Jana argued with Inge about the theory
'Jana argued with Inge about the theory.'

b. Jana stritt sich mit Inge über die Theorie.
Jana argued self with Inge about the theory
'Jana argued with Inge about the theory.'

(9) Jana hatte einen Streit mit Inge über die Theorie.
Jana had an argument with Inge about the theory
'Jana had an argument with Inge about the theory.'

In (8a) and (8b), we find the verb *streiten* ('to argue') and its counterpart *sich streiten* ('to argue'), respectively. In this context, there is no obvious difference in meaning that would be caused by choosing one verb over the other. Similarly, the multi word expression *einen Streit haben mit* ('to have an argument with') in (9) expresses the same type of situation as the sentences in (8). These three sentences are important because they exemplify the difficulty of identifying paraphrase relations within one language, and translation equivalents across languages.[6] In contrast to bilingual

6. An anonymous reviewer points out that another way of capturing such paraphrase relations would be to apply Mel'čuk's Meaning-Text Theory (Mel'čuk et al. 1988) and its Explanatory Combinatory Dictionaries. On this view, a

human speakers, who possess what Chesterman (1998: 39) calls translation competence ("the ability to relate two things"), multi-lingual NLP applications have to rely on MLLDs to supply information about translation equivalents. Without the inclusion of paraphrase relations and the different numbers and combinations of word senses across languages it will be difficult to solve problems such as those discussed above. With this overview, we now turn to a discussion of Frame Semantics and the structure of the English FrameNet database. In Section 5, we return to the linguistic issues discussed in this section and demonstrate how they can be tackled by MLLDs that employ semantic frames as an interlingua.

3. Frame Semantics

Frame Semantics, as developed by Fillmore and his associates over the past three decades (Fillmore 1970, 1975, 1982, Fillmore and Atkins 1992, 1994, 2000), is a semantic theory that refers to semantic "frames" as a common background of knowledge against which the meanings of words are interpreted (cf. Fillmore and Atkins 1992: 76–77).[7] An example is the `Compliance` frame, which involves several semantically related words such as *adhere*, *adherence*, *comply*, *compliant*, and *violate*, among many others (Johnson et al. 2003). The `Compliance` frame represents a kind of situation in which different types of relationships hold between so-called "Frame Elements" (FEs), which are defined as situation-specific semantic roles.[8] This frame concerns ACTS and STATES_OF_AFFAIRS for which PRO-

---

lexical function is a meaning relation between a keyword and other words or phraseological combinations of words. Using paraphrase mechanisms, we can link such paraphrases as *streiten* and *einen Streit haben* (cf. (8) and (9)) with lexical functions:

V0(argument) = argue
Oper1(argument) = have

See Mel'čuk & Wanner (2001) for a lexical transfer model using Meaning-Text Theory for machine translation.

7. For a detailed overview of Frame Semantics, see Petruck (1996).
8. Names of Frame Elements (FEs) are capitalized. Frame Elements differ from traditional universal semantic (or thematic) roles such as Agent or Patient in that they are specific to the frame in which they are used to describe participants in certain types of scenarios. "Tgt" stands for target word, which is the word that evokes the semantic frame.

TAGONISTS are responsible and which violate some NORM(S). The FE ACT identifies the act that is judged to be in or out of compliance with the norms. The FE NORM identifies the rules or norms that ought to guide a person's behavior. The FE PROTAGONIST refers to the person whose behavior is in or out of compliance with norms. Finally, the FE STATE_OF_AFFAIRS refers to the situation that may violate a law or rule (see Johnson et al. 2003).

With the frame as a semantic structuring device, it becomes possible to describe how different FEs are realized syntactically by different parts of speech. The unit of description in Frame Semantics is the lexical unit (henceforth LU), which stands for a word in one of its senses (cf. Cruse 1986). Consider the following sentences in which the LUs (the targets) *adhere*, *compliance*, *compliant*, *follow*, and *violation* evoke the `Compliance` frame. FEs are marked in square brackets, their respective names are given in subscript.[9]

(10) [$_{\text{<Protagonist>}}$ Women] take more time, talk easily and still *adhere*^{Tgt} [$_{\text{<Norm>}}$ to the strict rules of manners].

(11) It is also likely to improve [$_{\text{<Protagonist>}}$ patient] *compliance*^{Tgt} [$_{\text{<Norm>}}$ in taking the daily quota of bile acid].

(12) [$_{\text{<Protagonist>}}$ Patients] were^{Supp} [$_{\text{<Act>}}$ *compliant*^{Tgt}] [$_{\text{<Norm>}}$ with their assigned treatments].

(13) So now the Commission and other countryside conservation groups, have produced [$_{\text{<Norm>}}$ a series of guidelines] [$_{\text{<Protagonist>}}$ for the private landowners] to *follow*^{Tgt}.

(14) [$_{\text{<Act>}}$ Using a couple of minutes for private imperatives] was^{Supp} a [$_{\text{<Degree>}}$ serious] *violation*^{Tgt} [$_{\text{<Norm>}}$ of property rights].

The examples show that FEs may occur in different syntactic positions, and that they may fulfill different types of grammatical functions (subject, object, etc.). One of the major advantages of describing LUs in frame semantic terms is that it allows the lexicographer to use the same underlying semantic frame to describe different words belonging to different parts of speech. The design of the FrameNet database, to which we now turn, is influenced by and structured along frame-semantic principles.

9. Support verbs (Supp) such as *to be* or *to take* do not introduce any particular semantics of their own. Instead, they create a verbal predicate "allowing arguments of the verb to serve as frame elements of the frame evoked by the noun". (Johnson et al. 2003)

4. FrameNet

The FrameNet database developed at the International Computer Science Institute in Berkeley, California, is an on-line lexicon of English lexical units (LUs) described in terms of Frame Semantics. Between 1997 and 2003, the FrameNet team collected and analyzed lexical descriptions for more than 7,000 LUs based on more than 130,000 annotated corpus sentences (Baker et al. 1998, Fillmore et al. 2003a). The process underlying the creation of lexical entries in FrameNet involves several steps. First, frame descriptions for the words or word families targeted for analysis are devised. This procedure consists roughly of the following phases:

> (1) characterizing schematically the kind of entity or situation represented by the frame, (2) choosing mnemonics for labeling the entities or components of the frame, and (3) constructing a working list of words that appear to belong to the frame, where membership in the same frame will mean that the phrases that contain the LUs will all permit comparable semantic analyses. (Fillmore et al. 2003b: 297)

The second step in the FrameNet workflow concentrates on identifying corpus sentences in the British National Corpus exhibiting typical uses of the target words in specific frames. Next, these corpus sentences are extracted mechanically and annotated manually by tagging the Frame Elements realized in them. Finally, lexical entries are automatically prepared and stored in the database. An important feature of the FrameNet workflow is that it is not completely linear. That is, at each stage of the workflow, FrameNet lexicographers may discover new corpus data that might force them to re-write frame descriptions because of the need to include or exclude certain LUs in the frame. Similarly, if frames are found to include LUs whose semantics are too divergent, frames have to be "re-framed" (see Petruck et al. 2004), i.e., they have to be split up into separate frames (for a full overview of the FrameNet process, see Fillmore et al. (2003a) and Fillmore et al. (2003b)).

The FrameNet database (http://framenet.icsi.berkeley.edu) offers a wealth of semantic and syntactic information for several thousand English verbs, nouns, and adjectives. Each lexical entry in FrameNet is structured as follows: It provides a link to the definition of the frame to which the LU belongs, including FE definitions, example sentences exemplifying prototypical instances of FEs (For more information on the structure of the FrameNet database, please see Baker et al. (2003)). In addition, it offers information about various frame-to-frame relations (e.g., child-parent relation and sub-frame relation (see Fillmore et al. 2003b and Petruck et al. 2004)) and includes a list of LUs that evoke the frame.

The central component of a lexical entry in FrameNet consists of three parts. The first provides the Frame Element Table (a list of all FEs found within the frame) and corresponding annotated corpus sentences demonstrating how FEs are realized syntactically (see Fillmore et al. 2003b). In this part, words or phrases instantiating certain FEs in the annotated corpus sentences are highlighted with the same color as the FEs in the FE table above them. This type of display allows users to identify the variety of different FE instantiations across a broad spectrum of words and phrases. The Realization Table is the second part of a FrameNet entry. Besides providing a dictionary definition of the relevant LU, it summarizes the different syntactic realizations of the frame elements. The third part of the Lexical Entry Report summarizes the valence patterns found with a LU, that is, "the various combinations of frame elements and their syntactic realizations which might be present in a given sentence" (Fillmore et al. (2003a: 330)). As the first row in the valence table for *comply* in Figure 1 shows, the FE NORM may be realized in terms of two different types of external arguments: either as an external noun phrase argument, or as a prepositional phrase headed by *with*. Clicking on the link in the column to the left of the valence patterns leads the user to a display of annotated example sentences illustrating the valence pattern.[10]

Accessing the Lexical Entry Report for a given LU not only allows the user to get detailed information about its syntactic and semantic distribution. It also facilitates a comparison of the comprehensive lexical descriptions and their manually annotated corpus-based example sentences with those of other LUs (also of other parts of speech) belonging to the same frame. Another advantage of the FrameNet architecture lies in the way lexical descriptions are related to each other in terms of semantic frames. Using detailed semantic frames which capture the full background knowledge that is evoked by all LUs of that frame makes it possible to systematically compare and contrast their numerous syntactic valency patterns.

Our discussion of FrameNet shows that it is different from traditional (print) dictionaries, thesauri, and lexical databases in that it is organized

10. Frame Elements which are conceptually salient but do not occur as overt lexical or phrasal material are marked as null instantiations. There are three different types of null instantiation: Constructional Null Instantiation (CNI), Definite Null Instantiation (DNI), and Indefinite Null Instantiation (INI). See Fillmore et al. (2003b: 320–321) for more details.

around highly specific semantic frames capturing the background knowledge necessary to understand the meaning of LUs. By employing semantic frames as structuring devices, FrameNet thus differs from other approaches to lexical description (e.g. ULTRA (Farwell et al. 1993), WordNet (Fellbaum (1998), or SIMuLLDA (Janssen 2004)) in that it makes use of independent organizational units that are larger than words, i.e., semantic frames (see also Ohara et al. 2003, Boas 2005). In the following sections I show how the inventory of semantic frames can be utilized for the construction of MLLDs. Drawing on data from Spanish, Japanese, and German I demonstrate the individual steps necessary for the construction of parallel FrameNets.

Number Annotated	Patterns		
3 TOTAL	Act	Norm	
(3)	NP Ext	PP[with] Dep	
1 TOTAL	Norm	Norm	Protagonist
(1)	NP Ext	PP[with] Dep	CNI --
17 TOTAL	Norm	Protagonist	
(2)	PP[with] Dep	CNI --	
(15)	PP[with] Dep	NP Ext	
2 TOTAL	Norm	State_of_Affairs	
(1)	DNI --	NP Ext	
(1)	PP[to] Dep	NP Ext	

Figure 1. FrameNet entry for *comply*, Valence Table

5. Using semantic frames for creating multilingual lexicon fragments

5.1. Producing FrameNet-type descriptions for other languages

In order to construct a non-English FrameNet, we first download the English FrameNet MySQL database (see Baker et al. 2003 for a detailed description of the FN database structure). Next, all English-specific information is removed from the language-specific database tables. This includes, for example, all information about Lexical Units in the top left part of the original FrameNet database tables in Figure 2 (e.g. Lemma, Part of Speech, Lexeme, Lexeme Entry, Word Form), as well as all information relating to annotated corpus example sentences in the lower left part of the original FrameNet database tables in Figure 2 (e.g. Corpus, Sub-corpus, Document, Genre, Paragraph).

Once all English-specific information is removed, only information not specific to English remains in the database tables. This includes conceptual information in the upper right of the FrameNet database diagram in Figure 2, such as the Frames table, the FrameRelation table, the FERelation table, the FrameElements table, among other information. Once the FrameNet database has been stripped of its English-specific lexical descriptions and accompanying information, work begins on the second stage, namely re-populating the database with non-English lexical descriptions.

The first step consists of choosing a semantic frame from the stripped-down original database. For example, one might choose the `Communication_response` frame, which deals with communicating a reply or response to some prior communication or action (Johnson et al. 2003). English LUs belonging to this frame include the verbs *to answer, to counter*, and *to rejoin*, as well as the nouns *answer*, *response*, and *reply*, among others. In the FrameNet database we learn from the FrameElement table that this frame contains the FEs ADDRESSEE, MESSAGE, SPEAKER, TOPIC, and TRIGGER.

The second step in re-populating the database to arrive at a full-fledged non-English FrameNet is to identify with the help of dictionaries and parallel corpora lists of LUs in other languages that evoke the same semantic frame. This process is similar to the initial stages of English FrameNet (see Fillmore et al. 2003a), except for the fact that it is easier to compile lists of LUs because one already has access to existing frame descriptions and frame relations.[11] Our compilation of LUs for the `Communication_response` frame yields a list that includes German verbs and nouns such as *beantworten* ('to answer'), *entgegnen* ('to reply'), *die Ant-*

11. The availability of a stripped-down FN database with existing frames and FEs means that non-English FrameNets do not have to go through the entire process of frame creation (Fillmore et al. 2003: 304–313). It is important to keep in mind that at present FrameNet covers about 8900 lexical units in more than 600 frames. This means that its coverage of the English lexicon is somewhat limited when compared with other resources such as WordNet. Similarly, FrameNets for other languages will exhibit comparable limitations until FrameNet covers much larger areas of the English lexicon (or, even full coverage).

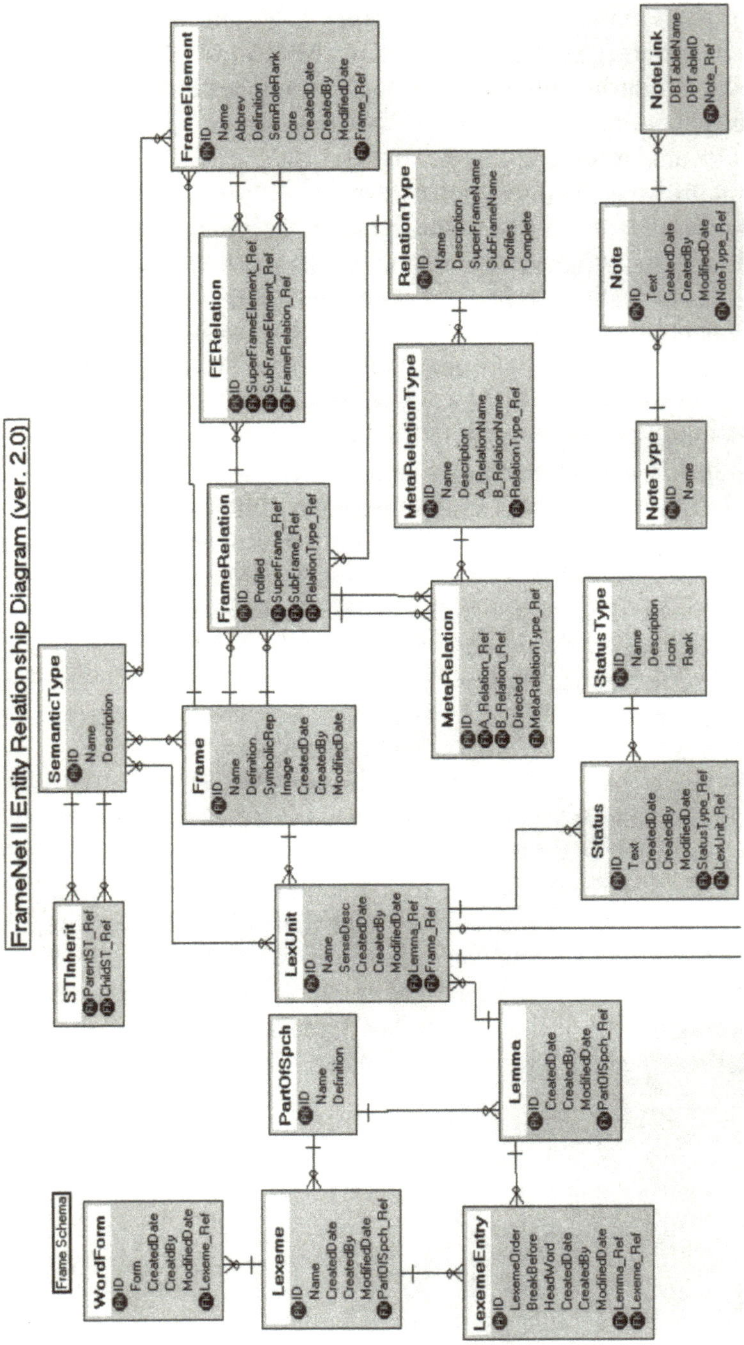
FrameNet II Entity Relationship Diagram (ver. 2.0)
Frame Schema
STInherit
ParentST_Ref
ChildST_Ref
SemanticType
ID
Name
Description
FrameElement
ID
Name
Abbrev
Definition
SemRoleRank
Core
CreatedDate
CreatedBy
ModifiedDate
Frame_Ref
FERelation
ID
SuperFrameElement_Ref
SubFrameElement_Ref
FrameRelation_Ref
FrameRelation
ID
Profiled
SuperFrame_Ref
SubFrame_Ref
RelationType_Ref
Frame
ID
Name
Definition
SymbolicRep
Image
CreatedDate
CreatedBy
ModifiedDate
RelationType
ID
Name
Description
SuperFrameName
SubFrameName
Profiles
Complete
MetaRelationType
ID
Name
Description
A_RelationName
B_RelationName
RelationType_Ref
MetaRelation
ID
A_Relation_Ref
B_Relation_Ref
Directed
MetaRelationType_Ref
LexUnit
ID
Name
SenseDesc
CreatedDate
CreatedBy
ModifiedDate
Lemma_Ref
Frame_Ref
PartOfSpch
ID
Name
Definition
Lemma
ID
CreatedDate
CreatedBy
ModifiedDate
PartOfSpch_Ref
WordForm
ID
Form
CreatedDate
CreatdBy
ModifiedDate
Lexeme_Ref
Lexeme
ID
Name
CreatedDate
CreatedBy
ModifiedDate
PartOfSpch_Ref
LexemeEntry
ID
LexemeOrder
BreakBefore
HeadWord
CreatedDate
CreatedBy
ModifiedDate
Lemma_Ref
Lexeme_Ref
StatusType
ID
Name
Description
Icon
Rank
Status
ID
Text
CreatedDate
CreatedBy
ModifiedDate
StatusType_Ref
LexUnit_Ref
Note
ID
Text
CreatedDate
CreatedBy
ModifiedDate
NoteType_Ref
NoteType
ID
Name
NoteLink
DBTableName
DBTableID
Note_Ref

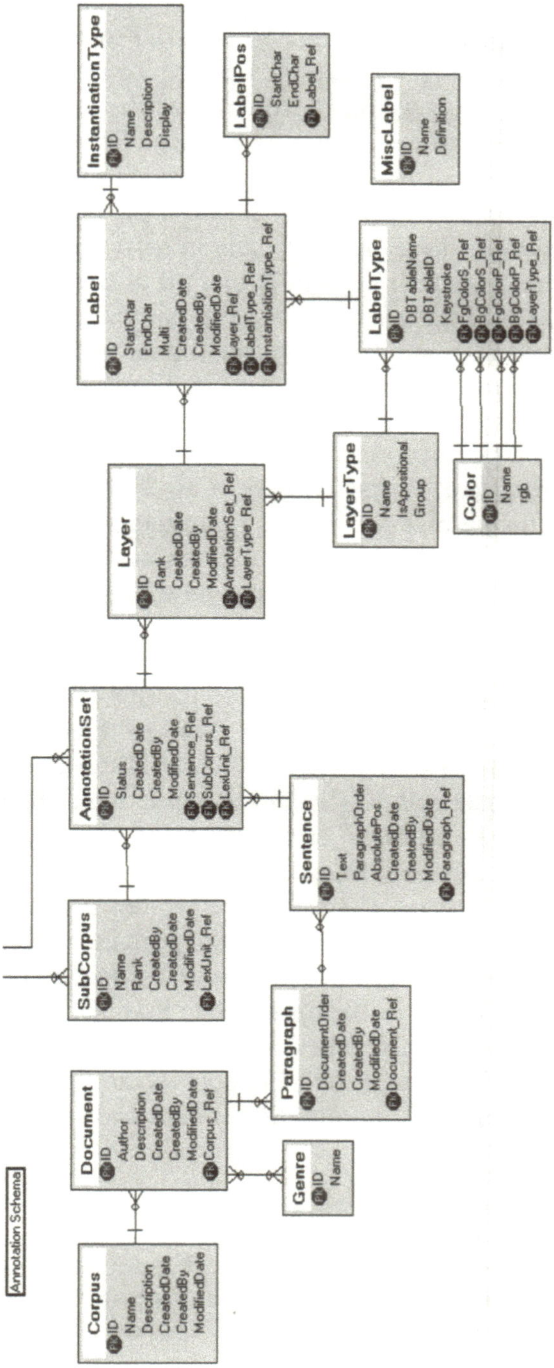

Figure 2. Structure of the FrameNet database (cf. Baker et al. 2003)

wort ('answer'), and *die Entgegnung* ('reply'). For Japanese, we find verbs such as *uke-kotae suru* ('to answer') and *ootoo suru* ('to reply') and nouns such as *kotae* ('answer'), which evoke the `Communication_response` frame. Similarly, in Spanish we find verbs such as *desmentir* ('deny') and *responder* ('to respond') and nouns such as *respuesta* ('response').

At this point it is necessary to briefly mention some similarities and differences among non-English FrameNets. Between the Spanish, Japanese, and German FrameNets there are differences in software setup and data sources used. Whereas Spanish FrameNet uses all of the original English FrameNet software (and has compiled its own corpus) (see Subirats and Petruck 2003), Japanese FrameNet is developing its own set of software tools to augment the tools provided by English FrameNet (see Ohara et al 2003). There are two projects concerned with developing FrameNet-type descriptions for German. The SALSA project at the University of the Saarland (Saarbrücken, Germany) (Erk et al. 2003) has developed its own annotation software and set of tools to annotate the entire TIGER corpus (König and Lezius 2003) with semantic frames. Its goal is to apply English-based frames to the TIGER corpus data, inventing new frames where necessary. In contrast, German FrameNet (Boas 2002), currently under construction at the University of Texas at Austin, is adapting the original FrameNet tools and aims to provide parallel lexical entries that are comparable in breadth and depth to those of English FrameNet. Another project, BiFrameNet (Fung and Chen 2004) focuses on the lexical description of Chinese and English for machine translation purposes. It differs from other FrameNets in that it takes a statistically-based approach to producing bilingual lexicon fragments.

To illustrate the process by which the stripped-down FrameNet database is repopulated with non-English data, the remainder of this section focuses primarily on the workflow of the Spanish FrameNet project (Subirats and Petruck 2003).[12] Once the appropriate lists of LUs evoking the frame are compiled for Spanish, they are added to the database using FrameNet's Lexical Unit Editor (cf. Fillmore et al. 2003b: 313–315). More specifically, for each LU information is stored about "(1) its name,

12. Spanish FrameNet currently contains about 80 annotated frames (with about 480 lexical units) as well as 500 frames that have not yet been annotated. Currently, SALSA has annotated approximately 540 lexical units, totaling more than 25,000 verb instances in the TIGER corpus. As both Japanese FrameNet and German FrameNet are currently in their beginning stages, no data have yet been made public.

(2) its part of speech, (3) its meaning, and (4) information about its formal composition" (Fillmore et al. 2003: 313). After adding all of the relevant information about each LU belonging to a frame to the database, a search is conducted in a very large corpus in order find sentences that illustrate the use of each of the LUs in the frame. This approach is parallel to the procedure employed by the original Berkeley FrameNet. Spanish FrameNet uses a 300 million-word corpus, which includes a variety of both New World and European Spanish texts from different genres such as newspapers, book reviews, and humanities essays (Subirats and Petruck 2003). To search the corpus and to create different subcorpora of sentences for annotation, the Spanish FrameNet project employs the Corpus Workbench software from the Institut für Maschinelle Sprachverarbeitung ('Institute for Natural Language Processing') at the University of Stuttgart (Christ 1994). Using an electronic dictionary of 600,000 word forms and a set of deterministic automata, a number of automatic processes select relevant example sentences from the corpus and subsequently compile subcorpora for each syntactic frame with which an LU may occur (cf. Subirats and Ortega 2000 and Ortega 2002). As in the creation of the original FrameNet, the subcorpora are then manually annotated with frame semantic information in order to arrive at clear example sentences illustrating all the different ways in which frame elements are realized syntactically. For annotation and database creation, Spanish FrameNet (SFN) employs the software developed by the original Berkeley FrameNet project. Figure 3 illustrates how the FrameNet Desktop Software is used by SFN to annotate part of an example sentence in the `Communication_response` frame.

Figure 3. Annotation of a Spanish sentence in the `Communication_response` frame (Subirats and Petruck 2003)

The top line shows the example sentence *La respuesta positiva de los trabajadores al acuerdo* with the target noun *respuesta* ('response'), which evokes the `Communication_response` frame. Underneath the top line are three separate layers, one each for information pertaining to frame element names (FE), grammatical functions (GF), and phrase types (PT). After having become familiar with the frame and frame element definitions, annotators mark whole constituents with the appropriate colored tags representing the different frame elements of the `Communication_response` frame. In Figure 3, *positiva* ('positive') is tagged with the FE MESSAGE, *de los trabajadores* ('by the workers') is tagged with the FE SPEAKER, and *al acuerdo* ('to the accord') is marked with the FE TRIGGER. Once example sentences are marked with semantic tags, syntactic information about grammatical functions (GF) and phrase types (PT) is added semi-automatically and hand-corrected if necessary. Figure 4 shows only a small part of the software used for semantic annotation by members of the Spanish FrameNet team. Recall that manual semantic annotation covers the full range of examples of sentences illustrating each possible syntactic configuration in which a lexical item may occur. As such, Figure 4 gives a more complete illustration of the FrameNetDesktop Annotator software graphical user interface.

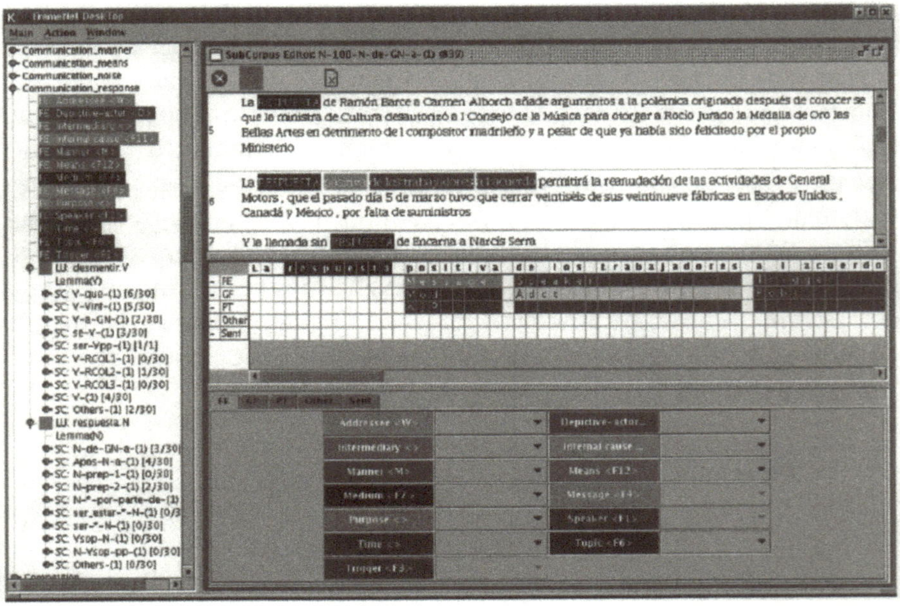

Figure 4. Annotation of a Spanish sentence using the FrameNet Annotator (Subirats and Petruck 2003)

The FrameNet Annotator window is divided into four main parts. The left part is the navigation frame that allows annotators to directly access all frames as well as their respective frame elements and lexical units contained in the MySQL database. The navigation frame shows different communication frames (`Communication_manner` and `Communication_noise` among others), where `Communication_response` is highlighted by an annotator to reveal the frame's FEs (ADDRESSEE, MEDIUM, and SPEAKER, among others). Clicking on a frame name reveals a list of LUs evoking the frame, in this case *desmentir* ('deny') and *respuesta* ('response') with their corresponding subcorpora containing example sentences previously extracted from the 300 million-word corpus (Subirats and Petruck 2003).

Selecting a lexical unit's subcorpus displays its respective example sentences in the top right part of the FrameNet Annotator window, in this case three example sentences with the target noun *respuesta*, which is highlighted in black. Clicking on one of the corpus sentences allows annotators to view it with the full set of layers in the middle part on the right of the Annotator window (see also Figure 3). The fourth part on the bottom right of the Annotator window displays the content space with the specifications for the different frame elements of the `Communication_Response` frame.[13]

Using the Annotator tool, members of the Spanish FrameNet team annotate a set of relevant corpus sentences in each subcorpus (see description above), thereby arriving at an extensive set of annotated subcorpora for each LU. As with the original FrameNet, the resulting annotated sentences represent an exhaustive list of the ways in which frame elements may be realized syntactically with a given target word. Once annotation is completed, the lexical units are stored with their annotated example sentences in the FrameNet MySQL database, which at the end of the workflow described in this section has evolved from a FrameNet database whose tables have been stripped of all of their English-specific data into a corresponding Spanish FrameNet database. Thus, Spanish FrameNet (and, to some degree, the corresponding Japanese and German FrameNets) is comparable in structure with that of the original English FrameNet database in that it contains the same set of frames and frame relations. It differs from English FrameNet in that the entries for argument taking nouns, verbs, and adjectives are in Spanish. Users may access the Spanish FrameNet database by the same set of web-based reports as for the original English FrameNet, i.e., for each LU in the database it is possible to display an Annotation Report, a Lexical Entry Report, and the corresponding valence tables. With this overview in mind, we now look at

13. Frame Elements are automatically annotated with grammatical function (GF) and phrase type (PT) information.

how semantic frames may be used to connect parallel lexicon fragments. More specifically, I show that the frame-semantic approach to MLLDs overcomes many of the problems faced by other MLLDs discussed in Section 2.

5.2. Linking parallel lexicon fragments via semantic frames

With FrameNets for multiple languages in place, the next step towards the creation of MLLDs on frame-semantic principles consists of linking the parallel lexicon fragments via semantic frames in order to be able to map lexical information of frame-evoking words from one language to another language (see also Heid and Krüger 1996, Fontenelle 2000, Boas 2002). Since the MySQL databases representing each of the non-English FrameNets are similar in structure to the English MySQL database in that they share the same type of conceptual backbone (i.e., the semantic frames and frame relations), this step involves determining which English lexical units are equivalent to corresponding non-English lexical units.

Table 3. Partial Realization Table for the verb *answer*

FE Name	*Syntactic Realizations*
Speaker	NP.Ext, PP_by_Comp, CNI
Message	INI, NP.Obj, PP_with.Comp, QUO.Comp, Sfin.Comp
Addressee	DNI
Depictive	PP_with.Comp
Manner	AVP.Comp, PPing_without.Comp
Means	PPing_by.Comp
Medium	PP_by.Comp, PP_in.Comp, PP_over.Comp
Trigger	NP.Ext, DNI, NP.Obj, Swh.Comp

To exemplify, consider the `Communication_response` frame discussed in the previous section. Suppose this frame, along with its frame elements and frame relations is contained in multiple FrameNets, where each individual database contains language-specific entries for all of the lexical units that evoke the frame in that language. Once we identify with the help of bilingual dictionaries a lexical unit whose entry we want to connect to a corresponding lexical unit in another language, we have to carefully consider the full range of valence patterns. This is a rather lengthy and complicated process because it is necessary that the different syntactic frames associated with the two lexical units represent translation equivalents in context. This procedure is facilitated by the use of parallel-aligned corpora, which allow a comparison between the LUs when they are embedded in different types of context (see, e.g. Wu 2000, Salkie 2002).[14] Consider, for example, the verb *answer*, whose individual frame elements may be realized syntactically in many different ways.[15] The realization table (in Table 3) is an excerpt from the FrameNet lexical entry for *answer*, which contains an excerpt from the valence tables as well as the corresponding annotated corpus sentences.

The column on the left contains the names of Frame Elements belonging to the `Communication_Response` frame, the column on the right lists their different types of syntactic realizations. For example, the FE SPEAKER may be realized either as an external noun phrase or a prepositional phrase complement headed by *by*. Alternatively, the FE SPEAKER does not have to be realized at all as in imperative sentences such as *Never answer this question with a straight no*.

Table 4. Excerpt from the Valence Table for *answer*

	Speaker	*TARGET*	*Message*	*Trigger*	*Addressee*
a.	NP.Ext	answer.v	NP.Obj	DNI	DNI
b.	NP.Ext	answer.v	PP_with.Comp	DNI	DNI
c.	NP.Ext	answer.v	QUO.Comp	DNI	DNI
d.	NP.Ext	answer.v	Sfin.Comp	DNI	DNI

Recall from Section 4 that each lexical entry also gives a full valence table illustrating the various combinations of frame elements and their syntactic realizations, which might be present in a given sentence. The valence table for the verb *answer* lists a total of 22 different linear sequences of Frame Elements, totaling 32 different combinations in which these sequences may be realized syntactically. As the full valence table for *answer* is rather long, we focus on only one linear sequence of Frame

14. We are currently looking into the possibility of automating this process by using a script that matches non-English examples expressing a specific constellation of FEs with their corresponding English examples expressing the same constellation of FEs.
15. We focus on verbs here, but similar procedures are followed for nouns and adjectives.

Elements, namely the one in which the FE SPEAKER is followed by the target LU *answer* and the FE MESSAGE. The annotated example sentences in (15) correspond to the valence table excerpt in Table 4.

(15) a. Every time [<Speaker> you] *answer*^{Tgt} [<Message> no], I shall adorn you with these pegs. [<Trigger> DNI] [<Addressee> DNI]

b. [<Speaker> She] *answered*^{Tgt} [<Message> with another question]. [<Trigger> DNI] [<Addressee> INI]

c. [<Speaker> He] *answered*^{Tgt}, [<Message> This beer is expensive] [<Trigger> DNI] [<Addressee> DNI]

d. [<Speaker> He] *answered*^{Tgt} [<Message> that he had gone too far now and that the country expected a dissolution]. [<Trigger> DNI] [<Addressee> DNI]

Table 4 is an excerpt from the full valence table for the verb *answer* and shows how one of the 22 different linear sequences of FEs may be realized in four different ways at the syntactic level. That is, besides sharing the same linear order of Frame Elements with respect to the position of the target LU *answer*, all four valence patterns have the FE SPEAKER realized as an external noun phrase, and the FEs TRIGGER and ADDRESSEE not realized overtly at the syntactic level, but null instantiated as Definite Null Instantiations (DNI). In other words, in sentences such as *He answered with another question* the FEs TRIGGER and ADDRESSEE are understood in context although they are not realized syntactically.

With both the language-specific as well as the language-independent conceptual frame information in place, we are now in a position to link this part of the lexical entry for *answer* to its counterparts in other languages. Taking a look at the lexical entry of *responder* ('to answer') provided by Spanish FrameNet, we find a list of Frame Elements and their syntactic realizations that is comparable in structure to that of its English counterpart in Table 4.

Spanish FrameNet also offers a valence table that includes for *responder* a total of 23 different linear sequences of Frame Elements and their syntactic realizations. Among these, we find a combination of Frame Elements and their syntactic realizations that is comparable to the English in Table 4 above. For example, the Frame Element MESSAGE may be realized as an adverbial phrase functioning as an object (AVP.AObj), a direct object quotation phrase (QUO.DObj), or a direct object phrase headed by *que* (queSind.DObj). Alternatively, it may not be realized syntactically, and therefore be understood as a definite null instantiation (DNI) based

Table 5. Partial Realization Table for the verb *responder*

FE Name	*Syntactic Realizations*
Speaker	NP.Ext, NP.Dobj, CNI, PP_por.COMP
Message	AVP.AObj, DNI, QUO.Dobj, queSind.DObj, queSind.Ext
Addressee	NP.Ext, NP.IObj, PP_a.IObj, DNI, INI
Depictive	AJP.Comp
Manner	AVP.AObj, PP_de.AObj
Means	VPndo.AObj
Medium	PP_en.AObj
Trigger	PP_a.PObj, PP_de.PObj, DNI

Table 6. Excerpt from the Valence Table for *responder*

	Speaker	*TARGET*	*Message*	*Trigger*	*Addressee*
a.	NP.Ext	responder.v	QUO.DObj	DNI	DNI
b.	NP.Ext	responder.v	QueSind.DObj	DNI	DNI

on the context. Because of space limitations, we cannot discuss here all 23 linear sequences of Frame Elements and their syntactic realizations. Instead, we focus on only the one linear sequence that corresponds to the English counterpart(s), namely sentence (a) in Table 4. Consider the excerpt from the valence table of *responder* in Table 6.

Comparing Tables 4 and 6, we see that *answer* and *responder* exhibit comparable valence combinations with the Frame Elements SPEAKER and MESSAGE realized at the syntactic level, and the Frame Elements TRIGGER and ADDRESSEE not realized syntactically, but implicitly understood (they are both definite null instantiations). Having identified corresponding semantic frames, lexical units, and their semantic and syntactic combinatorial possibilities, it is now possible to link the parallel English and Spanish lexicon fragments by establishing correspondence links between the parts of the entries of the two lexical units shown it Tables 3–6 via semantic frames.

It is important to keep in mind that at this stage it is not yet possible to automatically connect lexical entries of the source and target languages. For example, although bilingual lexicon fragments might match in terms of their syntactic and syntactic valences, they might differ in terms of domain, frequency, connotation, and collocation in the two languages. This means that one must carefully compare each individual part of the valence table of a lexical unit in the source language with each individual part of the valence table of a lexical unit in the source language with each individual part of the valence table of a lexical unit in the target language. This effort requires at the first stage a detailed comparison using bilingual dictionaries and mono-lingual as well as parallel corpora in order to ensure matching translation equivalents (cf. also Boas 2001, Teubert 2002, Subirats and Petruck 2003, Ohara et al. 2004).[16] Once the translation equivalents are identified, it is possible to link the parallel lexicon fragments. As Figure 5 illustrates, the semantic frame serves as an interlingual representation between the valence and realization tables of the LUs in English and Spanish, thereby effectively establishing links between translation equivalents (annotated corpus sentences are not included).

In Figure 5, *answer* and *responder* are indexed with 'a'. This index points to the respective first lines in the valence tables of the two verbs and identifies the two syntactic frames as being translation equivalents of each other. At the top of the box in Figure 5 we see the verb *answer* with one of its 22 linear sequences of Frame Elements, namely SPEAKER, TRIGGER, MESSAGE, and ADDRESSEE (cf. Table 4 above). For this linear sequence, Figure 5 shows one possible set of syntactic realizations of these Frame Elements, that given in row (a) in Table 4 above. The 9a-designation following *answer* indicates that this lexicon fragment is the ninth linear configuration of Frame Elements out of a total of 22 linear sequences. Of the ninth linear sequence of Frame Elements 'a' indicates that it is the first of a list of various possible syntactic realizations of these Frame Elements (there are a total of four, cf. Table 4 above). As pointed out above, SPEAKER is realized syntactically as an external noun phrase, MESSAGE as an object noun phrase, and both TRIGGER and ADDRESSEE are null instantiated. The bottom of Figure 5 shows *responder* with the first of the 17 lin-

16. An anonymous reviewer has pointed out that bilingual dictionaries may not include all the necessary information. This suggests that in order to find appropriate translation equivalents it is necessary to rely on multiple resources simultaneously (dictionaries, corpora, intuitions of bilingual speakers, etc.). At the same time it is important to keep in mind that any of the individual resources used for creating bilingual lexicon fragments may have particular shortcomings (e.g. coverage).

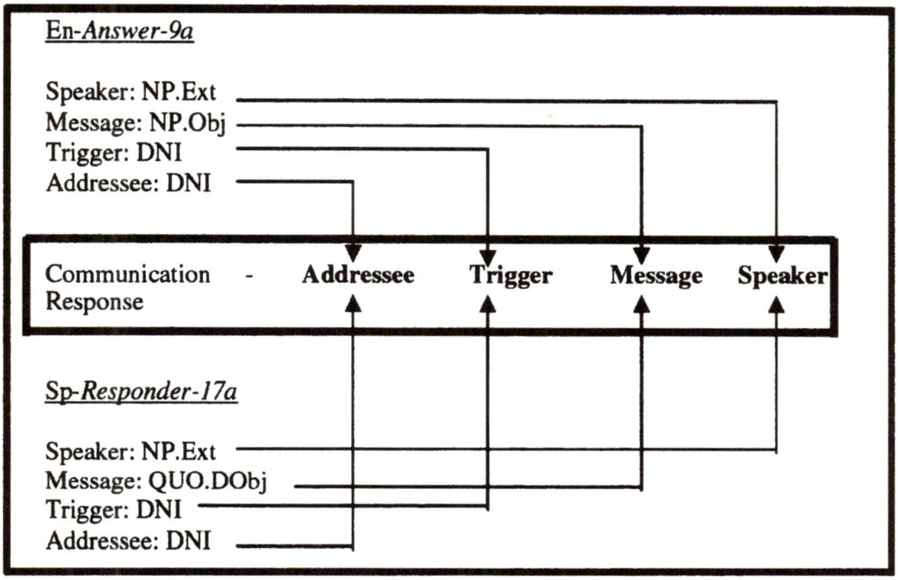

Figure 5. Linking partial English and Spanish lexicon fragments via semantic frames

ear sequences of Frame Elements (recall that there are a total of 23 linear sequences). For one of these linear sequences, we see one subset of syntactic realizations of these Frame Elements, namely the first row catalogued by Spanish FrameNet for this configuration (see row (a) in Table 6).

We can now link the two independently existing partial lexical entries at the top and bottom of Figure 5 by indexing their specific semantic and syntactic configurations as equivalents within the `Communication_Response` frame. This linking is indicated by the arrows pointing from the top and the bottom of the partial lexical entries to the mid-section in Figure 5, which symbolizes the `Communication_Response` frame at the conceptual level, i.e. without any language-specific specifications. The linking of parallel lexicon fragments is achieved formally by employing Typed Feature Structures (Emele 1994) that allow us to co-index the corresponding entries in a systemized fashion (see, e.g. Heid and Krüger 1996).

It is important to keep in mind that the English and Spanish data discussed in this section represent only a very small set of the full lexical entries of *answer* and *responder* in the `Communication_Response` frame. As such, these examples serve to illustrate how to systematically link parallel English and Spanish FrameNet fragments.[17] More specifically, in Figure 5 we have only looked at one possible syntactic realization out of one set of Frame Elements in a specific linear order. For the same order of Frame Elements there are four additional syntactic configurations (cf. Tables 4 and 6 above). For each of these sets, similar entries are needed in order to link them to each other. Recall that FrameNet provides for *answer* in the `Communication_Response` frame a total of 22 linear sequences of Frame Elements, totaling 32 different combinations in which these sequences may be realized syntactically. In order to arrive at a complete parallel lexicon fragment for *answer* and *responder*, it is necessary to create entries for each of the 32 combinations of *answer* and subsequently linking them to their corresponding Spanish counterparts. The same process is applied to link other lexical units across multilingual FrameNets.[18]

Clearly, the procedure outlined here appears to be very time intensive as currently the translation equivalents for each Frame Element Configuration (FEC) are largely determined manually, with the help of parallel corpora and bilingual dictionaries. Demanding though this procedure may be, it provides a solid basis for overcoming the types of linguistic problems typically encountered in the creation of multilingual lexical databases.

17. The current architecture of German FrameNet is based on identical (i.e., translation equivalent) texts. Using multilingual corpora such as the Europarl corpus (Koehn 2002), frame-evoking words are identified and subsequently explored in monolingual corpora in order to determine the full range of their uses. Then, other words in the same frame are explored (see Boas 2002). One problem not addressed in this paper (and currently under investigation) concerns translation mismatches where a single semantic frame or Frame Element may not be sufficient as an interlingual representation to map from one language to another language (see Section 2.3 for an example). Clearly, this is an important issue that needs to be addressed in future work. EuroWordNet (Vossen 2004) has developed a set of equivalence relations in combination with an Inter-Lingual-Index (ILI) in order to address mismatches between languages.
18. As this process is very time and labor intensive, efforts are currently under way to arrive at different ways for extracting parallel lexicon fragments automatically. A first step is to use parallel corpora to automatically identify translation equivalents in context in order to determine frame membership of lexical units across languages. For approaches incorporating automatic acquisition of lexical information from parallel corpora see Wu (2000), Farwell et al. (2004), Green et al. (2004), and Mitamura et al. (2004).

Another important point to keep in mind is that in this paper semantic frames do not serve as a true interlingua in which a concept is realized independently of a source language. However, the model presented here is neither a purely transfer-based system, because semantic frames are understood as an independently existing conceptual system that is not tied to any particular language. At this early point, semantic frames have been developed primarily on the basis of English, so it may appear as if they can only be used to describe the semantics of English LUs and one or two other languages. However, this is not the case. Because at this point semantic frames are best characterized as entities that combine aspects of true interlinguas and of transfer-based systems, I am using the term 'interlingual representation.' Once more languages are described using the FrameNet approach we may arrive at true universal semantic frames (e.g. communication, motion, etc.), which may then serve as a true interlingua. The remaining culture-specific frames (e.g. calendric unit frame; see Petruck and Boas 2003) will then have to be modeled using a transfer-based approach (see also Mel'čuk and Wanner (2001: 28), who propose the inclusion of transfer-mechanisms for systems that utilize true interlinguas).

5.3. Advantages of MLLDs based on Frame Semantics

Applying frame semantic principles to the design of MLLDs overcomes a number of theoretical and practical issues outlined in Section 2. With regard to polysemy we have seen that assigning different senses of words to individual semantic frames allows us to capture their syntactic and semantic distribution in great detail. This step shifts issues surrounding polysemy from the level of words to the level of semantic frames and FEs. As such, it is not only possible to describe overlapping polysemy effectively, but also diverging polysemy.

Table 7. Syntactic frames highlighting different parts of the `Communication_Statement` frame (Boas 2002: 1370)

1	[<speaker> They] *announced*^{Tgt} [<message> the birth of their child].
2	[<medium> The document] *announced*^{Tgt} [<message> that the war had begun].
3	[<speaker> The conductor] *announced*^{Tgt} [<message> the train's departure] [<medium> over the intercom].

For example, consider the `Communication_Statement` frame, which describes situations such as the following: the SPEAKER produces a (spoken or written) message, the ADDRESSEE is the person to whom the message is communicated, the MESSAGE identifies the content of what the SPEAKER is communicating to the ADDRESSEE, the MEDIUM is how the message is communicated, and the TOPIC is the subject matter to which the MESSAGE pertains. The verb *announce* is extremely flexible with respect to different types of perspectives it may take on a communication statement event.

Consider the examples in Table 8 discussed by Boas (2002). In each of the sentences, *announce* highlights different Frame Elements and their relations to each other. In German, each of the different uses of *announce* requires a different verb as a translation equivalent depending on the Frame Element Configuration and the type of perspective it takes on the communication statement scenario.

When *announce* occurs with only the SPEAKER and the MESSAGE frame elements, German prefers the use of *bekanntgeben*, *bekanntmachen*, *ankündigen*, and *anzeigen*, but not *ansagen* and *durchsagen*.[19] This is because the latter two verbs are primarily used in cases in which a MEDIUM frame element represents some sort of (electronic) equipment used to communicate

Table 8. Different syntactic frames of *announce* and corresponding German verbs (Boas 2002: 1370)

1	**speaker**	**TARGET**	**message**	
	NP.Ext	announce.v	NP.Obj	
	bekanntgeben, bekanntmachen, ankündigen, anzeigen			
2	**medium**	**TARGET**	**message**	
	NP.Ext	announce.v	Sfin_that.Comp	
	bekanntgeben, ankündigen, anzeigen			
3	**speaker**	**TARGET**	**message**	**medium**
	NP.Ext	announce.v	NP.Obj	PP_over.Comp
	ankündigen, ansagen, durchsagen			

19. In reality, a much finer-grained distinction (including contextual background information) is needed to formally distinguish between the semantics of individual verbs. E.g., *anzeigen* is used in a much more formal sense than the other verbs. In contrast, *ankündigen* is primarily used to refer to an event that will occur in the future (see Boas 2002).

the MESSAGE to the ADDRESSEE such as in the third sentence in Table 7. This demonstrates that it is not sufficient to simply generalize over senses of words that may be used as synonyms of each other. Instead, it is necessary for MLLDs to capture the full range of possible translation equivalents before arriving at decisions about which German verbs may serve as possible equivalents to a specific syntactic frame listed in an entry for an English lexical unit.[20]

MLLDs based on frame semantic principles may also help with overcoming problems surrounding word sense disambiguation caused by analogous valence patterns. Our discussion of *cure* and *get* in Section 2 illustrated that the proper identification of verb senses occurring with multiple syntactic frames is often difficult. By detailing how different types of syntactic frames are used to express diverse semantic concepts represented by semantic frames it becomes possible to correctly identify a word sense not only within a single language, but also mapping that sense to appropriate translation equivalents across languages.[21] For example, when *cure* occurs with the [NP, V, NP] syntactic frame, it may express either the preservation sense (*The mother cured the ham*), or the healing sense (*The mother cured the child*), depending on the choice of semantic object. Explicitly stating the different semantics of the postverbal object and other constituents in frame semantic terms as part of the lexical entry not only allows us to disambiguate the two senses straightforwardly. It also enables us to identify the proper translation equivalent for other languages by

20. Note that it will not suffice to only map a lexical unit's equivalents to German. Instead, a MLLD based on frame semantic principles has to map each syntactic frame of a German lexical unit back to a syntactic frame of an English lexical unit in order to ensure that the two are capable of expressing the same semantic space. Whenever there are discrepancies, a revision of mappings between lexical entries will be necessary. This example illustrates that although parallel corpora may be helpful for the automatic acquisition of bilingual lexicon fragments, it is still necessary to manually check the translation equivalents before finalizing any parallel lexicon fragments (see Boas 2001, 2002).
21. Syntactic frames alone are not sufficient for identifying the correct word sense. Instead, it is necessary to first determine the semantic types of the verb's arguments (using other lexical resources such as WordNet). Once we have information about the semantic types of the verb's arguments, it then becomes possible to link the syntactic frame to specific semantic frames, thereby correctly identifying word senses. For details about the linking of semantic and syntactic information for each of a word's multiple senses, see Goldberg (1995), Rappaport Hovav & Levin (1998), and Boas (2001).

using semantic frames to map the senses across languages. For German, we thus find *pökeln* for the preservation sense of *cure*, and *heilen* for the healing sense of *cure*.

Another advantage of employing semantic frames for the structuring of MLLDs is that knowledge about different lexicalization patterns can be accounted for systematically at the level of Frame Elements. The differences in lexicalization patterns between English and Japanese motion verbs discussed in Section 2.3 have shown that the two languages vary in the types of PATH Frame Elements. Whereas English exhibits only one general PATH FE, Japanese makes a more fine-grained distinction into ROUTE and BOUNDARY (cf. Ohara et al. 2004). To account for these differences, it is necessary to introduce the notion of Frame Element sub-categories that identify ROUTE and BOUNDARY as subtypes of the more general PATH FE. When mapping a PATH FE from English to Japanese it is thus important to rely on the valence patterns to determine the subtype of PATH FE for Japanese. For example, in English *the bridge* and *the river* may appear as a PATH FE with verbs such as *go*, *pass*, and *traverse*. As we have seen in Section 2.3, *wataru* ('go across') behaves similarly to English in that it may occur with *hasi* ('the bridge') and *kawa* ('the river'). In contrast, *koeru* ('go beyond') only occurs with *kawa*, but not with *hasi*. In a frame-based MLLD this difference is accounted for in terms of lexical entries that specify for each lexical unit the different combinations of FEs with which it occurs. Using the mapping and numerical indexing mechanisms outlined in the previous section, we can then link English and Japanese lexicon fragments according to the equivalent Frame Element Configurations. It is at this level that the fine-grained differences between the ROUTE and BOUNDARY subcategories of Japanese path FEs and their English PATH counterpart are encoded.

6. Differences to other MLLDs

Frame-based MLLDs differ from other MLLDs in a number of significant ways. The first difference is in their overall architecture. For example, EuroWordNet (Peters et al. 1998, Vossen 2004) consists of individual databases for eight European languages structured along the original Princeton WordNet for English (Fellbaum 1998). As such, EuroWordNet relies on decontextualized concepts for lexical descriptions. The sense relations between semantically related words (synsets) such as hyponymy, antonymy, meronymy, etc. differ from semantic frames in that they represent ontological relations holding between synsets. These sense relations are internal to the conceptual architecture of EuroWordNet. In contrast, frame-based MLLDs are based on linguistically motivated concepts (semantic frames) that are external to the units of analysis. As such, frame-based MLLDs and MLLDs based on WordNet such as EuroWordNet offer complementary types of information.

The second difference between frame-based MLLDs and other MLLDs is the combination of syntactic and semantic information. Some lexical databases provide detailed conceptual ontologies representing hierarchies of different lexical relations. For example, SIMuLLDA (Janssen 2004) provides a fine-grained formal concept analysis for nouns in English and French. But it does not offer any significant information about their syntactic distribution such as different types of modification. EuroWordNet (Vossen 2001, 2004) offers a detailed semantic analysis of lexical semantic relations between synsets, but it only contains partial syntactic information in the form of one or two example sentences illustrating how a word is used in context. In contrast, other lexical resources such as SIMuLLDA and EuroWordNet differ from frame-based MLLDs in that they provide different types of conceptual information as well as access to ontological information which is not currently available in frame-based dictionaries. Moreover, WordNet and its multilingual counterpart EuroWordNet offer a much broader coverage than FrameNet and its multilingual extensions.

Another difference concerns the methodology used to create and link MLLDs. In EuroWordNet, each language-specific WordNet is an autonomous language-specific ontology where each language has its own set of concepts and lexical-semantic relations based on the lexicalization patterns of that language (cf. Vossen 2004).[22] EuroWordNet differentiates between language specific and language-independent modules. The language-independent modules consist of a top concept ontology and an unstructured Inter-Lingual-Index (ILI) that provides mappings across individual language WordNet structures and consists of a condensed universal index of meaning (so far, 1024 fundamental concepts) (Vossen 2001, 2004). Each ILI record consists of a synset and an English gloss specifying its meaning and source. Although most concepts in each WordNet are

22. In EuroWordNet, there are no concepts for which there are not words or expressions in a language. In contrast, GermaNet (Hamp & Feldweg 1997, Kunze & Lemnitzer 2002), which is a spin-off from the German EuroWordNet consortium, uses non-lexicalized, so-called artificial concepts for creating well-balanced taxonomies.

ideally related to the closest concepts in the ILI, there is a set of equivalence relations that map between individual WordNets and the ILI (cf. Vossen 2004: 164–167).

Identifying equivalents across languages with EuroWordNet requires three steps. First, one must identify the correct synset to which the sense of a word belongs in the source language. Next, using an equivalence relation (e.g. EQ_HAS_HYPERONYM (when a meaning is more specific than any available ILI record), Vossen 2004: 164) the synset meaning is mapped to the ILI (which is linked to a top-level ontology). Finally, the corresponding counterpart is identified in the target language by mapping from the ILI to a synset in the target language.

Frame-based MLLDs differ from the EuroWordNet architecture in that all meanings are described directly with respect to the same semantic frame. Differences between the languages are thus to be found in the various ways in which the conceptual semantics of a frame are realized syntactically. On this approach, semantic frames are only used to identify and link meaning equivalents (Frame Elements). As we have seen in Section 5.2, the linking of the syntactic valence patterns is established by directly identifying the translation equivalents (on the basis of parallel corpora) and indexing them with each other.[23] Differences between languages are thus to be found in the various ways in which the conceptual semantics of a frame are realized syntactically.

It is important to keep in mind that at this early stage FrameNets for Spanish, German and Japanese are only linking their entries to existing English FrameNet entries, but not to entries across all the languages. The next step involves linking lexical entries across languages in order to test the applicability of semantic frames as a cross-linguistic metalanguage. Extending the FrameNet approach to different languages is in its preliminary stages. Clearly, much research on frame-based MLLDs remains to be done. One of the open questions concerns the description and mapping of adjectives and nouns across languages that differ in lexicalization patterns. This question has already been addressed by other MLLDs such as EuroWordNet. Another important issue concerns mismatches between languages. That is, we need to carefully consider the different strategies

---

23. Our approach differs from Fontenelle's (2000) analysis in that Fontenelle primarily relies on data from existing bilingual dictionaries to establish parallel lexicon fragments. Another difference is that Fontenelle augments his approach with additional semantic layers from Mel'čuk's Meaning-Text Theory in order to establish lexical functions.

that should be employed when encountering translation mismatches. Here, too, frame-based MLLDs may benefit from a variety of other resources to solve these problems: the detailed conceptual information contained in other resources such as EuroWordNet (Vossen 2004), information about complex translation mismatches provided by Acquilex (Copestake et al. 1995), statistical information on translation matches and mismatches provided by BiFrameNet (Fung and Chen 2004), or paraphrase relations as proposed by Mel'čuk's Meaning-Text Theory (Mel'čuk et al. 1988; see also Fontenelle 2000).

7. Conclusions and outlook

This paper has outlined the methodology underlying the design and construction of frame-based MLLDs. Starting with a discussion of the Berkeley FrameNet for English, I have shown how its semantic frames can be systematically employed to create parallel lexicon fragments for Spanish, Japanese, and German. In discussing the individual steps necessary for the creation of multilingual FrameNets, I have demonstrated how the use of semantic frames overcomes a number of linguistic problems traditionally encountered in cross-linguistic analyses. These include diverging polysemy structures, lexicalization patterns, and identifying and measuring paraphrase relations and translation equivalents.

At the center of the work-flow in the creation of frame-based MLLDs are the following three steps: (1) identification of translation equivalents based on existing English FrameNet entries, parallel corpora, and bilingual dictionaries; (2) attestation and semantic annotation of translation equivalents based on examples in both parallel corpora and large monolingual corpora; (3) creation of parallel lexical entries that are linked to English FrameNet entries on the basis of semantic frames. Since not all steps can be automated, this process is rather time and labor intensive.

The construction of frame-based MLLDs is only in its first phase. Clearly, future work will have to be extended to domains beyond those discussed in this paper to achieve broader coverage (i.e. beyond the 8,900 Lexical Units currently offered by FrameNet). Other multi-lingual resources such as EuroWordNet not only provide much broader coverage, but also contain useful conceptual information not currently encoded by FrameNet that may support this effort. Another important point will be to determine the feasibility of a truly independent metalanguage based on semantic frames for connecting multiple FrameNets. The idiosyncratic syntactic realizations of Frame Elements in the communication domain discussed in this paper for English and Spanish has shown that this is not an easy task. The fact that the large number of idiosyncratic valence patterns of verbs may evoke the same frame (or only certain aspects of a frame) suggests that it might be necessary to distinguish between truly universal frames and language-specific frames. The former would be modeled by linking the syntactic valence patterns of a lexical unit directly to a semantic frame. In this case semantic frames would serve as an interlingua as outlined in Section 5.3 above. The latter would be modeled by employing transfer rules between language pairs where specific transfer rules would have to specify how specific frames (or parts of frames) are mapped from one language to another. However, at this point it is too early to provide a definite answer to this problematic issue. It can only be addressed thoroughly once coverage has been extended significantly (both in terms of Lexical Units and of languages analyzed).

Future efforts will have to concentrate on finding mechanisms that allow for greater automation of the processes described in this paper, in particular the identification of translation equivalents in parallel corpora. Finally, it must be seen how multi-lingual FrameNets can be used to improve current and future machine translation systems.

References

Alsina, V. and J. DeCesaris
2002 Bilingual lexicography, overlapping polysemy, and corpus use. In: B. Altenberg and S. Granger (eds.), *Lexis in Contrast*, 215–230. Amsterdam/Philadelphia: Benjamins.

Altenberg, B. and S. Granger
2002 Recent trends in cross-linguistic lexical studies. In: B. Altenberg and S. Granger (eds.), *Lexis in Contrast*, 3–50. Amsterdam/Philadelphia: Benjamins.

Atkins, B.T.S.
1994 Analyzing the verbs of seeing: A frame semantic approach to corpus lexicography. In: C. Johnson et al. (eds.), *Proceedings of the Twentieth Annual Meeting of the Berkeley Linguistics Society*, 42–56. Berkeley: Berkeley Linguistics Society.

Atkins, B.T.S., N. Bel, F. Bertagne, P. Bouillon, N. Calzolari, C. Fellbaum, R. Grishman, A. Lenci, C. MacLeod, M. Palmer, G. Thurmair, M. Villegas, and A. Zampolli
2002 From resources to applications. Designing the multilingual ISLE lexical entry. In: *Proceedings of LREC 2002*, 687–693, Gran Canaria, Spain.

Baker, C.F., C.J. Fillmore, and J.B. Lowe
1998 The Berkeley FrameNet Project. In: *COLING-ACL'98: Proceedings of the Conference*, 86–90.

Baker, C.F., C.J. Fillmore, B. and Cronin
2003 The structure of the FrameNet Database. *International Journal of Lexicography* 16: 281–296.

Béjoint, H.
2000 *Modern Lexicography*. Oxford: Oxford University Press.

Boas, Hans C.
2001 Frame Semantics as a framework for describing polysemy and syntactic structures of English and German motion verbs in contrastive computational lexicography. In: P. Rayson, A. Wilson, T. McEnery, A. Hardie, and S. Khoja (eds.), *Proceedings of Corpus Linguistics 2001*, 64–73.

Boas, Hans C.
2002 Bilingual FrameNet dictionaries for machine translation. In: M. González Rodríguez and C. Paz Suárez Araujo (eds.), *Proceedings of the Third International Conference on Language Resources and Evaluation*, 1364–1371. Las Palmas, Spain.

Boas, Hans C.
2005 From theory to practice: Frame Semantics and the design of FrameNet. In: S. Langer and D. Schnorbusch (eds.), *Semantisches Wissen im Lexikon*, 129–160. Tübingen: Narr.

Chesterman, A.
1998 *Contrastive Functional Analysis*. Amsterdam/Philadelphia: John Benjamins.

Chodkiewicz, C., D. Bourigault, and J. Humbley
2002 Making a workable glossary out of a specialized corpus: Term extraction and expert knowledge. In: B. Altenberg and S. Granger (eds.), *Lexis in Contrast*, 249–270. Amsterdam/Philadelphia: Benjamins.

Christ, O.
1994 A modular and flexible architecture for an integrated corpus query system. In: *COMPLEX'94*, Budapest, 1994.

Copestake, A., T. Briscoe, P. Vossen, A. Ageno, I. Castellon, F. Ribas, G. Rigau, H. Rodriguez, and A. Samiotou
1995 Acquisition of lexical translation relations from MRDs. *Machine Translation* 9: 183–219.

Cruse, A.
1986 *Lexical Semantics*. Cambridge: Cambridge University Press.

Emele, M.
1994 TFS – The typed feature structure representation formalism. In: *Proceedings of the International Workshop on Sharable Natural Language Resources (SNLR)*, Nara, Japan, 1994.

Erk, K., A. Kowalski, and S. Padó
2003 Towards a resource for lexical semantics: A large German cor-

pus with extensive semantic annotation. In: *Proceedings of ACL 2003*, Sapporo.

Farwell, D., L. Guthrie, and Y. Wilks
1993 Automatically creating lexical entries for ULTRA, a multilingual MT system. *Machine Translation* 8: 183–219.

Farwell, D., S. Helmreich, B. Dorr, N. Habash, F. Reeder, K. Miller, L. Levin, T. Mitamura, E. Hovy, O. Rambow, and A. Siddharthan
2004 Interlingual annotation of multilingual text corpora. In: *Proceedings of the North American Chapter of the Association for Computational Linguistics Workshop on Frontiers in Corpus Annotation*, 55–62. Boston, MA.

Fellbaum, C.
1998 *WordNet: An Electronic Lexical Database*. Cambridge, Mass.: MIT Press.

Fillmore, C.J.
1970 The grammar of hitting and breaking. In: R.A. Jacobs and P.S. Rosenbaum (eds.), *Readings in English Transformational Grammar*, 120–133. Ginn and Company.

Fillmore, C.J.
1975 An alternative to checklist theories of meaning. In: C. Cogen et al. (eds.), *Proceedings of the First Annual Meeting of the Berkeley Linguistics Society*, 123–131. Berkeley: Berkeley Linguistics Society.

Fillmore, C.J.
1982 Frame Semantics. In: Linguistic Society of Korea (ed.), *Linguistics in the Morning Calm*, 111–138. Seoul: Hanshin.

Fillmore, C.J. and B.T.S. Atkins
1992 Toward a frame-based lexicon: The semantics of RISK and its neighbors. In: A. Lehrer and E. Kittay (eds.), *Frames, Fields and Contrasts: New Essays in Semantic and Lexical Organization*, 75–102. Hillsdale: Erlbaum.

Fillmore, C.J. and B.T.S. Atkins
1994 Starting where the dictionaries stop: The challenge for computational lexicography. In: B.T.S. Atkins and A. Zampolli (eds.), *Computational Approaches to the Lexicon*, 349–393. Oxford: Oxford University Press.

Fillmore, C.J. and B.T.S. Atkins
2000 Describing polysemy: The case of 'crawl'. In: Y. Ravin and C. Leacock (eds.), *Polysemy*, 91–110. Oxford: Oxford University Press.

Fillmore, C.J., C.R. Johnson, and M.R.L. Petruck
2003a Background to FrameNet. *International Journal of Lexicography* 16: 235–251.

Fillmore, C.J., M.R.L. Petruck, J. Ruppenhofer, and A. Wright
2003b FrameNet in action. The case of attaching. *International Journal of Lexicography* 16.3: 297–333.

Fontenelle, T.
2000 A bilingual lexical database for frame semantics. *International Journal of Lexicography* 14.4: 232–248.

Fung, P. and B. Chen
2004 BiFrameNet: Bilingual Frame Semantics resource construction by cross-lingual induction. In: *Proceedings of COLING 2004*. Geneva, Switzerland.

Goddard, C.
2000 Polysemy: A problem of definition. In: Y. Ravin and C. Leacock (eds.), *Polysemy*, 129–151. Oxford: Oxford University Press.

Goldberg, A.
1995 *Constructions: A Construction Grammar approach to argument structure*. Chicago: University of Chicago Press.

Green, R., B. Dorr, and P. Resnik
2004 Inducing frame semantic verb classes from WordNet and LDOCE. In: *Proceedings of the Workshop on Text Meaning and Interpretation*, Association for Computational Linguistics, Barcelona, Spain.

Hamp, B. and H. Feldweg
1997 GermaNet: A lexical-semantic net for German. In: P. Vossen, N. Calzolari, G. Adriaens, A. Sanfilippo, and Y. Wilks (eds.), *Proceedings of the ACL/EACL-97 Workshop on automatic information extraction and building of lexical semantic resources for NLP applications*, 9–15. Madrid.

Heid, U. and K. Krüger
1996 Multilingual lexicon based on Frame Semantics. In: *Proceedings of the AISB Workshop on Multilinguality in the Lexicon*. Brighton.

Janssen, M.
2004. Multilinguallexical databases, lexical gaps, and SIMuLLDA. *International Journal of Lexicography* 17.2: 137–154.

Johnson, C.R., M.R.L. Petruck, C.F. Baker, M. Ellsworth, J. Ruppenhofer, and C.J. Fillmore
2003 *FrameNet: Theory and Practice*. Technical Report. Berkeley: International Computer Science Institute.

Koehn, P.
2002 *Europarl: A multilingual corpus for evaluation of machine translation*. Ms., University of Southern California.

König, E. and W. Lezius
2003 *The TIGER language – A description language for syntax graphs, formal definition*. Technical report Institut für Maschinelle Sprachverarbeitung, University of Stuttgart.

Kunze, C. and L. Lemnitzer
2002 GermaNet – representation, visualization, application. In: *LREC 2002 Proceedings* Vol. V: 1465–1491.

Laecock, C. and Y. Ravin
2000 *Polysemy*. Oxford: Oxford University Press.

Mel'čuk, I., N. Arbatchewsky-Jumarie, L. Dagenais, L. Elnitsky, L. Iordanskaja, M.-N. Lefebvre, and S. Mantha
1988 *Dictionnaire explicatif et combinatoire du Français contemporain. Recherches lexico-sémantiques*. Montréal: Les Presses de l'Université de Montréal.

Mel'čuk, I. T. and Wanner
2001 Toward a lexicographic approach to lexical transfer in machine translation (Illustrated by the German-Russian Language Pair). In: *Machine Translation* 16: 21–87.

Mitamura, T., K. Miller, B. Dorr, D. Farwell, N. Habash, S. Helmreich, E. Hovy, L. Levin, O. Rambow, F. Reeder, and A. Siddharthan
2004 Semantic annotation for interlingual representation of multilingual texts. In: *Proceedings of the Workshop on Beyond Named Entity Recognition: Semantic Labeling for NLP Tasks*, LREC.

Ohara, K., S. Fujii, H. Saito, S. Ishizaki, T. Ohori, and R. Suzuki
2003 The Japanese FrameNet Project: A preliminary report. In: *Proceedings of the Pacific Association for Computational Linguistics (PACLING03)*, 249–254.

Ohara, K., S. Fujii, H. Saito, S. Ishizaki, T. Ohori, and R. Suzuki
2004 The Japanese FrameNet Project. An introduction. In: *Proceedings of the satellite workshop on building lexical resources from semantically annotated corpora*, 9–11. Fourth international Conference on Language Resources and Evaluation (LREC) 2004.

Ortega, M.
2002 *Intersección de autómatas y transductores en el análisis sintáctico de un texto*. MA Thesis, Polytechnic University of Catalonia, Spain.

Peters, W., I. Peters, and P. Vossen
1998 The reduction of semantic ambiguity in linguistic resources. In: A. Rubio, N. Gallardo, R. Catro, and A. Tejada (eds.), *Proceedings of the First International Conference on Language Resources and Evaluation*, 409–416. Granada.

Petruck, M.R.L.
1996 Frame Semantics. In: J. Verschueren, J-O Östman, J. Blommaert and C. Bulcaen (eds.), *Handbook of Pragmatics*, 1–13. Amsterdam/Philadelphia: Benjamins.

Petruck, M.R.L. and H.C. Boas
2003 All in a day's week. In: E. Hajičová, A. Kotěšovcová, and J. Mírovský (eds.), *Proceedings of the 17th International Congress of Linguists*, CD-ROM. Prague: Matfyzpress.

Petruck, M.R.L., C.J. Fillmore, C.F. Baker, M. Ellis, and J. Ruppenhofer
2004 Reframing FrameNet data. In: *Proceedings of The 11th EURALEX International Congress*, 405–416. Lorient, France.

Rappaport Hovav, M. and B. Levin
1998 Building verb meaning. In: M. Butt and W. Geuder (eds.), *The Projection of Arguments*, 97–134. Stanford: CSLI Publications.

Salkie, R.
2002 Two types of translation equivalence. In: B. Altenberg and S. Granger (eds.), *Lexis in Contrast*, 51–72. Amsterdam/Philadelphia: Benjamins.

Sinclair, J.
1996 An international project in multilingual lexicography. In: J. Sinclair, J. Payne, and P. Hernández (eds.), Corpus to corpus: A study of translation equivalence. Special issue of the *International Journal of Lexicography* 9: 179–196.

Subirats, C. and M. Ortega
2000 Tratamiento automático de la información textual en español mediante bases de información lingüistica y transductores. *Estudios de Lingüistica del Espanol* 10.

Subirats, C. and M. Petruck
2003 *Surprise: Spanish FrameNet.* Presentation at the workshop on Frame Semantics, International Congress of Linguists, July 29th, 2003, Prague.

Svensén, B.
1993 *Practical lexicography. Principles and methods of dictionary-making.* Oxford: Oxford University Press.

Talmy, L.
1985 Lexicalization patterns: semantic structures in lexical forms. In: T. Shopen (ed.), *Language Typology and Syntactic Description*, 57–149. Cambridge: Cambridge University Press.

Talmy, L.
2000 *Toward a Cognitive Semantics.* Cambridge, MA: MIT Press.

Teubert, W.
2002 The role of parallel corpora in translation and multilingual lexicography. In: B. Altenberg and S. Granger (eds.), *Lexis in Contrast*, 189–214. Amsterdam/Philadelphia: Benjamins.

Viberg, Å.
2002 Polysemy and disambiguation cues across languages: The case of Swedish *få* and English *get.* In: B. Altenberg and S. Granger (eds.), *Lexis in Contrast*, 119–150. Amsterdam/Philadelphia: Benjamins.

Vossen, P.
1998 Introduction to EuroWordNet. In: N. Ide, D. Greenstein, and P. Vossen (eds.), Special Issue on EuroWordNet. *Computers and the Humanities* 32: 73–89.

Vossen, P.
2001 Condensed meaning in EuroWordNet. In: P. Bouillon and F. Busa (eds.), *The language of word meaning*, 363–383. Cambridge: Cambridge University Press.

Vossen, P.
2004 EuroWordnet: A multilingual database of autonomous and language specific wordnets connected via an inter-lingual-index. *International Journal of Lexicography* 17.2: 161–173.

Wu, D.
2000 Bracketing and aligning words and constituents in parallel text using stochastic inversion transduction crammars. In: J. Veronis (ed.), *Parallel Text Processing: Alignment and Use of Translation Corpora*. Dordrecht: Kluwer.

4. The Kicktionary – a multilingual lexical resource of football language

Thomas Schmidt

1. Introduction

This paper presents the *Kicktionary*, an electronic multilingual (English, German, French) lexical resource of the language of football.[1] The Kicktionary was constructed predominantly on the basis of frame semantic principles, and is therefore perhaps best described as a multilingual, domain-specific FrameNet.[2] However, the objectives of the Kicktionary project are in many ways more restricted than those of the Berkeley FrameNet project. My primary goal was (and remains) to produce a lexical resource usable by *humans* for purposes of understanding, translating or otherwise paraphrasing texts in the domain of football. In contrast to much work currently being carried out by FrameNet and by related projects, the Kicktionary does thus not claim to make contributions to fields like machine translation, question answering or other sub-areas of natural language processing or artificial intelligence. By restricting the scope of research to computer-assisted lexicography for human users, I want to offer some answers to the following questions:

---

1. I use the British English term "football", to denote "association football", i.e., "soccer", not "American football".
2. The work presented here was carried out during my stay as a guest researcher with the team of the FrameNet project at ICSI in Berkeley, with the help of a research grant by the German Academic Exchange Service (DAAD). I am grateful to the FrameNet team (Charles Fillmore, Collin Baker, Michael Ellsworth, Josef Ruppenhofer) and its visitors (Kyoko Ohara, Jan Scheffczyk, Carlos Subirats) for their support. Miriam R.L. Petruck, Hans C. Boas and Josef Ruppenhofer have provided valuable comments on this paper. I owe the original idea for this project to Seelbach's (2001, 2002 and 2003) and Gross' (2002) work on the lexicography of football language in the lexicon grammar framework.

(1) What types of information and what means of navigation can a dictionary structured according to frame semantic principles offer which other (printed or electronic) lexical resources do not provide?
(2) How does a frame semantic approach support the inclusion of empirical language material (i.e. corpus examples) into a dictionary?
(3) How does a frame semantic approach support the construction of *multilingual* lexical resources?
(4) How does a frame semantic approach support the construction of *domain-specific* lexical resources?
(5) What difficulties arise in a frame semantic analysis of a multilingual domain-specific vocabulary? What are the limitations of such an approach and how can they be overcome?
(6) Does Frame Semantics have something to say about the integration of multi-medial elements into a lexical resource?

This paper is structured as follows: Section 2 gives a short review of Frame Semantics and shows how it can be applied to the domain of football. Section 3 explains how empirical evidence from a text corpus is used in that approach. Section 4 discusses aspects related to the multilinguality of the Kicktionary. Section 5 concerns difficulties and limitations of a frame semantic approach that were encountered in the analysis of football vocabulary. Section 6 introduces the concept of semantic relations which is used to overcome some of these limitations. Section 7 describes how the resulting Kicktionary is currently presented to users via a website. Finally, Section 8 provides a discussion of some broader issues relating to the use of Frame Semantics in a multilingual, domain specific lexicographic analysis.

2. Theoretical background: Scenes and frames in football

The same reasons that make the commercial transaction event a good illustration of frame semantic principles in general (see Fillmore 1977a, b) also make football vocabulary a promising object of study for a frame semantic approach. According to Fillmore (1978: 282), a frame can be defined as "a lexical set whose members index portions or aspects of some conceptual or actional whole [i.e. a scene, T.S.]." In other words: a *frame* is a structural entity used to group linguistic expressions which share a common *perspective* on a given conceptual *scene*. Whereas a scene is defined in terms of pieces of abstract (and possibly non-linguistic) knowledge, the notion of a frame is concerned with the properties of concrete linguistic means of expressing this kind of knowledge.[3]

As in a commercial transaction, the activities in a football match are governed by a set of conventionalized rules. These rules cannot be stated in linguistic terms alone, but they are essential to the understanding of any linguistic way of referring to it. A football match furthermore has a clearly definable set of actors and props taking part in it, and it is in the nature of the game that these participants take distinct perspectives on the event which can be reflected in different lexical choices.[4] Last but not least, a football match as a whole is naturally decomposable into smaller subevents, each of which comes with its own regularities concerning the actors and perspectives involved in it and the corresponding lexical items.

As a first example, consider the following sentences:[5]

---

3. My understanding of the terms *scene* and *frame* is based more on Fillmore's earlier papers about Frame Semantics than on more recent work on FrameNet. Petruck (1996: 2) notes that, "[i]n the early papers on Frame Semantics, a distinction is drawn between scene and frame, the former being a cognitive, conceptual, or experiential entity and the latter being a linguistic one [...]. In later works, scene ceases to be used and a frame is a cognitive structuring device, parts of which are indexed by words associated with it and used in the service of understanding [...]." In the Kicktionary and in this paper I maintain the explicit distinction between the notions of *scene* (a conceptual entity) and *frame* (a linguistic entity) referred to in this quote (see also section 8.3). The more recent literature on FrameNet (e.g., Ruppenhofer et al. 2006) uses terms like *scenario*, *background frame*, *non-lexical frame* and *non-perspectivized frame* all of which bear in some way on the same issues as the *scene/frame* distinction. I have, however, decided to work only with the latter because it seemed to me the most-clear cut, and also the most useful for the purpose of dictionary-making. In some parts of the web presentation of the Kicktionary, however, the term *scenario* is used. This is an accidental inconsistency – *scenario* in this context is to be understood in precisely the same sense as *scene*.
4. *Actors* and *props* are terms used by Fillmore in his earlier papers. For instance, the commercial transaction event has a buyer and a seller as actors, and the goods and the money exchanged as props (Fillmore 1978). When actual scenes and frames are defined, actors and props are represented as FEs (see below).
5. These and all following examples are based on attested corpus examples from the corpus described in section 3, but have been shortened and/or simplified for the purpose of this paper.

(1) a. [Zahovaiko]$_{\text{OPPONENT\_PLAYER}}$ *challenged* [Manou Schauls]$_{\text{PLAYER\_WITH\_BALL}}$ [in the penalty area]$_{\text{AREA}}$.

b. [He]$_{\text{PLAYER\_WITH\_BALL}}$ turned inside to *take on* [Roma]$_{\text{OPPONENT\_PLAYER}}$ and finish with his left foot from close range.

c. [Hector Font]$_{\text{PLAYER\_WITH\_BALL}}$ tried to *nutmeg*[6] [Ioannis Skopelitis]$_{\text{OPPONENT\_PLAYER}}$.

d. [Ronaldo]$_{\text{OPPONENT\_PLAYER}}$ *dispossessed* [Wisla goalkeeper Radoslaw Majdan]$_{\text{PLAYER\_WITH\_BALL}}$ [on the edge of the box]$_{\text{AREA}}$.

The lexical units (henceforth: LUs) *challenge*, *take on*, *nutmeg* and *dispossess* in these examples all evoke the same scene, namely a one-on-one situation in which a fixed set of actors and props (henceforth: frame elements – FEs[7]) takes part: a player in possession of the ball (PLAYER_WITH_BALL) is attacked by an opponent (OPPONENT_PLAYER) at some location (AREA) on the field.[8] Each example, however, imposes a somewhat different perspective on that scene. Thus, in (1a) and (1b), the temporal focus is on the event itself, while (1c) and (1d) relate the event from the perspective of its outcome. Similarly, (1a) and (1d) foreground the point of view of the opponent player, while (1b) and (1c) focus on the player in possession of the ball. This way of relating different LUs to one another

6. To *nutmeg* an opponent means to beat him in a one-on-one situation by playing the ball through his legs, rounding him, and collecting the ball again behind his back.
7. Given the explicit distinction between scenes and frames explained above, it would be more consistent to call these actors and props *Scene Elements*, since they are conceptual, rather than linguistic entities and remain constant across different frames belonging to the same scene. However, as this is bound to create confusion among readers who are familiar with FrameNet terminology, I decided to use the term *Frame Element* in this paper. Here and in the remainder of the paper, the following conventions are used: LUs are written in italics (*nutmeg*), FEs are written in small capitals (PLAYER_WITH_BALL), the names of frames are written in an equidistant font (`Challenge`), and the names of scenes are in bold face (**One-on-One**).
8. Due to space limitations it is not always possible to provide full descriptions of the frames, scenes, and parts thereof. Please point your internet browser to [http://www.kicktionary.de] to get access to complete descriptions.

by associating them with the same scene and differentiating them according to the perspective they impose on that scene is useful for structuring a large number of vocabulary items. Thus, LUs like *beat*, *outstrip* or *sidestep* have similar properties with respect to this scene-and-perspective distinction as the verb *nutmeg*. These LUs are therefore all assigned to the same frame `Beat`. Likewise, the verbal LU *tackle* and the nominal LU *sliding tackle* share their perspective on the **`One-on-one`** scene with the verb *challenge*. These LUs are therefore all assigned to the same frame `Challenge`.

A similar scenes-and-frames analysis can be carried out for many other areas of football vocabulary. For example, the **`Foul`** scene refers to a prototypical sequence of events as in the following description:

1. A player (the OFFENDER) or a whole team (the OFFENDER_TEAM) commits some kind of infringement of the laws of the game, typically (but not necessarily) involving a player of the opponent team (the OFFENDED_PLAYER), e.g., a foul, an offside position or a handball.
2. The REFEREE reacts to this infringement (the OFFENSE), by imposing a sanction on the OFFENDER (e.g. cautioning him) and/or by awarding a COMPENSATION (e.g., a penalty kick) to the opponent team (the OFFENDED_TEAM).

The following set of sentences demonstrates what different lexical choices can be made to foreground one aspect of this scene and background, or even omit others:

(2) a. [Costinha]$_{\text{OFFENDER}}$ *tripped* [Ignashevich]$_{\text{OFFENDED\_PLAYER}}$.
b. [The referee]$_{\text{REFEREE}}$ *awarded* [a penalty]$_{\text{COMPENSATION}}$ [to CSKA Moscow]$_{\text{OFFENDED\_TEAM}}$.
c. [Ignashevich]$_{\text{OFFENDED\_PLAYER}}$ *won* [a penalty]$_{\text{COMPENSATION}}$ [for CSKA Moscow]$_{\text{OFFENDED\_TEAM}}$.
d. [Costinha]$_{\text{OFFENDER}}$ *conceded* [a penalty]$_{\text{COMPENSATION}}$ [by tripping Ignashevich]$_{\text{OFFENSE}}$.
e. [The referee]$_{\text{REFEREE}}$ *cautioned* [Costinha]$_{\text{OFFENDER}}$ [for his foul on Ignashevich]$_{\text{OFFENSE}}$.

Further examples of prototypical events around which football scenes are constructed include shots, passes, goals, substitutions or the match as a whole. With this overview, I now turn to a discussion of the workflow that underlies the Kicktionary project.

3. Workflow

Once a given LU is identified as belonging to a specific scene and frame, example sentences can be searched for in a corpus and annotated according to that analysis.[9] This involves identifying the actual form of an LU as well as the realizations of its FEs (see the examples 1 and 2 above).

More than half of the LUs in the Kicktionary are nominal expressions, which have been analyzed and annotated using the same principles used for verbal LUs. The following sentences illustrate different annotations for the (compound) noun *overhead kick*, which is part of the `Shoot` frame.

(3) a. [Davide Furlan's]$_{\text{SHOOTER}}$ *overhead kick* found Francesco Ruopolo on the penalty spot.

b. [Francesco Ruopolo]$_{\text{SHOOTER}}$ answered by attempting an *overhead kick* at the opposite end.

In (3a), the FE SHOOTER is integrated as a specifier into the noun phrase which has the LU as its head. In (3b), a support verb *attempt* connects the LU with its FE syntactically. Support verbs are systematically recorded in this way for all nominal LUs. The far less frequently occurring adjectival or adverbial LUs are treated in a similar fashion as example (4) illustrates for the LU *ahead* in the `Lead` frame:

(4) By now Celtic were aware that [Shakhtar]$_{\text{LEADER}}$ were [2-0]$_{\text{SCORE}}$ *ahead* [against Barcelona]$_{\text{TRAILER}}$ in the Ukraine.

Having discussed how different types of English LUs are annotated as part of the workflow, I now turn to a discussion of how LUs from different languages are treated in the Kicktionary.

9. The corpus used for the construction of the Kicktionary consists of English, French and German football match reports taken from the website of the Union of European Football Associations (UEFA, www.uefa.com). For each language, about 500 such texts, amounting to roughly 250,000 words, were used. The German part of the corpus was supplemented with about 1,000 similar reports (approximately 700,000 words) from the website of the journal Kicker (http://www.kicker.de) and with a small number of transcriptions of live commentary from German radio (approximately 10,000 words).

4. Interlingual scenes, multilingual frames

The question of how to link lexical information from different languages is one major issue in the creation of multilingual lexical resources. The Kicktionary project suggests that scenes and frames are useful for this purpose since they are by definition independent of specific languages. It thus seems plausible to assume that, at least as far as the domain of football is concerned, a native speaker of English has a very similar abstract knowledge of prototypical events in that domain as a native speaker of German or French (provided, of course, that they have comparable levels of knowledge about football). Given this state of affairs, it should be possible to use a scenes-and-frames analysis of a given domain in one language as a type of language-neutral structural backbone of a multilingual resource. This is comparable to what Boas (2005a: 457) describes as "stripping the FrameNet database of its English-specific lexical descriptions" and then "re-populating the database with non-English lexical descriptions". One major difference to Boas' (2005a: 457) proposals is that in the Kicktionary workflow frames are "populated" more or less simultaneously with lexical material from English, German, and French, as it was planned as a multilingual resource from the outset. The result is a scenes-and-frames hierarchy which can be applied in principle across individual languages, and frames which can contain LUs from different languages.

Between the LUs of a given frame or scene, various types of cross-linguistic correspondences and divergences can be found, and a frame semantic analysis helps to classify and explain these relationships.

First, consider cases in which a LU and its translation equivalent, if it exists, are members of the same frame. In the simplest case, this is a pair of LUs in two languages whose meanings, parts of speech, and argument structure are largely identical, such as with the English LU *nutmeg* and its German counterpart *tunneln* ('to (make a) tunnel'[10]) – both part of the `Beat` frame in the **`One-On-One`** scene:

(5) a. [Hector Font]$_{\text{PLAYER\_WITH\_BALL}}$ tried to *nutmeg* [Ioannis Skopelitis]$_{\text{OPPONENT\_PLAYER}}$.

b. [Ailton]$_{\text{PLAYER\_WITH\_BALL}}$ *tunnelte* [Chris]$_{\text{OPPONENT\_PLAYER}}$ und spielte so Klasnic frei.

---

10. Here and in what follows, the English glosses for French or German LUs attempt to capture the literal (i.e., non-metaphoric) meaning of the item in question.

Second, consider cases where two LUs share the same semantic characteristics and argument structures, but differ in their part of speech. They are nevertheless assigned to the same frame, as the nominal French LU *petit pont* ('little bridge') in (6), which is arguably the best translation of the English verb *nutmeg* in the `Beat` frame, illustrates.

(6) [Bastian Schweinsteiger]$_{\text{PLAYER\_WITH\_BALL}}$ manquait le cadre après avoir réussi un *petit pont* [sur William Gallas]$_{\text{OPPONENT\_PLAYER}}$.

Next, there are also cases of translation equivalence where the meaning and part of speech of two LUs are identical, but the grammatical properties of the LUs differ in some aspect. In such cases, the annotated examples are useful for detecting these differences. Thus, the sentences in (7) indicate that the English LU *play* in the `Match` frame (in the **`Match`** scene) and its German equivalent *spielen* behave differently with respect to number agreement (TEAM1 is plural in English, singular in German), and may differ with respect to the form of their object (direct object in English, prepositional object in German):

(7) a. On that day [Northern Ireland]$_{\text{TEAM1}}$ *play* [England]$_{\text{TEAM2}}$ [at Old Trafford]$_{\text{MATCH\_LOCATION}}$.

b. [Wales]$_{\text{TEAM1}}$ *spielt* [in Cardiff]$_{\text{MATCH\_LOCATION}}$ [gegen Nordirland]$_{\text{TEAM2}}$.

In those cases where no direct translation equivalent for a given LU exists, the information encoded in the scenes-and-frames structure of the Kicktionary can be helpful in identifying potential paraphrases in the target language. For example, (8) is an annotated example of the French LU *coup du sombrero* ('sombrero move'), which means (the act of) getting past an opponent by lobbing the ball over him, rounding him and retrieving the ball behind his back.

(8) [Ronaldinho]$_{\text{PLAYER\_WITH\_BALL}}$ [lui]$_{\text{OPPONENT\_PLAYER}}$ faisait le *coup du sombrero.*

Neither English nor German offer a lexicalized way of expressing the same concept. The available alternatives include using a complex paraphrase like the one given in the previous paragraph, or using an LU that expresses the same general idea, but is less specific than the source expression such as a verbal hypernym. If such LUs exist, they will again be members of the same frame. For (8), the relevant frame `Beat` could, for instance, provide the user with LUs such as the English verb *round* or the

German verb *ausspielen* ('out-play'), both of which are fairly adequate (if less specific) translations of *(faire le) coup du sombrero.*

In other cases, it is possible to compensate for a missing translation equivalent by using another member of the corresponding frame together with an appropriate FE. For instance, German does not have a LU expressing the same idea as the English *side-foot,* i.e., to shoot with the side of the foot:

(9) [He]$_{\text{SHOOTER}}$ calmly rounded Marshall before *side-footing* [the ball]$_{\text{BALL}}$ [into the net]$_{\text{TARGET}}$.

However, the frame `Shot`, which contains the LU *side-foot*, offers several German verbs whose annotated examples indicate that and how a FE PART_OF_BODY can be used with them. Via the frame assignment, a user of the resource can thus discover a way of paraphrasing (9) by employing, for instance, the German LU *bugsieren*:

(10) [Er]$_{\text{SHOOTER}}$ spielte Marshall aus und *bugsierte* [den Ball]$_{\text{BALL}}$ [mit dem Innenrist]$_{\text{PART\_OF\_BODY}}$ [ins Netz]$_{\text{TARGET}}$.

There are also cases where a particular frame is language-specific, i.e., where one language offers a way of linguistically expressing a certain perspective on a given scene, while another language does not. While these are not very common in the football domain, (11) shows a particular usage of *take on*, which profiles a one-on-one situation from the perspective of the player with the ball:

(11) [Maris Verpakovskis]$_{\text{PLAYER\_WITH\_BALL}}$ *took on* and beat [centre-half Nowotny]$_{\text{OPPONENT\_PLAYER}}$ before squaring the ball for Kleber.

Whereas French offers *défier* ('defy') as a good direct translation equivalent, German does not have a lexicalized means of expressing the same perspective on a one-on-one scene. In other words, the corresponding frame `Take_On` contains only English and French, but no German LUs. In order to arrive at an adequate German translation of (11), the Kicktionary user will consult other frames belonging to the same scene. The description of the corresponding scene **`One-On-One`**, for instance, reveals that LUs in the frame `Challenge` take the opposite perspective of those in the frame `Take_On`. They relate a one-on-one situation from the perspective of the attacking player. Among the German LUs in this frame is the verb *angreifen* ('attack'), which, if passivized, adequately paraphrases (11) as shown in (12):

(12) [Maris Verpakovskis]$_{\text{PLAYER\_WITH\_BALL}}$ *wurde* [von Innenverteidiger Nowotny]$_{\text{OPPONENT\_PLAYER}}$ *angegriffen*, umdribbelte ihn und spielte einen Querpass auf Kleber.

Alternatively, the frame `One-On-One` contains LUs taking a neutral perspective on the same scene. The German noun *Zweikampf* ('two-fight') is a member of this frame and provides another means of paraphrasing (11) as shown in (13):

(13) [Maris Verpakovskis und Innenverteidiger Nowotny]$_{\text{PLAYERS}}$ <u>lieferten sich</u> einen *Zweikampf*. Verpakovskis setzte sich durch und spielte einen Querpass auf Kleber.

5. Difficulties and limitations of the scenes-and-frames analysis

As described in Section 2, lexical items from the football domain often lend themselves very naturally to a frame semantic approach. However, as with all lexicographic work, there are also cases where an unequivocal analysis of a given lexical item becomes more difficult.

Nouns whose main function is to denote persons and objects (like *goalkeeper*, *substitute*, *byline*, *penalty area*) rather than to describe processes or activities (like most LUs exemplified in the previous sections) constitute a class of words that are especially difficult to characterize. In this case the concept of scenes and frames loses a lot of its intuitiveness.[11] The notion of perspective, needed to characterize the relationship between a scene and the frames that belong to it, is therefore less easily applicable in "static" scenes (e.g. **`Actors`** or **`Field`**) which were introduced to the Kicktionary to accommodate such words.

Another type of difficulty arises from the lack of clear boundaries between the scenes of a football match. For instance, the fact that the match is restarted by a kick-off after a goal has been scored may be an argument in favor of including the LU *kick-off* (as a member of an appropriate frame) in the **`Goal`** scene. At the same time, an argument against such an analysis is the fact that a kick-off is carried out at a different loca-

11. This is also likely to be one of the reasons for the general language FrameNet to neglect such words: "[...] we do not annotate many nouns denoting artefacts and natural kinds [...]. In this area, we mostly defer to WordNet [...]." (Ruppenhofer et al. 2006: §1.1). It is worth noting, however, that, at least in the football domain, such nouns constitute a significant portion (more than 25%) of the overall vocabulary.

tion on the field, and by actors who do not have a direct connection to any FE of the rest of the **Goal** scene. In this particular case, I decided not to treat the kick-off event as a part of the **Goal** scene, mainly because it would have meant the introduction of a new FE to the scene exclusively for the description of this one LU. This decision, however, is arguably based more on pragmatic considerations (e.g., economy of design) than on purely linguistic principles.

A similar problem was encountered in the assignment of the LU *free-kick* to its "correct" frame and scene. Since a free-kick is by necessity preceded by an infringement of the laws of the game and a subsequent referee intervention, it seems plausible to regard it as belonging to a final stage of the **Foul** scene (see above). However, as with the LU *kick-off*, the FEs used with the LU *free-kick* are different from the FEs of the rest of the scene – the player who executes a free-kick is not necessarily identical to the OFFENDED_PLAYER, and the TARGET or the RECIPIENT of a free-kick are two further FEs that do not figure anywhere else in the **Foul** scene:

(14) a. [Sonck]$_{\text{EXECUTING\_PLAYER}}$ sent a *free-kick* [into the top right corner]$_{\text{TARGET}}$ [from 20 metres]$_{\text{SOURCE}}$.

b. [Anton Naumov]$_{\text{EXECUTING\_PLAYER}}$ floated a *free-kick* [into the penalty box]$_{\text{TARGET}}$ [for defender Tomas Mikuckis]$_{\text{RECIPIENT}}$.

In fact, (14a) and (14b) demonstrate that, instead of emphasizing its role as a compensation for a foul, a free-kick might equally well be analyzed as a special type of shot or pass and thus be assigned to an appropriate frame in the **Shot** or **Pass** scene, respectively. In this case, I chose the first alternative (i.e. assign *free-kick* to a frame `Set-Piece` in the **Foul** scene). Again, this was not based on an irrefutable linguistic analysis, but rather on pragmatic considerations about which analysis would result in the most economic data structure and thus in an organization of the lexicon which is maximally transparent to a user.

Another kind of difficulty arose with the definition and delineation of frames within a scene. Thus, the scene **Shot** must provide appropriate frames to accommodate both LUs like *shot* and *shoot*, as well as LUs describing an opponent's interaction with a shot. The verbs *block* and *fist* are examples of such LUs:

(15) a. [Jon Dahl Tomasson's point-blank shot]$_{\text{SHOT}}$ *was blocked* [by Greek defender Kostas Katsouranis]$_{\text{INTERVENING\_PLAYER}}$.

b. [Casillas]$_{\text{GOALKEEPER}}$ *fisted* [away]$_{\text{INTERVENTION\_TARGET}}$ [Candela's deflected shot]$_{\text{SHOT}}$.

There are good reasons to include these two LUs in the same frame, or alternatively, to create two separate frames for them. On the one hand, the label GOALKEEPER in (15b) is only a more specific label for the INTERVENING_PLAYER of (15a). Seen from a sufficiently abstract point of view, their role in and perspective on the scene is the same, hence the two verbs could go into the same frame. On the other hand, it may be argued that a goalkeeper's interaction with a shot is sufficiently distinct from an arbitrary player's interaction to regard the two as different possible outcomes of the same event, and hence to make two different frames for the LUs in question. Again, the actual decision was taken on the basis of pragmatic considerations: since there was a large number of LUs both for describing the more general interventions of an arbitrary player (e.g., *deflect*, *clear*, *turn*) and for describing the more specific interventions of a goalkeeper (e.g. *parry*, *punch*, *palm*), I decided to have two separate frames (`Intervention` and `Save`, respectively) and to state their close relatedness in the verbal description of the corresponding **`Shot`** scene.

6. Synonymy, translation equivalence and other semantic relations

So far, the scene-and-frame hierarchy does not include information about basic semantic relations. Consider, for example, the frame `Shot`, which contains the following English, German, and French LUs, among many others:

(16) a. *shot, drive, thunderbolt, volley, bicycle kick, overhead kick, header, diving header*

b. *Schuss, Torschuss, Hammer, Volley, Direktabnahme, Fallrückzieher, Kopfball, Kopfstoß, Flugkopfball, Kopfballtorpedo*

c. *tir, frappe, boulet de canon, vollée, retourné, tête, coup de tête, tête plongeante*

Grouping these nouns together is justified by an analysis that assumes that they all impose the same perspective (namely the shooter's) on the same prototypical scene (namely a shot). While a scene-and-frames analysis thus captures an important commonality between these words on a relatively abstract semantic level, it does not provide information about a number of other, more basic, semantic relations between them such as the following:

1. Synonymy. The LUs *Kopfball* ('head ball') and *Kopfstoß* ('head kick') are synonymous, as are *bicycle kick* and *overhead kick*, as well as *tête* ('head') and *coup de tête* ('head kick'). Whereas synonymy in these cases is also reflected by a morphological component common to both members of the pairs, other synonym pairs such as *shot* and *drive*, *Direktabnahme* ('direct connection') and *Volley* ('volley'), and *tir* ('shot') and *frappe* ('shot') consist of morphologically unrelated LUs.
2. Hyponymy. A *thunderbolt* is a special kind of *shot* – specifically, a very powerful one. The same hyponymy relation holds between the German LUs *Hammer* ('hammer') and *Schuss* ('shot') and the French LUs *boulet de canon* ('cannon ball') and *tir* ('shot'). Of course, if a given LU is a hypernym of another, the relation can be extended to all synonyms of both items. In that sense, the synonym set {*Kopfball*; *Kopfstoß*} can be called a hypernym set of {*Flugkopfball*; *Kopfballtorpedo*}.
3. Translation equivalence. The German LU *Volley* and the French LU *vollée* are both translation equivalents of the English LU *volley*. As with synonymy within one language, translation equivalence across languages can, but need not be, reflected in morphological commonalities between items. An example of morphologically unrelated translation equivalents in the `Shot` frame is the set {*bicycle kick* / *Fallrückzieher* / *retourné*}.[12] Again, the translation equivalence relation can be extended to all members of a pair of synonym sets. For example, since *Kopfball* is a synonym of *Kopfstoß*, and *header* is a translation equivalent of *Kopfball*, *header* must also be a translation equivalent of *Kopfstoß*.

Two further types of semantic relations can be found with verbal and nominal LUs, respectively, in other parts of the vocabulary:[13]

4. Troponymy. The verbal equivalent of the hyponymy/hypernymy relation is troponymy, holding between verbs X and Y if "to X is to Y in some way" (cf. Fellbaum 1990: 285ff). This relation is also widely encountered in football vocabulary. Thus *thrash* and *beat* – both members of the `Victory` frame in the **`Match`** scene – are related to another via troponymy, because to thrash an opponent is to beat them in a very clear manner:

12. In this and the following synsets, English words come first, followed by German and French words. Words of the same language are separated by a semicolon, words from different languages by a slash.
13. Other semantic relations – in particular antonymy relations between adjectival LUs – have not yet been taken into account in the Kicktionary.

(17) a. [Olympique Lyonnais]$_{\text{WINNER}}$ *beat* [Fenerbahçe SK]$_{\text{LOSER}}$ [3-1]$_{\text{FINAL\_SCORE}}$ [in Istanbul]$_{\text{MATCH\_LOCATION}}$.

b. [NK Dinamo Zagreb]$_{\text{WINNER}}$ *thrashed* [Beveren]$_{\text{LOSER}}$ [6-1]$_{\text{FINAL\_SCORE}}$.

Similar relations hold, for instance, between the German verbs *ausspielen* (*'out-play'*) and *austanzen* ('out-dance') in the `Beat` frame, or between the French verbs *perdre* ('lose') and *s'effondrer* ('break down') in the `Defeat` frame.

5. Meronymy. Nominal LUs may also be related to one another via a part/whole relationship – if X is a constituent part or a member of Y, X is a meronym of Y, and Y a holonym of X. The meronymy/holonymy relation is especially prominent in the more static scenes. Thus, many LUs belonging to frames in the **`Field`** scene are connected to one another via this semantic relation: the *six metre box* is a part of the *penalty box* which, in turn, is a part of the *field*; the *goalpost* is a part of the *goal*, etc. Likewise, the frames in the **`Actors`** scene contain many meronym/holonym pairs like English *forward* – *attack*, French *défense centrale* ('central defence') – *défense* ('defence') or German *Schiedsrichter* ('referee') – *Schiedsrichtergespann* ('referee team').

The question is how to supplement a scenes-and-frames hierarchy with the types of semantic relations above. One possible approach would be to extend or refine the concept of scenes and frames such that different semantic relations between LUs can be derived from their assignment to frames and/or from different relations of frames to one another or to the corresponding scenes. For example, frames could be constructed such that all the LUs in any single one of them are synonymous, and additional similarities between lexical units are represented by an appropriate relation between such minimal frames. Thus, there could be a frame `Volley` containing only the noun *volley*, its verbal counterpart *volley* and its German and French equivalents, another frame `Header` containing the noun *header*, the verb *head* etc. and a Frame `Shot` containing LUs like *shot, shoot, drive*, etc.; the `Volley` and `Header` frames could be connected to the `Shot` frame via a relation stating that the former are more specific versions of the latter. Up to a certain degree, this kind of solution is pursued by the Berkeley FrameNet project where the notion of 'frame inheritance' is, at least partly, related to the notion of troponymy/hyponymy between lexical units (see Ruppenhofer et al. 2006: §6).

For the Kicktionary, I decided to model these semantic relations *independently* of the scenes-and-frames structure of the resource, because I wanted to avoid having to add a further semantic dimension to existing frame and scene descriptions. Thus, I first partitioned the complete list of lexical units into synsets. The notion of a synset is borrowed from WordNet, where it is defined as "[a] synonym set; a set of words that are interchangeable in some context" (cf. WordNet Glossary). To capture similarities in the three languages, I extended the notion of synset to include translation equivalence across languages as well as synonymy within one language.[14]

On the basis of the partition of LUs into multilingual synsets, I then established additional semantic relations between synsets, leading to three different kinds of synset hierarchies. The first is the hyponymy/hypernymy relation between nominal synsets, which yielded, for example, a taxonomic tree of multilingual terms for players' positions:[15]

(18) {*player* / *Spieler* / *joueur*}
    {*goalkeeper*; *custodian* / *Torhüter*; *Torwart* / *gardien*}
    {*defender* / *Verteidiger*; *Abwehrspieler* / *arrière*; *défenseur*}
        {*central defender* / *Innenverteidiger* / *défenseur central*}
            {*sweeper* / *Abräumer* /}
            {/ *Libero* / *libero*} [...]

As mentioned above, the meronymy/holonymy relation is especially important for structuring lexical units in the static scenes, like those describing the playing field and its components:

(19) {*field*; *pitch* / *Platz*; *Spielfeld* / *champ*; *terrain*}
    {*half* / *Hälfte*; *Spielhälfte* / *moitié de terrain*}
      {*penalty box*; *area* / *Sechzehner* / *surface de réparation*} [...]
    {*touchline* / *Außenlinie*; *Seitenlinie* / *ligne de touche*} [...]

Concerning the troponymy relation between verbal synsets, Fellbaum's (1990: 287) observation that the resulting "verb hierarchies tend to have a

14. This approach differs from Euro WordNet (Vossen et al. 1997), which also proposes to link synsets across different languages, but which uses an unstructured interlingual index as a separate structural entity.
15. In this tree, LUs in consecutive lines are in a hyponymy relation to one another. Thus, a *sweeper* is a (kind of) *central defender*, a *central defender* is a (kind of) *defender*, a *defender* is a (kind of) *player* and so forth.

more shallow, bushy structure than nouns" was confirmed.[16] The following is an example of such a shallow hierarchy:

(20) {*beat*; *defeat* / *bezwingen*; *schlagen* / *battre*; *vaincre*}
{*thrash* / *deklassieren*; *überrollen* / *écraser*; *balayer*}

7. The Kicktionary

The Kicktionary is the result of the workflow described in the previous sections. As Table 1 shows, it currently contains close to 2,000 LUs in English, German and French:

Table 1. LUs in the Kicktionary

	English	*German*	*French*	*All*
Lexical Units (total)	599	792	535	1926
Nouns	318	451	290	1059
Verbs	248	305	201	754
Other	33	36	44	113

For each of these LUs, between one and fifteen example sentences are annotated, as Table 2 illustrates:

Table 2. Examples and annotations in the Kicktionary

	English	*German*	*French*	*All*
Examples	2374	3551	2239	8164
Examples/LU	3.96	4.48	4.19	4.24
Annotated FEs	3882	5731	3647	13260
Annotated supports	293	554	340	1187

16. It also seems that, in general, the problematic cases of deciding on lexical relations between LUs (including synonymy) were far more frequent in the verbal than in the nominal domain.

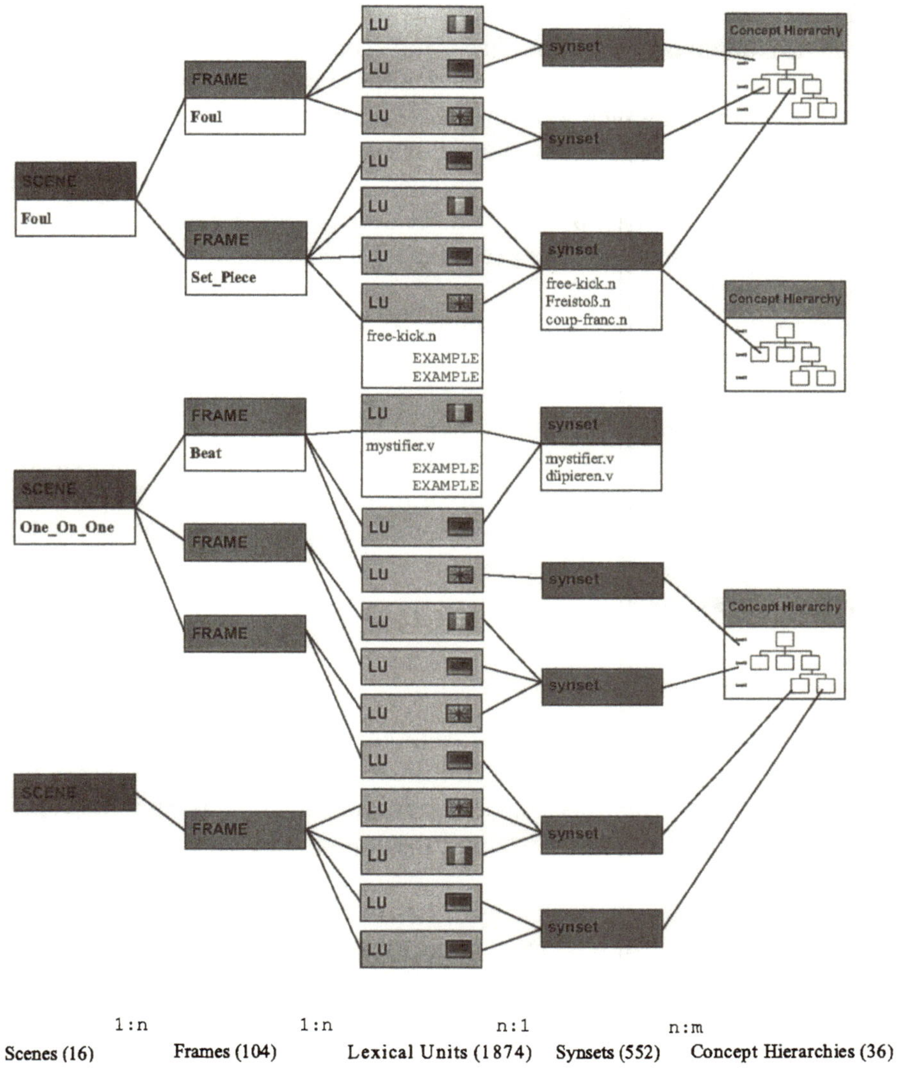

Figure 1. Organization of the Kicktionary

The basic unit of the Kicktionary is the LU, together with a set of annotated example sentences. As described above and illustrated in Figure 1 below, the list of LUs is further structured along two lines: (1) each LU is assigned to one of 104 frames, where each of these frames belongs to one of 16 scenes; (2) the list of LUs is partitioned into 552 synsets, and these synsets are further organized into a number of concept hierarchies using the semantic relations of hyponymy/hypernymy (20 hierarchies), meronymy/holonymy (6 hierarchies) and troponymy (10 hierarchies). In contrast to all other assignments, the mapping of synsets to concept hierarchies is neither complete nor unique – i.e., whereas each LU belongs to exactly one frame and exactly one synset, and each frame to exactly one scene, some synsets may not be assigned to a concept hierarchy at all, while others may be part of two or more concept hierarchies.

For purposes of editing and processing, the Kicktionary data are stored in a small number of XML files – one large file containing all the LUs together with their annotated examples as well as their assignments to a frame and to a synset, one file containing the different concept hierarchies, and 16 files containing descriptions of the scenes and information about what frames they consist of.

For presentation to the user, HTML files are generated on the basis of these XML files (mostly with the help of XSL style sheets) and disseminated via the freely available Kicktionary website (http://www.kicktionary.de). The following subsections describe the HTML presentation of the Kicktionary in more detail.

7.1. Presentation of LUs

As Figure 2 shows, the top line of each entry indicates the base form of the LU together with part of speech information and to which frame and which scenario the LU is assigned. The frame and scene names are hyperlinked to the presentations of the corresponding entities (see Section 7.2 below).

This description is followed by a list of FEs used in the annotation of the LU. Apart from a label indicating their semantic type[17] (e.g., 'On_The_Field_Location'), no further information about FEs is given at this level – since FEs are defined with respect to a superordinate scene, and not to individual LUs, I decided that the level of scenes is the best place to provide this definition (see next section).

The annotated example sentences are displayed in the center of the screen. Annotated FEs are indicated by a set of square brackets, with the FE name appended as a subscript. The form of the LU is printed in bold,

---

17. This assignment of FEs to semantic types – a kind of broader ontological classification of FEs (see Schmidt 2006) – is a further level of structure in the resource which was, however, not fully developed, and is, therefore, not treated in this paper.

drill.v

Scenario Shot **Frame** Shot

BALL [Ball]
PATH [On_The_Field_Location]
SHOOTER [Player]
SOURCE [On_The_Field_Location]
TARGET [On_The_Field_Location]

---

1. [Henry]$_{\text{SHOOTER}}$ cut inside from the right and laid the ball in to Ljungberg inside the penalty area, collecting the Swede's back-heeled return to **drill** [into the corner of the net]$_{\text{TARGET}}$. [1077218 / p6]
2. Poland's seventh came five minutes before the end when Tomasz Rzasa again exploited the visitors weak right side and cut back to substitute [Marek Saganowski]$_{\text{SHOOTER}}$ who spun in the area before **drilling** [the ball]$_{\text{BALL}}$ [home]$_{\text{TARGET}}$. [75339 / p8]
3. In the final minutes of the opening period Simão, Petit and Nuno Assis all took turns to try to level the score with audacious efforts from distance while CSKA's only attempt of note during this period fell to [Rolan Gusev]$_{\text{SHOOTER}}$, who also **drilled** [wide]$_{\text{TARGET}}$ [from long range]$_{\text{SOURCE}}$. [79954 / p6]
4. Krzynówek deservedly scored himself on 72 minutes, when [he]$_{\text{SHOOTER}}$ came off the left wing and **drilled** [high]$_{\text{PATH}}$ [past Kramarenko]$_{\text{TARGET}}$ [from the angle of the area]$_{\text{SOURCE}}$. [75339 / p7]

LU	BALL	PATH	SHOOTER	SOURCE	TARGET
drill			Henry		into the corner of the ne...
drilling	the ball		Marek Saganowski		home
drilled			Rolan Gusev	from long range	wide
drilled		high	he	from the angle of the are...	past Kramarenko

Synonyms	hämmern.v / jagen.v / knallen.v / dreschen.v blast.v / fire.v / rifle.v / drill.v catapulter.v / propulser.v
Troponyms [Move_Ball]	draufhalten.v / abziehen.v / schießen.v kick.v / shoot.v shooter.v / tirer.v / frapper.v

Figure 2. Presentation of the LU *drill*

and supports are underlined. Following each example sentence, information is given about the corpus text from which it was excerpted. Clicking on this information will take the user to a full text presentation of the match report in question.

A second, schematic representation of the examples in the form of a table allows users to study commonalities and differences between examples with respect to the surface forms of LUs and their FEs. The table hides all but LUs and FEs and lists the FEs name-by-name instead of in order of appearance in the sentence.

The lower part of the screen shows information about semantic relations of a LU with other LUs in the Kicktionary. First, the corresponding synset is displayed, providing the user with hyperlinks to all existing synonyms in the same language and translation equivalents in the other languages. Where appropriate, this is followed by a similar display of superordinate synsets from one or more of the concept hierarchies. Additionally, users are given a link to a complete presentation of the respective concept hierarchy (see below) and can explore hyponyms, co-hyponyms, meronyms and troponyms via this level.

7.2. Presentation of scenes and frames

Recall that in the Kicktionary, several frames make up a scene. When representing this relation, it is important to keep in mind that a scene, by definition, corresponds to a kind of knowledge that is not (or not exclusively) linguistic in nature. From the point of view of a dictionary, this means that a textual description, a short film or a schematic diagram may all be equally adequate representations of a scene. In fact, if the role of a scene as an interlingual mediator in the organization of a multilingual vocabulary is emphasized, there are even good reasons to prefer non-linguistic forms of presenting a scene over linguistic ones.

In its present form, the Kicktionary illustrates most scenes with one or more schematic diagrams such as the **Shot** scene in Figure 3:

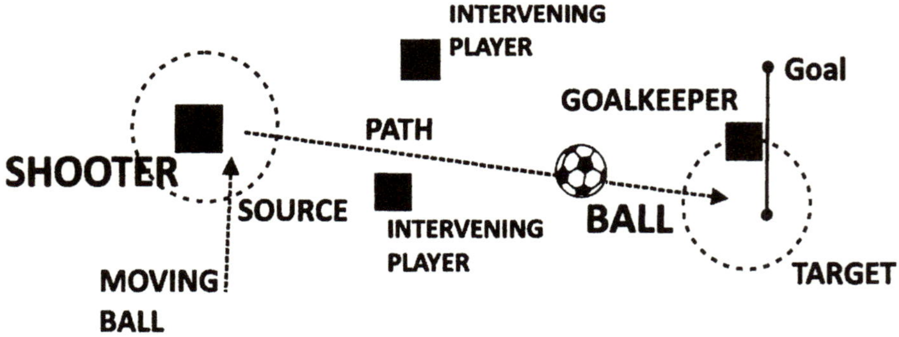

Figure 3. A schematic diagram of the **Shot** scene

The diagram in Figure 3 shows the main actors of the **Shot** scene (and the corresponding FE names), and represents their spatial constellation on the field while conveying a general idea of the temporal dynamics of the scene. A short film, possibly with appropriate subtitles and/or some graphical means of highlighting certain portions, would probably serve the same purpose in an even better way. In some instances, I also found that a scene or a part of a scene can be very adequately illustrated by a single photo or drawing which captures in some way a prototypical mental image associated with that scene. This was the case, for instance, for the `Celebration` frame in the **Goal** scene and for the **Substitution** scene as in Figure 4:

Figure 4. Images illustrating the `Celebration` frame and **Substitution**[18] scene, respectively

The graphic information is supplemented with a prose description of the scene, which lists the FEs, explains their roles in the action, and sketches the typical course of events in the scene. After the scene is explained in that way, the user is given links to the various corresponding frames, as is shown in Figure 5.

> The **Shot** scene is centered around the event of a player directing the ball to a target on the field. Typically, the target is the opponent's goal, and the shot is carried out with the intention of scoring a goal. The main protagonist of the scene is the SHOOTER. Using a PART OF HIS BODY, the shooter directs the BALL towards the opponent's goal. The ball moves from the SOURCE location on the field along a PATH to a TARGET location. In some cases, the MOVING BALL (typically a pass from a team-mate) that brought the shooter into a position to carry out the shot can be mentioned. Sometimes, a shot is construed as the final stage of a MOVE by the shooter's team.
>
> The frame `Shot` contains LUs which describe a shot from the shooter's point of view. The `Finish` frame contains LUs that construe a shot as the last stage of a move by the shooter's team. [...]

Figure 5. The text introducing the **Shot** scene

18. Images taken from [http://www.drblank.com/slaw3.htm].

Flick_On [Scenario: Pass]

1. RECIPIENT
2. PASS
3. SECOND_RECIPIENT
4. BALL
5. PART_OF_BODY
6. DIRECTION
7. FLICK_ON_TARGET

*	1	2	3	4	5	6	7
verlängern.v	■	■	■	■	■		■
Verlängerung.n	■	■					
weiterleiten.v	■	■	■	■			
flick_on.n	■						
flick_on.v	■	■	■				
touch_on.v	■	■	■				
prolonger.v	■	■	■		■	■	

Figure 6. Schematic overview of the content of the frame `Flick_On`

Given that all the contextual knowledge needed to understand the definition of a certain frame is already provided at the level of the superordinate scene, the presentation of a frame is restricted to a schematic overview of the relevant LUs and the FEs encountered with them. In Figure 6, this is done in the form of a table in which the LUs of a frame (sorted first by language, then alphabetically) are listed row-by-row and the FEs used in the annotation are listed column-by-column. The table cells indicate which FE is encountered with which LU. Clicking on any of the LUs will take the user to the corresponding LU representation.

7.3. Other elements of the presentation

In addition to the information outlined above, the web version of the Kicktionary provides a separate visualization of the organization of LUs into hierarchies of synsets (similar to WordNet, see Fellbaum 1998). There is a two-way-link between these representations and the representations of individual LUs so that a user can navigate from a given LU to one of its hyponyms or co-hyponyms via such a hierarchy, as illustrated in Figure 7.

The Kicktionary also provides a full-text display of the corpus texts, which can be accessed via the link provided in the example section of the LU presentation (see Figure 2 above). This allows users to study the larger

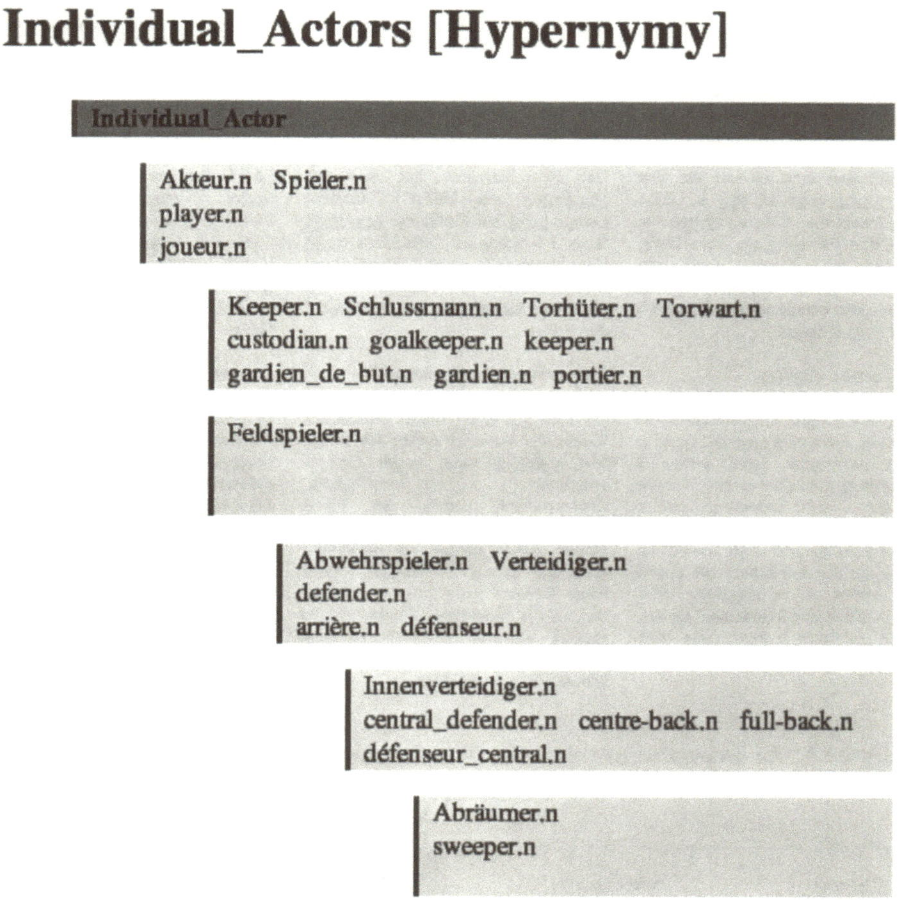

Figure 7. Presentation of the 'Individual_Actors' concept hierarchy

context in which the annotated example sentences appear. Finally, several means for top-level navigation provide the user with points for exploring the full list of LUs and their various forms of organization. For a bottom-up access to the Kicktionary, a simple alphabetical list of LUs, separated by language, is provided. Alternatively, users can start with an annotated parallel text in which occurrences of LUs are linked to the respective entries in the resource, as is shown in Figure 8.

For top-down access, the user can either start with an overview of scenes and frames or with a list of concept hierarchies, as Figure 9 illustrates.

English text	German text	French text
Barcelona glee in Glasgow Tuesday , 14 September 2004 By Alex O ' Henley at Celtic Park	**Barcelona mit historischem Sieg** Dienstag , 14. September 2004 Von Alex O ' Henley aus dem Celtic Park	**Le Barça jubile à Glasgow** Mardi , 14 septembre 2004 Par Alex O ' Henley à Celtic Park
FC Barcelona became the first visiting team to win a UEFA Champions League match at Celtic FC as goals from Deco, Ludovic Giuly and the homecoming Henrik Larsson secured maximum points in their Group F opener .	Der FC Barcelona hat als erste Mannschaft ein UEFA Champions League-Spiel bei Celtic FC gewonnen. Beim 3:1-Erfolg im Celtic Park trafen Deco, Ludovic Giuly und "Heimkehrer" Henrik Larsson und sicherten so den Katalanen zum Auftakt in der Gruppe F drei Punkte.	Le FC Barcelona est la première équipe à remporter un match d'UEFA Champions League à Celtic Park. Deco, Ludovic Giuly et Henrik Larsson, qui effectuait son grand retour, ont marqué et offrent les trois points au Barça dans le Groupe F.
Larsson clincher	**Entscheidung durch Larsson**	**Larsson buteur**
Larsson's goal, on his return to the club where he scored 242 goals in a seven-year spell, sealed a victory which had looked in doubt after Chris Sutton grabbed a dramatic equaliser for Celtic just short of the hour mark . Barcelona coach Frank Rijkaard had named Larsson as a substitute with Brazilian ace Ronaldinho coming in to form a front three with Ludovic Giuly and Samuel Eto ' o.	Larssons Tor gegen seinen ehemaligen Verein, für den er in sieben Jahren 242 Mal getroffen hatte, sorgte für die endgültige Entscheidung. Zwischendurch nahm die Partie dramatische Züge an, als nach etwa einer Stunde Chris Sutton der umjubelte Ausgleich gelang. Barcelonas Trainer Frank Rijkaard hatte Larsson zunächst nur auf die Ersatzbank gesetzt, um im Angriff mit dem brasilianischen Star Ronaldinho sowie Ludovic Giuly und Samuel Eto'o zu beginnen.	Le but de Larsson , pour son grand retour au club pour lequel il a marqué 242 buts en sept ans , scellait une victoire qui ne semblait pas acquise après l'égalisation de Chris Sutton à l'approche de l'heure de jeu . Le coach du Barça , Frank Rijkaard, décidait de reléguer Larsson sur le banc des remplaçants, alors que le prodige brésilien Ronaldinho faisait son entrée pour former un trio de tête avec Ludovic Giuly et Samuel Eto'o.

Figure 8. An annotated parallel text, linked to the lexical resource

Chance 3 frames 26 lexical units	Chance (10 LUs) Create_Chance (7 LUs) Miss_Chance (9 LUs)
Motion 7 frames 88 lexical units	Ball_Bounce (13 LUs) Ball_Escape (3 LUs) Ball_Land (12 LUs) Ball_Move (19 LUs) Goalkeeper_Advance (6 LUs) Player_Move (10 LUs) Player_Move_With_Ball (25 LUs)
Substitution 3 frames 27 lexical units	Bring_Off (8 LUs) Bring_On (12 LUs) Substitute (7 LUs)

Hypernymy / Hyponymy

Individual_Actors (143 lexical units)
Team_Parts (20 lexical units)
Moving_Balls (175 lexical units)
Matches (38 lexical units)
Goals (37 lexical units)
One_On_One_Situations (16 lexical units)
Match_Outcomes (27 lexical units)
Offences (43 lexical units)
Individual_Actions (76 lexical units)
Substitutions (9 lexical units)
Dead_Ball_Situations (48 lexical units)

Figure 9. Overview of scenes, frames and concept hierarchies

8. Evaluation

Since the Kicktionary can, in essence, be regarded as a multilingual, domain-specific adaptation of the methodology underlying the FrameNet project (Fillmore et al. 2003), a large part of the discussion in this section is concerned with a comparison of these two resources.

8.1. The multilingual aspect

Concerning the *construction* of a multilingual resource, the strategy of carrying out a scenes-and-frames analysis on several languages simultaneously has proven feasible, generally supporting Boas' (2005a) claim that semantic frames are useful as interlingual representations. Concerning the *use* of the Kicktionary for translation or similar tasks, examples like the ones discussed in Section 4 provide further evidence that diverse cases of cross-linguistic (non-)correspondences can be partly accounted for in frame semantic terms in a way that should be transparent and beneficial to dictionary users.

Furthermore, the concept of a scene provides a theoretically substantiated justification for introducing non-linguistic methods of description into dictionaries. As has been argued in the lexicographic literature (e.g. Storrer 2001), and as existing commercial electronic dictionaries show, the fact that computer technology facilitates the use of pictures, diagrams, films etc., alongside textual material opens interesting perspectives for monolingual as well as for multilingual dictionaries. Because Frame Semantics is, among other things, concerned with systematically relating linguistic forms to non-linguistic knowledge, a scenes-and-frames analysis can help define what kinds of information such multi-medial elements should convey, and determine at which level a resource should place it.

8.2. The domain-specific aspect

To my knowledge, the Kicktionary is one of the first attempts to apply frame semantic principles systematically to the vocabulary of a specific domain. This has a number of advantages.

First, football is a particularly rewarding domain because most of its scenes can be associated in a straightforward manner with concrete mental images – the notion of a scene (as understood here) is arguably much more intuitively applicable for LUs like *foul*, *goal* and *scissors kick* than it is for many parts of the general vocabulary which denote more abstract concepts, such as *depend*, *necessity* or *tolerant* (all from the FrameNet database). For similar reasons, difficulties in distinguishing literal and metaphorical uses of words hardly arise in the language of football.

Second, restricting the analysis to a specific domain also entails a limitation to a closed set of LUs, which means that there is a definable line beyond which LUs will not be taken into account because they fall outside the domain.[19] This limitation can be seen as an advantage from a methodological point of view: it allows for a manner of proceeding in which first a reasonably extensive (if not complete) list of LUs and example sentences is extracted from the corpus. Scenes and frames are then built on top of that list and the completeness of the resulting structure is continually checked with respect to the list.[20] This is different from FrameNet, which proceeds frame by frame, selecting candidate LUs for frames mainly through linguistic introspection, and only then consulting the corpus for evidence in favor of the tentative analysis.[21] An advantage of the Kicktionary methodology is that it makes it much easier to estimate the effects of an individual decision on the resource as a whole. For instance, many of the problems discussed in Section 5 were resolved[22] by considering which one of a number of potential alternative analyses would result in a more economic,

19. In the case of the Kicktionary, the set of lexical units was further limited by the relatively small size of the corpus – between 250,000 and 1,000,000 words for each language as compared to the 100,000,000 words of the BNC on which the FrameNet database is based. With few exceptions, words that could not be found in this small corpus were not considered for integration into the resource.
20. This is of course a simplified picture. In reality, the list could only be assembled with the help of a preliminary scenes-and-frames analysis of the football domain, which was then "thrown away" and rebuilt from scratch. The crucial point, however, is that developing scenes and frames and determining the LUs which are to become part of them can be regarded as two separate processes for the Kicktionary whereas they are inseparably interwoven for FrameNet.
21. In a discussion on the lexicography mailing list, this methodology is criticized as follows: "FrameNet proceeds frame by frame, not word by word. This may seem a trivial point, but it isn't. Although FrameNet uses empirical data, it does not use an empirical methodology." [Patrick Hanks, http://groups.yahoo.com/group/lexicographylist/]
22. And, conversely, some of these problems arose exactly *because* the scenes-and-frames structure of the Kicktionary was constructed to accommodate the entirety of LUs found in the corpus. Proceeding frame-by-frame always involves a certain risk of leaving exactly those LUs unanalysed that are ambivalent with respect to their framing characteristics.

homogeneous, balanced or useful overall structure of scenes and frames; and, of course, such a process presupposes that the majority of the LUs to be integrated into the structure be known at the time of analysis.

8.3. Scenes and frames, frame inheritance, and other entities and concepts

Although both resources are constructed on the basis of frame semantic principles, the Kicktionary and FrameNet differ in important points both with respect to their form, i.e., the actual data structures they use to represent their respective frame semantic analyses, and with respect to their content.

For example, FrameNet takes a much more comprehensive approach to the annotation of examples. Each LU is illustrated with a much larger number of sentences from the corpus than in the Kicktionary, and the annotation of these sentences is also much more extensive: in addition to the information about FEs, their grammatical functions (e.g., object, dependent) and their phrase types (e.g., noun phrase, prepositional phrase) are recorded. Time restrictions precluded this level of detail for the Kicktionary. Similarly, FrameNet uses the concept of null instantiation of FEs for "FEs that are conceptually salient, [but] do not show up as lexical or phrasal material in the sentence for annotation" (Ruppenhofer et al. 2006: §3.2.3). The Kicktionary does not make use of null instantiation; this does not mean that it was considered unimportant, but only that I lacked the time to integrate it into my analyses. The same holds for a number of other details of the FrameNet database like the notion of coreness, the bundling of FEs into core-sets or the annotation of extra-thematic FEs (see Fillmore et al. 2003).

Another difference between the two resources is that in FrameNet, the only top-level structural entities are frames (including specific types such as non-lexical frames, non-perspectivized frames, see Ruppenhofer et al. 2006: §6.2), which are related to one another via an elaborate system of frame-to-frame relations (e.g., inheritance, causative_of, inchoative_of, subframe, etc.). In contrast, the scene is the Kicktionary's top level entity, and it is explicitly understood as a unit substantially different from (and superordinate to) that of a frame. Each frame is associated with exactly one such scene, and this frame-to-scene assignment is also the only explicit way of relating frames to one another. Whereas a similar relationship can be expressed in FrameNet by connecting a lexical frame to a non-lexical frame via the "subframe" relation, nothing in the design of the FrameNet database *requires* such a frame-to-scene-assignment.[23] The notion of a scene and the distinction between scenes and frames are thus much more central to the Kicktionary than they are to FrameNet.

8.4. Frame Semantics and other analyses

Work on the Kicktionary suggests that an ideal lexicographic analysis for the purpose of dictionary-making will require both a methodologically motivated restriction of the role of Frame Semantics to certain areas of the vocabulary and an appropriate use of other approaches to semantic analysis.[24] By organizing the vocabulary of football language both in a scenes-and-frames hierarchy and in a WordNet-like system of synsets and concept hierarchies, the Kicktionary has partly explored the second of these requirements. One observation in this respect is that WordNet-style analyses often seem to be most profitable in precisely those areas where frame semantic analyses are less intuitively applicable or less informative (see also Boas 2005b). For instance, I argued in Section 5 that a scenes-and-frames analysis of LUs referring to parts of the playing field is made difficult by the fact that the notion of perspective is not easily applied to such a static "scene". At the same time, example (19) shows that this set of LUs can be very intuitively structured on the basis of semantic relations like synonymy and meronymy. Conversely, it was found that troponymy between verbal LUs seems to be a semantic relation that is more difficult to detect or analyze and/or less widely encountered than hyponymy or meronymy relations between nominal LUs. In this area, then, the kind of relation that a scenes-and-frames analysis establishes between verbal LUs may be the more useful one from the point of view of a dictionary user. Since real conflicts between the two approaches were not encountered, a tentative conclusion to be drawn from these observations is that FrameNet- and WordNet-style analyses should be viewed more as complementary, rather than in opposition to each other.[25]

---

23. And, in fact, most lexical frames in the FrameNet database are *not* related to a superordinate non-lexical frame.
24. As Fillmore (1978) states for semantic theory in general: "I think that semantic theory must reject the suggestion that all meanings need to be described in the same terms. I think, in fact, that semantic domains are going to differ from each other according to the kind of 'definitional base' which is most appropriate to them."
25. That is, there were no cases where an analysis according to one approach would positively contradict or be incommensurable with an analysis according to the other approach.

9. Summary and outlook

In this paper I discussed the theoretical background and the workflow underlying the Kicktionary, a multilingual, domain-specific lexical resource based on Frame Semantics. My comparison of the structure and content of the Kicktionary with more general lexical resources such as FrameNet and WordNet has resulted in several insights. First, a hierarchy of scenes and frames is an efficient way of grouping sense-related *domain-specific* vocabulary items on a level which abstracts over linguistic form, and thus constitutes a connection between linguistic and "world" knowledge. Second, FrameNet-style annotations provide an efficient way of including empirical language material in electronic dictionaries. Systematically relating the labels used in these annotations to the hierarchy of scenes and frames opens further possibilities for the dictionary user to discover and exploit relationships between lexical items. Third, the scenes-and-frames approach lends itself very well to the construction of a *multilingual* resource that can be helpful in various translation tasks. Fourth, decisions about frame and scene membership of a LU are not always straightforward. Often, pragmatic considerations about the economy of the dictionary design are a way of dealing with such difficulties. Fifth, a scenes-and-frames analysis is easier and more fruitful in those areas of the vocabulary which deal with dynamic activities than in more static areas. For the latter, WordNet-style concept hierarchies seem like the more intuitive and more useful approach. As such, a scenes-and-frames analysis and a WordNet style analysis of the lexicon are complementary to each other. Finally, the concept of a scene providing information about prototypical events gives dictionary writers a useful place for integrating multi-media elements like pictures or films that aid in the comprehension of words in foreign languages.

When constructing multilingual lexical resources, it is important to keep in mind that football is probably not a prototypical case of a special domain. Other specialized domains are likely to exhibit larger, more deeply nested, and more systematic taxonomic systems. Dynamic aspects, and hence the benefits of a scenes-and-frames organization of the lexicon, may play a less prominent role in their analysis. In contrast to football language, they will tend to avoid, rather than abound with, synonymy and near-synonymy so that the task of establishing links between lexical items is different. Work by Dolbey et al. (2006) on "Bio FrameNet" is an example of such a more typical specialized lexical resource.

At this point in time, the Kicktionary is complete in the sense that a reasonably large number of LUs from the football domain has been analyzed and integrated into the described architecture.[26] It is also complete in the sense that this architecture is accessible via a website. There are, however, various ways in which it could be improved and extended.

First, an extension of the corpus is likely to uncover new LUs and a larger corpus could be used to increase the number of annotated examples for existing LUs. In both cases, the additional material may make it necessary to remodel parts of the scenes-and-frames hierarchy and parts of the concept hierarchies. Further text materials from the UEFA website (about 250,000 tokens for English, French and German) have been acquired for this purpose and are presently being processed.

Second, user feedback for the Kicktionary website should make it possible to evaluate the quality of the resource and its presentation. One possible way of improving the presentation might be the inclusion of additional films and pictures into the description of scenes.

Third, the existing architecture, together with the concordancing and annotation tool developed for the analysis, should make it relatively easy to supplement the Kicktionary with data from other languages. Italian, Portuguese, Spanish, Russian and Japanese corpus materials are available for lexicographers interested in producing versions for these languages.

Finally, I would like to suggest that the Kicktionary should be regarded as a promising test case for the development and application of methods for collaborative creation of specialized multilingual lexical resources, because (1) football is a well-delimited special domain with a large, but manageably-sized vocabulary, and (2) contrary to many other specialized areas, it is not too difficult to find "experts" who are competent users of that vocabulary (in different languages) and who may be able and willing to contribute to such a collaborative effort either as lexicographers or as evaluators of the resulting resource.[27] First steps towards a client-server architecture in which dictionary creators and dictionary users can work together to construct an improved version of the Kicktionary have already been taken.

26. "Reasonably large" means that (a) the number of lexical units in the Kicktionary is considerably higher than in comparable printed dictionaries (e.g. Yıldırım 2006, Colombo et al. 2006) and that (b) a further analysis of the corpus would turn up no or very few additional LUs.
27. So far, online feedback shows that the Kicktionary seems indeed capable of getting both linguists and laymen interested in lexicography.

References

Boas, Hans C.
2005a Semantic frames as interlingual representations for multilingual lexical databases. In: *International Journal of Lexicography* 18.4: 445–478.

Boas, Hans C.
2005b From theory to practice: Frame Semantics and the design of FrameNet. In: S. Langer and D. Schnorbusch (eds.), *Semantik im Lexikon*, 129–160. Tübingen: Narr.

Colombo, Roberta, Klaus Heimeroth, Olivier Humbert, Michael Jackson, Frank Kohl, and Josep Ràfols
2006 *PONS Fußballwörterbuch*. Stuttgart: Ernst Klett Verlag.

Dolbey, Andrew, Michael Ellsworth, and Jan Scheffczyk
2006 BioFrameNet: A domain-specific FrameNet Extension with links to biomedical ontologies. In: *Proceedings of the International Workshop "Biomedical Ontology in Action"*, November 8, 2006, in Baltimore, MD.

Fellbaum, Christiane
1990 English verbs as a semantic net. In: G.A. Miller et al. (eds.), WordNet – an Online Lexical Database. *International Journal of Lexicography* 3.4: 278–301.

Fellbaum, Christiane
1998 *WordNet: an electronic lexical database*. Cambridge: MIT Press.

Fillmore, Charles J.
1977a The case for case reopened. In: P. Cole and J. Sadock (eds.), *Syntax and Semantics 8: Grammatical Relations*, 59–82. New York: Academic Press.

Fillmore, Charles J.
1977b Scenes-and-frames semantics, linguistic structures processing. In: A. Zampolli (ed.), *Fundamental Studies in Computer Science*, No. 59, 55–88. Dordrecht: North Holland Publishing.

Fillmore, Charles J.
1977c Topics in lexical semantics. In: R. Cole (ed.), *Current Issues in Linguistic Theory*, 76–138. Bloomington: Indiana University Press.

Fillmore, Charles J.
1978 On the organization of semantic information in the lexicon. In: D. Farkas et al. (eds.), *Papers from the Parasession on the Lexicon*, Chicago Linguistic Society, April 14–15, 1978. Reprint in: Fillmore, Charles J., *Form and Meaning in Language: Volume I, Papers on Semantic Roles*, Stanford: CSLI Publications, 261–289.

Fillmore, Charles J., Christopher Johnson, and Miriam R.L. Petruck
2003 Background to FrameNet. In: *International Journal of Lexicography* 16.3: 235–250.

Gross, Gaston
2002 Comment décrire une langue de spécialité? In: *Cahiers de lexicologie: revue internationale de lexicologie et lexicographie* 80: 179–200.

Petruck, Miriam R.L.
1996 Frame Semantics. In: J. Verschueren et al. (eds.), *Handbook of Pragmatics*, 1–13. Amsterdam/Philadelphia: John Benjamins.

Ruppenhofer, Josef, Michael Ellsworth, Miriam R.L. Petruck, and Chris Johnson
2006 FrameNet: Theory and Practice. http://framenet.icsi.berkeley.edu/book/book.html

Schmidt, Thomas
2006 Interfacing lexical and ontological information in a multilingual soccer FrameNet. In: *Proceedings of OntoLex 2006 – Interfacing Ontologies and Lexical Resources for Semantic Web Technologies*. Genoa, Italy, May, 24–26, 2006.

Seelbach, Dieter
2001 Das kleine multilinguale Fußball-Lexikon. In: W. Bisang and G. Schmidt (eds.), *Philologica et Linguistica. Historia, Pluralitas, Universitas*, 323–350. Trier.

Seelbach, Dieter
2002 La traduction des verbes avec adverbes appropriés et des verbes à particule allemands. In: *Traduire au XXIème siècle: Tendances et perspectives, Proceedings 2002*, 504–515. Facultés des lettres UATH Athens.

Seelbach, Dieter
2003 Separable Partikelverben und Verben mit typischen Adverbialen. Systematische Kontraste Deutsch-Französisch / Französisch-Deutsch. In: U. Seewald-Heeg et al. (eds.), *Sprachwissenschaft, Computerlinguistik, Neue Medien*, 103–115. Königswinter.

Storrer, Angelika
2001 Digitale Wörterbücher als Hypertexte: Zur Nutzung des Hypertextkonzepts in der Lexikographie. In: I., Lemberg, B. Schröder, and A. Storrer (eds.), *Chancen und Perspektiven computergestützter Lexikographie. Hypertext, Internet und SGML/XML für die Produktion und Publikation digitaler Wörterbücher*, 88–104. Tübingen: Niemeyer.

Vossen, Piek, Pedro Díez-Orzas, and Wim Peters
1997 Multilingual design of EuroWordNet. In: P. Vossen, N. Calzolari, G. Adriaens, A. Sanfilippo, and Y. Wilks (eds.), *Proceedings of the ACL/EACL-97 workshop on Automatic Information Extraction and Building of Lexical Semantic Resources for NLP Applications*. Madrid, July 12th, 1997.
WordNet Glossary: http://wordnet.princeton.edu/gloss

Yıldırım Kaya
2006 *Fußballwörterbuch in 7 Sprachen*. Kauderwelsch (203). Osnabrück: Reise-Know-How Verlag Peter Rump GmbH.

Part II. FrameNets for typologically diverse languages

5. Spanish FrameNet: A frame-semantic analysis of the Spanish lexicon

Carlos Subirats

1. Introduction

The goal of the Spanish FrameNet[1] (SFN) project is to apply Frame Semantics (Fillmore 1976, 1977a, 1977b, 1982, 1985) to develop a semantic analysis of the Spanish lexicon for verbs, nouns, prepositions, and adjectives, as well as adverbs, conjunctions, and entity names. Our aim is to develop a semantically and syntactically annotated lexical resource with broad lexical coverage in Spanish which can be used as a training corpus for applications aimed at automatic semantic role labeling (see Erk and Padó 2006). From a 370 million word Spanish corpus, sentences are extracted for further semantic and syntactic analysis. Certain project tasks are carried out automatically – for instance, the automatic extraction of syntactic constructions from the corpus, – while others are done semi-automatically or manually, like the semantic annotation of corpus sentences. The results of this project can be browsed on the web using several web report generators which support a variety of queries about the general description of semantic frames and their frame elements. The semantically and syntactically annotated corpus sentences display the syntactic realiza-

1. This project is being developed both at the Autonomous University of Barcelona and at the International Computer Science Institute (ICSI) in Berkeley, in cooperation with the FrameNet project. I would like to thank Collin Baker, Hans C. Boas, Michael Ellsworth, Charles J. Fillmore, Mercedes García de Quesada, Covandonga López-Alonso, Katie McGuire, and Marc Ortega for their help. This project has been sponsored by a three year grant of the Department of Science and Technology of Spain (TIC2002-01338). Additional funding has also been provided by a one-year grant from the Autonomous University of Barcelona (PNL2004-49 and PRP2006-04), and of the Department of Education of Spain (TSI2005-01200). I also thank the Department of Education for awarding me the fellowships that have enabled me to complete several research stays at ICSI.

tions of frame elements as well as their respective phrase types and grammatical functions.[2]

This paper demonstrates how parts of the design of the original Berkeley FrameNet project have been re-used for the construction of SFN and what kinds of theoretical and practical problems we encountered. The paper is structured as follows. Section 2 provides a brief summary of how Frame Semantics, the theory underlying the construction of SFN, can be applied to Spanish. More specifically, the discussion of *promesa* ('promise') shows how a frame-semantic analysis of the Spanish lexicon captures important information about the syntactic realizations of semantic knowledge necessary for the interpretation of words. Section 3 presents the computational infrastructure (corpus, software) underlying the workflow of the SFN project and shows which parts of the original Berkeley FN software have been re-used. Section 4 discusses the workflow of SFN by focusing on automatic sentence extraction and semantic annotation. Sections 5 and 6 highlight two theoretically important issues that arise during the annotation process, namely the annotation of nouns and metaphors, respectively. Finally, section 7 concludes and provides an outlook on future research.

2. Applying Frame Semantics to the Spanish lexicon

The basic assumption of Frame Semantics is that the meaning of lexical items must be described in relation to the frames that they evoke (Petruck 1996). A semantic frame is a schematic representation of a situation involving various participants, props, and other conceptual roles, each of which is an element belonging to this same frame, which is called a frame element (FE) (Fillmore et al. 2003). SFN describes the meaning of lexical units (LUs) (words in a particular sense) by directly appealing to the frames which underlie them and studies the grammatical constructions where these lexical units are instantiated by asking how frames and their constituent FEs are given syntactic form.

The syntactic realizations of a given predicating word are analyzed in terms of the frame to which it belongs. Consequently, the syntactic argument structure of this predicating word, following a lexical syntax approach (Subirats 2001), does not always coincide with the most relevant

2. The SFN project results are publicly available, and they can be accessed over the web or other interfaces on the SFN web page: http://gemini.uab.es/SFN.

construction for a frame semantic analysis in terms of its FEs. For example *a ver al presidente* ('to see the president') in (1) is a complement belonging to the syntactic argument structure of the verb *ir* ('go'), since the preposition *a* ('to'), which is heading the phrase, is determined by the verb *ir*.[3]

(1) [*Jordi* $_{\text{THEME}}$] ***fue*** [*a Madrid* $_{\text{GOAL}}$]
Jordi went to Madrid

[*a ver al presidente* $_{\text{INTENTION}}$]
to see to-the president

[*para pedirle dinero* $_{\text{PURPOSE}}$].
in order to ask-him money[4]

'Jordi went to Madrid in order to see the President and ask him for money.'

However, *a ver al presidente* is the INTENTION FE of the verb *ir*, which evokes the `Motion` frame[5], and INTENTION is not a core FE in this frame (i.e. it is not conceptually necessary) since it is not a definitional aspect of a motion event (see Ruppenhofer et al. 2006: 29). We may also encounter the opposite situation as in (2) where the prepositional phrase *sobre este tema* ('on this issue') is an adjunct which is not syntactically determined by the predicating noun *comentario* ('comment').

(2) [Max $_{\text{SPEAKER}}$] *hizo un* ***comentario*** *inoportuno*
Max made a comment inappropriate

[*sobre este tema* $_{\text{TOPIC}}$].
on this issue

'Max made an inappropriate comment regarding this issue.'

However, *comentario* is an event noun which belongs to the `Statement` frame[6], and, in this frame, TOPIC, i.e. the subject matter over which

3. In our examples, the target words of a given frame are always in boldface.
4. Word by word translations of example sentences are only provided when they contibute to clarify relevant aspects of the example. In all other cases, only one translation is given.
5. The definition of the `Motion` frame in FN can be found at: http://framenet.icsi.berkeley.edu/index.php?option=com_wrapper&Itemid=118&frame=Motion&
6. See the definitions of the `Statement` frame, its FEs, and other frame information on the FN website: http://framenet.berkeley.edu/index.php?option=com_wrapper&itemid=118&frame=Statement&

the comment is made, is a core FE.[7] Therefore, a core FE, such as TOPIC in the `Statement` frame, may well be mapped onto a constituent which is not a syntactic argument of the target word. As a result, the FEs evoked by a target word (an instance of an LU in the context of a particular sentence) in a given frame are realized in different syntactic constructions, all semantically relevant, regardless of whether the resulting sentence constituents are syntactic arguments or not.

We derive from Frame Semantics the basic assumption that targets select specific lexical material that may be optionally present, in order to evoke a particular frame. It is precisely within this frame that the target word is defined and understood. The semantic analysis of a given lexical unit[8] (henceforth: LU), therefore, consists of (1) the identification of the frame which houses this LU in just one of its senses, and (2) the specification of how the FEs are realized in syntactic constructions headed by the above mentioned target.

Frame Semantics, which underlies Spanish FrameNet, differs from other semantic approaches, such as Castellón et al. (2006), in that it does not use a fixed set of semantic roles, such as agent, patient, addressee, etc., for the semantic characterization of all the target words of a language. Studies by Fillmore (1976, 1977a, 1982, and 1985) have not only shown the difficulty in establishing a set list of labels to study the lexicon of natural languages, but they have even stated the impossibility of a frame semantic analysis of the lexicon following this same procedure. For this reason, the FEs used in SFN are always defined in terms of a specific frame involving various participants, props, etc., and the semantic analysis of the lexicon is based upon the FEs specifically defined for a given semantic frame. In this way, even when two (or more) different frames share the same FE, they are considered distinct, since they belong to different frames. These distinct types, regardless of the name identity, are explicitly connected to semantically related FEs in other frames when possible.

To illustrate, consider the predicate noun *promesa* ('promise') which evokes the `Commitment` frame[9] that describes scenarios in which a

7. A lexical unit is a word sense expressed by the relation between a lemma and the frame it evokes.
8. See the definition of the `Commitment` frame on the English FN website: http://framenet.icsi.berkeley.edu/index.php?option=com_wrapper&Itemid=118&frame=Commitment&
9. It is true that the sentence *Me hizo la promesa de que me mataría* ('He made me the promise that he would kill me') seems perfectly natural. Nevertheless, if someone says to his addressee, *Te prometo que te voy a matar* ('I promise

SPEAKER makes a commitment – which may be expressed through a MESSAGE or a TOPIC FE – to an ADDRESSEE, about a state of affairs or future event. This may be an action desirable (as with *promesa*[10]) or not desirable (as with *amenaza* 'threaten') to the ADDRESSEE. (3) is a canonical example of the eventive noun *promesa* evoking the `Commitment` frame.

(3) [*El juez* SPEAKER] [*le* ADDRESSEE] *hizo la* ***promesa***
the judge him/her made the promise
[*de que atendería su petición* MESSAGE].
of that would-consider his/her petition
'The judge made {him/her} the promise that he would accept {his/her} petition.'

The noun phrase *el juez* is the realization of the SPEAKER FE, the clitic pronoun *le* plays the role of the ADDRESSEE, and the subordinate clause *de que atendería su petición* is the MESSAGE, through which the SPEAKER expresses to the ADDRESSEE his commitment to carry out an action. In general, a target evokes a frame and the FEs are part of the frame it evokes; in this way, for example, *promesa* evokes the `Commitment` frame, which has the FEs SPEAKER, ADDRESSEE, and MESSAGE.

The sentence in (3) illustrates that the syntactic valence required by a given target word (here: *promesa*) is analyzed with respect to the frame that it evokes. The semantic valence properties of a target are expressed in terms of the kinds of entities that can participate in the frames evoked by the corresponding target. As such, the semantic valence of a target can be expressed through several syntactic constructions. For example, consider cases that involve null instantiations of core FEs, i.e. cases where conceptually actual salient FEs do not show up as constituents in a sentence. In Spanish, null instantiation of external arguments (i.e. subjects) is very common[11] and null instantiation of internal arguments is also applicable to most predicates. Thus, it is possible that all FEs of a target word remain unexpressed, as in (4).

---

that I will kill you'), it is unlikely that the addressee could say to a third person that someone has made him or her a promise; the addressee would rather say that someone has threatened him.

10. See Subirats (2001: 92, 94) for further discussion.
11. Support verbs are non-evoking LUs that combine with a state or event noun to create a predicate, allowing arguments of the noun to fill the slots of the frame elements of the frame evoked by the noun in a sentential construction. Support verbs do not introduce any significant semantics of their own (see Ruppenhofer et al. 2006: 52–55, Subirats 2001: 89–91).

(4) *Hizo una* ***promesa****.* (ECNI Speaker, DNI Addressee, Content)
made a promise
'{He/she} made a promise.'

In (4), the Speaker is an external constructional null instantiation (ECNI), i.e. a null instantiation of an external argument, which is licensed by a sentential construction with a support verb.[12] Moreover, the Addressee and the Message are not overtly realized but are understood as an anaphoric or definite null instantiation (DNI), in which the missing element is recoverable from the context (Fillmore et al. 2003: 245–246, Ruppenhofer et al. 2006: 33–36). Constructions of the type in (4) are interesting, as they exhibit all possible null instantiations of the FEs of a target word. Spanish differs from English in that it is generally possible to have unexpressed external arguments in sentential constructions. ECNI is not lexically dependent, but is constructionally determined by sentential constructions with predicative or support verbs, and it is regulated by contextual and pragmatic constraints (Enríquez 1984, and Enríquez and Albelda 2006).

In addition to the support constructions and their null instantiation possibilities we have just considered, the FEs of *promesa* can also be mapped onto different syntactic constructions. The first is a construction without a support verb, where *promesa* is the head of a noun phrase. In this case, the Speaker is an adjunct headed by the preposition *de* ('of') as in (5), or by the multi-word preposition *por parte de* ('on the part of, by') as in (6). Moreover, the FE Message can be realized by a sentential complement or infinitival complement headed by the preposition *de*, as *de que duplicaría el presupuesto de investigación en los próximos años* ('that he would double the research budget for the next years') in (5), or *de estudiar sus reivindicaciones* ('to study they claims') as in (6). Likewise, in all the above mentioned constructions, null instantiation of the FE Addressee may be found, as (5) and (6) demonstrate.

(5) *Uno de las cuestiones más sorprendentes fue la* ***promesa*** [*de Zapatero* $_{\text{SPEAKER}}$] [*de que duplicaría el presupuesto de investigación en los próximos años* $_{\text{MESSAGE}}$]. (DNI Addressee)
'One of the most surprising issues was the promise by Zapatero that he would double the research budget for the next years.'

---

12. For the purpose of its identification in the corpus, a word is any chain of alphabetical characters between two spaces, i.e., a blank space, return, tabulator, or consecutive combinations of them. We thus exclude from the word count figures, punctuation signs, and also alphanumeric combinations which are usually corpus misprints.

(6) *Los presos en huelga de hambre escucharon las* ***promesas***
[*por parte de las autoridades marroquíes* $_{\text{SPEAKER}}$]
[*de estudiar sus reivindicaciones* $_{\text{MESSAGE}}$]. (DNI ADDRESSEE)

'The prisoners on hunger strike listened to the promises by the Moroccan authorities to study their claims.

The FEs of *promesa* can also be realized in constructions where the support verb is a passive past participle, as *hechas* ('made') or *realizadas* ('made, declared') in (7) and (8). In these examples, the support verbs are postponed modifiers of *promesa*.

(7) *Los huelguistas exigieron el cumplimiento de las* ***promesas***
[*hechas* $_{\text{SUPP}}$] [*por la institución* $_{\text{SPEAKER}}$]. (DNI ADRESSEE, MESSAGE)

'The protesters claimed the fulfillment of the promises made by the institution.'

(8) *No mencionó las* ***promesas*** [*realizadas* $_{\text{SUPPORT}}$] [*a las organizaciones humanitarias* $_{\text{ADDRESSEE}}$]. (DNI SPEAKER, MESSAGE)

'He didn't mention the promises made/declared to the humanitarian organizations.'

Our discussion has shown that the valence patterns of a target word are determined by the syntactic realizations of the FEs of the frame which it evokes. For this reason, the main aim of SFN is to characterize the meaning of LUs by directly appealing to the frames and to characterize their meanings by determining how FEs belonging to a frame are realized in specific syntactic constructions associated with actual LUs. Our discussion in section 4 of how SFN conducts semantic annotation will illustrate how the study of meaning begins with the analysis of the mapping of FEs onto a set of specific syntactic constructions. Before we get to this point, we offer a brief overview of the computational infrastructure of SFN in the following section.

3. The SFN corpus and its search tools

Similar to the workflow of the Berkeley FrameNet project (see Fillmore et al. 2003), SFN starts with a corpus analysis of the syntactic constructions that bear the argument structures of the target words. This approach offers a more objective and accurate account than one provided by mere linguistic intuition and allows us to document precisely the constructions in which a target word occurs.

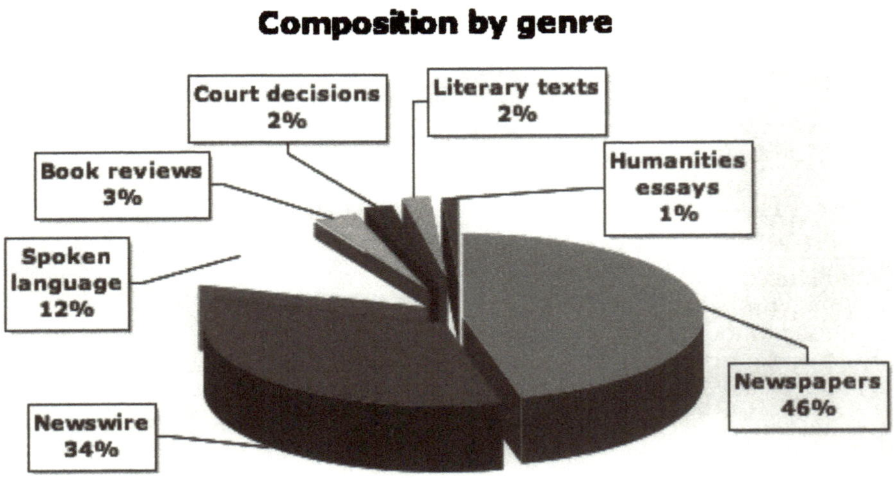

Figure 1. Different textual genres and percentages in the overall corpus of Spanish FrameNet

The SFN Corpus is a 370 million-word electronic corpus, containing 18 million sentences.[13] It includes both New World (60%) and European (40%) Spanish texts, covering seven different genres (see also Fig. 1): (1) newspapers from Spain (*Diario ABC*, *El Mundo*) and Latin America (*El Norte*, *El Tribuno*); (2) news from Latin American and Spanish news agencies (*Spanish Newswire Text*, Vol. 2, Linguistic Data Consortium); (3) cultural press (*ABC Cultural*); (4) humanities essays (philosophy, anthropology, literature, etc.); (5) legal texts (Spanish Constitutional Court verdicts); (6) literary texts (novels, short stories, poetry); and (7) transcriptions from spoken language (European and Spanish Parliament sessions).

The SFN Corpus is a file with XML markup which specifies (1) where the text comes from (for example, *Diario ABC*, etc.); (2) the file name where the text is found; (3) the genre to which the text belongs (e.g. *literary*, *essay*, *journalistic*, etc.); (4) the title of the text, as it has been referenced in the list of the SFN Corpus texts; and (5) the paragraph number

13. Controller verbs share one FE with their argument predicate noun, such as *superar* ('overcome') in *Drácula nunca pudo superar su* ***aversión*** *a los espejos* ('Dracula could never overcome his aversion to mirrors') (see section 4).

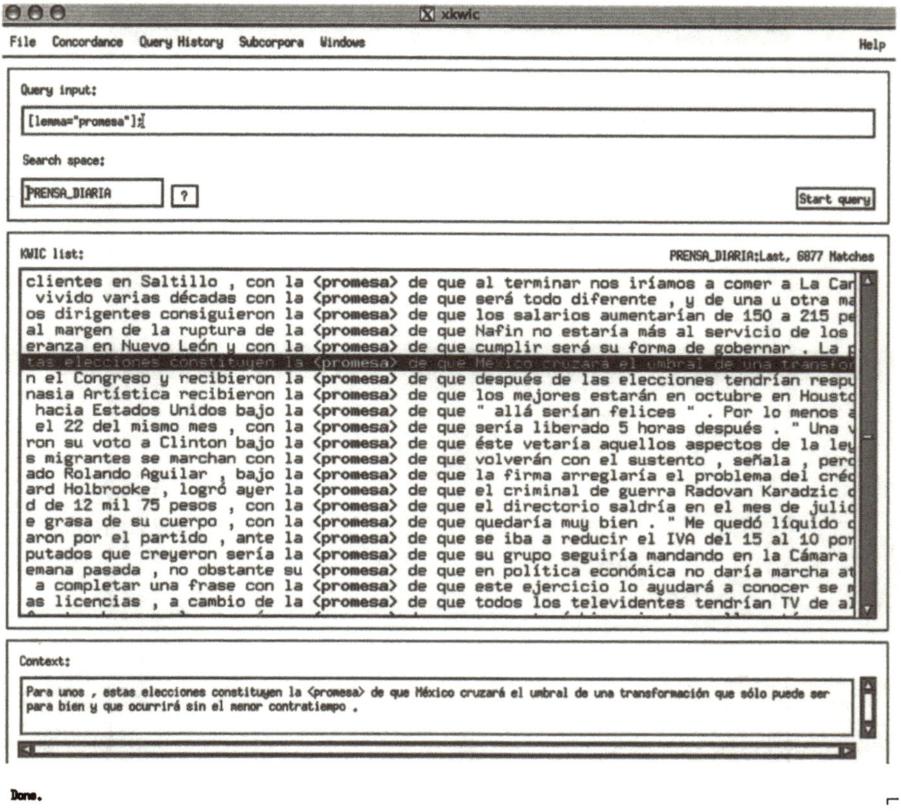

Figure 2. XKWIC display of all SFN Corpus sentences containing *promesa* ('promise'). In the central window, the different examples are browsed in the lower box, complete sentences are displayed after being selected in the central window

within the SFN Corpus. This information allows for eventual retrieval of contextual information, where the annotated sentences can be found.

Parallel to the workflow of the Berkeley FrameNet project, the SFN project queries its corpus with the Corpus Query Processor (CQP) and the graphic interface XKWIC (Key Word in Context Xwindows), both developed by the *Institut für Maschinelle Sprachverarbeitung* of the University of Stuttgart, Germany (see Christ 1994). One basic application of XKWIC is making quick queries in order to display all the sentences where a specific lemma occurs. Fig. 2, for instance, shows the search hits for sentences containing the lemma *promesa* ('promise').

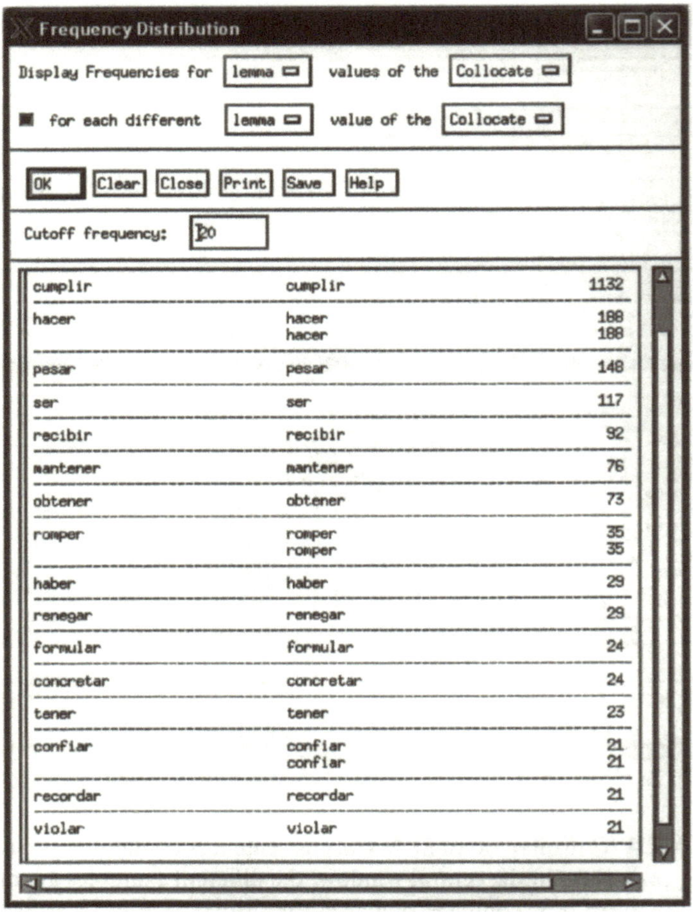

Figure 3. XKWIC snapshot showing the number of occurrences of the most frequent verbal lemmas occurring to the left of *promesa* 'promise'

In like manner, XKWIC allows carrying out further operations on the selected subcorpora. For the purpose of our research, it is worth mentioning the following applications:

(1) arranging the search results in alphabetical order;
(2) reducing the number of lines in the list, by assigning a maximum number or percentage to the results;
(3) automatically identifying the most frequent collocations, found both to the left and right of the searched word.

In Figure 3 we see the most frequently occurring verbs to the left of the target noun *promesa*. These include *cumplir* ('fulfill'), *hacer* ('make, do'), *ser* ('be'), etc. This information is particularly valuable for determining the most common support verbs, such as *hacer* ('make'), *ser* ('be'), *tener* ('have'), *recibir* ('receive'), and *obtener* ('obtain'), found with the target. Such collocation figures also allow us to determine the most frequent controller verbs[14], such as *cumplir* ('fulfill'), *romper* ('break'), or *formular* ('formulate'), etc., which are controllers of *promesa* (see Fig. 3). Once the syntactic contexts of a target are identified, SFN proceeds to the next stages in the workflow, namely automatic sense extraction and semantic annotation (see the following section). While specific pieces of software differ from those resources used by the Berkeley FrameNet, the overall workflow follows that of FrameNet, thereby demonstrating the cross-lingual applicability of its approach to lexical description.

4. Automatic sentence extraction and semantic annotation

At this stage, SFN uses GramCreator to create regular expressions that define the main formal aspects of the grammatical constructions that have to be automatically extracted from the corpus (see Figure 4 below). GramCreator allows us to use readily available templates and to choose those which allow automatic recognition and extraction of the selected syntactic constructions in which we are interested. For example, Figure 4 shows how GramCreator is used to automatically extract a subcorpus of sentences in which *promesa* ('promise') is followed by the preposition *de* ('of'), optionally followed by a noun phrase or the conjunction *que* ('that'). If GramCreator does not supply the appropriate regular expression for the recognition of a given syntactic construction, the regular expression can be edited manually. GramCreator then automatically veri-

14. ALIA is a piece of software developed by Marc Ortega at the Autonomous University of Barcelona that includes an automata intersection algorithm. The regular expressions created by GramCreator are converted into subsequential transducers. Actually, the regular expressions are representations of the language accepted by the transducer. Sentence extraction is performed by intersecting the transducers generated by GramCreator with the corpus sentences which have been previously POS tagged and lemmatized, then they were converted into linear automata, where ambiguities are bound to transitions between two states.

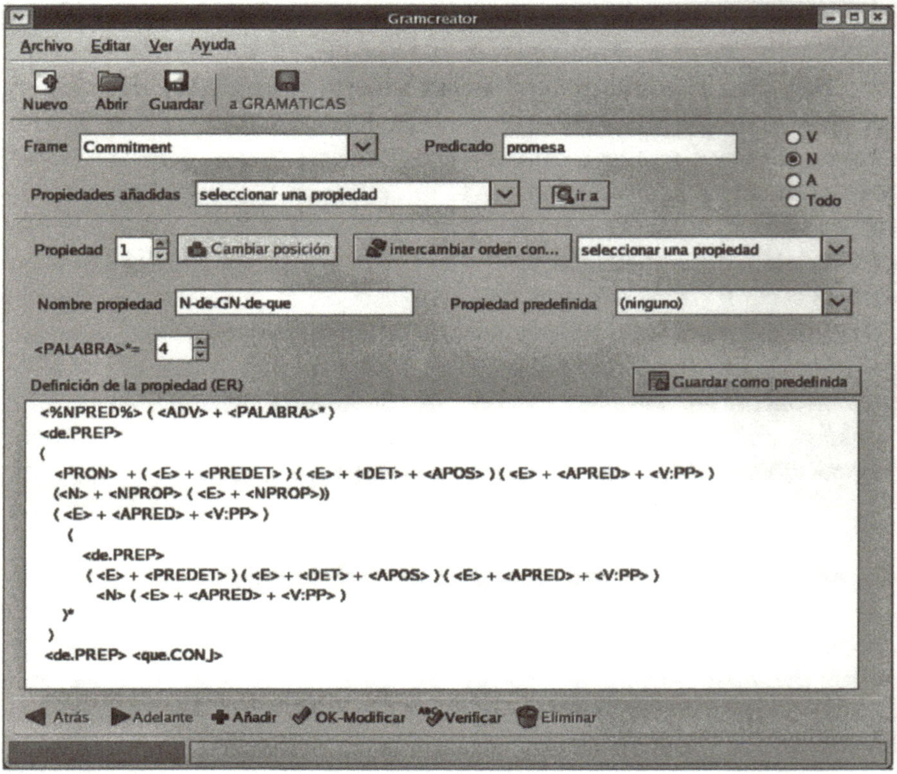

Figure 4. Semi-automatic creation of regular expressions with GramCreator

fies the syntax of the new regular expression and records it in the same application in a form optimized for later re-use.

The regular expressions created by GramCreator allow another program called ALIA[15] (Ortega 2002) to automatically extract all those syntactic constructions from the corpus that have the formal properties specified in the regular expressions. From each of the automatically extracted

15. The original FNDesktop had to undergo minor changes in order to get adapted to the annotation of Spanish sentences. One of the basic changes was introduced in the Classifier, which is a module of the original FNDesktop which is designed to automatically add the grammatical function and the phrase type once annotators have selected and annotated a constituent. The Classifier module which is used by the FNDesktop adapted to Spanish is completely different since both the tags it uses and the grammatical rules that are built in are specific for Spanish.

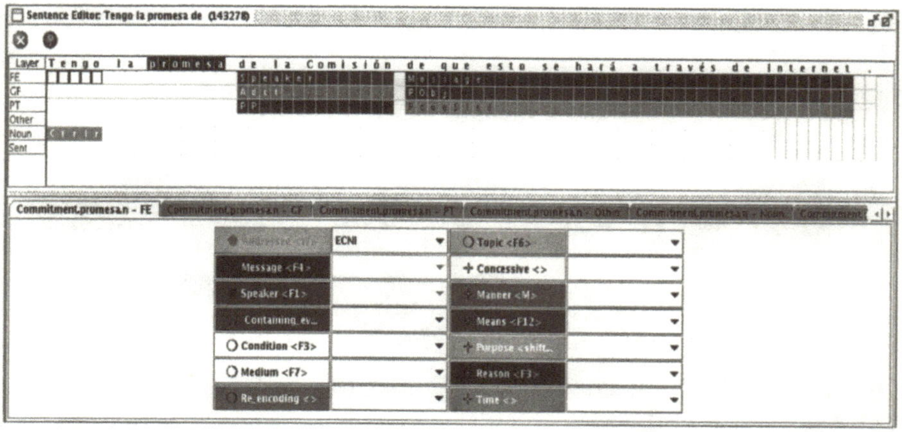

Figure 5. Annotation of the sentence *Tengo la promesa de la Comisión de que esto se hará a través de Internet* ('I have the promise from the commission that this will be done through the Internet') with the FNDesktop software adapted to Spanish

subcorpora, 30 sentences are randomly selected for annotation. Once the extraction has been performed, a subcorpus containing the syntactic constructions related to a specific target is created. Then, these subcorpora are tagged, lemmatized, and imported into the SFN database for further semantic and syntactic annotation.

The sentence annotation of the imported corpus sentences is performed by using FNDesktop, a tool created by the English FrameNet project (see Fillmore et al. 2003), which has been adapted to Spanish.[16] As Figure 5 shows, the constituents which are to be tagged are selected in the upper window. In the lower window, the list of FEs associated with the frame to which the target belongs is displayed. Once we select the constituent, we pick up the appropriate FE in the lower navigation window. For example, once the constituent *de que esto se hará a través de Internet* ('that this will be done through the internet') has been selected, we right-click the FE MESSAGE, and the selected constituent is tagged in the color assigned to this FE. Given that the annotation process is semi-automatic, the grammatical function and phrase type tags are usually automatically supplied and need not to be manually assigned. As Figure 5 illustrates,

16. See http://nlp.cs.nyu.edu/meyers/NomBank.html

01	Addressee + hacer + **promesa.N** + Message + (Speaker)
01	Addressee + recibir + **promesa.N** + Speaker + Message
01	Addressee + recibir + **promesa.N** + Topic + Condition + (Speaker)
01	Message + ser + **promesa.N** + Speaker + Time + Medium + (Addressee)
01	Speaker + formular + Time + **promesa.N** + Topic + Re encoding + (Addressee)
01	Speaker + hacer + **promesa.N** + Time + (Addressee) + (Message)
04	Speaker + **promesa.N** + Message + (Addressee)
01	Time + obtener + **promesa.N** + Speaker + Message + (Addressee)
01	cumplimiento + Speaker + **promesa.N** + Purpose + (Addressee) + (Message)
01	cumplimiento + **promesa.N** + Speaker + Message + (Addressee)
01	Cumplir + Speaker + **promesa.N** + Message + Concessive + (Addressee)
01	Formular + **promesa.N** + Purpose + (Addressee) + (Message) + (Speaker)
01	Hacer + **promesa.N** + (Speaker) + (Addressee) + (Message)
01	incumplimiento + Speaker + **promesa.N** + (Message) + (Addressee)
01	mantener + Speaker + **promesa.N** + Message + (Addressee)
01	mantenerse + **promesa.N** + Message + (Speaker) + (Addressee)
01	Obtener + **promesa.N** + Speaker + Message + (Addressee)
01	**Promesa.N** + Message + (Speaker) + (Addressee)
05	**Promesa.N** + Speaker + Message + (Addressee)
01	**Promesa.N** + realizar + Addressee + (Speaker) + (Message)
01	Romper + Speaker + **promesa.N** + Message + (Addressee)
02	tener + **promesa.N** + Speaker + Message + (Addressee)
01	Violar + **promesa.N** + Speaker + Message + (Addressee)
01	violar + Speaker + **promesa.N** + Message + (Addressee)

Figure 6. FrameSQL's automatic organization of the annotation data related to the eventive noun *promesa* ('promise'). Null instantiated core FEs are in parenthesis; support verbs are underlined, and controller verbs and nouns are shaded

the grammatical function of the constituent is automatically labeled as prepositional object (abbreviated *PObj*) and the phrase type is automatically marked as a clausal prepositional object with the main verb in the indicative (abbreviated *PqueSind*). Other FEs in this sentence are annotated with the same format, resulting for each constituent in a triplet of information about the name of the FE, its grammatical function (GF), and its phrase type (PT).

The annotated sentences can be visualized with several applications which can automatically handle the annotation data. For example, in Figure 6 the FrameSQL software adopted from the Berkeley FrameNet project and adapted to Spanish (Sato 2007) automatically organizes all the sentences containing the target *promesa* ('promise'), semantically annotated with FNDesktop. In Figure 6 we see (1) the order in which the FEs occur, (2) the support verbs (underlined) and controller verbs (shaded), and (3) the position of *promesa* in each of the annotated sentences. Null instantiations of core FEs are also displayed in parentheses. With this overview of the workflow underlying SFN, we now turn to a discussion of a number of important linguistic issues that have come up during the annotation process. We show that the choice of a particular linguistic analysis has direct consequences for how this linguistic information is stored in the SFN database.

5. Annotation of nouns: support verbs and controllers

Nominal predications are such an important part of the lexicon that there are whole research projects such as Nombank that are completely devoted to their study.[17] SFN is also allocating a significant effort to the study of nominal predicates, since its study is crucial not only for a frame semantic study of the Spanish lexicon, but also to use the SFN database for Spanish NLP applications such as automatic semantic role labeling. This is further evidenced by the fact that nominal and other non-verbal predications are as central as verbal predications in our Spanish corpus.[18] More spe-

17. See Castellón et al. (2006), and García-Miguel and Albertuz (2005) describing two semantic corpus annotation projects for Spanish where only verbs are annotated.
18. See the definition of the `Experiencer_subject` frame on the English FrameNet website at: http://framenet.icsi.berkeley.edu/index.php?option=com_wrapper&Itemid=118&frame=Experiencer_subj&

cifically, SFN is particularly interested in the annotation of eventive and stative nouns, because they constitute an important part of the frame evoking elements of the Spanish lexicon.

The annotation of nominal targets is problematic since some FE fillers occur locally inside the noun phrase headed by the target. Others, in contrast, may occur as external arguments of support or controller verbs. During the annotation of stative or eventive nouns (as well as adjectives) we encountered similar issues in relation with support verbs and controllers. For example, support verbs such as *tener* ('have') in (9) which occur with predicate nouns, are not independent frame evoking LUs. Their main function is to allow the valence of the associated predicate noun target to be expressed in a verb-headed clause whose subject must be understood as a participant in the event denoted by the supported noun (see Ruppenhofer et al. (2006), and Subirats (2001: 89–91)). In (9), the support verb *tener* allows the stative noun *aversión* ('aversion'), which evokes the `Experiencer_subject` frame, to project its FEs EXPERIENCER and TOPIC onto a clausal construction. The resulting construction is in part determined by the support verb *tener*, since *aversión* is a direct object of *tener*, and *Drácula*, the EXPERIENCER of *aversión*, is the subject of *tener* (it therefore agrees with it both in number and person). But the construction in (9) is also determined by *aversión*, since *espejos* ('mirrors'), the TOPIC of *aversión*, is not selected by *tener* but by *aversión*, and it is actually its prepositional object.

(9) [*Drácula* $_{\text{EXPERIENCER}}$] *tiene* ***aversión*** [*a los espejos* $_{\text{TOPIC}}$].
Dracula has aversion to the mirrors
'Dracula has an aversion to mirrors.'

Since support verbs are not independent frame evoking LUs, they usually do not introduce any significant semantics of their own. As a result, constructions such as in (9) that involve eventive or stative nouns with support verbs denote a similar state of affairs to a noun phrase headed by *aversión*, followed by the syntactic realization of its FEs inside the noun phrase. This is illustrated by the following example.

(10) *la* ***aversión*** [*de Drácula* $_{\text{EXPERIENCER}}$] [*a los espejos* $_{\text{TOPIC}}$]
the aversion of Dracula to the mirrors
'Dracula's aversion to mirrors.'

Controller verbs (or nouns) are different from support verbs in that they evoke a separate frame from that evoked by their governed noun, while still sharing an FE with the event denoted by the noun (see Ruppenhofer et al. 2006: 45–46). The constituent (or filler) representing the shared participant is typically the subject of the controller. For instance, consider (11), which contains an external argument as well the argument of the controller verb *superar* ('overcome'), namely, *Drácula*. In this case the controller is shared by the stative noun *aversion*, since *Drácula* (the PROTAGONIST FE of *superar*) also expresses the EXPERIENCER FE of *aversión*.

(11) [*Drácula* $_{\text{EXPERIENCER}}$] *no* [*superó* $_{\text{CONTROLLER}}$] *la* ***aversión***
Drácula not overcome the aversion

[*a los espejos* $_{\text{TOPIC}}$].
to the mirrors

'Dracula didn't overcome the aversion to mirrors.'

Verbs can control nouns as in (11), but the reverse is also true: nouns can also control verbs, and they can both share the same FE. In (12), for instance, the stative noun *seguridad* ('security') governs the verb *actuar* ('behave'). In addition, both the noun and the verb share an FE, since the COGNIZER of *seguridad* and the AGENT of the target *actuar* ('act') are expressed by the same constituent, which is an external constructional null instantiation (ECNI) of *tener* ('have').

(12) *Tengo la seguridad de* ***haber actuado*** *con rectitud*
have the security of have behaved with rectitude

en este caso. (ECNI AGENT)
in this case

'I am certain that I have behaved with rectitude in this case.'

However, there is an important difference between *seguridad* in (12) and *superar* in (11): In (12), it is the noun *seguridad* that selects the verb *actuar*. In contrast, in (11) it is *aversión* that selects the controller *superar*. It is precisely because predicate nouns select the controllers which govern them that it is lexicographically relevant to study the controllers that can co-occur with nouns. This is because their study can account for significant semantic properties of both controllers and nouns.

Controller verbs may, in turn, be governed by other verbs, and these verbs may also share an FE with both the controller and the target noun. In (13), for example, *gustar* ('to like') is a governor of the controller verb *superar* ('overcome') which shares an FE with the noun *aversión*, and the shared FE of *gustar*, *superar*, and *aversión* is *Drácula*, which in turn is the indirect object of *gustar*. In these cases, *Drácula* expresses the FE EXPERIENCER and external argument of *aversión*, and *superar* as a controller verb of *aversión*.

(13) *A* [*Drácula* $_{\text{EXPERIENCER}}$] *le* *gustaría* [*superar* $_{\text{CONTOLLER}}$]
to Dracula him would-like overcome
la ***aversión*** *a* *los espejos.*
the aversion to the mirrors
'Dracula would like to overcome his aversion to mirrors.'

Controller verbs are also annotated whenever the shared constituent of the controller and its governed noun is not realized with the same constituent. Consider (14), where *Drácula* is the PROTAGONIST FE and the external argument of the controller verb *superar*. Here, *su* (the EXPERIENCER of *aversion*) refers to *Drácula*, which is the FE shared by both *superar* and *aversión*. Note, however, that *superar* and *aversión* in (14) do not share the same constituent expressing the shared FE, since *Drácula* and *su* (although they are coreferent) are two different constituents. In this case, both *Drácula* and *su* are annotated as the EXPERIENCER of *aversión*.

(14) [*Drácula* $_{\text{EXPERIENCER}}$] *nunca superó* [*su* $_{\text{EXPERIENCER}}$]
Drácula never overcame his
aversión *a* *los espejos.*
aversion to the mirrors
'Dracula never overcame his aversion to mirrors.'

Another interesting case is when a controller verb appears in a sentence where its external argument, which is shared by its governed noun, cannot be overtly realized because it is not licensed by the corresponding grammatical construction. In this case, the external argument is referred to as a constructional null instantiation (CNI). For example, in (15) the *se*-passive construction does not license an overt reference to the external argument of the controller verb *formular* ('formulate'), which is the FE

SPEAKER shared by both *formular* and *promesa*. Thus, the SPEAKER is annotated as a constructional null instantiation.

(15) *Durante las elecciones, se* [*formularon* CONTOLLER]
during the elections, 3rd person clitic formulate

promesas, *aunque se sabía que no se*
promises, though 3rd person know that not 3rd person clitic

podían cumplir. (CNI SPEAKER, DNI MESSAGE)
could fulfill

'During the elections, promises were made, though it was known that they could not be fulfilled.'

Next, consider eventive nouns occurring with support verbs or governed by controllers. These may co-occur with modifiers or relative clauses that also include other support verbs or controllers. For example, in (16) the plural eventive noun *promesas* ('promises') is governed by the controller verb *cumplir* ('fulfill') while it is also followed by a relative clause containing the support verb *hacer* ('make'). Such cases are classified as involving two different events, namely *cumplir una promesa* ('fulfill a promise') and *hacer una promesa* ('make a promise'). This difference has direct consequences for our semantic annotation as we need to represent these different relationships. In other words, the fact that there are two different events requires different types of annotations.

(16) *No* [*cumplió* CONTOLLER] *las* ***promesas*** *que* [*había hecho* SUPPORT] *durante la campaña.*

'He didn't fulfil the promises that he had made during the campaign.'

Similarly, in (17) *promesa* is governed by the controller verb *violar* ('violate') and is modified by *formulada* ('formulated, made'), which is a past participle of another controller verb. As in (16), there are two different events encoded, namely *violar una promesa* ('violate a promise') and, *formular una promesa* ('formulate, make a promise'). Examples like these illustrate how the same sentence can be annotated in different ways. This state of affairs needs to be captured appropriately by our semantic annotation. This means that if we are annotating a single target in sentences like (16) or (17), we can choose the event we want to annotate. However, once we conduct full text annotation, we have to annotate both events, even though only one occurrence of the target occurs in the sentence.

(17) *Ucrania* [*violó* CONTROLLER] *la* ***promesa*** [*formulada* CONTROLLER] *cuando se unió al organismo europeo de defensa de los derechos humanos.*

'Ukraine violated the promise made when it joined the European organization for the defense of human rights.'

Finally, note that eventive nouns may control other eventive nouns as in (18) and (19). In (18), the controller noun *cumplimiento* ('fulfillment') shares an FE with the eventive noun *promesa*: *por parte de Estados Unidos* ('on the part of the United States'), which is the AGENT of *cumpimiento* and the SPEAKER of *promesa.* In (19), the controller noun *incumplimiento* ('non-fulfillment') shares an FE with the eventive noun *promesa: por parte de la dirección* ('on the part of the directorship'), which is the AGENT of *incumplimiento*, and *la dirección*, which is the SPEAKER of *promesa.*

(18) *El* [*cumplimiento* CONTOLLER] [*por parte de Estados Unidos* SPEAKER] *de la* ***promesa*** *de reducir las emisiones de* CO_2 *fue aplaudida internacionalmente.*

'The fulfillment, on the part of the United States, of the promise to reduce CO_2 emissions was internationally applauded.'

(19) *El* [*incumplimiento* CONTROLLER] [*por parte de la dirección* SPEAKER] *de las* ***promesas*** *formuladas a los trabajadores ha tenido un impacto negativo en las negociaciones.*

'The non-fulfillment on the part of the directorship of the promises made to the workers has had a negative impact on negotiations.'

In this section we outlined the role of support verbs as well as controller verbs and nouns in relation to the annotation of nominal predicators. Support verbs have shown how nominals can map their syntactic valencies onto sentential constructions. Controllers, in turn, have shown how noun targets can share FEs with other LUs which are selected by the targets. We now turn to another important issue for SFN, namely the annotation of metaphors.

6. Metaphor annotation

The annotation of metaphors is often difficult, because they cannot typically be interpreted literally. A metaphor involves understanding one conceptual domain, i.e. a coherent organization of experience, in terms of another conceptual domain (Lakoff and Johnson 1980). The conceptual domain from which we draw metaphorical expressions is the source domain; the conceptual domain that is understood this way is called the target domain. The target domain is more abstract than the source domain which usually has an experiential basis, for instance, understanding life (the abstract target concept) in terms of a container (a more concrete source concept) as in *Su vida está vacía* ('His/her life is hollow'), *Las drogas no llenan el vacío de la vida* ('Drugs don't fill the emptiness of life'), etc. In frame semantic terms, we can explain a metaphor as a mapping between two different frames, a source frame and a target frame.

Although the study of metaphors is not central to SFN, the study of metaphors is important because they structure our conceptual system (Lakoff and Johnson 1980). In fact, during the annotation of motion predicators in SFN, many metaphorical uses of motion verbs and nouns have been found that can only be accurately described as mapping their concrete physical meaning onto more abstract domains. SFN is also interested in the annotation of sentences whose targets are used metaphorically, since they show one of the ways the conceptual system is structured in Spanish. Thus, following the original Berkeley FrameNet project, SFN annotates metaphorical sentences by adding a specific sentence-level tag that indicates that the target of the corresponding sentence is used metaphorically, as Figure 7 illustrates.

Figure 7 shows the results of the annotation and tagging of a sentence with a metaphor tag. With this tag in place, it is possible to use FrameSQL to automatically query sentences tagged as metaphors via the web, whether at the LU level, the frame level or even in relation with the whole SFN database.The annotation of sentences in the motion-related frame `Collapse`[19] has produced a number of sentences with metaphorical interpretations. As (22) and (23) show, the physical motion denoted by a target such as *desplome* ('fall'), is meant to be conceptualized metaphorically in more abstract terms.

19. The SFN definition of the frame `Collapse` – which does not exist in FrameNet – is the following: "A THEME which is an entity collapses and falls by gravity or other natural, physical forces to a GOAL. The source of the motion event is deprofiled in this frame: *El techo del teatro se desplomó sobre el patio de butacas* ('The ceiling of the theater fell on the stalls.')".

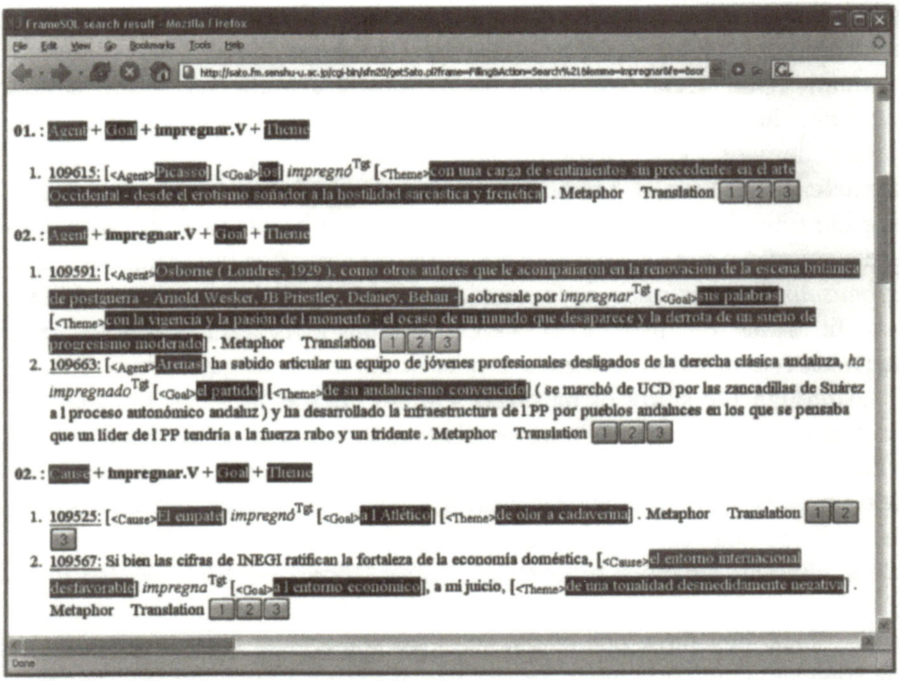

Figure 7. Automatic extraction, using FrameSQL, of metaphoric uses associated with *impregnar* ('impregnate') from the frame `Filling`[19]

(22) *El **desplome** [electoral* $_{\text{DOMAIN}}$*] de ese hombre inteligente y temerario significa, parafraseando a Gabriel Zaid, el haber sido incapaz de demostrar que se puede ser un político católico y moderno.*

'The drop in the electoral turnout for that smart and reckless man means, quoting Gabriel Zaid, having been unable to prove that it is possible to be a catholic and a modern politician.'

(23) *El **desplome** [bursátil* $_{\text{DOMAIN}}$*] de la semana pasada se inició en Hong Kong, un país que mantiene una paridad fija, en tanto que Argentina ha sufrido un mayor impacto de la turbulencia financiera que México.*

'Last week's stock market drop began in Hong Kong, a country which maintains a pegged exchange rate, while Argentina has suffered greater financial turbulence than Mexico.'

A frame semantic analysis of the metaphorical uses of *desplome* in (22) and (23) would allow us to give a precise description of both metaphors as a mapping between two different frames. As such, the metaphors in (22) and (23) could be explained as a mapping from the `Collapse` frame onto the `Progress` frame, which evokes scenarios where an entity changes from a pre-state to a post-state leading to improvement or deterioration.[20] A more detailed analysis of the metaphorical use of *desplome* in (22) and (23) above should also indicate the underlying conceptual metaphor which enables the understanding of the target frame in terms of the source frame. Thus, we would have to explain that in (22) and (23) a change, like *el desplome electoral* ('the drop in the electoral turnout') or *el desplome bursátil* ('the stock market drop'), is conceived of in terms of motion – since *desplome* in Spanish implies motion – and one entailment of this conceptual metaphor is that the lack of control over a change implies a lack of control over motion (Lakoff and Johnson 1980 and 1999). So far, we are not including this additional information in Spanish FrameNet. But in cases like (22) and (23), where the target has a modifier like *electoral* ('electoral') or *bursátil* ('stock market') indicating the type or subtype of the mapping in the target domain (in this case a subframe in the politics and economy domains), SFN annotates these modifiers with the DOMAIN FE. The metaphorical sentences annotated by SFN will be an important source of information for later research to understand how conceptual metaphors function in Spanish and how they differ from other languages.

7. Conclusion and outlook

Since 2003, the Spanish FrameNet project has performed an analysis of about 600 LUs, spread over 100 semantic frames from the domains of cognition, communication, emotion, and motion. Differences in lexicalization patterns in Spanish and English have been reported for emotion predicates (Subirats and Petruck 2003); constructional differences in English and Spanish motion verbs (Subirats and Sato 2004) have also been documented and analyzed, offering additional evidence of expressional dif-

20. See the definition of the `Progress` frame on the English FrameNet website at: http://framenet.icsi.berkeley.edu/index.php?option=com_wrapper&Itemid=118&frame=Progress&.

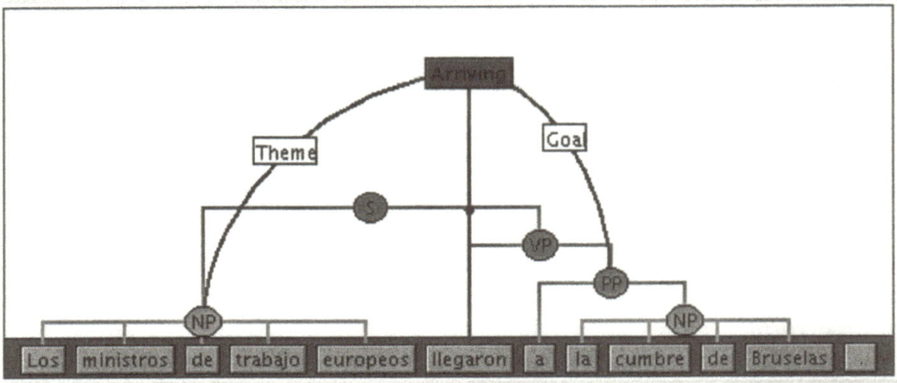

Figure 8. Automatic semantic role labeling of the sentence *Los ministros de trabajo europeos llegaron a la cumbre de Bruselas* ('The European labor secretaries arrived at the Brussels summit') with Shalmaneser (Erk and Padó 2006) trained on SFN data

ferences in motion events between Germanic and Romance languages (Slobin 1996). Besides being a monolingual and multilingual semantic dictionary, SFN is also used as a training corpus for automatic semantic role labeling applications (see Figure 8). In the future, SFN will also allow the development of new applications for automatic semantic analysis of texts in Spanish. Following Scheffczyk et al. (2006), we will link SFN to various ontologies, which will mean a step forward in the development of computer-based reasoning in NLP, especially, for applications aimed at the semantic web in Spanish.

This paper has shown that the workflow of SFN is similar to that of the Berkeley FrameNet project. As such, it has demonstrated that the Berkeley workflow can in principle be applied to other languages. Nevertheless, there are some language-specific differences in the computational infrastructure and the workflow of SFN. For example, the corpus processing tools described in sections 3 and 4 (POS taggers and lemmatizers), as well as the parsers that have been used to extract specific constructions from the corpus to be imported into the FNDesktop, are specific to Spanish.

The Berkeley FrameNet Project started in 1997 with English. Other proposals have followed thereafter aimed at the creation of FrameNets for other languages, in favor of applying the same theory, the same methodology and, sometimes, even the same annotation software. In this way, the initial project for English has evolved into a global, cooperative endeavor to cover other languages such as German, Japanese, and Spanish. Two research groups with different foci are currently investigating FrameNet-designs for German: (1) *SALSA II. The Saarbrücken Lexical Semantics Acquisition Project* (Burchardt et al. 2006), being developed at the Saarland University, under the direction of Prof. Manfred Pinkal (http://www.coli.uni-saarland.de/projects/salsa/), and (2) *German FrameNet* at the University of Texas at Austin (Boas 2002), under the direction of Prof. Hans C. Boas (http://gframenet.gmc.utexas.edu/). The *Japanese FrameNet* project: *An online Japanese lexicon based on Frame Semantics* (Ohara et al. 2004), under the direction of Prof. Kyoko Ohara, is building a FrameNet-based lexicon for Japanese at the University of Keio in Japan (http://jfn.st.hc.keio.ac.jp/). The fact that these projects pursue analogous theoretical models and methodologies, and compatible software (see Boas 2002, 2005), will enable future contrastive semantic studies (Ellsworth et al. 2006) and further development of tools aimed at multilingual queries of annotated data. For example, FrameSQL, a web-based tool developed at the University of Senshu (Japan) by Prof. Hiroaki Sato, allows users to search and view existing FN annotations in a variety of ways. This application allows the comparison of annotated data in English and Spanish, on the one hand, and in English and German, on the other, forming the embryo of a future online multilingual semantic dictionary.

References

Baker, Collin F., Charles J. Fillmore and Beau Cronin
2003 The structure of the FrameNet database. *International Journal of Lexicography* 16.3: 281–296.

Boas, Hans C.
2002 Bilingual FrameNet Dictionaries for Machine Translation. In: Manuel González Rodríguez and C. Paz Suárez Araujo (eds.), *Proceedings of the Third International Conference on Language Resources and Evaluation*, Vol. IV: 1364–1371. Las Palmas, Spain.

Boas, Hans C.
2005 From theory to practice: Frame Semantics and the design of FrameNet. In: Stefan Langer and Daniel Schnorbusch (eds.), *Semantisches Wissen im Lexikon*, 129–160. Tübingen: Narr.

Boas, Hans C.
2006 A frame-semantic approach to identifying syntactically relevant elements of meaning. In: Petra Steiner, Hans C. Boas, and Stefan Schierholz (eds.), *Contrastive Studies and Valency. Studies*

in Honor of Hans Ulrich Boas, 119–149. Frankfurt/New York: Peter Lang.

Burchardt, Aljoscha, Katrin Erk, Annette Frank, Andrea Kowalski, Sebastian Padó and Manfred Pinkal
2006 The SALSA Corpus: a German corpus resource for lexical semantics. In: *Proceedings of LREC 2006*, Genoa: http://www.coli.uni-saarland.de/%7Epado/pub/papers/lrec06_burchardt1.pdf

Castellón, Irene, Ana Fernández, Gloria Vázquez, Laura Alonso, and Joan A. Capilla
2006 The Sensem Corpus: a corpus annotated at the syntactic and semantic level. In: *Proceedings of LREC 2006*: http://grial.uab.es/archivos/LREC2006def.pdf

Christ, Oliver
1994 A modular and flexible architecture for an integrated corpus query system. *3rd Conference on Computational Lexicography and Text Research*. Budapest: http://www.ims.unistuttgart.de/projekte/CorpusWorkbench/Papers/christ:complex94.ps.gz.

Ellsworth, Michael, Kyoko Ohara, Carlos Subirats and Thomas Schmidt
2006 Frame-semantic analysis of motion scenarios in English, Japanese, and Spanish. In: Seiko Fujii, Takahiro Morita and Chie Sakuta (eds.), *ICCG-4. Proceedings of the Fourth International Conference on Construction Grammar*. The University of Tokyo, 75–76.

Enríquez, Emilia V.
1984 *El pronombre personal sujeto en la lengua española hablada en Madrid.* Madrid, Consejo Superior de Investigaciones Científicas.

Enríquez, Emilia and Marta Albelda
2006 El pronombre personal. In C. Hernández (ed.), *Estudio gramatical del español hablado en América*. Valladolid: Instituto Interuniversitario de Estudios de Iberoamérica y Portugal.

Erk, Katrin and Sebastian Padó
2006 Shalmaneser. A flexible toolbox for semantic role assignment. *Proceedings of LREC* 2006: http://www.coli.uni-saarland.de/~pado/pub/papers/lrec06_erk.pdf.

Fillmore, Charles J.
1976 Frame semantics and the nature of language. In: *Annals of the New York Academy of Sciences: Conference on the Origin and Development of Language and Speech*, Vol. 280: 20–32.

Fillmore, Charles J.
1977a. Scenes-and-frames semantics, Linguistic Structures Processing. In: Antonio Zampolli (ed.), *Fundamental Studies in Computer Science*, 55–88. Dordrecht: North Holland Publishing.

Fillmore, Charles J.
1977b The need for a frame semantics in linguistics. In: Hans Karlgren (ed.), *Statistical Methods in Linguistics* 12: 5–29.

Fillmore, Charles J.
1982 Frame Semantics. In: Linguistic Society of Korea (ed.), *Linguistics in the Morning Calm*, 111–137. Seoul, Hanshin Publishing Co.

Fillmore, Charles J.
1985 Frames and the semantics of understanding. In *Quadernie di Semantica* 6.2: 222–254.

Fillmore, Charles J., Christopher Johnson and Miriam R.L. Petruck
2003 Background to FrameNet, *International Journal of Lexicography* 16.3: 235–250.

García-Miguel, Juan M. and Francisco J. Albertuz, Francisco
2005 Verbs, semantic classes, and semantic roles in the ADESSE Project. In: Katrin Erk, Alissa Melinger and Sabine Schulte im Walde (eds.), *Proceedings of the Interdisciplinary Workshop on the Identification and Representation of Verb Features and Verb Classes*, Saarbrücken:
http://webs.uvigo.es/adesse/textos/saarb05.pdf

Lakoff, George and Mark Johnson
1980 *Metaphors We Live By*. Chicago: University of Chicago Press.

Lakoff, George and Mark Johnson
1999 *Philosophy in the Flesh. The embodied mind and its challenge to Western thought.* New York: Basic Books.

Ohara, Kyoko Hirose, Seiko Fujii, Toshio Ohori, Ryoko Suzuki, Hiroaki Saito, and Ishizaki Shun
2004 The Japanese FrameNet Project: An introduction. In: *Proceedings of the Satellite Workshop "Building Lexical Resources from Semantically Annotated Corpora"*, LREC 2004, 9–11.
http://jfn.st.hc.keio.ac.jp/publications/JFN30July2004.pdf

Ortega, Marc
2002 *Interseccion de autómamatas y transductores en el análisis sintáctico de un texto.* MA Thesis, Polytechnic University of Catalonia, Spain.

Petruck, Miriam R. L.
1996 Frame Semantics. In: J. Verschueren, J.-O. Östman, J. Blommaert y C. Bulcaen (eds.), *Handbook of Pragmatics*, 1–13. Amsterdam/Philadelphia: John Benjamins.

Ruppenhofer, Josef, Michael Ellsworth, Miriam R.L. Petruck and Christopher Johnson
2006 *FrameNet: Theory and Practice*:
http://framenet.icsi.berkeley.edu/book/book.pdf.

Sato, Hiroaki
2007 The search tool FrameSQL for cross-lingual FrameNets (in Japanese), *Universals and Variation in Language* vol. 2, 165–176, Senshu University.
http://sato.fm.senshu-u.ac.jp/_web/papers/200703.pdf.

Scheffczyk, Jan, Collin F. Baker and Srini Narayanan
2006 Ontology-based reasoning about lexical resources. *OntoLex 2006: Interfacing Ontologies and Lexical Resources for Semantic Web Technologies*: http://www.icsi.berkeley.edu/~snarayan/fn_reasoning.pdf

Slobin, Dan. I.
1996 Two ways to travel: Verbs of motion in English and Spanish. In: Masayoshi Shibatani and Sandra A. Thompson (eds.), *Grammatical Constructions: Their Form and Meaning,* 195–220. Oxford: Clarendon Press.

Subirats, Carlos
2001 *Introducción a la sintaxis léxica del español.* Madrid/Frankfurt: Iberoamericana/Vervuert.

Subirats, Carlos and Miriam R.L. Petruck
2003 Surprise: Spanish FrameNet! In: E. Hajicova, A. Kotesovcova y J. Mirovsky (eds.), *Proceedings of CIL 17*. Prague: Matfyzpress: http://www.icsi.berkeley.edu/%7Eframenet/papers/SFNsurprise.pdf.

Subirats, Carlos and Hiroaki Sato
2004 Spanish FrameNet and FrameSQL. In: *Proceedings of Building lexical Resources from Semantically Annotated Corpora*, European Language Resources Association (LREC), Lisbon, 13–16.

6. Frame-based contrastive lexical semantics in Japanese FrameNet: The case of *risk* and *kakeru*

Kyoko Hirose Ohara

1. Introduction

Following Fillmore and Atkins' (1992) pioneering study of the English `Risk` frame, this paper proposes a contrastive analysis of linguistic expressions in Japanese and English pertaining to the concept of RISK, encountered during the creation of Japanese FrameNet (hereafter JFN). It examines the advantages and limitations of a frame-based approach to contrastive lexicography, and considers polysemy structures across typologically unrelated languages (cf. Fillmore and Atkins 2000; Boas 2001, 2005; Subirats and Petruck 2003). In particular, the paper analyzes correspondences between English and Japanese expressions pertaining to the `Risk` frame by investigating translation equivalents of the English verb *risk* and by examining the polysemy structure of one of the corresponding Japanese lexical units (hereafter LUs).

The paper is based on data from the JFN project (Ohara et al. 2004), whose goal is to create a FrameNet-style lexicon of Japanese described in terms of Frame Semantics by annotating corpus examples with frame elements (hereafter FEs). The resulting JFN database will thus contain valence descriptions of Japanese LUs and a collection of annotated corpus attestations. JFN asks two important research questions. First, to what extent is the Frame Semantics approach suitable for analyzing the Japanese lexicon? Second, to what extent are the existing English-based semantic frames suitable for characterizing Japanese LUs?

Furthermore, JFN will eventually link its database to those of FrameNets for other languages, so that the integrated databases can be used as frame-based multilingual lexical databases (cf. Boas 2001, Fontenelle 2000, Subirats and Sato 2004).[1] Boas (2005) has already suggested frames

1. A joint project between FrameNet and JFN on "Frame-based Japanese-English bilingual lexicon", linking FrameNet and JFN data, started in April,

as interlingual representations for multilingual lexical databases. Under such a view, lexicon fragments are linked to each other via semantic frames, which function as interlingual representations. However, the hypothesis has not been examined systematically for typologically unrelated languages such as English and Japanese. The present work begins to fill this gap.

Investigating whether semantic frames may serve as an interlingua between English and Japanese, this paper discusses English-Japanese correspondences in both directions. First, it focuses on the English verb *risk* and examines its Japanese translation equivalents, exploring whether the Japanese expressions should indeed be defined as LUs in the same set of frames as *risk*. The paper then analyzes the Japanese verb *kakeru*, one of whose senses is comparable to that of English *risk*, and considers the semantic frames that the Japanese verb evokes.

The paper is structured as follows. Section 2 first summarizes previous analyses of semantic frames related to the concept of RISK and presents the senses of the English verb *risk*, the basis for the discussion of Japanese data in the rest of the paper (Section 2.1). It then analyzes Japanese translation equivalents of the verb *risk* (Section 2.2) and discusses the English-Japanese correspondences via frames (Section 2.3). Section 3 describes the semantic network of the Japanese verb *kakeru* and compares it with that of *risk*. Finally, Section 4 concludes the discussion.

2. The `Risk` frame: *risk*.v and its Japanese translation equivalents

The complexity of the `Risk` frame makes it particularly appropriate for studying polysemy structures of lexical items in English and Japanese: while the frame itself is static, it evokes a hypothetical scenario (Hasegawa and Ohara 2006: 356); and yet, since every culture needs to deal with the concept, every language will have a means of expressing it. While the `Risk` frame and the LUs that evoke it have been studied extensively for English (Fillmore and Atkins 1992, 1994, Fillmore et al. 2003, Pustejovsky 2000), the Japanese lexical material that pertains to the concept of RISK has not been examined at all until recently (Ohara 2006).

2007 and continued until March, 2009. The joint project was being supported by the Japan Society for Promotion of Science (JSPS) under the Japan-U.S. Cooperative Science Program.

First, as a summary of the previous work on RISK-related frames and of the senses of the English verb *risk*, I present the analyses by Hasegawa et al. (2006). They will be the basis for the discussion of the Japanese data and for the contrastive analysis of English and Japanese in the rest of the paper. They provide the most recent and updated treatment of the frames and of the verb by one of the co-authors of the seminal papers on the topic (Fillmore and Atkins 1992, 1994). Next, to determine whether semantic frames may function as interlingual representations for LUs in the two languages, the Japanese translation equivalents of English *risk*.v in each of the frames are discussed. Finally, it is shown that even if it is possible to posit the same semantic frames for the purpose of analyzing both Japanese and English, sometimes seemingly corresponding words and expressions in the two languages may overlap only partially in their distributions across the semantic frames.

2.1. The `Risk` frame

The schema, or the situation type, for the `Risk` frame, taken from Hasegawa et al. (2006: 2), is shown in Figure 1:

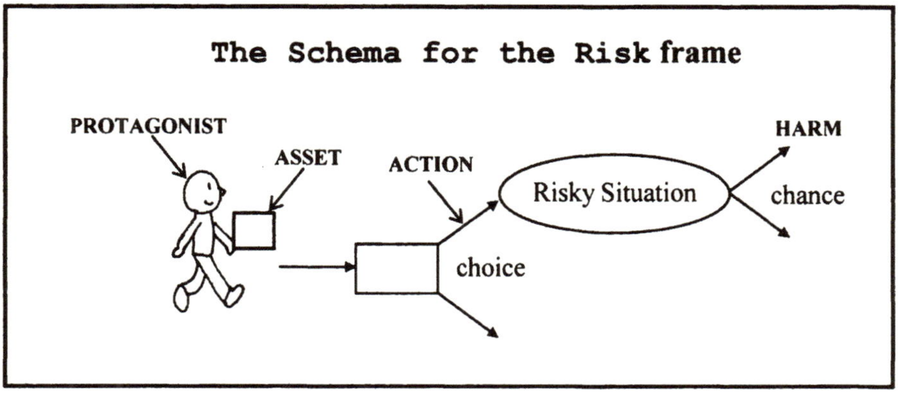

Figure 1. The schema for the `Risk` frame

Currently FrameNet classifies FEs into three levels: core, peripheral, and extra-thematic, based on their centrality to a particular frame (Ruppenhofer et al. 2006: 26). A core FE instantiates a conceptually necessary component of a frame, while making the frame unique and different from other frames (ibid.). The core FEs pertaining to the `Risk` frame are captured by the following definitions[2]

The core FEs of the `Risk` frame[3]

ACTION: the act of the PROTAGONIST that has the potential of incurring HARM (*a trip into the jungle, swimming in the dark*).

ASSET: a valued possession of the PROTAGONIST, seen as potentially endangered in some situation (*health, income*).

HARM: a potential unwelcome development coming to the PROTAGONIST (*infection, losing one's job*).

PROTAGONIST: the person who performs the ACTION that results in the possibility of HARM occurring.

Following Hasegawa et al. (2006: 5), I analyze the senses of *risk*.v as distinguishable by positing three frames, differing from one another in terms of which FEs are foregrounded (Fillmore et al. 2003). They are the `Jeopardizing`, `Incurring`, and `Daring` frames.[4] In the `Jeopardizing` frame, the PROTAGONIST and ASSET are foregrounded and encoded as core FEs,[5] as in (1), where the PROTAGONIST is realized as the subject and the ASSET as the direct object of the verb. In the `Incurring` frame,

2. According to Hasegawa et al. 2006, the peripheral FEs of the `Risk` frame include the following: CHANCE: the uncertainty about the future. RISKY SITUATION: the state of affairs within which the ASSET might be said to be at risk. These FEs are not realized linguistically in *risk*.v sentences.
3. In the previous analyses, the FEs are given slightly different names, but their definitions are essentially the same (Fillmore and Atkins 1992: 81–84; Fillmore and Atkins 1994: 16; Fillmore et al. 2003: 241): ACTION: formerly DEED (Fillmore and Atkins 1992), RISK_ACTION (Fillmore et al. 2003); ASSET: formerly VALUED OBJECT (Fillmore and Atkins 1992), POSSESSION (Fillmore and Atkins 1994); HARM: formerly BAD (Fillmore and Atkins 1994), BAD_OUTCOME (Fillmore et al. 2003); PROTAGONIST: formerly ACTOR (Fillmore and Atkins 1992).
4. The current FrameNet analysis of the senses of *risk*.v, however, places them in a family of frames with relation to other frames. The `Jeopardizing` and `Incurring` uses of *risk*.v are analyzed as different perspectives on a generalized scenario (see the `Risk_scenario` and `Risky_situation` frames). The `Daring` sense of *risk*.v is in a separate frame, `Daring`, which is a subtype of the `Intentionally_act` frame (Russell Lee-Goldman, personal communication). See also Pustejovsky (2000).
5. In determining which FEs are considered core, FrameNet also considers some formal properties that provide evidence for core status. For example, when a FE always must be overtly specified, it is core (Ruppenhofer et al. 2006: 26).

the PROTAGONIST and the HARM are foregrounded, as in (2), where the PROTAGONIST is the subject and the HARM is the direct object. In the `Daring` frame, as shown in (3), the PROTAGONIST and the ACTION are foregrounded as the subject and the direct object, respectively.

(1) `Jeopardizing` frame

He	risked	**his life**	{for a man he did not know}.
PROTAGONIST		ASSET	BENEFICIARY

(2) `Incurring` frame

He	risked	**losing his life savings**
PROTAGONIST		HARM

{by investing in such a company}.
ACTION

(3) `Daring` frame

I	wouldn't risk	**talking like that in public**.
PROTAGONIST		ACTION

By stating the facts about the direct object of the verb in terms of the FEs ASSET, HARM, and ACTION, the three frames allow the verb senses to be described perspicuously and accounted for straightforwardly.[6]

I argue that each of the `Jeopardizing`, `Incurring`, and `Daring` frames bears a particular relation to the `Risk` frame which may be characterized as a type of frame-to-frame relation, namely that of *Perspective_on* (Ruppenhofer et al. 2006: 103–108). FrameNet currently defines eight types of frame-to-frame relations: Inheritance, Perspective_on, Subframe, Precedes, Inchoative_of, Causative_of, Using, and See_also. Each frame relation in the FrameNet data is a directed (asymmetric) relation between two frames, where one frame (the less dependent, or more abstract) may be called the Super_frame and another (the more dependent, or less abstract) the Sub_frame. In the Perspective_on relation, a more specific and infor-

6. Even though the three frames reflect the three 'dictionary senses' of *risk*.v, which are partly constrained by the condition of substitutability, they do not correspond to different schemas (cf. Fillmore and Atkins 1994: Figure 5). In Frame Semantics, "polysemy exists when the use of a word instantiates different schemas." (ibid: 18) Therefore, it is debatable whether it is appropriate to characterize the three frames as describing a polysemy structure in the strict Frame Semantics sense. For the time being, however, I treat the three frames as describing the polysemy structure of *risk*.v.

mative name is given to the Super_frame and the Sub_frame: Neutral frame and Perspectivized frame, respectively. The Perspective_on relation is characterized as "(t)he use of [the Perspective_on] relation indicates the presence of at least two different points-of-view that can be taken on the Neutral frame" (brackets are mine).

According to Ruppenhofer et al. (2006), a Neutral frame is normally Non-lexical and Non-perspectivized. Also, a single Neutral frame generally has at least two Perspectivized frames, but in some cases, words of the Neutral frame are consistent with multiple different points-of-view while the Perspectivized frame is consistent with only one. Whenever there is a state of affairs that is describable by a frame in a Perspective_on relation, all the other frames connected to it by the frame relation can also be used to describe the same state of affairs (ibid.: 106–7).

An example of sets of frames that have Perspective_on relations are the `Commerce_goods_transfer`, the `Commerce_buy`, and the `Commerce_sell` frames. The `Commerce_goods_transfer` frame is the Neutral frame, which is Non-lexical and Non-perspectivized; the `Commerce_buy` and `Commerce_sell` frames are Perspectivized frames, which are evoked by verbs like *buy* and *sell* respectively.

In the case of the RISK-related frames, the `Risk` frame is the Neutral frame and the `Jeopardizing`, `Incurring`, and `Daring` frames are the Perspectivized frames. English *risk*.v is consistent with the three points-of-view associated with the `Jeopardizing`, `Incurring`, and `Daring` frames. That a state of affairs describable by one of the three frames can also be described by the other two frames is shown in the following sentences, which may be construed as describing the same scene:

(4) `Jeopardizing` frame

He	risked	**his life**	{for a man he did not know}.
PROTAGONIST		ASSET	BENEFICIARY

(5) `Incurring` frame

He	risked	**losing his life**	{for a man he did not know}.
PROTAGONIST		HARM	BENEFICIARY

(6) `Daring` frame

He	risked	**saving a man he did not know**.
PROTAGONIST		ACTION

English *risk*.v is peculiar since it is compatible with multiple perspectives. In contrast to *buy*.v, which is compatible only with the perspective of the `Commerce_buy` frame and *sell*.v, which is compatible only with the `Commerce_sell` frame, *risk*.v is compatible with the perspective of any of the `Jeopardizing`, `Incurring`, and `Daring` frames.

Having discussed the senses of English *risk*.v, the semantic frames that the verb evokes, and the relations among the frames, let us now turn to the Japanese translation equivalents of the English verb to see whether the 'corresponding' Japanese expressions involve the same semantic frames.

2.2. The Japanese translation equivalents of *risk*.v

English *risk*.v in the `Jeopardizing`, `Incurring`, and `Daring` frames and the Japanese translation equivalents are shown in (I) through (III). The Japanese expressions that correspond to English *risk*.v are indicated by the bold type in sentences (1a) through (3a).

(I) `Jeopardizing` frame

PROTAGONIST	risk.v	ASSET
NP.Ext	target	NP.Obj

(7) [He $_{\text{Protagonist}}$] **risked** [his life $_{\text{Asset}}$] [for a man he did not know $_{\text{Beneficiary}}$].

Corresponding Japanese Expressions: *kakeru, tosu, kiken ni sarasu*

(8) naze [syooboosi wa $_{\text{Protagonist}}$] [hito no tame ni $_{\text{Beneficiary}}$]
why firefighters TOP people GEN sake DAT

[inoti o $_{\text{Asset}}$] **kakeru** no ka.
life ACC NMLZ Q

'Why do firefighters risk their lives for others?'

(9) ... [syoku o $_{\text{Asset}}$] **tosi** ta yuuki ni atama ga sagaru.
career ACC PERF bravery DAT head NOM descend

'(I) take off my hat for the bravery of risking her career.'

(10) ... [kanozyo wa $_{\text{Protagonist}}$] iraku ni itte [inoti o $_{\text{Asset}}$]
she TOP Iraq GOAL go life ACC

kiken ni sarasita.
risk DAT expose-PAST

'She went to Iraq and risked her life.'

(II) `Incurring` frame

PROTAGONIST	risk.v	HARM
NP.Ext	target	PPby.Obj

(11) [He $_{\text{Protagonist}}$] **risked** [losing his life savings $_{\text{Harm}}$]
{by investing in such a company $_{\text{Action}}$}.

Corresponding Japanese Expression: *kiken o okasu*

(12) ... [sizi kiban kara no hanpatu no $_{\text{Harm}}$]
support base ABL GEN objection GEN

kiken o okas azaru o enakatta ...
risk ACC take could.not.help

'(He) had to risk objections from (his) support base.'

(III) `Daring` frame

PROTAGONIST risk.v ACTION
NP.Ext target VPing.Obj

(13) `Daring` frame

[I $_{\text{Protagonist}}$] wouldn't **risk** [talking like that in public $_{\text{Action}}$].

Corresponding Japanese Expression: *aete*

(14) ... buka no temae, tataka e nai to yuu koto
subordinates GEN front fight can NEG COMPL say thing

wa, sazo iinikukatta ni tigainai ga,
TOP how was.difficult.to.say DAT must CONJ

sono zyoo wa sutete, **aete**
that emotion TOP abandon daringly

[hakkiri yuu beki desita $_{\text{Action}}$].
explicitly say should PAST

'It must have been very difficult (for him) to say in front of the men under his command that (Japan) cannot fight, but (he) should have abandoned such an emotion and (he) should have risked saying it explicitly.'

Risk.v in the `Jeopardizing` frame may be translated into Japanese using either of the verbs *kakeru* or *tosu*, or a multi-word verbal expression *kiken_ni_sarasu*, as shown in sentences (8) through (10). Among the three Japanese expressions, *kakeru* will be discussed in more detail in Section 2.3.1 below.

Risk.v in the `Incurring` frame is usually translated into Japanese with the multi-word form *kiken_o_okasu*, literally meaning 'to commit a risk'.[7] When the noun *kiken* 'risk' is modified by a linguistic realization of the notion HARM, the whole sentence is interpreted as pertaining to the `Incurring` frame as in (12). Uses of *kiken_o_okasu* will be discussed in more detail in Section 2.3.2 below.

`Daring`.*risk*.v is usually translated into Japanese NOT using a verb but instead using an adverb *aete* 'daringly' as in (14). That is, in the case of `Daring` sentences, the possibility of expressing the concept of RISK as a clausal head does not exist in Japanese (See also Section 2.3.3 below and Hasegawa et al. 2006: 10).[8]

2.3. English-Japanese correspondences via semantic frames

First, informal representations of the correspondence between *risk*.v and *kakeru*.v in the `Jeopardizing` frame are given. Next, issues concerning the multi-word form *kiken_o_okasu* are discussed, namely, which of the three `Risk`-related uses it can have and under what conditions, as well as whether it should be recognized as an LU in each of the three `Risk`-related frames. Lastly, the correspondence in the `Daring` frame is discussed.

2.3.1. Risk.*v and* kakeru.*v*

The uses and the valence patterns of `Jeopardizing`.*kakeru*.v closely correspond to those of `Jeopardizing`.*risk*.v. In addition to the core FEs PROTAGONIST and ASSET, *kakeru* can also be accompanied by an

---

7. There is a variant form *risuku_o_okasu* with the noun *risuku* 'risk' instead of *kiken*:

   (i) ... [nihon gawa kara taiwa o utikiru $_{\text{Harm}}$]
   Japan side ABL dialogue ACC cut.off
   risuku wa okasi taku nai ...
   risk TOP take want NEG
   '(We) don't want to risk cutting off the dialogue from the Japanese side ...'

8. Other so-called interpretation predicates in English such as *manage, deign* and *condescend* are also translated into Japanese as adverbials, with almost no possibility of expressing the idea in a main verb. This seems to be due to differences in basic clause structure between English and Japanese and suggests profound semantic-typological differences between the two languages (Hasegawa et al. 2006: 13).

expression encoding one of the following FEs: BENEFICIARY (16), PURPOSE (18), or MOTIVATION (20):

(15) `Jeopardizing` frame

Why did [he $_{\text{Protagonist}}$] **risk** [his life $_{\text{Asset}}$]
[for a man he did not know $_{\text{Beneficiary}}$]?
(Fillmore and Atkins 1992: 88)

[NP-*ga* $_{\text{Protagonist}}$] [NP-*no tame ni* $_{\text{Beneficiary}}$] [NP–*o* $_{\text{Asset}}$] *kakeru*

(16) naze [syooboosi wa $_{\text{Protagonist}}$] [hito no tame ni $_{\text{Beneficiary}}$]
why firefighters TOP people GEN sake DAT

[inoti o $_{\text{Asset}}$] **kakeru** no ka.
life ACC NMLZ Q

'Why do firefighters risk their lives for others?'

(17) `Jeopardizing` frame

Why should [he $_{\text{Protagonist}}$] **risk** [his life $_{\text{Asset}}$]
[to try to save Brooks $_{\text{Purpose}}$]? (Fillmore and Atkins 1992: 89)

[NP-*ga* $_{\text{Protagonist}}$] [NP-*no tame ni* $_{\text{Purpose}}$] [NP-*o* $_{\text{Asset}}$] *kakeru*

(18) "doosi" to ie ba, mukasi wa
QUOTE say COND formerly TOP

keppan o osite,
petition-sealed-with-blood ACC seal

[kyootuu no mokuteki no tame ni $_{\text{Purpose}}$]
common GEN purpose GEN sake DAT

inoti o $_{\text{Asset}}$] **kakeru** nakama desita.
life ACC buddy COP-PAST

'In the past, *doosi* referred to buddies among whom people risked their lives for a common goal, by sealing (documents) with blood.'

(19) `Jeopardizing` frame

I have **risked** [all that I have $_{\text{Asset}}$] [for this noble cause $_{\text{Motivation}}$].
(Fillmore and Atkins 1992: 89)

[NP-*ga* $_{\text{Protagonist}}$] [NP-*ni* $_{\text{Motivation}}$] [NP–*o* $_{\text{Asset}}$] *kakeru*

(20) . . . [yamanoi husai no $_{\text{Protagonist}}$] akumademo
Mr. and Mrs. GEN persistently

[onore no yume ni $_{\text{Motivation}}$]
self GEN dream DAT

[inoti o $_{\text{Asset}}$] **kakeru** sono sugata ...
life ACC that attitude

'... the attitude of Mr. and Mrs. Yamanoi, who risked their lives for the sake of their own dream...'

Among the three `Risk`-related frames, the use of the Japanese verb *kakeru* is restricted to that of `Jeopardizing`. Thus, it seems appropriate to define the Japanese LU *kakeru* as evoking the `Jeopardizing` frame (But see Section 3 below). Tables 1 and 2 below summarize relevant valence information for `Jeopardizing`.*risk*.v and `Jeopardizing`.*kakeru*.v, respectively.

Table 1. Valence table for *risk* in the `Jeopardizing` frame

a.	[PROTAGONIST: NP.Ext] *risk*.v [ASSET: NP.Obj]
b.	[PROTAGONIST: NP.Ext] *risk*.v [ASSET: NP.Obj] [BENEFICIARY: PP_*for*.Dep]
c.	[PROTAGONIST: NP.Ext] *risk*.v [ASSET: NP.Obj] [PURPOSE: VP*to*.Dep]
d.	[PROTAGONIST: NP.Ext] *risk*.v [ASSET: NP.Obj] [MOTIVATION: PP_*for*.Dep]

Table 2. Valence table for *kakeru* in the `Jeopardizing` frame

a.	[PROTAGONIST: NP.Ext.-*ga*] [ASSET: NP.Dep.-*o*] *kakeru*
b.	[PROTAGONIST: NP.Ext-*ga*] [BENEFICIARY: NP.Dep. -*no tame ni*] [ASSET: NP.Obj.-*o*] *kakeru*
c.	[PROTAGONIST: NP.Ext-*ga*] [PURPOSE: NP.Dep. -*no tame ni*] [ASSET: NP.Obj.-*o*] *kakeru*
d.	[PROTAGONIST: NP.Ext.-*ga*] [MOTIVATION: NP.Dep. -*ni*] [ASSET: NP.Obj.-*o*] *kakeru*

Based on the valence descriptions, the partial correspondence between the two LUs is represented in Figure 2.[9]

9. The actual correspondence between the valence tables of the two LUs is quite large. In fact, one of the aims of the Japan-U.S. joint project "Frame-based Japanese-English bilingual lexicon" funded by JSPS was precisely to pursue ways in which correspondences between LUs via semantic frames in the two languages may be best represented and described (See also Note 1).

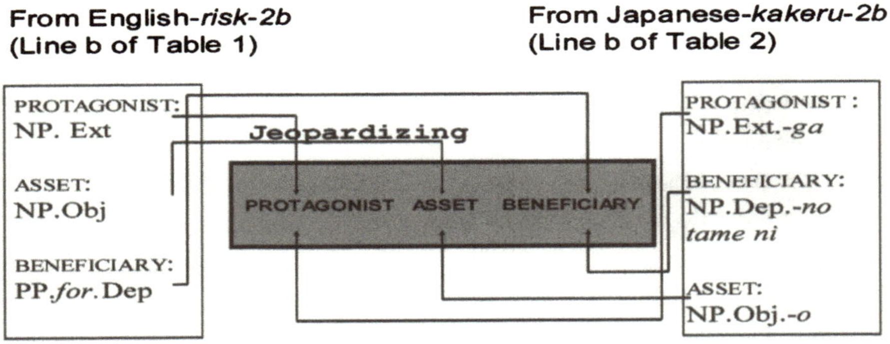

Figure 2. Linking relevant English and Japanese lexicon fragments via the `Jeopardizing` frame

2.3.2. Risk.*v and* kiken_o_okasu.*v*

The multi-word phrase *kiken_o_okasu*, presented as a translation equivalent of `Incurring`.*risk*.v in Section 2.2, also pertains to the `Jeopardizing` and the `Daring` frames as well. First, when the noun *kiken* in the multi-word form *kiken_o_okasu* is modified by linguistic material that expresses an ASSET, the sentence is interpreted as evoking the `Jeopardizing` frame, as shown in (21).

`Jeopardizing`: [NP-*no* $_{\text{Asset}}$] *kiken o okasu*

(21) ... [inoti/seimei no $_{\text{Asset}}$] **kiken o okasite** mo
life GEN even

[syoogensi $_{\text{Action}}$] te kureru yuiitu no hito deatta ...
testify sole GEN person COP-PAST

'... (she) was the only person who would testify even risking (her) life...'

Occurrences of the `Jeopardizing` sense with *kiken_o_okasu* seem to be restricted to cases where the modifying phrase of *kiken* contains either of the two nouns *inoti* and *seimei*, both meaning 'life'.

Second, when the multi-word phrase is used sentence-medially followed by an ACTION VP with no modification on the noun *kiken*, the sentence is interpreted as evoking the `Daring` frame, literally meaning "the PROTAGONIST, taking a risk, performed the ACTION," or "the PROTAGONIST took a risk and performed the ACTION." In other words, in such a sentence, the multi-word expression as a whole is functioning as an adverbial modifying the following ACTION VP, as seen in (22).

Daring: *kiken o okasi(te)* [VP $_{\text{Action}}$]

(22) ... [kookai zyuusatusareru otooto o
public execution-PASS younger.brother ACC
sukuoo to $_{\text{Purpose}}$] **kiken o okasite**
rescue COMPL risk ACC take
[saigon (gen hootimin) si e sinnyuusuru $_{\text{Action}}$] ...
Saigon present Ho Chi Minh City GOAL enter
lit. '(She) entered Saigon (present Ho Chi Minh City), taking a risk, to rescue her brother from public execution.'
'(She) risked entering Saigon (present Ho Chi Minh City) to rescue her brother from public execution.'

The multi-word expression in question appears sentence-medially in the default continuative form *kiken_o_okasi* or in the *-TE* form *kiken_o_okasite* (22), and thus not as the main predicate of the sentence. Moreover, unlike the Incurring use in (12), the multi-word expression is not preceded by a modifier expressing a HARM. Instead, a VP encoding an ACTION follows *kiken_o_okasi(te)*.

Based on examples such as (21) and (22) pertaining to the Jeopardizing and Daring frames, in addition to the Incurring uses in (12), it thus seems appropriate to define *kiken_o_okasu* as a multiword LU in each of the three Risk-related frames.

2.3.3. Risk.*v and* aete.*adv*

As pointed out in Section 2.2, Daring.*risk*.v can only be translated into Japanese using an adverbial, i.e., *aete*.adv. There seems to be no possibility of expressing the concept of the Daring frame using a clausal head in Japanese (See also Note 8). The correspondence between English *risk*.v and Japanese *aete*.adv via the Daring frame is a case in which semantic frames as an interlingua representation link words belonging to distinct parts of speech in two languages.

Let us summarize the above discussions concerning English-Japanese correspondences via semantic frames. The analyses of the Japanese translation equivalents of English *risk*.v have revealed three different types of English-Japanese correspondences. First, as for *risk*.v and *kakeru*.v, their uses may be regarded as corresponding to each other in the sense that they both evoke the same Jeopardizing frame. That is, both *risk*.v and *kakeru*.v are compatible with the perspective of the Jeopardizing frame. Second, as for *kiken_o_okasu*.v, it is compatible with any of the perspectives of the Jeopardizing, Incurring, and Daring frames, just like *risk*.v. Finally, English Daring.*risk*.v corresponds to Japanese Daring.*aete*.adv, even though they belong to different parts of speech.

The above analyses, especially those pertaining to Jeopardizing.*kakeru*.v and Incurring.*kiken_o_okasu*.v, suggest that when contrasting the semantics of words in different languages, it is not sufficient to examine only the corresponding senses of the words in the two languages. It is also necessary to take into account the entire polysemy structure of each word within the language before trying to link the words in the two languages. Let us now turn to the analysis of the semantic network of the Japanese verb *kakeru*, since among the LUs which are construed as translation equivalents of *risk*.v, *kakeru*.v's correspondence to the English verbs via the Jeopardizing frame seems to be the most straightforward in that it is a one-to-one correspondence.

3. Japanese *kakeru*.v and its frames

This section discusses the semantic network for *kakeru*, one of the translation equivalents of *risk*.v. In most English-Japanese bilingual dictionaries, the verb *kakeru* indeed occurs as one of the equivalents of *risk*. It should be noted in passing that in Japanese there are several sets of characters used for the same sound sequence. However, the fact that the same characters 賭ける are used for each of the senses described below motivates hypothesizing their semantic interconnectedness, at least synchronically. In the rest of this section, I will first provide the network diagram of the senses of *kakeru*, following the semantic network analyses of English *crawl* and French *ramper* by Fillmore and Atkins (2000). I will then discuss the overlaps and mismatches between the senses of *risk* and *kakeru* and finally consider how far these two verbs are true equivalents. The semantic network for *kakeru* is given in Figure 3.

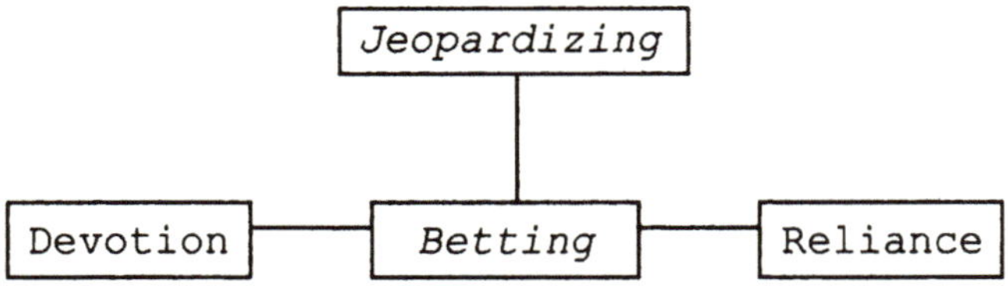

***kakeru* 賭ける**

Figure 3. Semantic Network for the Verb *kakeru*

In Figure 3, each of the senses is identified by a frame name, which will be described below. The senses 'shared' with *risk* are shown in italics. The lines can be thought of as representing sense extensions.

In addition to being used in the `Jeopardizing` sense, *kakeru* is used in the `Betting` sense as well, just like *risk*. The `Betting` frame may be characterized as showing a relationship between PROTAGONIST, INVESTMENT, and a chance-involved entity or event CHANCE. The PROTAGONIST exposes the INVESTMENT to loss by wagering it on a CHANCE (see also Fillmore and Atkins 1992: 100).

`Betting` frame

(23a) [We $_{\text{Protagonist}}$] **risked** [all that money $_{\text{Investment}}$] [on a horse $_{\text{Chance}}$].
(Fillmore and Atkins 1992: 100)

(23b) [kare wa $_{\text{Protagonist}}$] [3000 en o $_{\text{Investment}}$]
he TOP 3000 yen ACC

[sono uma ni $_{\text{Chance}}$] **kaketa**.
that horse DAT bet PAST

'He <u>bet</u> 3000 yen on that horse.'

Let us now examine the uses of *kakeru*, which are not shared by *risk* (non-italicized in Figure 3 above). Unlike *risk*, *kakeru* may be used in the `Devotion` frame, which involves a situation in which the PROTAGONIST expends an ASSET, usually time or energy, to perform some ACTIVITY in order to achieve some meaningful goal. Here, *kakeru* means 'devote' or 'dedicate.'

`Devotion` frame

(24a) [I $_{\text{Protagonist}}$] am **devoting** [myself $_{\text{Asset}}$] [to this mystery $_{\text{Activity}}$].
because I want to be a man. (from *British National Corpus*)

(24b) [kare wa $_{\text{Protagonist}}$] [seesyun o $_{\text{Asset}}$] [yakyuu ni $_{\text{Activity}}$] **kaketa**.
he TOP youth ACC baseball DAT PAST

'He <u>devoted</u> his youth to (playing) baseball.'

Kakeru may also be used in the `Reliance` frame. The `Reliance` frame is currently defined in FrameNet as follows.[10] "A PROTAGONIST needs a MEANS_ACTION performed for their BENEFIT. The relevant MEANS_

10. At the time of writing this paper, the `Betting` and `Devotion` frames have not yet been defined in FrameNet.

ACTION is often evoked only by reference to an INTERMEDIARY who performs it. Also, if the PROTAGONIST performs the MEANS_ACTION himself, the INSTRUMENT that they use may be referred to in place of the MEANS_ACTION." In this frame, *kakeru* means 'rely on.'

`Reliance` frame

(25a) [She $_{\text{Protagonist}}$] had to **rely on** [friendly passers-by $_{\text{Intermediary}}$].
[to give directions $_{\text{Benefit}}$]. (from *British National Corpus*)

(25b) [kare wa $_{\text{Protagonist}}$] [syoosin o $_{\text{Benefit}}$]
he TOP promotion ACC

[tyokuzoku zyoosi ni $_{\text{Intermediary}}$] **kaketa**.
direct supervisor DAT rely PAST

'He relied on his direct supervisor for a promotion.'

Finally, let us consider how far *kakeru* and *risk* are true equivalents. Although *kakeru* seems to have the same uses as *risk* in the `Jeopardizing` and `Betting` frames, it cannot be used in the `Incurring` and `Daring` uses and is instead used in the `Devotion` and `Reliance` frames. I suspect that the following may be the reason for the divergences: While both of the notions of CHANCE and HARM are central to *risk*, what is crucial for the senses of *kakeru* is the notion of CHANCE only (see also Fillmore and Atkins 1992: 80).

In its use in the `Jeopardizing` and `Betting` frames *kakeru* seems to be equivalent to *risk*. The `Jeopardizing` and `Betting` frames involve both of the notions of CHANCE and HARM. That is, both frames have to do with uncertainty about the future and possible loss of an ASSET, i.e., a HARM. In `Jeopardizing`.*kakeru* sentences, the noun *inoti* 'life' often appears instantiating the ASSET as in (26). In `Betting`.*kakeru* sentences, the ASSET is restricted to something that can be regarded as INVESTMENT, such as money as in (27).

(26) `Jeopardizing` frame

[tai tero butai wa $_{\text{Protagonist}}$]
anti terrorist team TOP

[hitoziti kyuusyutu ni $_{\text{Purpose}}$] [inoti o $_{\text{Asset}}$]
hostages rescue DAT life ACC

kaketa.
risk PAST

'The antiterrorist team risked their lives to rescue the hostages.'

(27) `Betting` frame

[kare wa Protagonist] [hitoziti kyuusyutu seikoo ni Outcome]
he TOP hostages rescue success DAT

[100 doru o Asset] **kaketa**.
dollar ACC bet PAST

'He bet 100 dollars on the success of the hostage rescue operation.'

The `Devotion` frame also pertains not only to the notion of CHANCE but also HARM. However, whereas the HARM involved in the `Jeopardizing` and `Betting` frames is usually losing an ASSET, the HARM pertaining to the `Devotion` frame is wasting the ASSET, e.g. time or energy. In (28), for example, failing to create *sake* with a new taste does not usually involve dying.

(28) `Devotion` frame

[kore made ni naku karuku, sukkirisita sake o
this until DAT non-existent light pure ACC

tukuridasu koto ni Purpose] [zinsei o Asset] **kaketa**.
create thing DAT span.of.life ACC dedicate PAST

'(He) dedicated his life to creating *sake* which tastes lighter and purer than has ever been tasted.'

The `Reliance` frame does not directly involve the notion of HARM (29) and pertains to CHANCE only (30).

`Reliance` frame

(29) [kantoku wa Protagonist]
manager TOP

[kare no gizyutu to keiken ni Instrument] **kaketa**.
he GEN technique and experience DAT rely PAST

'The (baseball) manager counted on his technique and experience.'

(30) [ato no iti-wari ni Instrument] **kakeru**.
rest GEN 10% probability DAT

'Rely on the last 10 percent probability.'

As discussed in Section 2.1, the `Jeopardizing`, `Incurring` and `Daring` frames describe the same scene but they are associated with different points of view. Further analysis is needed, but at least the reason why *kakeru* does not have the `Incurring` use appears to be due to the fact that the notion of HARM, which is foregrounded in the `Incurring` frame, is not central to the senses of *kakeru.*

4. Conclusion

This paper investigated lexical correspondences between English and Japanese, a typologically unrelated pair of languages, with respect to the viability of semantic frames as an interlingua for the two languages. It demonstrated the complexity of lexical correspondences between two languages. Specifically, I analyzed the correspondences between the English and Japanese expressions involving the concept of RISK. Assuming the same set of semantic frames for the concept in the two languages, I examined the Japanese translation equivalents of the English verb *risk.* Some seemingly corresponding words in Japanese only involve one perspective on a RISK-related scene, while at least one Japanese expression, namely, *kiken_o_okasu,* is compatible with all the perspectives associated with the English verb *risk.*

I also explored the polysemous verb *kakeru* and showed that the different senses of the Japanese verb rely on the knowledge structured in four different frames, only one of which corresponds directly to the frame for English *risk*.v. While it is always possible that we are dealing with a language specific irregularity or a word peculiarity, it is necessary to continue to question the viability of frames as an interlingua for cross-lingual FrameNet lexical resource development.

References

Boas, Hans C.
2001 Frame Semantics as a framework for describing polysemy and syntactic structures of English and German motion verbs in contrastive computational lexicography. In: Rayson, Paul, Andrew Wilson, Tony McEnery, Andrew Hardie, and Shereen Khoja (eds.), *Proceedings of the Corpus Linguistics 2001 Conference. Technical Papers*, Vol. 13, 64–73. Lancaster, UK: University Centre for computer corpus research on language.

Boas, Hans C.
2005 Semantic frames as interlingual representations for multilingual lexical databases. In: *International Journal of Lexicography* 18.4: 445–478.

Ellsworth, Michael, Kyoko Ohara, Carlos Subirats, and Thomas Schmidt
2006 *Frame-semantic analysis of motion scenarios in English, Japanese, Spanish, and German*. Paper presented at ICCG-4, Tokyo.

Fillmore, Charles J. and B.T.S. Atkins
1992 Towards a frame-based organization of the lexicon: The semantics of RISK and its neighbors. In: Lehrer, A. and E. Kittay (eds.), *Frames, Fields, and Contrast: New Essays in Semantics and Lexical Organization*, 75–102. Lawrence Erlbaum Associates, Hillsdale.

Fillmore, Charles J. and B.T.S. Atkins
1994 Starting where the dictionaries stop: The challenge for computational lexicography. In: B.T.S. Atkins and A. Zampolli (eds.), *Computational Approaches to the Lexicon*, 349–393. Oxford: Oxford University Press.

Fillmore, Charles J. and B.T.S. Atkins
2000 Describing polysemy: The case of 'Crawl'. In: Y. Ravin and C. Leacock (eds.). *Polysemy: Theoretical and Computational Approaches*, 91–110. Oxford: Oxford University Press.

Fillmore, Charles J., Christopher Johnson, and Miriam R.L. Petruck
2003 Background to Framenet. *International Journal of Lexicography* 16.3: 235–250.

Fontenelle, Thierry
2000 A bilingual lexical database for Frame Semantics. *International Journal of Lexicography* 13.4: 232–248.

Hasegawa, Yoko, Kyoko Ohara, Russell Lee-Goldman and Charles J. Fillmore
2006 *Frame integration, head switching, and translation: RISK in English and Japanese*. Paper presented at ICCG-4, Tokyo.

Hasegawa, Yoko and Kyoko Ohara
2006 Charuzu Firumoa Kyoju ni Kiku (Interview with Professor Charles J. Fillmore). (In Japanese). *The Rising Generation* 152.6: 354–359.

Ohara, Kyoko
2006 Furemu Imiron to Nihongo Furemu Netto (Frame Semantics and Japanese FrameNet). (In Japanese). *Nihongogaku (Japanese Linguistics)* 25.6: 40–52.

Ohara, Kyoko, Seiko Fujii, Toshio Ohori, Ryoko Suzuki, Hiroaki Saito, and Shun Ishizaki
2004 The Japanese FrameNet Project: An introduction. In: *Fourth international conference on Language Resources and Evaluation (LREC 2004). Proceedings of the Satellite Workshop "Building Lexical Resources from Semantically Annotated Corpora"*, 9–11.

Pustejovsky, James
2000 Lexical shadowing and argument closure. In: Y. Ravin and C. Peacock (eds.), *Polysemy: Theoretical and Computational* Approaches, 68–90. Oxford: Oxford University Press.

Ruppenhofer, Josef, Michael Ellsworth, Miriam R.L. Petruck, Christopher Johnson, and Jan Scheffczyk.
2006 *FramNet II: Extended theory and practice.* Technical Report. Berkeley: International Computer Science Institute.
Subirats-Rüggeberg, Carlos and Miriam R.L. Petruck
2003 Surprise: Spanish FrameNet! In: E. Hajicova, A. Kotesovcova, and J. Mirovsky (eds.), *Proceedings of CIL 17.* CD-ROM. Prague: Matfyzpress.
Subirats, Carlos and Hiroaki Sato
2004 Spanish FrameNet and FrameSQL. In: *Fourth International Conference on Language Resources and Evaluation (LREC 2004). Proceedings of the Satellite Workshop "Building Lexical Resources from Semantically Annotated Corpora"*, 13–16.

Data

CD-Mainichi Newspaper 1992–2002.

7. Typological considerations in constructing a Hebrew FrameNet[1]

Miriam R. L. Petruck

1. Introduction

The FrameNet Project[2] implements the theoretical constructs of Frame Semantics (Fillmore 1977, 1982, 1985, Petruck 1996), including the semantic frame, frame elements, frame-to-frame relations, coreness status of frame elements, and semantic types. While FrameNet is being developed to determine the valence descriptions for the lexicon of contemporary English, and document these findings with corpus evidence, the working assumption is that the frames in the FrameNet hierarchy represent conceptual structure, not an application driven structured organization of the lexicon of contemporary English. The present work describes a project to develop Hebrew FrameNet, one of whose long-term goals is determining how the existing machinery of FrameNet would transfer to languages other than English,[3] in part by comparing frame structures of FrameNet frames with those needed for characterizing the lexicon of contemporary Hebrew. Because Hebrew (Semitic) is genetically distinct from English (Germanic), as well as from the other languages for which FrameNet (or FrameNet-like)[4] databases have been developed, it provides a unique testing ground for this research.

---

1. Parts of this paper derive from presentations at the 2nd Cross-Linguistic FrameNet meeting (held in Saarbrücken) and at the 23rd National Association of Professors of Hebrew International Conference on Hebrew Language and Literature (held at Stanford University), both in 2005.
2. http://framenet.icsi.berkeley.edu/~framenet.
3. For an overview, see Boas (2005).
4. FrameNet projects for other languages (i.e. Spanish and Japanese) are described in this volume. The German SALSA project does not develop a new frame if FrameNet hasn't defined it; hence it is only FrameNet-like.

Like the original FrameNet Project on which it is based, Hebrew FrameNet will create an on-line lexical resource for contemporary Hebrew based on the principles of Frame Semantics and supported by corpus evidence. An initial goal is to document the range of semantic and syntactic combinatorial possibilities (*valences*) of each word in each of its senses by annotating example sentences and compiling the results for display. Hebrew FrameNet will provide full-text annotation of frame evoking elements (FEEs)[5] for an existing newspaper corpus, as a means of (1) creating the infrastructure for using the FrameNet Desktop for the analysis of Hebrew texts and (2) investigating at what level of linguistic description and computational representation the lexicon of contemporary Hebrew can be characterized in the same terms as the lexicon of English, thereby necessarily considering the matter of transferability of FrameNet machinery to a language other than English. The investigation of how events and scenarios are expressed through the same or different frames will also document the different lexicalization patterns of Hebrew and English (Talmy 2000), thus contributing to cross-linguistic studies as well.

The present paper has four more sections. Section 2 summarizes the basic principles of Frame Semantics, also providing an overview of the work of FrameNet. Section 3 describes the current state of affairs in Hebrew Computational Linguistics and existing resources for the computational processing of Hebrew. Section 4 discusses the infrastructure for this project, specifically the software developed by FrameNet and issues relating to its use with Hebrew texts. An example Frame Semantics annotation of a sentence from the Hebrew newspaper corpus is included, illustrating how Hebrew instantiates two key constructs, the semantic frame and frame elements. Section 5 presents Talmy's motion event typology (further refined by Slobin) against which motion events in Hebrew can be characterized. A subset of motion frames in the FrameNet database and relevant to the Hebrew data is considered, also exemplifying frame-to-frame relations and semantic types, two additional important Frame Semantics (FS) constructs.

5. An FEE is a linguistic unit that evokes a frame, including primarily verbs, event nouns, adjectives, and adverbs. By *full text* annotation, we mean semantic annotation of FEEs, excluding named entities, such as persons, locations, organizations, numbers, and numerical expressions (e.g. dates, addresses), etc.

2. Frame Semantics and FrameNet

Frame Semantics was first introduced into linguistics (Fillmore 1975) as an alternative to what was characterized as "check-list theories of meaning", the latter covering theories in which a linguistic form is represented in terms of a checklist of conditions that have to be satisfied in order for the form to be appropriately or truthfully used. Importantly, in Frame Semantics, where a linguistic unit *evokes* a frame, the meaning of that linguistic unit is defined in terms of experience-based schematizations of the speaker's world – i.e. *frames,* script-like structures of inferences that characterize a type of situation, object, or event, and provide the background and motivation for the existence and everyday use of words in a language. For example, the word *tip* evokes a scene in which someone has paid for a service received, (typically) is satisfied with the service, and gives a monetary reward to the person who has provided the service. The information needed for speakers of English to understand the sentence *Marty gave the waiter a big tip* could not be itemized perspicuously as a list of conditions. Rather, speakers understand that Marty paid the waiter for the service and the reward is understood against the background of assumptions and practices of the evoked frame.

Fillmore (1978) characterized the frame as the most central and powerful kind of domain structure, paving the way for a frame-based organization of the lexicon (Fillmore and Atkins 1992), setting the stage for the development of FrameNet, and suggesting the utility of the semantic frame for cross-linguistic research. Other work expanded upon and further clarified different aspects of the theory (Fillmore 1977, 1982, 1985). While Frame Semantics has been used to provide accounts of a variety of lexical, syntactic, and semantic phenomena in a range of different languages (Östman 2000, Petruck 1995, Lambrecht 1984), the most highly developed instantiation of the theory is found in FrameNet, a computational lexicography project that provides for a substantial portion of the vocabulary of contemporary English, a body of semantically and syntactically annotated sentences from which reliable information can be reported on the valences or combinatorial possibilities of each item analyzed.

In its lexicographic work, FrameNet focuses on defining frames and analyzing lexical units (LUs). A FrameNet frame is a schematic representation of a situation involving various participants, props, and other conceptual roles each of which is a *frame element* (FE). A *lexical unit* is a word sense, expressed by the relation between a lemma and the frame that it evokes. To illustrate, the **Revenge** frame is characterized in terms of an AVENGER performing some PUNISHMENT on an OFFENDER as a response to an INJURY, inflicted on an INJURED_PARTY. Some of the LUs in the **Revenge** frame are *avenge*.v, *avenger*.n, *get back (at)*.v *get even*.v, *retaliate*.v, *retaliation*.n, *retribution*.n, *retributory*.a, *revenge*.v, *revenge*.n, *vengeance*.n, *vengeful*.a, and *vindictive*.a, where nouns, verbs, and adjectives are included, as are multi-word expressions. The linguistic realization of each FE highlights different participants and props of the frame, as shown in the following examples, where the *target* (the word being analyzed and with respect to which the FS annotation is done) is the verb *avenge*.[6]

(1) [Sven $_{\text{Avenger}}$] **avenged** [his brother $_{\text{Injured\_party}}$] [after the incident $_{\text{Time}}$].

(2) [El Cid $_{\text{Avenger}}$] **avenged** [the death of his son $_{\text{Injury}}$] [hastily $_{\text{Manner}}$].

(3) [The monkey $_{\text{Avenger}}$] **avenged** [himself $_{\text{Injured\_party}}$] [by growing to the size of a giant and setting fire to the city $_{\text{Punishment}}$].

(4) [Hook $_{\text{Avenger}}$] **avenged** [himself $_{\text{Injured\_party}}$] [on Peter Pan $_{\text{Offender}}$].

AVENGER, PUNISHMENT, OFFENDER, INJURY, and INJURED_PARTY are the *core* FEs of **Revenge**, since they uniquely define the frame. As with other events, an act of revenge can be described as having occurred, for example, at a particular TIME (as in 1), or in a particular MANNER (as in 2). TIME, and MANNER are two of the *peripheral* FEs of the frame, describing aspects of events more generally. For each FE that is annotated in an example sentence, FrameNet also records grammatical function (from a modified list of grammatical categories) and phrase type information, thereby collecting triples of information about each FE. Thus, in all of the above sentences AVENGER is recorded as an *External* NP.[7] The INJURED_PARTY in (1)–(3) is realized as an Object NP, as is INJURY in (2), while PUNISHMENT is realized as a PPing phrase, and OFFENDER as in (4) is realized as a PP. The peripheral FE TIME, as in (1), is instantiated as a PP and MANNER is instantiated as an AVP.

---

6. Examples (1)–(5) are based on sentences in the FN database, reflecting the same phenomena that occur in corpus attestations.
7. FrameNet uses *external* for the grammatical function of arguments that are subjects of target verbs, as well as for any constituent that controls the subject of a target verb.

When a conceptually necessary and salient (i.e. core) FE is not represented in the surface syntax of a sentence, FrameNet records it as a null instantiation, of which there are three types: constructional (CNI); definite (DNI); and indefinite (INI). Constructionally omitted constituents are licensed by a grammatical construction in which the target occurs. Examples of CNI are the omitted agent in a passive sentence and the omitted subject in an imperative, as in *Her honor was **avenged** by murdering her assailant* and ***Get even** with that bum*, where the AVENGER is not mentioned explicitly, although clearly understood as a participant in the event. The other types of null instantiation are lexically specific. In sentences (1)–(3), above, there is no lexical or phrasal material for the OFFENDER; FrameNet records that information because it provides lexicographically relevant information about omissibility conditions. In these examples, OFFENDER is omitted under DNI, since the referent is understood from the linguistic or discourse context. INI is the other lexically specific null instantiation, and it is illustrated with the missing objects of verbs such as *eat, bake*, and *sew*, which are usually transitive, but can be used intransitively. With such verbs the nature of the missing element can be understood without referring back to a previously mentioned entity in the discourse. In the Revenge frame, all of the verbs allow the FE PUNISHMENT to be omitted under INI; thus, for sentences (1), (2), and (4), the FrameNet database records PUNISHMENT as INI.

FrameNet also distinguishes a third type of FE, namely *extra-thematic*. A FE with extra-thematic status places the current frame against the backdrop of a larger situation, as seen in the following example, where the extra-thematic FE ITERATION indicates the number of times the event denoted by the target has occurred.[8]

(5) [The looters $_{\text{AVENGER}}$] revenged [themselves $_{\text{INJURED\_PARTY}}$] [again and again $_{\text{ITERATION}}$] during the demonstration.

FrameNet lexicographers annotate many example sentences for a given LU, to ensure coverage of all patterns in which it occurs. Automatic processes summarize the findings, and present them in displays that show explicit information about the mapping of semantic roles to syntactic structure. One such display is given in Figure 1, the valence table for the LU *avenge*.v, which on the FrameNet website also provides clickable links to the annotated sentences.

8. Ruppenhofer et al. (2006) provides a detailed description of FrameNet's FE types, and current annotation practices.

Number Annotated	Patterns				
(5) TOTAL	Avenger	Injured_Party	Injury	Offender	Punishment
(1)	CNI --	NP Ext	2nd --	INI --	INI --
(1)	NP Ext	2nd --	NP Obj	INI --	INI --
(1)	NP Ext	NP Obj	2nd --	INI --	INI --
(1)	NP Ext	NP Obj	PPing[for] Dep	PP[on] Dep	INI --
(1)	PP[by] Ext	2nd --	NP Obj	INI --	INI --
(3) TOTAL	Avenger	Injured_Party	Offender	Punishment	
(1)	CNI --	NP Ext	INI --	INI --	
(1)	NP Ext	NP Obj	INI --	INI --	
(1)	NP Ext	NP Obj	PP[on] Dep	INI --	

Figure 1. Valence Table for *avenge*.v

FrameNet also records frame-to-frame relations in the database, the most important of which are *Inheritance* and *Subframes*, with *Using* somewhat less significant. Frame inheritance is a relationship in which a child frame is a more specific elaboration of its parent frame. Thus, all of the FEs, other frame relations and (semantic) characteristics of the parent have equally or more specific correspondents in the child frame. For example, the `Revenge` frame inherits from the `Rewards_and_Punishment` frame, some of whose LUs are *discipline*.v, *reward*.n and *punitive*.a, and where the FE EVALUEE corresponds to the more specific FE OFFENDER in the `Revenge` frame. Subframes is a relationship characterizing the different sequential parts of a complex event in terms of the sequences of states of affairs and transitions between them, each of which can itself be separately described as a frame. For instance, the complex `Employment_scenario` frame consists of three simpler frames, including the following: `Employment_start`; `Employment_continue`; and `Employment_end`. When a specific frame refers in a general way to a more abstract, schematic frame, the *Using* relationship holds between the specific child frame and the more general parent frame. In this relation, only some of the FEs in the child frame have a corresponding entity in the parent frame, and they are more specific. To illustrate, the `Undressing` frame uses the `Removing` frame, with the FEs WEARER and CLOTHING of the former being more specific than the AGENT and THEME FEs (respectively) of the latter.[9]

3. Computational processing of Hebrew

Hebrew FrameNet draws upon resources developed for the computational processing of Hebrew, and will contribute to that area of research as well. The computational processing of Hebrew (and Semitic languages in general) presents a number of unique issues for computational linguistics. This section summarizes in brief the current state of affairs in Hebrew computational linguistics and describes the (publicly available) resources needed for the frame semantic annotation of Hebrew texts.

3.1. Hebrew computational linguistics: current state of affairs

Given its writing system, its rich and complex morphology, its characteristically Semitic word formation processes involving roots and patterns, and (until very recently) a dearth of resources, such as corpora and computational grammars, the computational processing of Hebrew presents a number of challenges, some of which go beyond what needs to be overcome for many of the languages that already have extensive computational resources. First of all, the writing system poses problems because the alphabet is not Latinate, it is written from right to left, and, except for children's books and learner's materials, written texts are unvocalized, thereby increasing the degree of ambiguity for any given word form. Next, although much of Hebrew inflectional morphology consists of adding suffixes to (baseform) words, there are also prefixes, as well as combinations of both kinds of affixation (with nouns and adjectives inflecting for number and gender and verbs inflecting for person, number, gender, and tense), which contributes to the difficulty in the computational processing of the language.

9. FrameNet also has the *causative of* and *stative of* relations to indicate the fairly regular relationship between causative, inchoative and stative frames, and has recently added the *precedes* and *perspective on* relations to its repertoire of frame-to-frame relations. The *precedes* relation and *perspective on* relation is a refinement of *using*. See Ruppenhofer et al. (2006) for further information.

Finally, the word formation apparatus, based on a system of roots and patterns in which, typically, three- or four-consonant roots fit into the empty slots of patterns – i.e. sequences of vowels or consonants and vowels – cannot be described computationally as easily as a concatenative process (Wintner 2004, Yona and Wintner 2005).

There have been numerous significant accomplishments in the computational processing of Hebrew, most notably the Bar Ilan Corpus of Modern Hebrew, a thirty million word, tagged computerized corpus of the language and *Rav-Milim* (Choueka 1997),[10] a computerized dictionary for which a set of tools (morphological analyzer and vocalizer) were also developed (Choueka 1990, 1993). Nevertheless, the publicly available computational infrastructure needed for the processing of Hebrew has been limited. Recently, however, Haifa University's computational linguistics laboratory (http://cl.haifa.ac.il) and the Knowledge Center for Processing Hebrew (http://www.mila.cs.technion.ac.il/website/english/index.html) at The Technion have begun to remedy the situation. Existing resources and tools in development to be used for constructing Hebrew FrameNet are itemized in the following section.[11]

3.2. Resources and tools for the annotation of Hebrew texts

While research on various aspects of and approaches to the computational processing of Hebrew has been in progress for several decades, publicly available resources and tools have only been in development for less than a decade. Those to be used in the development of Hebrew FrameNet are described here.

The *2000-sentence HaAretz Corpus* contains newspaper articles from 1991.[12] This corpus will be annotated with Frame Semantics annotations, recording semantic role, grammatical function, and phrase type information for each FEE, summaries of which will be provided in automatically produced reports, initially for internal use and eventually to the public via the Internet for research and teaching purposes. This corpus is available in various formats, one of which includes morpho-syntactic annotations, given in Figure 2, showing part of a sentence with XML tags defined for

10. Choueka (1997) is the original print edition.
11. These are either freely available or will be made available for research purposes upon completion.
12. http://mila.cs.technion.ac.il/website/english/resources/corpora/2000sentences/index.htm.

the Hebrew material. Some of the conventions for record-keeping of corpus information include a sentence identification number for each sentence and a token identification number for each word in each sentence. In addition, the Hebrew spelling and a transliterated form is supplied for each token of each word. Finally, the base form of the token is provided, along with grammatical information about the token, such as number (singular; plural), status (absolute; construct), and gender (masculine; feminine) for nouns, and tense (past; present; future), person (1st; 2nd; 3rd), number (singular; plural), and gender (masculine; feminine) for verbs.[13]

```
- <sentence id="2">
  - <token id="1" surface="תופעה" transliterated="twpyh">
    - <analysis id="1">
      - <base lexiconItem="תופעה" transliteratedLexiconItem="twpyh">
          <noun number="singular" status="absolute" gender="feminine"/>
        </base>
      </analysis>
    </token>
  - <token id="2" surface="זו" transliterated="zw">
    - <analysis id="1">
      - <base lexiconItem="זה" transliteratedLexiconItem="zh">
          <pronoun number="singular" person="3" gender="feminine"/>
        </base>
      </analysis>
    </token>
  - <token id="3" surface="התבררה" transliterated="htbrrh">
    - <analysis id="1">
      - <base lexiconItem="התברר" transliteratedLexiconItem="htbrr">
          <verb tense="past" number="singular" person="3" gender="feminine"/>
        </base>
      </analysis>
    </token>
  - <token id="4" surface="אתמול" transliterated="atmwl">
    - <analysis id="1">
      - <base lexiconItem="אתמול" transliteratedLexiconItem="atmwl">
          <adverb/>
        </base>
      </analysis>
    </token>
```

Figure 2. Hebrew corpus sentence fragment with XML tags

13. The XML schema definition (XSD) for the 2000-sentence *HaAretz* can be found at http://cl.haifa.ac.il/~shlomo/corpora/schema/hebrew_corpus.

In addition to the morphologically analyzed and disambiguated newspaper corpus, there are *raw corpora* totaling approximately 10 million words of newspaper text. These corpora, considered raw because they require morphological analysis and disambiguation, will be used to support and expand the frame semantic analysis of the frame evoking elements in the 2000-sentence *HaAretz* Corpus. The raw corpora will be processed with lemmatization tools.

Given the high degree of morphological productivity in Hebrew and the ambiguity in the written language, described briefly above, lemmatization calls for sophisticated morphological analysis and disambiguation. Hebrew FrameNet will use the following lemmatization tools: HAMASH,[14] a morphological analysis system for Hebrew; and a disambiguation module, currently under development.[15] Based on finite-state linguistically motivated rules and an extensive lexicon, HAMASH has the broadest coverage and is the most accurate freely available system for Hebrew. The disambiguation module will select the most likely analysis for each word in context with an accuracy of approximately 90%.[16]

Built as part of the MultiWordNet system[17] and as a counterpart to Princeton's English WordNet[18], *Hebrew WordNet* currently includes approximately 2500 synsets. Like other WordNet resources (Italian, Spanish, Romanian) which are aligned with English WordNet, Hebrew WordNet is being developed by assigning Hebrew lexical data to English synsets having determined an appropriate mapping between the Hebrew and the English (Ordan and Wintner 2005). Although it has limited coverage, Hebrew WordNet can serve as an aid to word-list development and sense discrimination in cases of polysemy. To illustrate, currently the verb *amar* occurs in two synsets, one for verbs that would be defined in a `Request`

14. HAMASH stands for Haifa Morphological System for Analyzing Hebrew.
15. The disambiguation module is being developed by the computational linguistics group at the University of Haifa under the direction of Dr. Shuly Wintner.
16. See Bar-Haim et al. (2005) for a system that does POS tagging of Hebrew (which is almost identical to morphological disambiguation, although not exactly the same) with accuracy of 90.5%. Habash and Rambow (2005) report approximately 95% accuracy for morphological disambiguation in Arabic. It is reasonable to assume comparable accuracy for Hebrew disambiguation.
17. http://multiwordnet.itc.it/online.
18. http://wordnet.princeton.edu.

frame (e.g. *request*, *order*, *tell*) and one for verbs in a `Statement` frame (e.g. *say*, *state*, *tell*); each would correspond to a separate frame.[19]

Along with detailed information about the grammar of a word (part of speech, morphological pattern (*binyan/miškal*), inflected forms), *Rav-Milim* lists synonyms (as in a thesaurus) and collocations in which a word occurs, making it a particularly useful resource for the present purposes. For instance, the entry for the noun *roš* – 'head' displays over 180 everyday phrases, expressions, and conventionalized idioms. Internet access to such information will facilitate development of word lists as well as syntactic and semantic analyses.[20]

4. Infrastructure

This section describes existing FrameNet infrastructure and its use for the development of Hebrew FrameNet, along with information about needed tools and processes for the project. In addition, an example sentence from the newspaper corpus illustrating frame semantic annotation is provided, also showing how contemporary Hebrew instantiates two key Frame Semantics constructs, the *semantic frame* and the *frame element*.

4.1. FrameNet infrastructure

The original FrameNet has designed a database, developed a suite of tools for input to the database, and a set of reports for displaying the data in a variety of ways (Baker et al. 2003, Fillmore et al. 2003). These are available for research purposes, and will be used to develop Hebrew FrameNet.

FrameNet data is stored in a relational database, whose structure models the conceptual structure of the project, to the extent possible.[21] Although implemented in a single MySQL database, it is simplest to characterize it in terms of its two parts: the lexical database (or *top* part), rep-

19. However, given known differences between English FrameNet and WordNet (Fellbaum 1998), we do not anticipate that every synset in Hebrew WordNet will map directly to a frame in the database.
20. Rav-Milim is available via the Internet (http://www.ravmilim.co.il) for a nominal annual subscription fee.
21. Boas (2005) characterizes the two parts of the database as *conceptual* and *lexical* (or *language specific*), the former for the frames, FEs, and their relations, and the latter for the LUs and associated annotation sets.

resenting the frames, FEs, LUs, etc.; and the annotation database (or *bottom* part), holding the example sentences and their annotations, the latter consisting of sets of layers. The annotation layers include information about the FE, grammatical function, and phrase type for each tagged constituent in a given sentence (Baker et al. 2003). Currently, the database contains over 800 frames, over 10,000 lexical units, of which approximately 6,000 are fully annotated.

The FrameNet Desktop is a suite of GUI tools used as a front-end to the database for defining frames, FEs, and lexical units, and annotating illustrative example sentences (Fillmore et al. 2003). It is written in Java, integrating the frame creation functions and the annotation functions, the latter of which includes a convenient display of the annotation layers. The basic model of the software has three parts: client, server, and database, which helps prevent collisions, ensures the integrity of transactions, and allows multiple users to share a cache on the application server, reducing database calls. The client application is thin and easily portable, and the design is clean and modular, making new features relatively easy to add.

An extensive report system, accessible from within the FrameNet Desktop and via the Internet, displays frames, annotations, and lexical entries including detailed tables of valence patterns. The report system will be adapted for displaying the Hebrew data, and will be made available publicly via the Internet. The web-based version of the FrameNet report system also facilitates the viewing of data from off-site locations.

4.2. Infrastructure for Hebrew FrameNet

The development of Hebrew FrameNet requires (1) acquiring the FrameNet database and adapting FrameNet software for use with Hebrew texts, (2) developing corpus tools and algorithms for use with the Hebrew newspaper corpus, which also requires special processing, and (3) annotating the 2000-sentence corpus for use in the FrameNet Desktop.

4.2.1. Acquiring and adapting FrameNet's database and software

The source code for the complete FrameNet software suite is available for research and testing. The FrameNet database and software are platform independent, and will be installed on a computer dedicated to the research of the present study. FrameNet has produced a non-English database structure, including the frames and associated labels (i.e. the *top* part), but not the English vocabulary or annotated sentences (i.e. the contents of *bottom* part). This package, created as a starting point for the development of FrameNets in languages other than English, will be used for the present research, as done for Spanish FrameNet (Subirats and Petruck 2003, Subirats and Sato 2004) and Japanese FrameNet (Ohara et al. 2003, 2004). Hebrew FrameNet adopts this approach for both practical and theoretical reasons. On a practical level, using the existing FrameNet database structure is far more efficient than creating it anew, even despite anticipated adjustments (in both parts of the database) given differences between English and Hebrew. Since FrameNet implements the theoretical constructs of Frame Semantics, determining whether and how the machinery of FrameNet would transfer to languages other than English is best accomplished by comparing existing FrameNet frame structures with those needed for characterizing the lexicon of contemporary Hebrew.

Storing and processing a full lexicon, including all word forms (some 50 million) is in principle feasible, even with the high degree of morphological productivity and orthographic ambiguity in Hebrew (Wintner 2007), but doing so would not serve the present purposes. Instead, Hebrew FrameNet will develop a mechanism for accessing lexical data (i.e. relating word forms to lemmas) from an outside source. FrameNet has developed its own XML format for importing corpora; therefore, it will be necessary to convert the Hebrew newspaper corpus into a compatible format.

Creating the infrastructure for using the FrameNet Desktop for the analysis of Hebrew texts is essential for the annotation. In addition (as with Spanish FrameNet and Japanese FrameNet, each of which have dealt with these issues to varying degrees), it provides the opportunity to consider what existing FrameNet software can be used, albeit with needed modifications to accommodate language specific requirements, and what might be necessary to create anew given known structural and typological differences between English and Hebrew. Adapting the FrameNet Desktop for the analysis of Hebrew texts in the current research will also demonstrate the feasibility of using the software for a Semitic language.[22]

4.2.2. Developing corpus tools and algorithms

Searching the morphologically analyzed corpus is crucial for finding attestations of target LUs and determining the syntactic and collocational con-

22. In principle, this will be useful for other Semitic languages, (e.g. Arabic), for which there are still quite limited language resources for computational development and research, despite the increased interest around the world in Semitic languages.

texts in which a target word occurs. A tool will be developed that includes browsing and sorting functions so that relevant corpus sentences with a particular lemma (or word form) can be viewed in a variety of ways, such as by a preceding or following part of speech, lemma, word form, or collocate within a given distance of the lemma (or word form) under consideration. An extraction tool is needed to select corpus examples of the target word that exhibit the syntactic patterns appropriate to the word sense and to group sentences matching the specified patterns into subcorpora. The extracted subcorpoa will be processed to comply with FrameNet's XML so that they can be imported into the Desktop and annotated.

4.2.3. Corpus annotation and frame development

In contrast to the original FrameNet, the development of Hebrew Frame-Net begins with a relatively small corpus, hence Hebrew FrameNet will provide full text annotation of FEEs from the outset of the project. The annotation of all FEEs in the 2000-sentence corpus drives the frame development and frame semantic analyses for Hebrew, thereby exploiting the existing infrastructure of FrameNet and enhancing the developing infrastructure of Hebrew FrameNet. Also, a commitment to full text annotation of FEEs will necessitate defining frames that have not yet been defined in the FrameNet database.

As has been the case for FrameNet projects in other languages (Subirats and Petruck 2003, Ohara, et al., 2003, 2004), Hebrew FrameNet adopts existing FrameNet frames, adapting them as needed for Hebrew. Importantly, it is in the adaptation of existing FrameNet frames that the question of transferability of FrameNet apparatus to a language other than English is addressed. In particular, Hebrew FrameNet asks whether existing English FrameNet frame definitions, including FE definitions, coreness statuses, semantic types, and frame-to-frame relations, are appropriate for characterizing (what appears to be) an analogous LU in Hebrew. Crucially, the adaptation does not assume a one-to-one correspondence between existing FrameNet frames and those developed for Hebrew, or between English LUs and Hebrew LUs (See also Ohara et al. 2006). As such, Hebrew FrameNet investigates the level of linguistic description and computational representation of the lexicon of contemporary Hebrew and asks whether it can be characterized in the same terms as the lexicon of English. Thus, in this "bottom-up" manner, it considers the universality of the semantic frame.

The remainder of this (sub-)section gives the frame semantic annotation of an example sentence from the 2000-sentence corpus focusing on its three predicates, and then identifies the frames needed for full text annotation of all the FEEs in the sentence. The example sentence is given in (6), with target predicates in boldface.

(6) [esrot anašim $_{\text{THEME}}$] **magi'im** [mi-tailand $_{\text{SOURCE}}$] [le'israel $_{\text{GOAL}}$]
tens (of) people reach from-thailand to-israel

[kše-hem $_{\text{REGISTRANT}}$] **niršamim** [ke-mitnadvim $_{\text{CATEGORY}}$]
as/when-they register as-volunteers

ax le-ma'ase **mešamšim** [ovdim sxirim zolim $_{\text{PURPOSE}}$]
but in-fact they function workers hired cheap

'Tens of people arrive in Israel from Thailand, registering as volunteers, but in fact they function as cheap hired workers.'

The verb *mag'im* (3rd person masculine plural present participle) – 'reach' evokes an `Arriving` frame, characterizing a situation in which a THEME moves in the direction of a GOAL, the latter either expressed explicitly or implied by the verb. The NP *esrot anašim* fills the role of THEME, and functions as the External argument; the GOAL is expressed by the PP *le-israel*; the example sentence also includes an optional SOURCE expression in the PP *mi-tailand*. *niršamim* – 'register' evokes a `Registration` frame, describing a scene in which a REGISTRANT puts an ENTITY on record at an INSTITUTION as belonging to a CATEGORY or as LICENSED for a specific PURPOSE or STATE. *kše-hem* expresses the REGISTRANT and functions as the External argument; the phrase *ke-mitnadvim* instantiates the FE CATEGORY. Finally, *mešamšim* evokes the `Function_as` frame, in which an ENTITY serves a FUNCTION or PURPOSE, the former for activities and the latter for states of affairs. Although not present in the maximal clause of the verb *mešamšim*, it is clear what fills the ENTITY role (*hem* in the previous clause), which is also indicated by the third-person masculine plural ending *-im* on the verb; the Object NP *sxirim zolim* expresses the PURPOSE.[23]

As indicated above, full text annotation will undoubtedly necessitate defining frames that do not (yet) exist in the FrameNet database. To illustrate, while FrameNet already defined an `Arriving` frame, which proved

23. The Object NP as it occurs in the example without *ke-* – 'as' is more typical of the spoken language than the written; this may suggest a change under way in written Hebrew.

suitable for the verb *higia*[24] – 'reach, arrive' (and related words), it had not yet defined either a Registration frame or a Function_as frame. Thus, in principle, this work will also provide a means of increasing coverage in FrameNet, for example, by suggesting frames to be defined and LUs to be considered for inclusion in them. Furthermore, in addition to the three predicates discussed briefly here, there are several other FEEs in example (6) above, each of which serves as the starting point for elucidating and validating the frame structure for the evoked frames (*anašim* – 'people' evokes a People frame; *ovdim* – 'workers' evokes a Being_employed frame, *sxirim* – 'hired' evokes a Hiring frame; and *zolim* – 'cheap' evokes an Expensiveness frame), following which they would be the focus of analysis and annotated with appropriate FE labels.

The following section examines several additional Arriving verbs in the context of a broader description of the expression of motion events in typologically distinct languages, and considers the larger structure of the FrameNet hierarchy of frames in which Arriving figures, also attending to frame-to-frame relations and semantic types.

5. Motion events

The description of motion events has proven to be a fruitful area for cross-linguistic research, hence especially relevant for the present work which seeks to determine cross-linguistic compatibility of Frame Semantics machinery (Subirats and Petruck 2003, Subirats and Sato 2004, Ohara et al. 2003, 2004). Interested in characterizing lexicalization patterns across languages, Talmy (1985, 1991, 2000) provided a typology of motion events, specifically concerning the expression of the path of movement of a "figure" with respect to a "ground". A basic distinction is drawn between what has come to be called verb-framed languages where path is expressed by the main verb in a clause (as in Hebrew, *nixnas* – 'enter' and *yaca* – 'exit'), and satellite-framed languages where path is expressed by an element of the clause that is associated with the verb (go *in*, go *out*). Moreover, Talmy's work inspired further study of motion events particularly aimed at documenting the ways that languages encode different aspects of motion, including those subsumed under the category of manner

24. While not depicted in Figure 3, the *precedes* relation holds between Departing and Arriving. Space limitations preclude depicting the *using* relation for these frames.

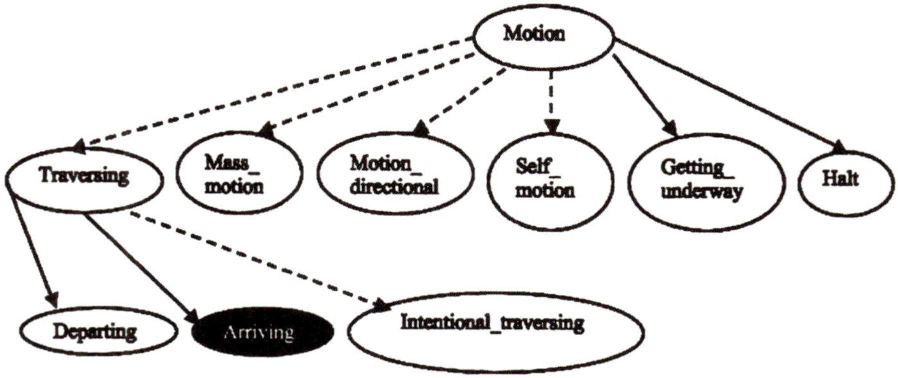

Figure 3. `Arriving` in the FrameNet Hierarchy

(covering meaning components such as force, rate, and attitude), and refining the typology (Slobin 2004a, Slobin 2004b, Ohara 2002).

The portion of the FrameNet hierarchy that includes `Arriving`, the frame evoked by *magi'im* – 'they (masc.) reach' (example (6) above), is shown in Figure 3 (where a dashed line indicates inheritance and a solid line represents subframes).[25] Note that `Arriving` is a subframe of `Traversing`, which inherits from `Motion`; currently, none of these frames specifies the semantic type "sentient" for THEME, the FE that would typically function as the External argument in `Arriving`. In addition, the hierarchy displayed in Figure 3 only represents actual motion, not fictive motion or metaphorical motion. The frame structures and frame-to-frame relations that are needed to characterize motion more generally in contemporary Hebrew may not parallel that which is provided for English.

Other frame semantic concepts might be needed: the coreness statuses of the FEs in the frames that capture the facts for Hebrew may differ from that of English; and there may be FE-to-FE relations (requires, excludes) specified. Such information is fundamental to addressing the question about the level of linguistic description at which Hebrew can be characterized in the same terms as English has been characterized in FrameNet.

Hebrew `Arriving` verbs serve as a starting point for a preliminary description of how motion events are expressed in the language, and how

25. Conventionally, Hebrew verbs are cited in the third person masculine singular of the past tense; *magi'im* (in the example sentence) is a third person masculine plural present participle.

they will be treated in Hebrew FrameNet. In addition to *higia* – 'arrive' (in (6), the above corpus example), the following verbs can be characterized in terms of the `Arriving` frame: *ba* – 'come', *nixnas* – 'enter', *xazar* – 'return', *šav*– 'return' (formal register); and *biker* – 'visit'.[26] As with the originally defined frame, the Hebrew verbs profile the GOAL; corpus examples are given in (7)–(9).

(7) [ha-mehagrim THEME] **ba'u** [me-'anglia SOURCE]
the-emigres came from-England

ve-hitnaxalu ba-cafon
and-settled in-the-north

'The emigres came/arrived from England and settled in the north.'

(8) kše-**nixnas** [šaron THEME] [le-misrad ha-šikun GOAL]...
when-entered Sharon to-office (of) the-housing...

'When Sharon entered the housing office...'

(9) [silber THEME] **xazar** ha-šavua [la-'universit GOAL]
silber returned this-week to-the-university

'Silber returned to the university this week.'

In (7), the deictic verb *ba* – 'come' anchors the motion event in the same location as the speech event. Thus, although not mentioned explicitly, as in (8) and (9), the sentence is understood as expressing motion towards a null-instantiated GOAL. While perhaps attributable to the language of newspaper reports, and hence an issue for further study, it is noteworthy that in each of these sentences the main verb expresses what Talmy calls *Path* (i.e. there are no other elements associated with the verb, such as a verb particle or adverb, that elaborate information about the Path of motion), thus illustrating the characteristic feature of Hebrew as a verb-framed language.[27] In contrast to English which also allows other elements associated with a verb to express Path information (e.g. *go in*/*enter*, *go back*/*return*), Hebrew does not offer such an alternative.

The example sentences that illustrate Hebrew verbs of `Arriving` here include an External THEME that is also an agent. However, the verb *higia* does not require an agentive THEME, as shown in example (10).

---

26. While related event nouns are not discussed here, they also evoke the `Arriving` frame, and would be included.
27. Talmy uses *path* to refer to the whole extent of the motion.

(10) be-ša'a 1500 **higia** [ha-'aron $_{\text{THEME}}$] [la-makom $_{\text{GOAL}}$]
at-hour 1500 reached the-coffin to-the-place
'At 3:00 PM, [the coffin $_{\text{THEME}}$] **reached** [the place $_{\text{GOAL}}$].'
? 'At 3:00 PM, the coffin **arrived** at the place.'

Note that Hebrew *higia* behaves somewhat differently than both English *reach* and *arrive*. First, with *reach* the GOAL is an Object NP, while in Hebrew the GOAL is a PP. Next, English *arrive* with a non-agentive theme is awkward (or impossible) in this sense, while *higia* allows both an agentive and a non-agentive THEME, suggesting that in Hebrew agency remains unspecified.[28] Alternatively, these data may suggest the existence of two different LUs in Hebrew, each in its own uniquely defined frame, and each including different semantic types for the FE that would typically function as the External argument. The daily work of Hebrew FrameNet provides for the empirical investigation of corpus data through which the matter of underspecifcation vs. polysemy can be addressed and the question of frame definition and frame membership be resolved. More generally, the annotation of corpus examples with contemporary Hebrew verbs of `Arriving`, as illustrated here, records information about semantic and syntactic combinatorial possibilities for each LU in the frame. Automatic summaries of the findings are displayed in table format and constitute the valence description of the LU.

Based on frame-semantic analyses of Hebrew corpus data, the development of Hebrew FrameNet, as described in the present work, builds upon existing tools and resources as well as an established methodology to investigate the transferability of FrameNet machinery to a Semitic language. The results will provide a new resource that includes subtle semantic information about the Hebrew lexicon, and new tools for the computational processing of Hebrew texts. The current research, along with that already under way for Spanish FrameNet (Subirats-Rüggeberg and Petruck 2003, Subirats-Rüggeberg and Sato 2004) and Japanese FrameNet (Ohara et al. 2003, 2004), will contribute to an understanding of the representation of conceptual structure in a computational lexical resource.[29]

---

28. However, a non-agentive THEME is allowed with *arrive* in the "delivery" context: *The books arrived at the office in the morning mail.*
29. Like Lönneker-Rodman (2007), an informative review of the theoretical and technical complexities of multilingual FrameNet development and practical consequences thereof, here the focus is on the *semantic frame* (with all that it entails) as the conceptual structure represented in a computational lexical resource.

References

Baker, Collin F., Charles J. Fillmore, and Beau Cronin
2003 The structure of the FrameNet database. *International Journal of Lexicography* 16.3: 251–280.

Bar-Haim, Roy, Khalil Sima'an, and Yoad Winter
2005 Choosing an optimal architecture for segmentation and POS-tagging of Modern Hebrew. In: Karim Darwish, Mona Diab and Nizar Habash (eds.), *Proceedings of ACL Workshop on Computational Approaches to Semitic Languages*, 39–46. Ann Arbor: Association for Computational Linguistics.

Boas, Hans C.
2005 Semantic frames as interlingual representations for multilingual lexical databases. *International Journal of Lexicography* 18.4: 445–478.

Choueka, Yaacov
1990 MLIM – a system for full, exact on-line grammatical analysis of Modern Hebrew. In *Proceedings of the Annual Conference on Computers in Education* 63, Yehuda Eizenberg (ed.), Tel Aviv.

Choueka, Yaacov
1993 Response to "Computerized analysis of Hebrew words". *Hebrew Linguistics* 37: 87.

Choueka, Yaacov
1997 *Rav-Milim: the complete dictionary of contemporary Hebrew*, Steimatzky, C.E.T. and Miskal, Tel-Aviv, 6 Vols. (Online interactive version, including updates at http://www.ravmilim.co.il)

Fellbaum, Christiane (ed.)
1998 *WordNet: An Electronic Lexical Database*. Cambridge: MIT Press.

Fillmore, Charles J.
1975 An alternative to checklist theories of meaning. In *Proceedings of the Annual Meeting of the Berkeley Linguistics Society*, 123–131. Berkeley: Berkeley Linguistics Society.

Fillmore, Charles J.
1977 Scenes-and-frames semantics. In: Antonio Zampolli (ed.), *Linguistic Structures Processing* (Fundamental Studies in Computer Science, No. 59), 55–88. Amsterdam: North Holland Publishing.

Fillmore, Charles J.
1978 On the organization of semantic information in the lexicon. In: Donka Frakas et al. (eds.), *Papers from the Parasession on the Lexicon*, 148–173. Chicago: Chicago Linguistic Society.

Fillmore, Charles J.
1982 Frame Semantics. In: Linguistic Society of Korea (ed.), *Linguistics in the Morning Calm*, 111–137. Seoul: Hanshin Publishing Co.

Fillmore, Charles J.
1985 Frames and the semantics of understanding. *Quderni di Semantica* 6.2: 222–254.

Fillmore, Charles J. and B.T.S. Atkins
1992 Towards a frame-based organization of the lexicon: The semantics of RISK and its neighbors. In: A. Lehrer and E. Kittay (eds.), *Frames, Fields, and Contrast: New Essays in Semantics and Lexical Organization*, 75–102. Hillsdale: Lawrence Erlbaum Associates.

Habash, Nizar and Owen Rambow
2005 Arabic Tokenization, Part-of-Speech Tagging and Morphological Disambiguation in One Fell Swoop. In: *Proceedings of the 43rd Annual Meeting of the Association for Computational Linguistics*, 573–580. Ann Arbor: Association for Computational Linguistics.

Itai, Alon and Erel Segal
2003 A Corpus based morphological analyzer for unvocalized Modern Hebrew. In: *Proceedings of the MT Summit IX Workshop on Machine Translation for Semitic Languages*. New Orleans.

Lambrecht, Knud
1984 Formulaicity, frame semantics, and pragmatics in German binomial expressions. *Language* 60.4: 753–796.

Lönneker-Rodman, Birte
2007 *Multiliguality and FrameNet*. Technical Report TR-07-001, Berkeley: International Computer Science Institute.

Ohara, Kyoko Hirose
2002 Linguistic encodings of motion events in Japanese and English: A preliminary look. *The Hiyoshi Review of English Studies* 41: 122–153.

Ohara, Kyoko, Seiko Fujii, Shun Ishizaki, Toshio Ohori, Hiroaki Sato, and Ryoko Suzuki
2003 The Japanese FrameNet Project: a preliminary report. In: *Proceedings of the Pacific Association for Computational Linguistics*, 249–254. Halifax: Pacific Association for Computational Linguistics.

Ohara, Kyoko, Seiko Fujii, Shun Ishizaki, Toshio Ohori, Hiroaki Sato, and Ryoko Suzuki
2004 The Japanese FrameNet Project: an introduction. In: Charles J. Fillmore, Manfred Pinkal, Collin F. Baker, and Katrin Erk (eds.), *Proceedings of the Fourth International Conference on Language Resources and Evaluation Post-conference Workshop on Building Lexical Resources from Semantically Annotated Corpora*, 9–12. Paris: LREC.

Ohara, Kyoko Hirose, Seiko Fuji, Toshio Ohori, Ryoko Suzuki, Hiroaki Saito, and Shun Ishikazi
2006 *Frame-based contrastive lexical semantics and Japanese FrameNet: The case of RISK and 'kakeru'*. Paper presented at the Fourth International Conference on Construction Grammar, Tokyo.

Ordan, Noam and Shuly Wintner
2005 Representing natural gender in multi-lingual lexical databases. *International Journal of Lexicography* 18.3: 357–370.

Östman, Jan-Ola
2000 Postcard discourse: placing the linguistic periphery at the center. *Sphinx 1999–2000*: 7–26.

Petruck, Miriam R. L.
1995 Frame semantics and the lexicon: nouns and verbs in the body frame. In: M. Shibatani and S. Thompson (eds.), *Essays in Semantics and Pragmatics*, 279–296. Amsterdam: John Benjamins.

Petruck, Miriam R. L.
1996 Frame Semantics. In: Jef Verschueren, Jan-Ola Östman, Jan Blommaert, and Chris Bulcaen (eds.), *Handbook of Pragmatics*, 1–11. Philadelphia: John Benjamins.

Ruppenhofer, Josef, Michael Ellsworth, Miriam R. L. Petruck, Christopher R. Johnson, and Jan Scheffczyk
2006 *FrameNet II: Extended Theory and Practice*. Web Publication (http://framenet.icsi.berkeley.edu/book/book.html).

Slobin, Dan I.
1996 Two ways to travel: Verbs of motion in English and Spanish. In: M. Shibatani and S. Thompson (eds.), *Grammatical Constructions: Their Form and Meaning*, 195–220. Oxford: Clarendon Press.

Slobin, Dan I.
2004a Relating narrative events in translation. In: Dorit Ravid and Hava B. Shyldkrot (eds.), *Perspectives on Language and Language Development: Essays in Honor of Ruth Berman*. Dordrecht: Kluwer.

Slobin, Dan I.
2004b The many ways to search for a frog: Linguistic typology and the expression of motion events. In: S. Strömqvist and L. Verhoeven (eds.), *Relating Events in Narrative: Typological and Contextual Perspectives*, 219–257. Mahwah: Lawrence Erlbaum.

Subirats-Rüggeberg, Carlos and Miriam R. L. Petruck
2003 Surprise: Spanish FrameNet! In: *Proceedings of Workshop on Frame Semantics*, International Congress of Linguists. Prague, Czech Republic. CD-Rom Publication.

Subirats-Rüggeberg, Carlos and Hiroaki Sato
2004 Spanish FrameNet and FrameSQL. In: Charles J. Fillmore, Manfred Pinkal, Collin F. Baker, and Katrin Erk (eds.), *Proceedings of the Fourth International Conference on Language Resources and Evaluation Post-conference Workshop on Building Lexical Resources from Semantically Annotated Corpora*, 13–16. Paris: LREC.

Talmy, Leonard
1985 Lexicalization patterns: semantic structure in lexical forms. In: T. Shopen (ed.), *Language Typology and Syntactic Description*, Volume 3: 57–149. Cambridge: Cambridge University Press.

Talmy, Leonard
1991 Path to realization: A typology of event conflation. In: *Proceedings of the Annual Meeting of the Berkeley Linguistics Society*, 480–519. Berkeley: Berkeley Linguistics Society.

Talmy, Leonard
2000 *Toward a Cognitive Semantics*. Cambridge: MIT Press.

Wintner, Shuly
2004 Hebrew computational linguistics: Past and future. *Artificial Intelligence Review* 21.2: 113–138.

Wintner, Shuly
2007 Finite-state technology as a programming environment. In: Alexander Gelbukh (ed.), *Computational Linguistics and Intelligent Text Processing*, 97–106. Berlin: Springer.

Wintner, Shuly and Shlomo Yona
2003 Resources for Processing Hebrew. In: *Proceedings of the MT Summit IX Workshop on Machine Translation for Semitic Languages*. New Orleans.

Yona, Shlomo and Shuly Wintner
2005 A Finite-state morphological grammar of Hebrew. In: Darwish, Karim, Mona Diab and Nizar Habash (eds.), *Proceedings of ACL Workshop on Computational Approaches to Semitic Languages*, 9–16. Ann Arbor.

Part III. Methods for automatically creating new FrameNets

8. Using FrameNet for the semantic analysis of German: Annotation, representation, and automation

Aljoscha Burchardt, Katrin Erk, Anette Frank, Andrea Kowalski, Sebastian Padó, and Manfred Pinkal

1. Introduction

This chapter reports on the Saarbrücken Lexical Semantics Annotation and Analysis (SALSA) project, whose main goals are (1) the exhaustive semantic annotation of a large German corpus resource with FrameNet frames and frame elements[1] (Fillmore et al. 2003), including the generation of a frame-based lexicon from the annotated data, and (2) the induction of data-driven models for automatic frame semantic analysis as well as their application in practical Natural Language Processing (NLP) tasks.

A fundamental assumption of this project, which began in the summer of 2002, is that English FrameNet frames can be re-used for the semantic analysis of German. This assumption rests on the nature of frames as coarse-grained semantic classes which refer to "prototypical situations" (Fillmore 1985). To the extent that these situations agree across languages, frames should be applicable cross-linguistically (see also Boas 2005). While this is clearly a very attractive assumption, it must be empirically validated.

Unlike ontologies, FrameNet's structuring principles do not rely exclusively on conceptual considerations, but are linguistically grounded. A sense of a lemma can evoke a frame, and thus form a lexical unit (LU) for this frame, if this sense is syntactically able to realize the core frame

1. The FrameNet concept of "frame element" (FE) corresponds to the more general concept of "semantic role".

elements (FEs) "that instantiate a conceptually necessary component of a frame" (Ruppenhofer et al. 2006: 26). Consequently, frames may not be applicable to other languages if the subcategorization properties of lemmas in this language differ significantly from their English translations.

Among the questions that SALSA examined is the extent to which cases of non-parallelism at the level of frames are correlated with typological differences across languages, in particular with respect to (syntactic) valency, and how to account for cross-linguistic divergences. In our work, we have found that the vast majority of frames can in fact be applied directly to the analysis of German – a language that is typologically close to English. The types of problems we encountered during our cross-linguistic work stem primarily from (1) general constructions in German that do not exist in English (such as particular uses of datives), and (2) lexicalization differences in particular semantic domains (such as movement).

The remainder of the paper is structured as follows. In Section 2, we describe the SALSA corpus annotation workflow, present our annotation scheme and process, and discuss various challenges that follow from particular choices of our approach, including (1) problems of coverage, (2) handling of special phenomena encountered in full text annotation (e.g., multiword expressions and metaphors), and (3) problems of vagueness and meaning distinctions. Section 3 discusses cross-lingual aspects of frame semantic annotation. We summarize our experience with frame semantic annotation for German on the basis of English FrameNet frames, as well as commonalities with and differences from related projects for other languages. The discussion also includes a description of our efforts in automated cross-lingual frame semantic resource creation. The final sections of the paper are devoted to the usage of the annotated corpus to induce automated analysis tools for NLP applications. In Section 4, we present SHALMANESER, a general shallow semantic parsing architecture for English and German. In Section 5, we discuss the SALSA RTE system, which utilizes frame semantic resources to investigate the usefulness of frame-semantic information for the NLP task of recognizing textual entailment (Dagan et al. 2005).

2. SALSA: Semantic Annotation and Lexicon Building for German

The main objective of the SALSA project is the creation of lexical semantic resources for German within the framework of Frame Semantics (Fillmore 1985). Similar to PropBank (Palmer et al. 2005), SALSA extends an existing German treebank, the TIGER treebank (Brants et al. 2002), with a layer of lexical semantic annotations, focusing on verbal predicates.

A first corpus was released in summer 2007 and consists of about 500 German verbal predicates of all frequency bands plus some deverbal nouns, totaling about 20,000 annotated instances.

2.1. Corpus-driven resource creation

The SALSA project differs from FrameNet in that it is primarily concerned with providing an exhaustive annotation of the entire corpus as a basis for obtaining large-scale NLP resources with as complete coverage as feasible. Therefore, SALSA analyzes the entire TIGER corpus lemma by lemma, whereas FrameNet proceeds frame by frame, extracting relevant examples from different sections of the British National Corpus. Since we regard ourselves more as users of the existing FrameNet resource than as creators of a comparable German FrameNet, we are released from the requirement of systematically describing all possible frames and their realization patterns, as FrameNet aspires to. At the same time, our exhaustive annotation policy forces us to analyze all instances of a lemma in the corpus, which often requires the creation of proto-frames on the fly, as described in Section 2.3. Also, exhaustive annotation requires addressing frequently occurring phenomena with limited compositionality (such as idioms or support verb constructions), as well as cases of ambiguity and vagueness (see Section 2.4). In contrast, FrameNet primarily analyzes predicates with a clear syntax-semantics mapping that illustrate lexicographically relevant "core" meanings. Despite these differences, the two methods are converging in practice in that FrameNet is starting to pursue corpus-driven full-text annotation, while SALSA is extracting a general lexicon resource from corpus annotations and spends considerable efforts on proto-framing.

2.2. Annotation scheme and annotation practice

To annotate, we employ SALTO, a graphical annotation tool designed and implemented for SALSA (Burchardt et al. 2006a), which is shown in Figure 1. Freely available for research purposes (see Section 7), SALTO supports annotation in a simple drag-and-drop fashion and can also be used more generally for the graphical annotation of treebanks with a wide range of relational information. SALTO uses SALSA/TIGER XML, a general XML format for input and output (see Section 4 for details), and additionally supports corpus management and quality control.

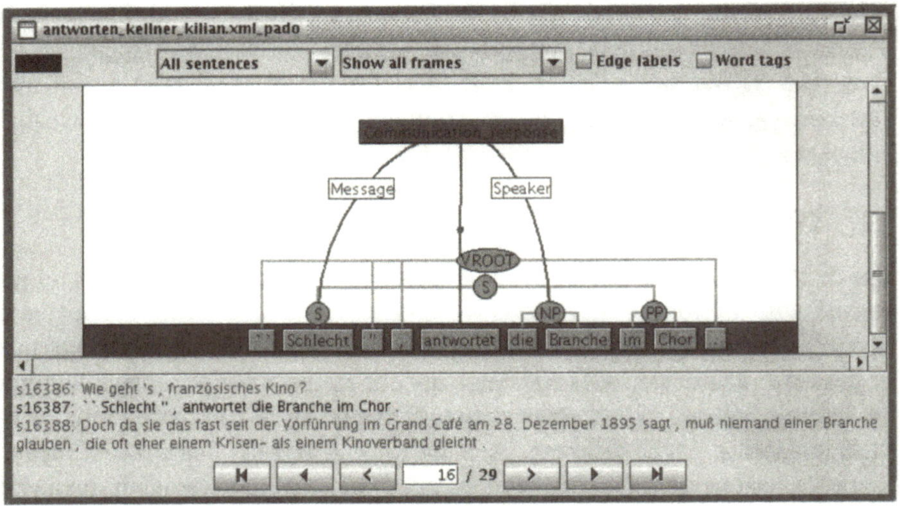

Figure 1. Annotation example: *"Schlecht", antwortet die Branche im Chor.* ("Badly", the industry sector answers in unison.)

We annotate frame-semantic information on top of the syntactic structure of the TIGER corpus, with a single flat tree for each frame: The root node is labeled with the name of a frame. The edges of the syntactic constituents are labeled with the names of FEs defined for the frame. Figure 1 shows a simple annotation instance: the verb *antwortet* ('answers') evokes the frame `Communication_response`. The NP subject *die Branche* ('the industry sector') is annotated with the FE SPEAKER and *schlecht* ('badly'), under a sentence (S) node, with the FE MESSAGE. In contrast to FrameNet, we annotate only *core* FEs (see Section 1). Moreover, we assign FEs to existing constituents where possible.

Like PropBank, SALSA follows a corpus-based approach, aiming at full-text corpus annotation by covering all instances of a particular lemma in the corpus. To make this procedure feasible for annotators, annotation proceeds lemma by lemma: for each lemma in the running text of the TIGER corpus, we extract all corpus sentences in which it occurs. The resulting subcorpora are given to pairs of annotators for parallel and independent annotation, together with a list of candidate frames that seem appropriate. The annotators consult the frame definitions in FrameNet, and may also choose additional frames from FrameNet for novel uses they encounter in a given subcorpus. As a result of our corpus-based full-text annotation practice, we face two major challenges: one concerns coverage, the other one the treatment of special linguistic phenomena.

2.3. Coverage and proto-frames

A major problem for exhaustive annotation is that FrameNet is still under development, and thus does not yet cover all senses of the lemmas that we annotate. Another, more subtle problem, are frequent usages whose meanings are clear in context, but difficult to relate to lexicographical prototypes.

To assess FrameNet coverage for a given lemma and to spot missing senses, we thus extract a small sample of sentences containing instances of this lemma in the TIGER corpus prior to annotation. For each instance, we check whether there is a FrameNet frame that provides an appropriate analysis. The decision is based on the two criteria detailed in Ellsworth et al. (2004: 18–19): (1) Does the meaning of the instance meet the frame definition? (2) Can all important semantic arguments of the instance be described in terms of the FEs? In unclear cases, we also check annotated FrameNet example sentences for similar usages to get a better understanding for the full range of a frame.

This process results in a list of instances for the current lemma which cannot be described in terms of existing frames. We group these into coarse-grained "sense groups" and construct a proto-frame for each group. The resulting proto-frames are lemma-specific, i.e., contain only a single lexical unit. Table 1 shows a proto-frame constructed for the "to be counted (among a group)" sense of *rechnen* ('to count as').

Table 1 illustrates that the SALSA proto-frames are similar to FrameNet frames – they have a textual definition, a set of FEs with

Table 1. Example of a proto-frame for one sense of *rechnen (zu)* ('count (as)')

Frame: `Rechnen.Unknown3`		
An ITEM is construed as an example or member of a specific CATEGORY. In contrast to CATEGORISATION, no COGNIZER is involved. In contrast to MEMBERSHIP, the CATEGORY does not have to be a social organisation.		
FEs	ITEM	**Die Philippinen und Chile** rechnen zu den armen Ländern der Region.
	CATEGORY	Die Philippinen und Chile rechnen **zu den armen Ländern der Region**.

FrameNet-style names, and annotated example sentences. They follow a simple naming convention, e.g., `Rechnen.Unknown3`, which marks the third proto-frame constructed for the lemma *rechnen*. The proto-frames are lemma-specific and not intended as final descriptions for the senses. They form a sense inventory for German that finds immediate application in our annotation process, allowing us to semantically annotate all corpus instances in the running text, even if not at the same level of generalization as provided by FrameNet frames.

We envisage that our proto-frames can form the input to a lexicographic generalization process for the further development of FrameNet. To support this integration, our proto-frames are defined at roughly the same level of granularity as FrameNet frames. In addition, we list frame-to-frame relations for proto-frames to indicate their relationship to both FrameNet frames and other proto-frames. For example, for `Rechnen.Unknown3` we record that it is identical to a proto-frame for *zählen* ('to count among'). In the example sentence in Table 1, *rechnen* can thus be paraphrased by *zählen*.

To illustrate the quantitative relation between the coverage of FrameNet and of our proto-frames, we computed preliminary statistics on a dataset of 12,437 annotation instances and found that the average number of frames per lemma was 2.33, composed of 1.6 FrameNet frames and 0.73 SALSA proto-frames. In other words, less than one third of the lemma senses in our corpus was not covered by FrameNet. To gauge the degree of semantic granularity of our proto-frames, we compared the average number of lexical units (i.e., frames) of our lemmas to the average number of synsets (i.e., senses) for verbs in GermaNet. We found that our annotation was more fine-grained (2.33 frames per lemma) than the 2.2 synsets per verb in GermaNet (Hamp and Feldweg 1997). This is at least partly due to our treatment of idioms and metaphoric readings as additional senses of lemmas (see Burchardt et al. 2006b for more details).

2.4. Special phenomena

In standard annotation cases, there is a strong one-to-one mapping between syntactic and semantic structure: a frame is evoked by a single word, and its FEs link to syntactic (i.e., subcategorized) arguments of the word. An example is shown in Figure 1 above. However, due to our exhaustive annotation policy, we frequently encounter cases of limited

Table 2. Phenomena with limited compositionality (LC)

	246 Lemmas		*nehmen*	
	Number	%	Number	%
Compositional	**10,820**	**87.0**	**42**	**17.4**
Metaphor	707	5.7	38	15.8
Support	597	4.8	132	45.8
Idiom	313	2.5	29	12.0
LC	**1,617**	**13.0**	**199**	**82.6**
Total	**12,437**	**100.0**	**241**	**100.0**

compositionality ("LC-phenomena") in which frame choice, argument choice, or both, diverge from such a straightforward mapping between syntax and semantics. Three prominent cases of LC-phenomena which we encounter in our annotation are support verb constructions, idioms, and metaphors. As Table 2 illustrates, they occur quite frequently, constituting almost one seventh of the 12,000-instance corpus sample mentioned above. For high-frequency (and typically highly polysemous) verbs such as *nehmen* ('to take'), they even make up the majority of instances. We now discuss our criteria for distinguishing the three LC-phenomena as well as our annotation schemes for each of them.

2.4.1. Support verb constructions

A support verb construction (SVC) is a combination of a verb with a "bleached" or abstract meaning (e.g. causation or perspectivization) with a predicative noun, which is typically its object. The noun constitutes the semantic head of the phrase and is usually treated as the frame-evoking element. An example is *Abschied nehmen* ('to take leave'), where *Abschied* evokes the `Departure` frame. Often, the SVC can be paraphrased with a morphologically related verb (e.g., *sich verabschieden* ('to say good-bye')). Currently, SALSA annotates verbal parts of SVCs with a pseudo frame `Support`, whose only FE SUPPORTED points to the supported noun phrase. This annotation makes SVCs retrievable and thus available for a subsequent more elaborate analysis of the syntax-semantics interaction between the verbs and nouns involved.

2.4.2. Idioms

We identify idioms by three criteria. They are multi-word expressions that are for the most part fixed, and which have to be understood as a whole while their figurative meaning is not recoverable synchronically from their literal meanings. An example is *(etwas) in Kauf nehmen* (literally 'to take (something) into purchase'), which means *to put up with (something)*. Figure 2 shows an instance of this idiom, *Die Gläubiger nehmen Nachteile in Kauf* ('the creditors put up with disadvantages'). As can be seen, we annotate the idiom as a whole as the frame-evoking element, which here evokes the frame `Agree_or_refuse_to_act`. The semantic arguments of the idiom are annotated as normal FEs – *die Gläubiger (the creditors)* fill the role SPEAKER, *Nachteile (disadvantages)* fill the role PROPOSED_ACTION.

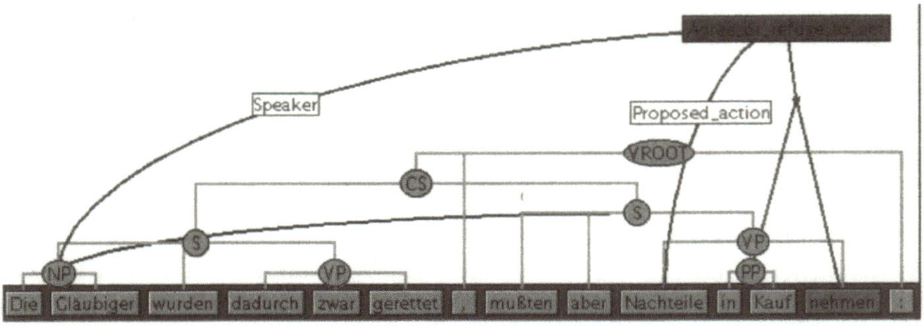

Figure 2. Multi-word target for idiom *in Kauf nehmen* ('to put up with s.th.')

2.4.3. Metaphors

Metaphors are distinguished from idioms through the existence of a figurative reading which is recoverable from their literal meaning. Following Lakoff's ideas on metaphorical transfer involving source and target domains (Lakoff and Johnson 1980), we annotate metaphorical expressions with two frames – a source frame representing the literal meaning, and a target frame representing the figurative meaning.

As an example, consider the metaphor *unter die Lupe nehmen* ('to put (literally: take) under a magnifying glass'). The source analysis is shown in Figure 3, where the verb *nehmen* ('take') is annotated as a frame-evok-

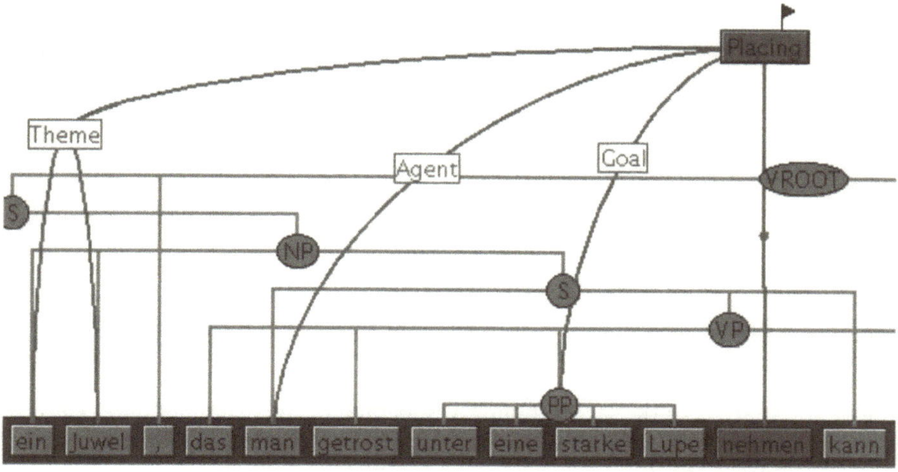

Figure 3. Analysis of the source (literal) reading of the metaphor *unter eine Lupe nehmen* (lit.: 'to take under a magnifying glass'). The frame `Placing` is introduced by the verb only

ing element, which introduces the frame `Placing`.[2] All arguments of *nehmen* are analyzed as ordinary FEs of `Placing`: *ein Juwel* ('a jewel') is the THEME that is taken, *man* ('one') is the AGENT who does the taking, and *unter die Lupe* ('under a magnifying glass') is the GOAL, the eventual position of the THEME. The corresponding target reading is shown in Figure 4. Here, the frame `Scrutiny` is introduced by the fixed part of the metaphor, *unter die Lupe nehmen*.

We often found target (figurative) meanings difficult to describe in terms of (existing) FrameNet frames. In order to maintain our rate of annotation, we chose to restrict the annotation of difficult cases to source readings. During a later phase, these samples will then be retrieved for a more comprehensive analysis.

The double annotation using a source and a target frame facilitates modeling the construction of this metaphor as a transfer from a (concrete)

2. The most salient sense of the German verb *nehmen* is best analyzed with the frame `Taking`. However, *nehmen* can also be used with a directional argument expressing a GOAL, as in the example at hand. These cases are better analyzed using the frame `Placing`.

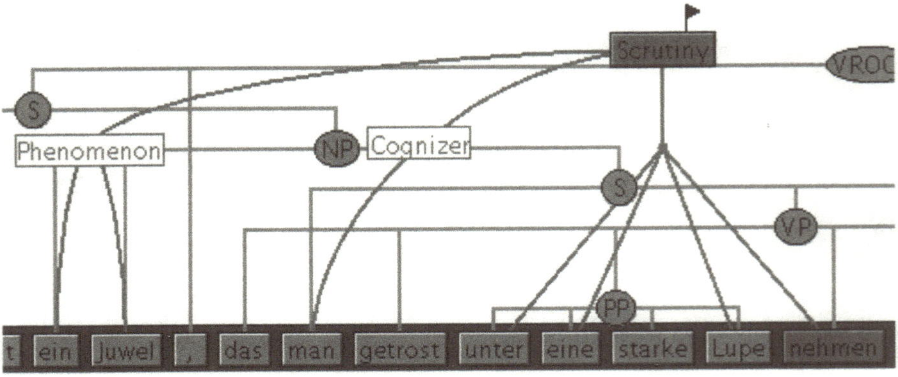

Figure 4. Analysis of the target (figurative) reading of the metaphor *unter eine Lupe nehmen* (lit.: 'to take under a magnifying glass'). The frame `Scrutiny` is introduced by the complete metaphor.

putting event to a (more abstract) investigation event. This illustrates that source and target frames describe complementary properties of metaphors: The source frame models the syntactic realization patterns of the arguments of the main predicate, while the target frame captures the figurative meaning.

Source/target frame pairs can be used to study *argument transfer* from source to target predicates. In simple cases, the transfer establishes a direct correspondence between source and target frames, including all arguments. In the example *Das Postfach explodiert* ('The mailbox explodes'), the source frame `Change_of_phase` with its role UNDERGOER directly maps onto the target frame `Expansion` with the role ITEM. As a more complex case, consider *unter eine **starke** Lupe nehmen* ('to put under a **strong** magnifying glass'). The corresponding transfer scheme in Figure 5 exemplifies a case of *argument incorporation*: the FE GOAL of the `Placing` frame is absorbed by the frame-evoking element of the SCRUTINY frame; in addition, the modifier *starke* ('strong'), which does not constitute a FE on the source side, constitutes the FE DEGREE of the target frame.

It is important to keep in mind that such transfer schemes do not answer the question about which factors trigger the metaphorical transfer for a specific utterance. However, they can model the interpretation process underlying metaphors to a certain degree. This, in turn, provides a description of the relation between source and target frames for specific metaphors, which facilitates expressing generalizations over patterns of FE shifts.

$$
\begin{bmatrix}
\text{Target:} & \textit{nehmen} \\
\text{Frame:} & \text{PLACING} \\
\text{Roles:} & \begin{pmatrix} \text{AGENT:} & \boxed{1}\ \text{man} \\ \text{THEME:} & \boxed{2}\ \text{ein Juwel} \\ \text{GOAL:} & \boxed{3}\ (\boxed{4}\ \text{starke})\ \text{Lupe} \end{pmatrix}
\end{bmatrix} \Rightarrow
\begin{bmatrix}
\text{Target:} & \textit{nehmen} \cdot (\boxed{3}/\boxed{4}) \\
\text{Frame:} & \text{SCRUTINY} \\
\text{Roles:} & \begin{pmatrix} \text{COGNIZER:} & \boxed{1} \\ \text{PHENOMENON:} & \boxed{2} \\ \text{DEGREE:} & \boxed{4} \end{pmatrix}
\end{bmatrix}
$$

Figure 5. Transfer scheme for *Die Klangkultur ist ein Juwel, das man getrost unter eine starke Lupe nehmen kann.* ('The sound is a jewel which stands up to any type of scrutiny.')

We now discuss the use of underspecification for difficult frame and FE distinctions.

2.4.4. *Underspecification*

It is well-known that there are cases of vagueness in semantic annotation, where the assignment of only a single label (such as a frame, or an FE) would not be appropriate, and annotators should be able to assign more than one label (see Kilgarriff and Rosenzweig 2000). Allowing this type of annotation makes it possible to retrieve vague cases and avoids forcing the annotators to adopt ad-hoc choices for decisions which are impossible to make reliably.

SALSA annotation faces the vagueness problem both at the level of frames and FEs. To illustrate, consider the verb *bemerken* ('to notice/comment') in (1), which typically introduces meaning components of two frames simultaneously, namely `Statement` (like *say*) and `Becoming_aware` (like *notice*). Neither frame alone conveys the complete meaning of *bemerken*, and forcing annotators to make an unambiguous decision would presumably result in inconsistent annotations.

(1) Kein Wunder, dass Gerhard Schäfer in seinem Buch derzeit eine "Renaissance der Verbindungen in den neuen Ländern" bemerkt. (TIGER s11777)

'(It is) not surprising that Gerhard Schäfer **notices/comments on** a "renaissance of fraternities in the new states".'

The metonymic sentence in (2) exemplifies a similar case at the FE level. Here, one frame is evoked, namely `Request`, but one of the FEs is vague. *Ein Antrag* ('a motion') describes the MEDIUM used to convey the demand, but it also refers metonymically to the SPEAKER. Again, no single annotation can capture the complete meaning.

(2) Die nachhaltigste Korrektur <u>fordert</u> [**ein Antrag** MEDIUM/SPEAKER].
'The most radical change is <u>demanded</u> by [**a motion** MEDIUM/SPEAKER].'

In such cases, SALSA annotators can assign more than one frame (or more than one FE of the same frame), connecting the multiple assignments by an underspecification link. Underspecification does not have an a priori disjunctive ("only one of the two labels fits, but it is impossible to decide which") or conjunctive ("both labels apply simultaneously to some extent") interpretation since it has been argued that this meta-level question is often as difficult to decide as the object-level question of which label to choose (see Kilgarriff and Rosenzweig 2000).

Underspecification is particularly useful for representing borderline instances of phenomena with limited compositionality. Notorious cases are the distinction between support constructions and metaphors, as well as between transparent metaphors and idioms that are no longer transparent.

2.4.5. Difficult role distinctions

FrameNet often uses ontological criteria to differentiate between closely related but mutually exclusive FEs. Such configurations arise, for example, in the form of pairs of FEs that stand in a systematic metonymical relationship (as opposed to incidental cases of metonymy discussed in the last paragraph). Since these are difficult to distinguish with annotations, we defined, where necessary, higher-level FEs which generalize over the problematic FEs.

For example, in the FrameNet frame `Waiting`, a PROTAGONIST waits for an EXPECTED_EVENT or a SALIENT_ENTITY associated with the event. While the two crossed-out roles can be distinguished in examples (3) and (4), example (5) contains an argument that is neither a clear-cut EXPECTED_EVENT nor a SALIENT_ENTITY. We have therefore defined a new FE, called EXPECTED_EVENT_SALSA in the `Waiting` frame. This FE allows us to describe all three instances in (3)–(5) in the same manner, generalizing over EXPECTED_EVENT, SALIENT_ENTITY, and problematic borderline cases.

(3) Luise wartet [darauf, dass das Telefon klingelt. ~~EXPECTED_EVENT~~ EXPECTED_EVENT_SALSA]
    'Luise waits [for the phone to ring ~~EXPECTED_EVENT~~ EXPECTED_EVENT_SALSA].'

(4) Luise wartet [auf ihren Mann ~~SALIENT_ENTITY~~. EXPECTED_EVENT_SALSA]
    'Luise is waiting for [her husband ~~SALIENT_ENTITY~~ EXPECTED_EVENT_SALSA].'

(5) Viele Wähler in Rußland haben immer [auf eine starke Sozialdemokratie EXPECTED_EVENT_SALSA] gewartet.
    'Many voters in Russia have always waited [for a powerful social democracy EXPECTED_EVENT_SALSA].'

2.5. Consistency control

Figure 6 shows the global structure of the annotation workflow in SALSA: Each dataset for a given lemma is annotated independently by two annotators (trained undergraduate students). Because of the double annotation process, a fair number of annotation mistakes can be detected automatically, and resolved in a double adjudication step: After annotation, the two annotated versions of a dataset are automatically merged into a single copy in which annotation differences are marked. The conflicts are resolved independently by two SALSA researchers. Almost all disagreements which remain after adjudication are truly difficult cases. Many are idiosyncratic problems, i.e., problems with particular instances. An example is that of referential ambiguities, which can lead to ambiguous FE assignments, or conceptual problems with respect to the FrameNet inventory. Examples of the latter are systematic problems in distinguishing FEs, or usages which meet frame descriptions only partially, or combine aspects of several frames. In cases where the adjudicators cannot reach an unanimous decision, underspecification is used as a last resort.

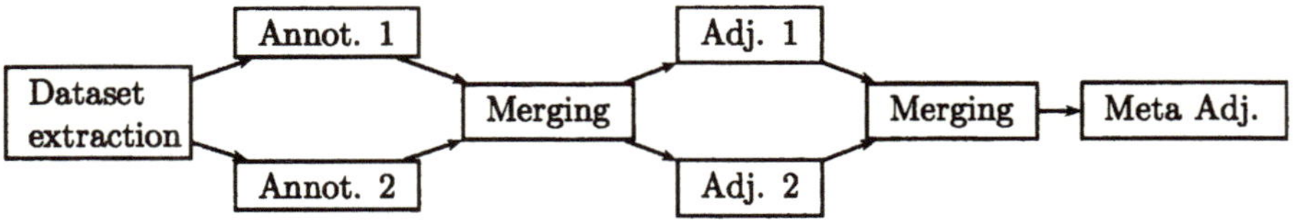

Figure 6. SALSA workflow: annotation and quality control

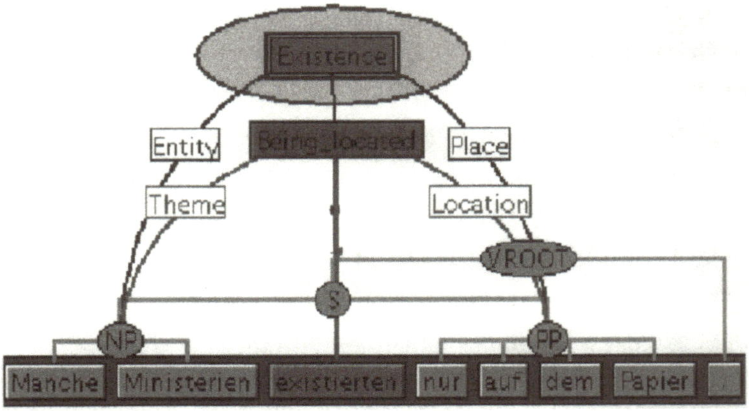

Figure 7. Inter-annotator difference: `Existence` vs. `Being_located`

The SALTO tool is used to manage the whole workflow, including dataset extraction and merging. In a special adjudication mode, SALTO guides the user specifically through those differences to allow for manual inspection and correction. Figure 7 shows an example of inter-annotator disagreement: One annotator tagged the word *existieren* ('exist') with the frame `Existence`, while the other annotator chose `Being_located`. The SALTO tool circled `Existence` to show that this is the next annotation choice to be either confirmed or denied by the adjudicator.

2.5.1. *Computing agreement*

It is best practice for annotation projects to report chance-corrected agreement, such as the kappa statistic (Siegel and Castellan 1988). However, as discussed in Burchardt et al. (2006b), kappa is only applicable to categorization tasks with fixed numbers of items and categories. Since these conditions do not apply to our setting, we do not report kappa; instead we report percentage agreements according to a strict evaluation metric (labeled exact match).

On the basis of two independently annotated and two adjudicated versions, we compute inter-annotator agreement and inter-adjudicator agreement. We consider frame selection and FEs assignment individually, due to their different characteristics. According to our method of computing agreement, inter-annotator agreement is 85% for frames and 86% for FEs for matching frames. Inter-adjudicator agreement is 97% for frames and 96% for FEs. Informally, annotators agree in more than 4/5 of all instances; adjudication creates consensus for another 4/5 of the disagreements. These numbers indicate substantial agreement, which demonstrates that the task is well-defined.

2.5.2. Limits of the four-eye principle

Quality control using inter-annotator agreement can only identify errors caused by individual annotation differences between annotators. If both annotators make the same error, it cannot be detected automatically. This limits the effectiveness of quality control by inter-annotator agreement with regard to systematic mistakes.

For this reason, we draw random samples from all completely annotated lemma-frame-pairs, which are then inspected for possible systematic annotation mistakes. We have also experimented with *intra*-annotator agreement, trying to automatically detect errors by finding "outliers" with non-uniform behavior. However, due to the LU-specific nature of semantic annotation, even correctly annotated datasets can show discrepancies.

2.6. From corpus to lexicon

One of the outcomes of the SALSA workflow illustrated in Figure 6 above is a frame-based lexicon model for German. This lexicon stores the information from the annotated corpus in a hierarchical model in description logics (Spohr et al. 2007). The model includes frame descriptions with their syntax-semantics linking patterns and frequency distributions.

Extracting a separate lexicon from the corpus offers a number of advantages. It allows the modular definition of generalizations over typically fine-grained annotation categories for individual instances as well as quantitative generalizations over these instances. The example in Table 3 shows that this kind of generalization is particularly crucial for information about the mapping between syntax and semantics. This information is extracted in ways similar to the FrameNet lexical entry reports. Fine-grained categories like NN (normal noun), NE (named entity), and PPER (personal pronoun) lead to the fragmentation of the corpus-derived mapping information and makes it susceptible to noise in the data. We therefore introduce generalized categories to discover linguistically meaningful and more robust regularities.

A second advantage of the separate lexicon is that it allows practically arbitrary "views" of the data, e.g., grouping information by lemma, by frame, or by phenomenon. All lexicon entries provide links to the annotation instances, thus grounding the lexicon in the corpus.

Table 3. Generalizations over syntactic categories in the lexicon

Frame.Role	Annotated Category	Generalized Category
Placing.Theme	NN	NounP
Placing.Theme	NE	NounP
Placing.Theme	PPER	NounP
Statement.Message	S	VerbP
Statement.Message	VP	VerbP

A benefit of the use of description logics for lexicon modeling is that it is a very general representation format. It supports consistency control of the annotated data and can serve as a machine-readable repository of lexical data for NLP applications, as well as a data source for linguistic research. The latter point is supported by the query mechanism SeRQL which allows the flexible retrieval of data from description logics databases.

3. Cross-lingual aspects

3.1. The applicability of FrameNet frames for the annotation of German

The fact that our German corpus annotation is based on frames and FEs that were originally created for English raises the question of the applicability of frame semantic descriptions to other languages (see Boas 2005). In our experience, the vast majority of FrameNet frames can be re-used fortuitously to describe German predicate-argument structures. Nevertheless, some FrameNet frames require adaptation and modification. Below, we discuss two central types of problems, namely missing FEs and differences in the linguistic realization of frame structures.

3.1.1. Missing Frame Elements

We found a number of frames derived on the basis of English that were well suited for the semantic description of German lexical units, but faced the problem that German verbs realize dative objects for which no appropriate FE is defined in the frame. Many of these cases are instances of the *external possessor construction*, in which a possessor of a verb's object is realized as an argument of the verb itself. While this construction is quite frequent in German, its use in English is known to be quite restricted; for example, Hole (2005: 238) recently noted that "English beneficiary objects are heavily constrained [...]".

As an example, consider the frame `Taking`, in which an AGENT takes possession of a THEME by removing it from a SOURCE. In English, the SOURCE, usually realized as a *from*-PP, can be either a source location or a former possessor. It is not possible to realize both as separate, full-fledged arguments of a predicate, although the possessor may be incorporated in the source location ("from his hand"). Thus, FrameNet does not distinguish between the two. In contrast, the German verb *nehmen* ('to take') can realize location and possessor simultaneously as arguments, as the following example illustrates:

(6) Er nahm [ihm POSSESSOR] [das Bier THEME]
He took him the beer

[aus der Hand SOURCE]
out of the hand

To handle such cases, we add new FEs – here a FE POSSESSOR, thereby splitting the FrameNet FE SOURCE into a location-type SOURCE and a distinct POSSESSOR.

3.1.2. Differences in the lexicalization of frames

The meanings of German verbs sometimes cut across the frame distinctions designed on the basis of English data. An example is the German verb *fahren* ('to drive'), which encompasses both English *drive* (frame `Operate_vehicle`, with the FE DRIVER) and *ride* (frame `Ride_vehicle`, with the FE PASSENGER). In German, context often does not disambiguate between the two frames, which makes it difficult to make a decision between these alternative frames. Consider (7), where German *fahren* is fully underspecified as to whether the people referred to (*they*) were drivers or passengers of the 14 vehicles.

(7) In 14 Armeefahrzeugen fuhren sie von dem abgezäunten Gelände, das der Besatzungsmacht 28 Jahre lang als Hauptquartier gedient hatte.

'With 14 army vehicles they departed from the enclosed area that had served the occupying forces as headquarters for 28 years.'

In the case at hand, FrameNet has introduced the frame `Use_vehicle`, which subsumes both `Operate_vehicle` and `Ride_vehicle`.

While this higher-level frame has no lexicalization in English, it is the right level to describe the meaning of German *fahren* in examples such as (7). In general, such cases need to be discussed from a multilingual perspective. In the ongoing annotation effort, we resort to underspecification (see Section 2.4.4). A possible area for future work is to find cross-lingually valid redefinitions for problematic frames, in cooperation with FrameNet and other partners.

3.2. SALSA and FrameNet projects for other languages

While SALSA frame annotation is done on a corpus with complete, deep syntactic annotation, Berkeley FrameNet (and FrameNet projects for other languages) annotate examples on the basis of unparsed corpus sentences, where syntactic information is added exclusively for annotated roles, either manually or semi-automatically. This is mirrored at the technical level in the choice of storage format: FrameNet's "lexical unit report" XML files represent annotations one frame at a time, and characterize role spans by way of character spans of the sentence string. In contrast, SALSA uses SALSA/TIGER XML (Erk and Padó 2004), an extension of TIGER XML, a description formalism originally used for syntax trees, and extended to semantic annotation. SALSA/TIGER XML can represent an arbitrary number of frames and roles (as shown in Figure 7, for example), defining their span in terms of (sets of) syntactic constituents. Several steps have been taken, however, to harmonize the different frame-semantic resources.

Our first goal was to allow the exchange of annotated data between projects. Mutually convertible data formats make it possible to develop common toolboxes, e.g., for modeling, consistency checking, or simply visualization using the SALTO tool (see Section 2.2). SALSA subcorpora and FrameNet lexical unit (LU) reports form the most appropriate level of granularity for data exchange: One SALSA subcorpus for a lemma corresponds to a set of LU reports, one for each reading of the lemma (i.e., frame). The direction SALSA → FrameNet is comparatively simple, since it only consists of removing most of the syntactic structures, retaining just the constituents labeled with FEs. The reverse direction (FrameNet → SALSA) is also fairly straightforward in that the span-based characterization of roles, in conjunction with categorial or functional information, can be used to define a partial syntactic and semantic structure in SALSA/TIGER XML. This is restricted to the annotated target word and FEs. In practice, the conversion direction was implemented in a different, pragmatically motivated way, in the context of developing a shallow semantic parser (see Section 4 for details): The conversion FrameNet → SALSA was implemented in the shape of an input filter that reads FrameNet LU reports, runs an automatic wide-coverage syntactic parser on the sentences, and converts the character-based annotation into a constituent-based annotation. Even though the accuracy of the automatic analysis cannot be guaranteed, this procedure makes it possible to train a shallow semantic parser directly on FrameNet data.

A further step, which builds directly on the ability to exchange annotated data, is to develop methods to compare and contrast data from more than one language in a flexible and comfortable manner. This goal has been realized in the lexicographical domain by FrameSQL, a database-oriented browser for the FrameNet database developed by Sato (2003). This tool has been extended to allow for the contrastive display of FrameNet information for different languages, first for the language pair English–Spanish (Subirats and Sato 2004), and later also for English–German.

As Figure 8 shows, it is possible to compare the lexical units of two languages for the same frame, and their valencies. This represents a first step to facilitate the study of cross-lingual commonalities and divergences in the frame semantic paradigm.

An important area for future research is the development of a cross-lingual, declarative lexicon model that is modular and powerful enough to represent both SALSA-style and FrameNet-style representations, together with annotated examples and statistical generalizations.

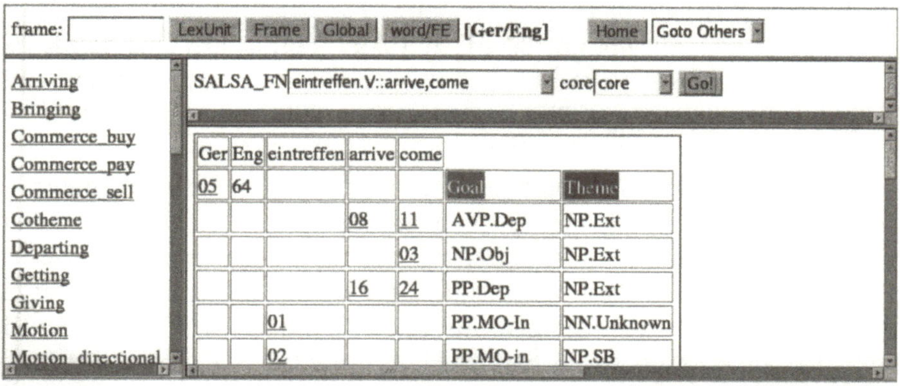

Figure 8. Sato Tool snapshot contrasting English *arrive* and *come* with German *eintreffen*

Our current efforts in building a frame-based lexicon from German corpus annotations in Spohr et al. (2007) is a first step towards this goal.

3.3. Cross-lingual projection for resource creation

As discussed above, English FrameNet frames are well suited to describe predicate-argument structures of different languages. In this context, the question arises as to how the annotation effort can be kept minimal whenever a new language is analyzed. More specifically, we are interested in methods which can automate at least part of this process.

At SALSA, we approached this task by using annotation projection, a strategy that exploits translational information from large parallel corpora to transfer semantic annotation across languages (see Pitel (this volume) for an alternative approach). More specifically, we re-used the manual effort expended on the creation of the English FrameNet to create comparable frame-semantic resources for French and German. This task naturally consists of two subproblems: (1) the induction of frame-semantic lemma classifications (i.e., lists of admissible frame-evoking elements for frames); and (2) the creation of a corpus of sentences with annotation of FEs.

With regard to (1), we developed a general language-independent architecture to bootstrap frame-semantic lemma classifications. We found that high-quality classifications can be induced for new languages by concentrating on translation pairs of source and target language lemmas which are especially likely to be frame-preserving. This property can be established even on the basis of shallow linguistic knowledge by exploiting the distributional profile of translation pairs in a large parallel corpus. For example, in experiments on the EUROPARL corpus (Koehn 2005), we constructed FrameNet-sized lemma classifications for both German and French with a precision of 65% to 70%, comparable to the size of Berkeley FrameNet (Padó and Lapata 2005a).

As for the induction of semantic role annotation for German sentences, provided that the frames match, the main task is to establish a mapping between subsentential phrases of source and target sentences that constitute possible roles. This problem can be phrased as a graph optimization problem, using word alignments to describe the pairwise cross-lingual similarity of phrases. In an experimental evaluation (Padó and Lapata 2005b), we demonstrated that FEs can be projected with an accuracy of up to 69% f-score (75% precision) when English manual FE annotation is used. When an imperfect state-of-the-art automatic shallow semantic parser is used to analyze the English text, the performance degrades to 57% f-score. However, this is mostly a problem of recall: the precision remains very high at 74%, indicating that it is possible to produce high-quality semantic annotation for new languages even from noisy data.

While the fully automatic methods for both types of information still fall short of the quality of manually created resources, their use can speed up resource development for new languages considerably, or serve as a "rough-and-ready" resource if no manual effort can be expended at all.

4. Automation

In this section, we present our strategies for shallow semantic parsing. Shallow semantic parsing is important for all NLP applications that benefit from deeper text understanding, such as the applications that Manning (2006) calls "Information Retrieval++": question answering, information extraction, and customer response systems. The availability of robust and accurate systems that can produce shallow semantic parses for free text is a crucial step towards the usability of role-semantic information in applications, such as the recognition of textual entailment (cf. Section 5). Shallow semantic parsing can be divided into Word Sense Disambiguation (WSD) (in FrameNet: an assignment of frames to frame-evoking elements) and Semantic Role Labeling (SRL) (in FrameNet, the assignment of FEs). While WSD is one of the oldest NLP tasks (Ide and Véronis 1998), SRL has only recently become a task of considerable interest in the computational linguistics community, beginning with the seminal study by Gildea and Jurafsky (2002).

4.1. SHALMANESER: A system for shallow semantic parsing

Research on shallow semantic parsing is in its early stages, requiring further steps both on the level of the analysis and its application. For this reason, we have developed a system for shallow parsing in SALSA, called SHALMANESER (the SHALlow seMANtic parSER). SHALMANESER fills the need for a shallow semantic parser which is publicly available and which can be used as a "black box" to obtain semantic role analyses of texts without the need to consider the intricacies of shallow semantic parsing (comparable to current syntactic parsers). While developed for English and German, the system is easily applicable to other languages as well.

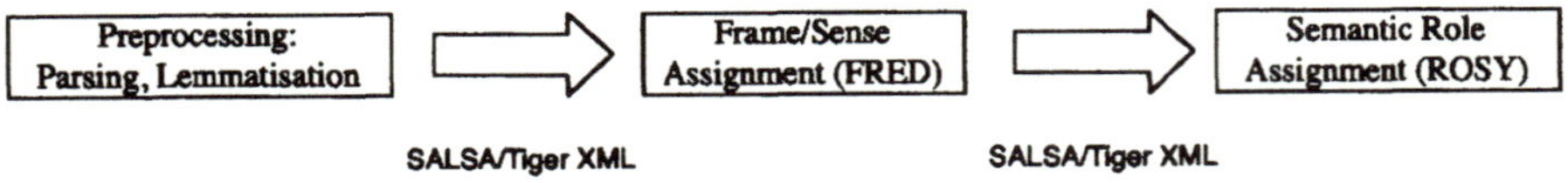

Figure 9. The SHALMANESER toolchain

The structure of SHALMANESER is illustrated in Figure 9. It takes plain text as input, which is first lemmatized, part-of-speech tagged, and syntactically analyzed. Semantic information is then added in two consecutive steps, WSD and SRL: First, the frame disambiguation system assigns semantic classes (senses) to lemmas. Then, the FE assignment system adds FEs to surrounding constituents. Both sense and FE assignments are modeled as supervised learning tasks. Sense assignment is decided on the basis of the lexical context and syntactic properties of lemmas (Erk 2005). For FE assignment, we rely both on syntactic features (e.g., path from FEE to constituent) and lexical features, which, although sparse, provide crucial information (see Erk and Padó 2005).

SHALMANESER uses the SALSA/TIGER XML format described in Section 3.2. Thus, the SALTO annotation tool can be used to inspect and manually modify the assigned frames and roles within a graphical interface. More generally, an open extensible architecture like the one offered by SHALMANESER allows for a modular view of semantic analysis. Semantic classes and roles are just one particular type among the many kinds of semantic information that are potentially helpful in NLP applications. The last years have seen impressive progress in the accurate computation of individual kinds of semantic information. These comprise lexical information (ontological status, lexical relations, polarity) and structural information (scope, modality, anaphoric and discourse structure).

4.1.1. Using SHALMANESER

SHALMANESER is designed with two application scenarios in mind. In an "end user scenario", pre-trained classifiers for English and German are available for exploring the use of role-semantic information in different NLP settings (see Section 7 for details). In a "research scenario", the modular architecture facilitates the integration of additional processing modules. Furthermore, we keep the processing components encapsulated to make them easily adaptable to new features, parsers, languages, or classification algorithms.

Researchers primarily interested in a robust system for shallow semantic analysis can use the pre-trained classifiers for English and German provided with SHALMANESER. A single command starts the analysis of plain text input, encompassing syntactic analysis, frame assignment and role assignment. More specifically, the training data for English is the FrameNet release 1.2 dataset, consisting of 133,846 annotated BNC examples for 5,706 lemmas. For German, the training data is a portion of the SALSA corpus (Erk et al., 2003), namely 17,743 annotated instances covering 485 lemmas.

The other aim of SHALMANESER is to allow research in semantic role assignment on a high level of abstraction and control. Studies in this area typically involve a comparative evaluation of different experimental conditions, e.g., the activation and deactivation of model features. In SHALMANESER, these parameters can be specified declaratively in experimental files.

4.2. Evaluation

The WSD and the SRL systems were evaluated against 10% held-out data from the FrameNet and SALSA datasets. The SHALMANESER WSD system obtained an accuracy of 93% (baseline: 89%) for English and 79% (baseline: 75%) for German. The high baseline for English is due to the fact that FrameNet, whose workflow progresses one frame at a time, provides an incomplete sense inventory for many words (but see below). The SHALMANESER SRL system was evaluated separately for the tasks of argument recognition (Is the constituent a role or not?) and argument labeling (If it is a FE, which FE is it?). The results are summarized in Table 4.

Table 4. SRL evaluation results

		argrec		*arglab*
Data	Prec.	Rec.	F	Acc.
English	0.855	0.669	0.751	0.784
German	0.761	0.496	0.600	0.673

4.3. Handling incomplete coverage

Adequate coverage is a general problem of automatic semantic analysis, and frame-based shallow semantic parsing is not an exception. The main problem is that FrameNet is still under development, and frames have not been defined for all senses of all lemmas. The most difficult class in this respect is formed by lemmas for which there are no existing frames. Processing these cases requires more lexicographic (and presumably manual) effort. However, there are two classes of lemmas with incomplete coverage that can be treated (semi-)automatically, namely (a) lemmas which are not listed in FrameNet, but presumably fall under an existing frame, and (b) lemmas that are listed, but for which at most a subset of the senses is covered by existing frames.

To provide an approximate semantic analysis for the lemmas in class (a) we developed the "Detour to FrameNet" system (Burchardt et al. 2005a). It exploits the larger coverage of WordNet (Fellbaum 1998) to (heuristically) assign existing FrameNet frames that approximate the lemma's meaning. The Detour system generates candidate frames on the basis of WordNet synonyms and hypernyms of the given lemma. It then selects the best fitting frame(s) with a weighting scheme. The Detour system can be used in combination with SHALMANESER to assign analyses to otherwise unknown lemmas. Alternatively, it can be used on its own, e.g., to generate suggestions for manual annotation in order to speed up the annotation process.

Lemmas of class (b) pose a problem because when one of the senses of a target word is missing from the lexicon, standard WSD algorithms will always incorrectly assign one of the existing senses, wrongly assuming that all applicable sense labels for a target word are known. An example is shown in Figure 10, where a sentence from the Hound of the Baskervilles has been analyzed by SHALMANESER. FrameNet lacks a sense of "expectation" or "being mentally prepared" for the verb *prepare*, so *prepared* is assigned the sense COOKING_CREATION, a possible but improbable analysis.[3] Such erroneous labels can be fatal when further processing builds on the results of shallow semantic parsing, e.g. for drawing inferences.

To address this problem, we developed an approach to detect occurrences of unknown senses (Erk 2006) based on the method of "outlier

3. Unfortunately, the semantic roles have been mis-assigned by the system. The word *I* should fill the FOOD role while *for a hound* should be assigned the optional RECEIVER role.

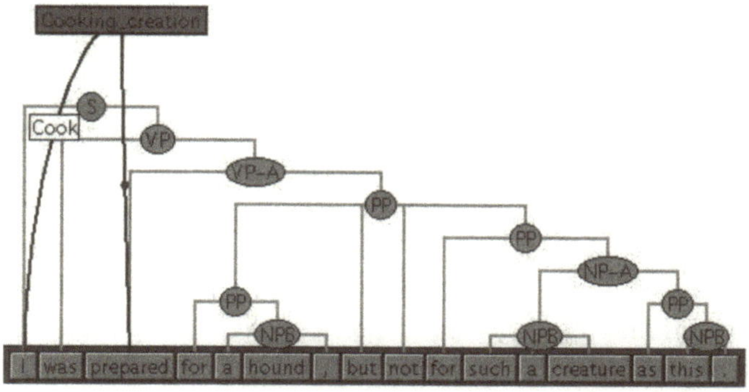

Figure 10. Wrong assignment due to missing sense: Example from "The Hound of the Baskervilles"

detection". An outlier detection model is trained on a set of positive examples only, deriving form it some model of "normality" to which new objects are compared. Its task is then to decide whether a new object belongs to the same set as the training data. For unknown sense detection, we constructed an outlier detection model based on the training occurrences of all senses of the target word. Whenever a new occurrence of the word is classified as an outlier, it is considered an occurrence of an unknown sense. In an evaluation of FrameNet 1.2 data, designating one sense of each lemma as an unknown sense, the best parameter set achieved a precision of 0.77 and a recall of 0.81 in detecting occurrences of unknown senses.

5. Applications

One of the aims of the SALSA project is to explore the usefulness of frame semantic descriptions in language technology. FrameNet descriptions differ from alternative lexical semantic descriptions, such as those found in PropBank, in that they combine different types of semantic information: (i) coarse-grained sense classification in terms of conceptual classes, i.e., frames, (ii) their predicate-argument structure, in terms of FEs, and (iii) semantic relations between frames, in terms of FrameNet's frame hierarchy (Fillmore et al. 2004). As a lexical-semantic framework, it crucially differs from truth-conditional semantic frameworks such as Montague Semantics or Discourse Representation Theory, in disregarding sentence-semantic phenomena such as tense, modality, quantification, or scope.

One application which has recently been successfully approached with frame-based processing is question answering (QA). In textual question answering (Fliedner (2006), Kaisser (2005)), frames present an attractive representation level for matching questions and potential answers. For question answering from structured knowledge bases, Frank et al. (2007) applied a somewhat different strategy, which also highlighted the cross-lingual appropriateness of frames. They used frames as an intermediate layer which enabled the automatic translation of (multilingual) natural language questions to structured queries over (language-independent) domain ontologies.

5.1. Textual entailment

In this section, we focus on a problem related to questions answering, namely Recognizing Textual Entailment. Textual Entailment is a relation holding between a text (T) and a hypothesis (H). It holds "if the meaning of H can be inferred from the meaning of T, as would typically be interpreted by people" (Dagan et al. 2005: 1). An example where textual entailment holds is given in (8).

(8) T: In 1983, Aki Kaurismäki directed his first full-time feature.
H: Aki Kaurismäki directed a film.

Checking for textual entailment can be taken as a semantic verification step for many information access tasks. For example, a summarization system might generate (8H) as a summary of (8T); in this context, textual entailment can subsequently be used to ensure the consistency of the summary with the original information.

Modeling Textual Entailment has been institutionalized in the form of the yearly PASCAL Recognizing Textual Entailment (RTE) Challenge, where training data in terms of Text-Hypothesis pairs is provided together with human judgments about whether textual entailment holds or not. The task is then to model this relation and to predict whether entailment holds or not for unseen test data.

5.2. The SALSA contribution to the RTE challenge

Our hypothesis for approaching the RTE task is that FrameNet's coarse-grained conceptual classification and role-semantic analysis offers a useful abstraction layer with a significant degree of normalization across lexical predicates, parts of speech and syntactic argument realization, i.e., diathe-

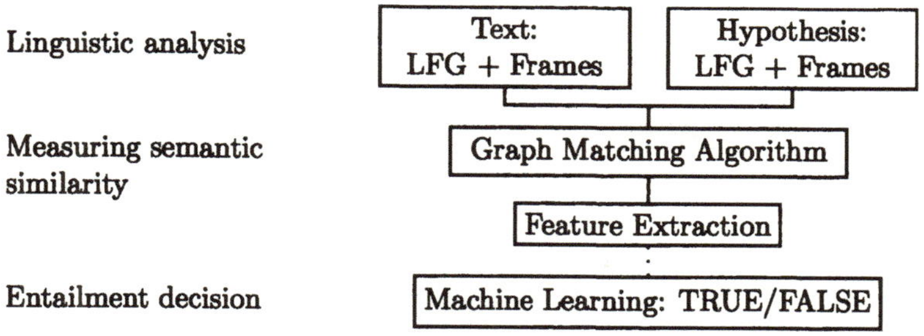

Figure 11. SALSA RTE Architecture

sis variations. Moreover, like WordNet, and based on its hierarchy of frames, FrameNet allows us to determine different types of semantic similarity measures (cf. Burchardt et al. 2005a).

Note, however, that frame semantic analysis on its own is not sufficient for the task. A theoretical issue that needs further consideration is that decisions about entailment often require additional types of information, such as fine-grained lexical information, (e.g., *rise* and *fall* are antonyms), sentence-level of information (e.g., negation or modality), or additional world knowledge. A more practical issue is coverage: At present, we cannot expect to always obtain complete analyses of free texts. We remedy this situation by combining different frame semantics with other resources in a layered approach that provides diverse kinds of information and supports a fall back in the case of missing or partial analyses.

The overall design of our system is shown in Figure 11. The linguistic analyses of H and T are graph structures. They are taken as input to a module that computes *semantic similarity* by way of a graph matching algorithm. Different types of matches (e.g. functional-syntactic, frame-semantic) are recorded and marked as safe or defeasible depending on the respective matching rules. Further measures of similarity are the size and connectedness of the resulting match graph. These similarities then serve as input to a statistically trained model which "decides" whether entailment holds or not.

The linguistic analysis part of the system is shown in Figure 12. It is centered around a frame-semantic projection on top of a symbolic LFG grammar (Frank and Erk 2004, Frank and Semecký 2004). We employ the English LFG grammar developed at PARC (Riezler et al. 2002), whose f-structure trees serve as an anchor for all information provided by the other resources. The frame-semantic annotations are produced by SHALMANESER and the Detour system (Burchardt et al. 2005a), and are

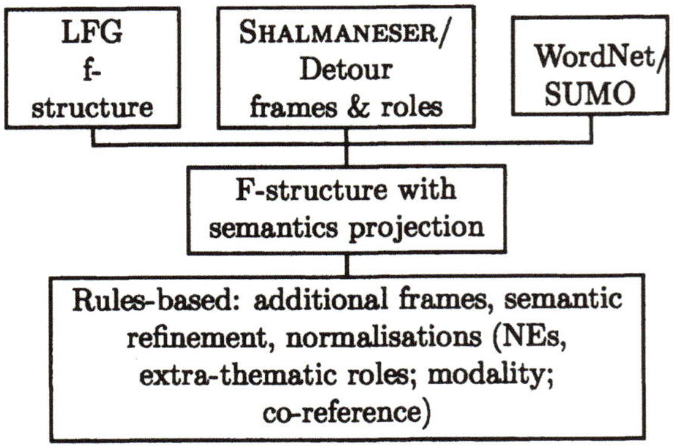

Figure 12. Linguistic analysis component of the SALSA RTE System

subsequently enriched with information from the WordNet and SUMO ontologies, using a WSD system (Banerjee and Pedersen 2003) and mappings from WordNet to SUMO (Niles and Pease 2003), respectively. Subsequently, the LFG f-structure is evaluated by a heuristic rule-based component to gather information about additional phenomena such as co-reference, modality, etc.

We now present a complete example. Figure 13 illustrates the LFG and frame semantic analysis of T and H of (8) in the two boxes. The LFG information is displayed on the left of each box, the corresponding frame semantic projection on the right side. The frame `Behind_the_scenes` has been assigned to *direct* and *film* by the automatic frame and FE assignment systems. Based on the Named Entity Recognizer of the LFG grammar, the `People` frame has been assigned in the rule-based refinement step. Because of a disambiguation problem, *feature* was not assigned a frame. However, in the graph matching process, both *feature* and *film* are recognized as a deep syntactic object (**dobj**) of the main predicate. At the same time, a defeasible match based on WordNet has been found to relate both predicates. This provides evidence that the semantic similarity between T and H is very high. H can thus be taken as "fully covered" by T and the statistical model successfully confirms entailment in this case.

The SALSA RTE system participated in the RTE-2 challenge (Burchardt and Frank 2006). With 59% accuracy, it scored in the middle range of all participating systems. We take this as evidence that frame semantic analysis integrated with syntactic, lexical, and other types of knowledge resources is a promising basis for large-scale semantic processing.

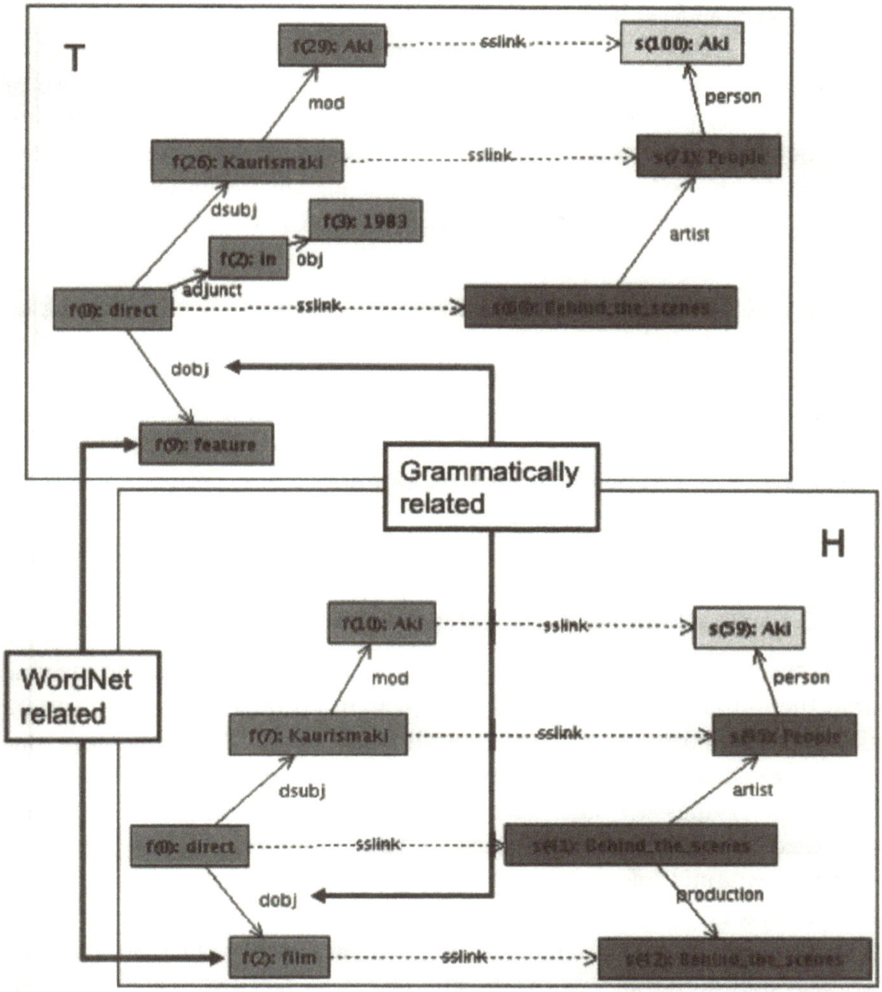

Figure 13. Analysis of example (8)

Ultimately, we envisage that frame-based analyses will be even more competitive in future years of the RTE Challenge, for which an extension to larger chunks of text is planned. We have already studied the interactions of frame semantic structures with discourse phenomena (Burchardt et al. 2005b), and found that frame semantic structures are tightly interrelated with discourse phenomena, and thus may serve as an informative component in models of discourse structure.

6. Summary and outlook

In this paper we discussed various aspects in which the current phase of the SALSA project has investigated the annotation, representation and implementation of Frame Semantics, as realized in Berkeley FrameNet. Our results are both practical and theoretical. On the practical side, we have made the following software tools and resources available to the research community:

- The SALTO tool provides a convenient graphical interface for frame-semantic annotation and supports the frame annotation workflow from corpus extraction to quality control;
- The SHALMANESER system is employed for shallow, statistical frame-semantic processing;
- The DETOUR system offers approximate frame descriptions for missing entries in the FrameNet database;
- The SALSA/TIGER corpus provides frame-semantic annotations for German newspaper texts, plus a queryable lexicon that stores the frame-semantic information extracted from the annotated corpus.

On the theoretical side, we gained a number of significant insights. First, the initial hypothesis that Frame Semantics provides an appropriate and powerful framework for cross-lingual meaning descriptions has been impressively corroborated by the large-scale re-usability of Berkeley FrameNet frames for the description of German predicate-argument structures. Our successful approach to automatic cross-lingual projection of frame-semantic information from English to German and French bolsters the claim.

Second, we explored the feasibility of large-scale exhaustive frame-semantic annotation of text documents. We demonstrated that the annotation of all kinds of borderline cases and special phenomena of limited compositionality is indeed feasible. Moreover, we showed that frame-semantic annotation supports the systematic modeling of phenomena such as metaphors in an interesting way.

Third, we successfully employed frame-semantic resources for language technology tasks like RTE and Question Answering, confirming our conviction that frame-semantic resources constitute a valuable tool for all kinds of semantically informed natural-language applications.

From our experience, the most pressing issue restricting the extensive use of frame information in language-technology applications is the somewhat limited coverage of frame-semantic resources. Manual lexicon development or manual semantic annotation appears to be too time consuming to quickly arrive at a full coverage high-quality frame-semantic lexicon within the next three to five years. Therefore, we will concentrate on the further development of automated techniques of lexical semantic acquisition in the next phase of SALSA. We thus intend to speed up the development of frame-semantic resources with broader coverage by exploring the use of linguistically informed data expansion techniques and ways to access and integrate complementary knowledge provided by upper-model ontologies into a frame-semantic lexicon.

Acknowledgements

The research reported here was funded by the German Research Foundation (DFG) under Grant PI 154/9-2. We are grateful to the Berkeley FrameNet team and the Cross-lingual FrameNet Group for fruitful collaboration.

7. Appendix: SALSA Resources

The SALSA resources listed below are freely available for academic research.

SALTO

The SALTO tool was implemented at CLT Sprachtechnologie GmbH under the direction of Daniel Bobbert. It is implemented in Java and was tested successfully under Windows, Linux, SunOS and Mac OS X. SALTO can be downloaded from the SALSA project homepage at http://www.coli.uni-saarland.de/projects/salsa/page.php?id=software.

SHALMANESER

The SHALMANESER semantic analysis system is written in Ruby. It makes use of several third-party software systems, as described in the documentation. The system has been tested successfully under Linux. SHALMANESER can be downloaded from http://www.coli.uni-saarland.de/projects/salsa/page.php?id=software.

A WordNet Detour to FrameNet

The Detour system is written in Perl, and is available from the CPAN archive at http://search.cpan.org/~reiter/FrameNet-WordNet-Detour/. It requires FrameNet and WordNet as external resources.

SALSA Release 1.0

The first SALSA release in 2007 contains a portion of the frame-annotated SALSA/TIGER corpus, together with FrameNet-style documentation of the FrameNet frames used in the annotation as well as the proto-frames developed by SALSA. This release includes a queryable lexicon model that stores the corpus-extracted lexicon data. The release is accessible from the SALSA homepage, at http://www.coli.uni-saarland.de/projects/salsa/page.php?id=release1.0.

8. References

Banerjee, Satanjeev and Ted Pedersen
2003 Extended gloss overlaps as a measure of semantic relatedness. In: *Proceedings of the Eighteenth International Joint Conference on Artificial Intelligence*, 805–810.

Boas, Hans C.
2005 Semantic frames as interlingual representations for multilingual lexical databases. In: *International Journal of Lexicography* 18.4: 445–478.

Brants, Sabine, Stefanie Dipper, Silvia Hansen, Wolfgang Lezius, and George Smith
2002 The TIGER treebank. In: *Proceedings of the Workshop on Treebanks and Linguistic Theories*: 24–41.

Burchardt, Aljoscha, Katrin Erk, and Anette Frank
2005a A WordNet Detour to FrameNet. In: Bernhard Fisseni, Hans-Christian Schmitz, Bernhard Schröder, and Petra Wagner (eds.), *Sprachtechnologie, mobile Kommunikation und linguistische Ressourcen (Computer Studies in Language and Speech 8.)*, 408–421. Frankfurt am Main: Peter Lang.

Burchardt, Aljoscha, Katrin Erk, Anette Frank, Andrea Kowalski, and Sebastian Padó
2006a SALTO – a versatile multi-level annotation tool. In: *Proceedings of the 5th International Conference on Language Resources and Evaluation.*

Burchardt, Aljoscha, Katrin Erk, Anette Frank, Andrea Kowalski, Sebastian Padó, and Manfred Pinkal
2006b The SALSA corpus: a German corpus resource for lexical semantics. In: *Proceedings of the 5th International Conference on Language Resources and Evaluation.*

Burchardt, Aljoscha and Anette Frank
2006 Approaching textual entailment with LFG and FrameNet frames. In: *Proceedings of the RTE-2 Workshop*, 92–97.

Burchardt, Aljoscha, Anette Frank, and Manfred Pinkal
2005b Building text meaning representations from contextually related frames – a case study. In: *Proceedings of the 6th International Workshop on Computational Semantics*, 66–77.

Dagan, Ido, Oren Glickman, and Bernardo Magnini
2005 The PASCAL recognizing textual entailment challenge. In: *Proceedings of the First Challenge Workshop, Recognizing Textual Entailment*, 1–8.

Ellsworth, Michael, Katrin Erk, Paul Kingsbury, and Sebastian Padó
2004 PropBank, SALSA and FrameNet: How design determines product. In: *Proceedings of the Workshop on Building Lexical Resources From Semantically Annotated Corpora at LREC 2004.*

Erk, Katrin
2005 Frame assignment as word sense disambiguation. In: *Proceedings of the 6th International Workshop on Computational Semantics.*

Erk, Katrin
2006 Unknown word sense detection as outlier detection. In: *Proceedings of the joint Human Language Technology Conference and Annual Meeting of the North American Chapter of the Association for Computational Linguistics*, 128–135.

Erk, Katrin, Andrea Kowalski, Sebastian Padó, and Manfred Pinkal
2003 Towards a resource for lexical semantics: A large German corpus with extensive semantic annotation. In: *Proceedings of the 41st Annual Meeting of the Association for Computational Linguistics*, 537–544.

Erk, Katrin and Sebastian Padó
2004 A powerful and versatile XML format for representing role-semantic annotation. In: *Proceedings of the 4th International Conference on Language Resources and Evaluation.*

Erk, Katrin and Sebastian Padó
2005 Analyzing models for semantic role assignment using confusability. In: *Proceedings of the joint Human Language Technology Conference and Conference on Empirical Methods in Natural Language Processing*, 668–675.

Fellbaum, Christiane (ed.)
1998 *WordNet: An electronic lexical database*. Cambridge, MA: MIT Press.

Fillmore, Charles J.
1985 Frames and the semantics of understanding. In: *Quaderni di Semantica* 4.2: 222–254.

Fillmore, Charles J., Collin F. Baker, and Hiroaki Sato
2004 FrameNet as a "Net". In: *Proceedings of the 4th International Conference on Language Resources and Evaluation.*

Fillmore, Charles J., Christopher R. Johnson, and Miriam R. L. Petruck
2003 Background to FrameNet. *International Journal of Lexicography* 16.3: 235–250.

Fliedner, Gerd
2006 Towards natural interactive question answering. In: *Proceedings of the 5th International Conference on Language Resources and Evaluation.*

Frank, Anette and Katrin Erk
2004 Towards an LFG syntax-semantics interface for Frame Semantics annotation. In: Alexander Gelbukh (ed.), *Computational Linguistics and Intelligent Text Processing*, 1–12. Heidelberg: Springer Verlag.

Frank, Anette, Hans-Ulrich Krieger, Feiyu Xu, Hans Uszkoreit, Berthold Crysmann, Brigitte Jörg, and Ulrich Schäfer
2007 Question answering from structured knowledge sources. *Journal of Applied Logic, Special Issue on Questions and Answers: Theoretical and Applied Perspectives* 5.1: 20–48.

Frank, Anette, and Jiří Semecký
2004 Corpus-based induction of an LFG syntax-semantics interface for Frame Semantic processing. In: *Proceedings of the 5th International Workshop on Linguistically Interpreted Corpora*, 39–46.

Gildea, Daniel and Daniel Jurafsky
2002 Automatic labeling of semantic roles. *Computational Linguistics* 28.3: 245–288.

Hamp, Birgit and Helmut Feldweg
1997 GermaNet: a Lexical-Semantic Net for German. In: *Proceedings of the ACL/EACL97 workshop on Automatic Information Extraction and Building of Lexical Semantic Resources for NLP Applications*, 9–15.

Hole, Daniel
2005 Towards a unified voice account of dative binding in German. In: Claudia Maienborn and Angelika Wöllstein (eds.), *Event Arguments: Foundations and Applications*, 213–242. Tübingen: Niemeyer.

Ide, Nancy and Jean Véronis
1998 Introduction to the special issue on word sense disambiguation: The state of the art. *Computational Linguistics* 24.1: 1–40.

Kaisser, Michael
2005 QuALiM at TREC 2005: Web-Question-Answering with FrameNet. In: *Proceedings of the 2005 Edition of the Text Retrieval Conference, TREC 2005.*

Kilgarriff, Adam and Joseph Rosenzweig
2000 Framework and results for English Senseval. *Computers and the Humanities. Special Issue on SENSEVAL 34* 1–2, 15–48.

Koehn, Phillip
2005 Europarl: A parallel corpus for statistical machine translation. In: *Proceedings of the MT Summit X.*

Lakoff, George and Mark Johnson
1980 *Metaphors we live by.* Chicago: University of Chicago Press.

Manning, Christopher D.
2006 *Local textual inference: It's hard to circumscribe, but you know it when you see it – and NLP needs it.* Manuscript, Stanford University. http://nlp.stanford.edu/~manning/papers/LocalTextualInference.pdf.

Niles, Ian and Adam Pease
2003 Linking lexicons and ontologies: mapping WordNet to the suggested upper merged ontology. In: *Proceedings of the International Conference on Information and Knowledge Engineering,* 412–416.

Ohara, Kyoko Hirose, Seiko Fujii, Toshio Ohori, Ryoko Suzuki, Hiroaki Saito, and Shun Ishizaki
2004 The Japanese FrameNet project: An introduction. In: *Proceedings of the Workshop on Building Lexical Resources from Semantically Annotated Corpora at LREC 2004.*

Padó, Sebastian and Mirella Lapata
2005a Cross-lingual bootstrapping for semantic lexicons. In: *Proceedings of the 22nd National Conference on Artificial Intelligence,* 1087–1092.

Padó, Sebastian and Mirella Lapata
2005b Cross-lingual projection of role-semantic information. In: *Proceedings of the joint Human Language Technology Conference and Conference on Empirical Methods in Natural Language Processing,* 859–866.

Palmer, Martha, Dan Gildea, and Paul Kingsbury
2005 The proposition bank: An annotated corpus of semantic roles. *Computational Linguistics* 31.1: 71–106.

Riezler, Stefan, Tracy H. King, Ronald M. Kaplan, Richard Crouch, John T. Maxwell III, and Mark Johnson
2002 Parsing the Wall Street Journal using a Lexical-Functional Grammar and Discriminative Estimation Techniques. In: *Pro-*

ceedings of the 40th Annual Meeting of the Association for Computational Linguistics, 271–278.

Ruppenhofer, Josef, Michael Ellsworth, Miriam R.L. Petruck, and Jan Scheffczyk
2006 FrameNet II: Extended Theory and Practice. http://framenet.icsi.berkeley.edu/index.php?option=com_wrapper&Itemid=126.

Sato, Hiroaki
2003 FrameSQL: A software tool for the FrameNet database. In: *Proceedings of the 3rd Conference of the Asian Association for Lexicography* 251–258.

Siegel, Sidney and N. John Castellan
1988 *Nonparametric statistics for the Behavioral Sciences*, 2nd edition. London: McGraw-Hill.

Spohr, Dennis, Aljoscha Burchardt, Sebastian Padó, Anette Frank, and Ulrich Heid
2007 Inducing a Computational Lexicon from a Corpus with Syntactic and Semantic Information. In: *Proceedings of the 7th International Workshop on Computational Semantics*, 210–221.

Subirats, Carlos and Miriam R.L. Petruck
2003 Surprise: Spanish FrameNet! In: *Proceedings of the Workshop on Frame Semantics, XVII. International Congress of Linguists.*

Subirats, Carlos and Hiroaki Sato
2004 Spanish FrameNet and FrameSQL. In: *Proceedings of the 4th International Conference on Language Resources and Evaluation.*

9. Cross-lingual labeling of semantic predicates and roles: A low-resource method based on bilingual L(atent) S(emantic) A(nalysis)

Guillaume Pitel

1. Introduction

Work on the Berkeley FrameNet project (Fillmore et al. 2003) has been underway since 1997 and is still continuing. This rather long period of time has led researchers working on other languages to ask how much time and resources are required to create new FrameNet-type resources for other languages (see Fontenelle 2000, Boas 2005). At the moment, there are two different approaches for creating FrameNets for other languages. The first is the original lexicographic approach, proceeding frame by frame and L(exical) U(nit) by LU, as practiced by the Berkeley FrameNet project for English (Fillmore et al. 2003), Spanish FrameNet (Subirats and Petruck 2003), and Japanese FrameNet (Ohara et al. 2004). The second approach, explored by the SALSA project for German (Burchardt et al. 2006a) as well as the original FrameNet more recently, focuses on annotation of continuous text.

Since both approaches are very time-consuming, there is a strong need for methods that would speed up the process of creating FrameNets for new languages. For instance, it is imaginable that the resource could be bootstrapped using a projection-based approach. In such an approach, information from the English resource is adapted to the new language in order to build a preliminary resource. Our work contributes to this approach, in that it deals with reusing data by projection from the English FrameNet into a French FrameNet, concerning both the *lexicon* and the *annotations*.

In this paper, we report on our efforts undertaken during the *Fr.FrameNet* project, the goal of which is to compare different options that can be taken into consideration in order to facilitate the task of building such a resource.[1] We propose two complementary approaches result-

1. Please see http://libresource.inria.fr/projects/framenet/.

ing from this research. The first approach, discussed in section 3, focuses on building a FrameNet lexicon for French on the basis of existing French-English word-by-word translation resources: the Semantic ATLAS (Ploux and Ji 2003) and the WordReference online French-English dictionary.[2] This approach is not language-independent, but can be adapted to many other languages, provided translation resources to English are available. The second approach, discussed in the remainder of this paper, is aimed at developing a robust automatic role classification system (which differs from automatic role labeling in that it does not handle role bracketing) that relies only on the English FrameNet in combination with generic cross-lingual information. We show that although the success rate using this method cannot compete with monolingual automatic labeling systems, our method is nevertheless valuable in that it can be used as a helpful annotation assistant for starting the development of a more complete resource. More precisely, our approach will require a similarity measure between text segments in two languages that we intend to obtain from a bilingual LSA vector space. In contrast to cross-lingual semantic role projection approaches (Padó and Lapata 2005b, Johansson and Nugues 2006), the approach outlined below requires fewer resources, and shows potential for a better coverage in terms of frames and frame elements, because it is not restricted to the availability of parallel data for each possible frame. This advantage makes our system an interesting complement to other approaches, or a viable standalone option for low-resource languages. As we show below, our approach mainly relies on the availability of a parallel corpus and is thus almost entirely language-independent.

2. Different methods for automatic role labeling

In this section we present existing work related to the use of lexical information in automatic semantic role labeling systems and cross-linguistic methods for semantic information projection. Automatic role labeling consists of segmenting sentences and classifying relevant segments as being particular arguments of a predicate evoked in the sentence. Figure 1 describes the four steps of a semantic role labeling system for a sentence where the target "ate" is already selected. Our contribution, described in section 4, focuses on the two last steps.

2. Acknowledgments for this go to Mike Kellogg, at WordReference.com, for granting me the use of his site's data for this experiment.

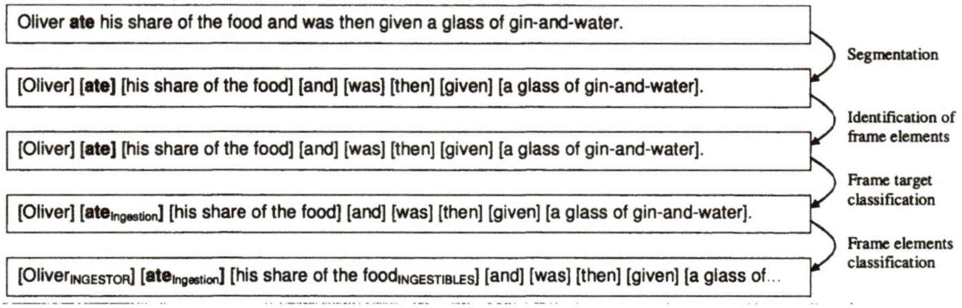

Figure 1. The four steps of an automatic semantic role labeling system (example taken from the FrameNet database)

2.1. Lexical information in automatic role labeling

In automatic role labeling, lexical information plays a major role (see, e.g. Erk and Padó 2005). For example, Gildea and Jurafsky (2002: 266–271) study several predictors for correct role labeling and show that a predictor based on the head lemma, phrase type and target word presents the highest accuracy of all predictors (87.4%). However, at the same time it has the lowest coverage (43.8%) because this predictor can only be used when the head lemma has previously been encountered in the training data. For this reason, current semantic role labeling systems are mostly based on syntax.

In order to improve this coverage, Gildea and Jurafsky propose generalizing the information on the head lemma with three different approaches: (1) Automatic clustering using term co-occurrence in predicate-object pairs; (2) Using the WordNet semantic hierarchy; and (3) Bootstrapping unannotated data, i.e. annotating new data using an automatic role labeling system without lexical generalization and then using this data to increase the number of known predicate-head lemma pairs.

Gildea and Jurafsky (2002: 271) conclude that automatic clustering seems to be the most promising method for increasing the coverage of lexical predictors. The accuracy obtained with this method for the classification of NPs reaches 79.7% with a coverage of 97.9%.

Another type of generalization over training data, which has been tested in Baldewein et al. (2004), is based on the relations defined between frame elements (FEs). This approach makes use of the several partial hierarchies over frames described in FrameNet, whose main types are *inheritance, use*, and *subframing* (Baker et al. 2003: 286). By using these relations it is possible to guess how the FEs in different frames are related to each other, and thus whether they can be grouped together to create a more general cluster for learning. Baldewein et al. (2004) also investigate the potential of grouping peripheral FEs based on their name. In other words, they consider classifying peripheral FEs that share the same name as one single cross-frame general FE. These methods are typically useful when too few annotations of a given FE are available in the training data. However, this method may also introduce some errors because particular frames have unique frame-specific FEs.

While the methods used by Gildea and Jurafsky (2002) and Baldewein et al. (2004) rely on manually annotated English sentences from FrameNet, the use of such data as a basis for automatic labeling in a new language with no or few manual FrameNet annotations is a different problem to which we now turn.

2.2. Cross-linguistic approaches to automatic role labeling

The most successful cross-lingual approach to automatic role labeling to date is proposed by Padó and Lapata (2005b) for English and German and by Johansson and Nugues (2006) for English and Swedish. This method relies on the projection of FEs into a large word-aligned bilingual corpus covering two languages, L1 and L2. In this framework, L1 must have a FrameNet resource while L2 is the language for which a FrameNet resource is created. The L1 side of the corpus is annotated, and frame as well as FE annotations are obtained manually or with an automatic role labeler. The ultimate goal is to use an automatic approach for obtaining the annotation for L1. Using alignment information, role labels are then projected into the L2 part of the corpus.

Considering the sparseness of word-alignment, one of the main issues of this paradigm is to obtain the correct span of FEs on the target side of the corpus. For this purpose, Padó and Lapata (2006: 1163–1165) obtain constituents from a chunker or a syntactic parser in order to test several models of constituent-level alignments and word or constituent filters. In contrast, Johansson and Nugues (2006: 440–441) use language-specific heuristics based on constituents to extend the scattered initial information into continuous segments of texts. Hence, an automatic role labeling system can be obtained using the projected data in the target language as training data. This approach is not free of problems. The most common ones are null-alignments and non-frame-conserving translations that may impede the coverage of the projected annotation, in terms of frames, FEs, and syntactic realizations.

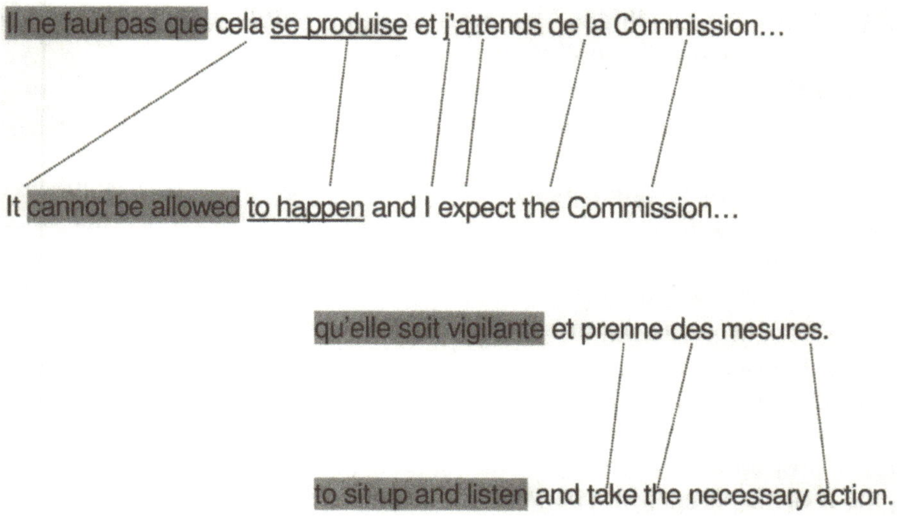

Figure 2. Example of null-alignments in the EuroParl corpus (id = 1151510)

Null-alignments are a problem even when using a perfect manual alignment as projection source, since some segments of the translations simply cannot be word-aligned even though they carry the same communicative purpose. Consider, for example, Figure 2, which illustrates how certain parts of sentences (marked in gray) have no word-to-word relations with their translations.

While it will not introduce errors into the projected side (being non-aligned, it is easy to avoid projecting the frames attached to these segments), it is possible that some expressions having systematically the same translations will never be projected, causing coverage problems. The second problem of this methodology, non-frame-conserving translations, is illustrated by the following sentences.

(1) «Si nous pouvons inciter les États membres à encourager une conduite automobile plus respectueuse de l'environnement, [la consommation $_{\text{THEME}}$] **suivra** $_{\text{Cotheme}}$ [rapidement $_{\text{MANNER}}$] [le mouvement $_{\text{COTHEME}}$].»

(Europarl:21546630:FR) constrained translation: "If we can encourage Member States to promote more environmentally conscious driving, the fuel consumption will quickly follow the movement."

(2) "If [we can encourage Member States to promote more environmentally conscious driving $_{\text{LANDMARK\_OCCASION}}$], [good driving patterns $_{\text{FOCAL\_OCCASION}}$] will [soon $_{\text{INTERVAL}}$] **follow** $_{\texttt{Relative\_time}}$." *(Europarl:21546630:EN)*

While a word-alignment system will link together *suivra* (follow + 3s + FUT) and *follow*, it is not the case that the two LUs express the same frame. The French LU evokes the `Cotheme` frame, related to the situation where something (the THEME) keeps close to a moving entity (the COTHEME). In contrast, the English LU evokes the `Relative_time` frame, the sequential meaning of "follow," where two events happen one after the other. This example is not a cross-lingual problem, since it is possible to express both frames in both languages. It is nevertheless a problem for a projection system relying on the assumption that word parallelism plus lexicon parallelism (parallel words can evoke at least one frame in common) means frame parallelism, as is the case with the system proposed by Padó and Lapata (2006).

Currently, FrameNet lexicons exist only for the languages for which a FrameNet project exists. This means that this approach only works for languages with existing resources, which would be useless, since such resources must first be built, either automatically (see, e.g., Padó and Lapata 2005a), or manually. Since we consider that a high quality semantic lexicon would improve the precision of an automatic labeling system, we propose in the next section a semi-automatic method for building such a resource at a reasonable cost.

3. Assisted manual construction of a frame-based lexicon for French

In this section, we describe and evaluate a method for the acquisition of lexical units (LUs) in a new language (here, French), based on the English FrameNet lexicon and several French/English dictionaries. The main idea behind this semi-manual method is to have the lexicographer focus on lexicon construction on a frame by frame basis. We show that with this method, creating a minimal FrameNet lexicon for a new language is a matter of one or two months for one lexicographer.

While it is not mandatory to have a FrameNet lexicon of the target language before starting a set of FrameNet annotations for a new language, its availability is useful for the FrameNet annotators to get quick advice about the frames potentially evoked by a lemma, thus avoiding some mis-

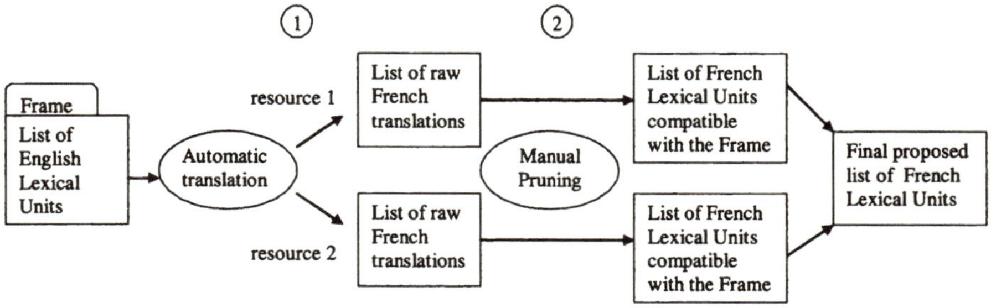

Figure 3. Schema of the procedure for the semi-automatic creation of a FrameNet lexicon for a new language

takes during the first phase of annotation. Such a resource is also useful for an automatic semantic role labeling system, in particular for guiding the Frame Target classification task (see below).

Building a lexicon for a new language is possible only because the frames of the Berkeley FrameNet have been shown to be useful as interlingual representations (see Boas 2005). In contrast to Padó and Lapata (2005a), who propose an unsupervised method for automatic lexicon construction based on frame information from the FrameNet database, we are interested in whether the English LUs contained in the FrameNet database can be "translated" manually into French at an affordable cost. This insight will help other researchers to identify the most effective method for constructing FrameNets for other languages. The main purpose of this undertaking is to provide an estimation of the time required for the creation of the whole lexicon.

Figure 3 represents the procedure we propose in order to arrive at a list of French LUs from an entry in the English FrameNet database. The procedure is the following: (1) For each frame in the FrameNet database, automatically extract all potential translations of its LUs, using available automatic translation resources; (2) This list must then be pruned manually: for each frame in the list and for each proposed LU, this LU must be tentatively mentally instantiated in one of the typical situations described in the frame description. The person performing the pruning has to think about the possible usage of a LU to describe one of the situations covered by the frame. A quick mental test is also to be performed in order to make the adequate choice: this test is about the similarity of the numbers and types of the arguments. This approach is mainly inspired by Fillmore et al. (2003b: 299–300) and Ruppenhofer et al. (2006: 11–13), and relies on the idea that when one attempts to find the frame(s) for each LU it may not always be necessary to check the validity of a choice against different frames.

We applied this procedure to the 15 most frequently occurring frames in the French gold standard corpus (see section 4.4.1), obtained as a set of translation lists from the English-French Semantic Atlas (Ploux and Ji 2003) and the WordReference online tool. We then manually pruned these two lists for each frame by removing the inappropriate entries after a careful reading of the English frame description. In a last step we merged for each frame the two pruned lists into one thereby creating a final LU list. Out of a total of 600 unique LUs, we removed 21 candidates that we judged inadequate at the final stage.

The Semantic Atlas (Ploux and Ji 2003) is a resource based on cross-language semantic mapping. This system maps words into a multi-dimensional space, based on information coming from bilingual dictionaries and synonym dictionaries in both languages. It currently covers only the French/English language pair and is freely available on the web. The WordReference online tool is a free resource for (at least) English/French, English/Italian, English/Spanish, and Spanish/Portuguese. Compared to the Semantic Atlas, the most significant difference is that the WordReference tool provides more multi-word expressions.

Using such language-specific resources makes this approach difficult for many languages, but it has the advantage of being independent of the frequency of the frames or LUs in a given corpus.

Table 1 shows the results of our translations of LUs from the selection of 15 FrameNet frames into French. The columns in Table 1 contain the following information for each of the processed frames:

- LU_{En}: the number of English LUs evoking a specific frame in the Berkeley FrameNet database;
- LU_{Fr}: the number of French LUs after automatically extracting all potential translations with the Semantic Atlas (SA) or the WordReference online tool (WR);
- LU_{Pr}: the number of remaining French LUs after manual pruning of each initial list;
- tim_{Pr}: the time (in seconds) spent on the manual pruning for each list of French LUs (SA and WR);
- LU_{Fin}: the final number of French LU after merging the pruned SA and WR lists, and after a final revision;
- tim_{Pr}/LU_{En}: the average number of seconds spent for each LU in the initial English list.

Table 1. Translations of FrameNet LUs into French

Frame	LU_{En}	LU_{Fr}		LU_{Pr}		tim_{Pr}		LU_{fin}	tim_{Pr}/LU_{En}
		SA	WR	SA	WR	SA	WR		
`Arriving`	19	165	527	28	20	290	671	27	50.5
`Awareness`	27	65	287	31	42	175	424	50	22.2
`Commerce_pay`	5	35	108	12	12	81	140	20	44.2
`Endangering`	4	2	4	1	4	15	8	4	5.8
`Event`	6	79	206	10	5	244	135	11	63.2
`Evidence`	28	175	391	38	41	295	444	49	26.4
`Giving`	21	135	367	33	22	257	333	37	28.1
`Hear`	2	16	39	2	3	65	42	3	53.5
`Judgment`	55	194	374	30	29	380	464	43	15.3
`Judgment_direct_address`	33	104	121	25	23	116	255	30	11.2
`Killing`	66	133	184	67	48	200	291	69	7.4
`Questioning`	12	35	85	5	11	59	167	13	18.8
`Removing`	40	276	347	54	30	476	648	59	28.1
`Request`	24	92	279	28	29	269	276	39	22.7
`Statement`	73	254	628	95	83	488	777	125	17.3
Total	415	1840	3879	459	402	3410	5075	579	20.4

Table 1 shows the divergence between SA and WR at the first step of the process, which is the production of translations from English to French. For instance, there is a minimal difference for `Judgment_direct_address`, for which SA produces 104 translations while WR produces 121 translations. The maximal difference is found in the frame `Awareness`, with 65 translations for SA and 267 for WR. The majority of pruned LUs resulted from polysemy-related errors. Many candidates from the WR resources were multi-word expressions, and a few of them were kept in the end, while the majority was easily pruned.

After the pruning phase, the difference between resources is largely reduced to a minimum: maximum divergence is about 30%, when the maximal divergence for the translation step is more than 400%. In addition, the ratio between the number of English LUs and the number of candidates after pruning is very consistent, ranging from 0.6 to 1.8 for frames with a significant number of candidates (for the whole set, mean = 1.09, standard deviation = 0.47). The ratios of the number of pruned candidates to initial English LUs are also consistent. For SA, mean = 1.16, standard deviation = 0.54. For WR, mean = 1.12, standard deviation = 0.47. From these results, we conclude that the lists of pruned LUs have characteristics relatively close to what is expected. The average ratio of the final number of French LUs (after merging of pruned lists from SA and WR) to the number of initial English LUs is 1.6, with a standard deviation = 0.76. Considering that French is known to have a slightly smaller vocabulary than English, this ratio should be less than 1. One way of expressing this is by saying that the way English LU lists are built does not guarantee that they are complete, since LUs are added manually by lexicographers. This is especially the case for adjectives, nouns and multiword expressions. The second factor is a loose pruning process, during which uncertain LUs are kept by default.

Table 2 describes four different ratios for SA, WR, and for the union of both: (1) the average number of French LUs (before pruning) per English LU, (2) the average number of French LUs (after pruning) per English LU, (3) the average number of seconds spent on pruning per French LU (from the raw lists of translations), and (4) the average time spent for pruning per English LU. The average pruning time per final French LU (after merging the two lists from SA and WR): 17.7 sec. (std = 9.9).

Table 2 demonstrates that SA and WR over-generate by a significant margin, with regard to the original English LU lists. It also shows that WR over-generates more than twice when compared to SA. It is interesting to note that despite this higher over-generation by a factor of 2.5 when

Table 2. Means and standard deviation values for the semi-manually built semantic lexicon (standard deviation in parentheses)

	Semantic Atlas	WordReference	All
LU_{Fr}/LU_{En}	5.2 (3.3)	12.8 (9.7)	18.1 (12.8)
LU_{Pr}/LU_{En}	1.2 (0.5)	1.1 (0.5)	2.3 (0.9)
tim_{Pr}/lu_{Fr}	0.5 (0.2)	0.8 (0.3)	0.6 (0.2)
tim_{Pr}/lu_{En}	12.3 (10.8)	15.3 (8.8)	27.7 (17.5)

using WR the average pruning time per English LU only differs by a factor of 1.25. Consequently, we consider that despite a high standard deviation, the average pruning time per English LU is a correct choice as a general predictor for the pruning time (while pruning time per French LU has a lower standard deviation, it would not be better to use it since the LU_{Fr}/LU_{En} ratio's standard deviation is equivalent to that of tim_{Pr}/LU_{En}). Also, the ratios LU_{Pr}/LU_{En} and LU_{fin}/LU_{En} show that using this procedure produces more LUs in French than what existed in English. This could be explained if French were known to have a larger vocabulary than English, but this is not the case. We suspect that our approach over-generates, or that English FrameNet still lacks some LUs in the relevant frames as we have more nouns and constructions with support verbs in our French data than found in the FrameNet database.

Table 3 shows how pruning improves the precision of the lists obtained, and how each of the resources contribute to the final result. Each row describes the precision and recall of one list compared to another. For instance, the first row gives, for the lists built from the SA resource, the score of the initial list compared to the list after pruning. The pruned list

Table 3. Precision and recall of each French LU list in the two following configurations: [raw translations] → [pruning] and [pruning] → [merging]

	Precision	Recall
LU_{Fr}/LU_{Pr} (SA)	24.9	100
LU_{Fr}/LU_{Pr} (WR)	10.3	100
LU_{Pr}/LU_{fin} (SA)	97.3	77.2
LU_{Pr}/LU_{fin} (WR)	97.7	67.8

thus contains 24.9% of the original list, which means that 75.1% of the initial candidates were removed. It is clear that despite lower over-generation, results obtained from the SA translation show a better precision compared to the pruned list and a better recall compared to the final list. Using WR in addition improves SA recall by 22.8%. This shows that in order to obtain a lexicon with good coverage, it is worth using several resources.

Based on these values, one can interpolate the time required to build a bootstrapped version of a lexicon for a new language using the equation in (i):

(i) $nbFrames \times frameInitTime + nbLU \times avgLUSelectTime$

In (i), *frameInitTime* denotes the time an annotator needs to read the description and the example annotations of a given frame, which we take to be about 4 minutes. With the 795 frames contained in FrameNet 1.3, and its 10195 LUs, the average expected time with this approach is about 132 hours, which is something quite acceptable even though the resulting data will not have the best accuracy and coverage. In the most extreme case, the maximum time per English LU (63 seconds for the frame `Event`) would add up to 232 hours of annotation time. However, these results should be regarded with some caution, given the fact that the annotator in our experiment had a previous knowledge of the English frames.

4. Robust LSA-based frame and frame element classification

In this section, we present our approach to cross-lingual semantic role annotation. The targeted tasks are to find the frame or FE evoked by a fragment of French text, using only the English data from the FrameNet database and a bilingual parallel corpus, which is used for training a LSA space.

FE classification in a monolingual set-up consists of linking a text segment to the FE it realizes based on a variety of features, such as the grammatical function (of the phrase covered by the text segment) and the head lemma. In a cross-lingual set-up, it is impossible to use grammatical features or raw lexical information, because these features are not transferred between languages (at least in the general case). As a consequence, we have to extract information that is not directly accessible in the linguistic form, but nevertheless transferred by the translation. Note that our goal is not to use rich annotation information in French to produce a full automatic role labeling of a text. Instead, we are interested in finding an efficient method for helping a human annotator in her task.

For our approach to work for a target language L, we require only the availability of the following three resources: (1) a bilingual, aligned corpus L/English; (2) English FrameNet annotations; (3) a part-of-speech tagger and a lemmatizer for English and the target language L (this should be optional). In our approach, no syntactic information is used, because we make the assumption that in a significant number of cases the semantic content of the sentence parts identified by a particular FE in a FrameNet annotation is *semantically coherent*, and thus may be used as a reference for FE classification. The measure of the cohesion of FEs will be discussed in section 4.2. Another significant advantage of our method is that it only relies on sentence-aligned parallel corpora, while projection-based methods require word-level alignments.

The meaning of "semantic" in this paper is the same as that in the L(atent) S(emantic) A(nalysis) approach, which is based on a singular value decomposition of a co-occurrence matrix (Landauer and Dumais 1997). More specifically, LSA allows, to some extent, a generalization to be performed over a co-occurrence matrix, making some relations appear between words where insufficient data would not in a normal vector space. The full process behind LSA learning is too long to be described here. The final product of LSA learning over a corpus is a multi-dimensional space where each word has a position (represented by a vector) related to its semantic content. Over this space we define a metric by which words with semantic relations are considered close to each other. We assume that a bilingual LSA space can be built and used to measure the similarity of a text segment in the target language with the vector representing a FE, computed from the English annotations of the original FrameNet. A bilingual LSA space would be one containing words in two languages. In such a space, a word in language L1 would be close to its translations in L2 as well as close to semantically related words in L1. By extension, a word in L1 would also be close to semantically related words in L2.

In order to evaluate our method, we adopt the following data preparation procedure: first, we choose and prepare the corpora in order to build the LSA vector spaces (the actual chosen corpora and the different preparations are discussed in section 4.1 below). Then, we build the monolingual and multilingual vector spaces (potentially with different parameters) and use them to verify our hypotheses, i.e., we measure the semantic cohesion of FEs, and measure the cross-lingual similarity in the bilingual spaces. Finally, for each FE in the FrameNet database, we extract all relevant annotations, transform them into a set of vectors in the LSA space and then create clusters out of these FE representations to distinguish important sub-groups of similar terms inside each FE. We hypothesize that this method will consequently improve the odds of finding the right similarity between sentence parts and FE reference vectors in the LSA space. In the following sections we provide a detailed discussion of the three steps used to evaluate our method.

4.1. Data preparation

4.1.1. Base corpora

We used several corpora for our project: (1) The multi-domain aligned Europarl corpus (Koehn 2005) contains 33.16 million French words and 28.65 million English words, and (2) the Hansard corpus (Roukos et al. 1995), which contains 19.8M words for English and 21.2M words for French. We also investigated a way to improve the lexical coverage of our training data (i.e. include more words in our LSA space), by the addition of monolingual data from the British National Corpus and bilingual data from Frantext.[3]

We experimented with three different data formats: (1) raw text, (2) concatenated part-of-speech and lemma, and (3) concatenated simplified part-of-speech (for instance: VV instead of VVZ, VVP or VVG) and lemma. We call "terms" the results of these transformations of the original words. These terms will be what is stored in an LSA space. For the bilingual data, we interleaved the terms, within segments provided by available markups (paragraphs and sentence marks). We used a classical point generation algorithm in order to guarantee the correct distribution of terms from both languages even when lengths of segments differ (see, e.g., Resnik and Melamed 1997).

Table 4 presents the three steps of our data preparation. The row at the top contains the original text, with a tag <P> marking the end of the paragraph (the example is short due to space reasons). The middle row contains the list of terms after the transformation (here using format 3, concatenated simplified part-of-speech). The bottom row contains the final interleaved data. Table 4 shows that despite the shortness of the example, the word *December* is ten terms away from its French equivalent. This makes it necessary to use a large co-occurrence window for the construction of the LSA space.

3. Frantext is a French corpus containing 3,737 texts of the following fields: sciences, arts, literature and engineering over 5 centuries (16th–20th). Subscription-based access at http://www.frantext.fr/.

Table 4. The three steps of corpus data preparation

	English	French
Original text	I declare resumed the session of the European Parliament adjourned on Friday 17 December 1999, and I would like once again to wish you a happy new year in the hope that you enjoyed a pleasant festive period. <P>	Je déclare reprise la session du Parlement européen qui avait été interrompue le vendredi 17 décembre dernier et je vous renouvelle tous mes voeux en espérant que vous avez passé de bonnes vacances. <P>
Transformed text	PPI VVdeclare VVresume DTthe NNsession INof DTthe NPEuropean NPParliament VVadjourn INon NPFriday NPDecember CCand PPI MDwould VVlike RBonce RBagain TOto VVwish PPyou DTa JJhappy JJnew NNyear INin DTthe NNhope INthat PPyou VVenjoy DTa JJpleasant JJfestive NNperiod <P>	PROje VERdéclarer VERreprendre DETle NOMsession PRPdu NOMparlement ADJeuropéen PROqui VERavoir VERêtre VERinterrompre DETle NOMvendredi NOMdécembre ADJdernier KONet PROje PROvous VERrenouveler PROtout DETmon NOMvoeux PRPen ADJespérant KONque PROvous VERavoir VERpasser PRPde ADJbon NOMvacance <P>
Interleaved result	<DOC><TEXT> PPI VVdeclare PROje VVresume DTthe VERdéclarer NNsession VERreprendre INof DETle DTthe NOMsession NPEuropean PRPdu NPParliament NOMparlement VVadjourn ADJeuropéen INon PROqui NPFriday VERavoir NPDecember CCand VERêtre PPI VERinterrompre MDwould DETle VVlike NOMvendredi RBonce NOMdécembre RBagain ADJdernier TOto KONet VVwish PROje PPyou PROvous DTa JJhappy VERrenouveler JJnew PROtout NNyear DETmon INin NOMvoeux DTthe PRPen NNhope ADJespérant INthat KONque PPyou PROvous VVenjoy VERavoir DTa JJpleasant VERpasser JJfestive PRPde NNperiod ADJbon NOMvacance </TEXT></DOC>	

4.1.2. Building LSA spaces

At the next stage, we computed the LSA spaces using the Infomap software (Flournoy et al. 1998). The available parameters for the computation of an LSA space are the following: pre/post terms window size,[4] rows (number of terms for which a vector is computed), columns (number of reference terms used as initial dimensions), singular values (max. number of final dimensions), and *singular vector decomposition* iterations (number of iterations in dimension reduction).

To illustrate the representation of terms in an LSA space, consider the first phrase annotated as a CONTAINER Frame Element (FE) in the frame

4. The term window is the segment of text taken into account for the calculation of the co-occurrence matrix. With a pre/post window size of 1, for instance, in the sentence *the little cat is playing with the dog, cat* will co-occur only with *little* and is.

`Apply_heat`, which is *in a large pan of boiling water*. After preprocessing (in the simple POS + lemma formatting case) the format of the phrase looks as follows: "INin DTa JJlarge NNpan INof VVboil NNwater". An interesting hint about the cohesion of the terms is given by the neighborhood of the centroid of these terms in the LSA semantic space.[5] The nearest neighbors of these terms in the LSA space are the following: NNpan (0.93), NNbowl (0.92), NNsaucepan (0.90), NNjug (0.89), VVpan (0.89), NNpeel (0.88), VVsprinkle (0.87), NNpot (0.86), NNtin (0.85), and NNcontainer (0.85).

The number associated with each term is the cosine of the angle between the centroid and the term's position in the semantic space:

$$s(P,t) = \cos\left(\sum \vec{v}(p \in P), \vec{v}(t)\right)$$

P is the phrase representing the FE (or all the phrases annotated for that FE), *t* is the term which is to be compared to P, v is a function returning the vector corresponding to a term in the LSA space. Cosine is often used as a similarity measure (see, e.g., Landauer and Dumais 1997, Lee 1999, and Karlgren J. and Sahlgren 2001: 303) with 1 being the maximum similarity and −1 the minimum.

4.1.3. Building representations of frame targets and Frame Elements

Recall that our main goal, illustrated in Figure 5, is to classify a segment of text that we will call the FE Evoking Text as one of the potential FEs of a given frame. This requires us to be able to evaluate the similarity of a FE Evoking Text such as *the revealing silk blouse she had worn in the show* with a given FE such as `Wearing`.CLOTHING. To this end, we must have a suitable FE Representation of the contents of the FEs, that is, all the annotations of a particular FE in the FrameNet database. We introduce the Frame Target (FT) Evoking Text and the FT Representation for the FT classification task.

Building a FE Representation consists of extracting the corresponding sentence subparts for each FE with an annotation (about 3,440), and of applying a transformation to the words coherent with the format chosen for the bilingual corpus. For instance, if we used the [simplified

5. The neighborhood of all non-empty FrameNet's Frame Elements can be found here (from a corpus of pure English): http://guillaume.work.free.fr/FramesText.Neighbors.en.html.

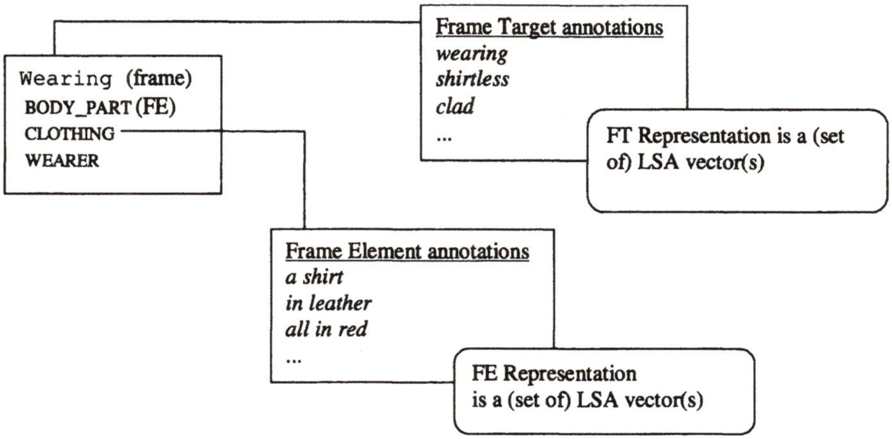

Figure 4. Building the Frame Element and Frame Target representations from the FrameNet database and an LSA space

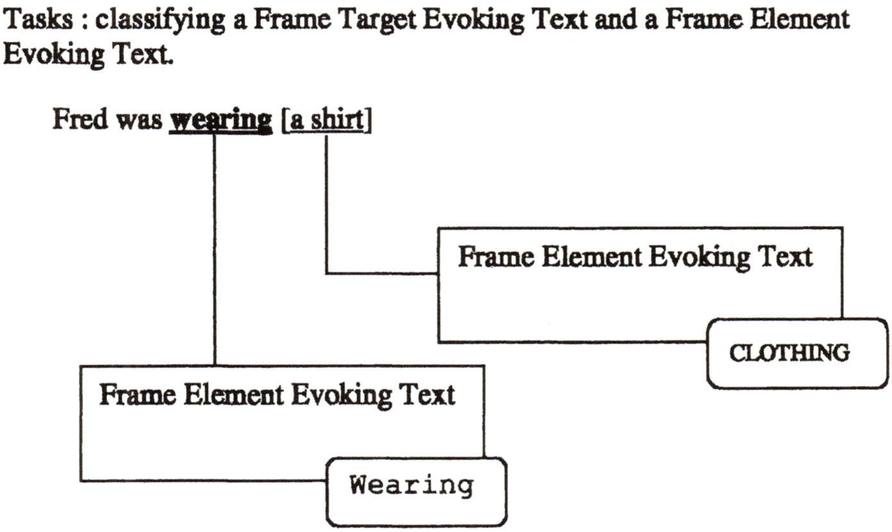

Figure 5. Schema of the Frame Element classification and Frame Target classification tasks

POS + lemma] format to build the LSA space from the corpus, the same transformation is applied to the words of the FE annotations. Once the list of all terms found in the text that evoke a frame (including its FEs) is built, three options are available.

1. The first option is to consider each term contained in the annotations of a FE, and to build an LSA vector out of it. In that case, the representation will be a potentially very large set of LSA vectors, which does not easily allow implementing a mechanism that takes into account only the most significant terms.
2. The second option is to add all the vectors of the FE terms, thus computing the centroid in the LSA high-dimensional space, of all the terms of the FE. This allows us to have a unique vector representing the whole FE. While this approach allows for a much faster similarity measure, it will lose many interesting features of the FE. For instance, if the FE is mainly characterized by four distinct categories of content words such as color (*white, blue,...*), matter (*silk, leather,...*), appearance (*shiny, mat, dirty,...*), and clothing type (*shirt, trouser,...*), the final vector will somehow blur these distinctive features, which is not necessarily a good thing since it means losing information about the FE's characteristics. With a blurred representation, the difference of similarity to a FE Representation between a good candidate and a bad one will decrease, and the classification will be less precise.
3. The third option is to make a clustering of the list of terms obtained in option (1) and to compute one vector per cluster. This option balances the two previous options in that it allows grouping similar terms while at the same time keeping distinct features separated.

We used the second approach in our pre-experiment evaluation of the semantic cohesion. We chose the last approach for the final classification task, which consists of selecting the most probable FE for a given French FE Evoking Text. As a clustering method we use the classical greedy agglomerative procedure (see Velldal 2003: 67–70).[6] We tested the results of the clustering using different arbitrary thresholds. Since the size of the clusters can be taken into account in the function that measures the similarity of a term with a FE Representation, small clusters, which are probably not significant for the FE, can be discarded. The potential of this method is limited since many FEs have too few annotations for a clustering to be considered useful. Also, the terms in a FE can be quite scattered semantically in which case the clustering will have no effect since no cate-

6. The greedy agglomerative clustering procedure starts with each element considered initially as a singleton cluster. Then clusters are iteratively merged with their nearest neighbor when their distance is below a given threshold.

gory will emerge. An extreme example of this is the FE TOPIC in the `Statement` frame.

Before proceeding to the classification experiment, we also wanted to validate our hypothesis that a significant number of FEs from the English FrameNet database have a high degree of semantic cohesion. We considered this to be a necessary step assuring that our approach was not bound to fail.

4.2. Semantic cohesion of FEs

In this section we characterize FEs by how likely they will lead to correct classifications. For example, we assume that if annotations for a FE only contain color adjectives it should lead to very good classification scores. In contrast, a FE whose annotations contain words from many different categories will be harder to classify correctly.

We understand semantic cohesion of a FE to denote the degree to which the individual words that make up the FE (i.e. word in text segments annotated with the FE) are semantically similar. This is comparable to the distance between synsets in WordNet (see Fellbaum 1998). For example, a high measure of semantic cohesion is expected for sets of semantically related LUs such as [*tomato, onion, potato, bean*], [*trouser, jeans, hat, shirt*], [*wrist, shoulder, leg, thigh*]. In contrast, a low score should be set for a list of unrelated terms such as [*tomato, shirt, leg*]. Analyzing semantic cohesion of frames and FEs is interesting for a number of reasons, because it may indicate that a semantic type can be attributed to a given FE.

To evaluate the coverage of our approach we first considered the percentage of FEs that seemed acceptable for automatic annotation based on the author's intuitive judgment. Before the experiment began, we computed a list of the mean similarity of the 100 nearest neighbors of each FE by using the FE centroid vector as a point of comparison.[7] The *LSA neighborhood* of a term (or, in this case, of a FE) represents the terms that surround it in the LSA space, giving us an important insight about its position in the semantic space. We found that the FEs with the highest Nearest Neighbors Similarity (NSS) appear to be related to a coherent list of terms, and appear to be coherent FEs, too. At the same time, FEs such as *.TOPIC, for which one could expect a scattered distribution, are all in

7. The full table of FEs sorted by average similarity is available at: http://guillaume.work.free.fr/FramesText.Neighbors.en.html/byavg.html.

the bottom 50% of the list and their NNS never exceeds 0.57 (the similarity measure being a cosine, its maximum value is 1). As a threshold, we chose 0.6 since at this value some neighborhoods begin to look less coherent, even though most are in fact coherent. In general, we found that the lower the NNS, the more likely it seems to imply a semantically scattered FE. If we consider only FEs representing more than 15 lemmas (1,841 out of 3,225 FEs in FrameNet version 1.2), and a NNS over 0.6 (986 out of 1,841), we find that those FEs are related to 285 frames (out of a total of 480).[8] This suggests that about 59% of FrameNet frames should each have an average of 3 FEs with high semantic cohesion and a number of annotations that seem sufficient to be useful for an automatic task. However, NSS presents an important drawback since it depends on the density of the surrounding semantic space. A better alternative is to compute the variance of the FE Representation, that is, the average distance of each annotation to the center of the FE Representation. The NSS was originally chosen because of its meaning for human annotators.

To evaluate our approach, we also wanted to verify the semantic coherence of the FEs after the experiment took place, using the results of the classification instead of manual evaluation. To this end, we considered the method of Padó and Boleda (2004) who evaluate the correlation between the quality of the automatic annotation and what they call "Argument Structure Uniformity" (ASU), which is related to the regularity of the pairings of grammatical functions with semantic roles (i.e., FEs). In order to measure the ASU of a frame, one must first compute the vector space associated with the frame (different from the LSA vector space above), each different pairing being one dimension of the vector space (Padó and Boleda 2004: 106). For instance, suppose that the frame `Awareness` is instantiated with patterns that consist of the following pairings of grammatical functions with FEs: {(COGNIZER, SUBJ), (CONTENT, COMP)} twice, and {(CONTENT, SUBJ), (COGNIZER, COMP)} once. Based on this information, we can define a vector space where the patterns are dimension labels of the vector space. At the same time, the probability of each pattern is then measured by the length of the vectors. Then one can measure the similarity of any annotation pairing in this space. The sum of all similarities between the pairings gives the frame a certain degree of uniformity. This method produces a syntax/semantics

8. The list of the Frames with at least one FE with an average over 0.6 may be read here: http://guillaume.work.free.fr/good_frames.txt.

correlation measure, which is not directly applicable for our purposes, but which can be adapted to our own approach.

Our objective is to determine the semantic cohesion of an FE, i.e., the semantic cohesion of the words composing the FE annotations. We propose to test both a measure based on the average term/FE Representation similarity, and a measure based on semantic neighborhood computed in an LSA vector space built from a monolingual corpus. We do not rely on a per-FE vector space because of the supplemental data provided by the LSA space. This will result in better similarity scores between terms that are considered semantically related in the LSA vector space.

Despite the apparent good cohesion measure presented by the neighborhood similarity measure as presented above in the pre-experiment situation, both the Pearson (linear) and Kendall (ordinal) correlations show no statistically significant relation between automatic annotation success and cohesion of FEs. The Pearson correlation factor computes the linear relation between two random variables. For instance, if x happens to be systematically equal to $N.y$, with N constant, then the Pearson correlation of x and y will be 1, the maximum correlation. The Kendall correlation, on the other hand, computes the correlation of two random variables based on the fact that the relation between the variables maintains the relative order.

4.3. Automatic classification methods

In this section we illustrate our methods for the automatic classification of French FEs and FT Evoking Texts, based on English data from the FrameNet database. We first present the method for FE classification, then the method for Frame Target classification.

4.3.1. Frame Element classification

As pointed out above, we do not expect a system using as little information as ours to be usable as a fully automatic role labeling system. Therefore, we only consider the case of classification of pre-segmented text, called the "unrestricted case" by Litkowski (2004: 11). We assume that both the target frame and the boundaries of FE Evoking Texts are known. The correct FE is chosen from all potential FEs of a frame, and not from the smaller subset of core FEs (see Atkins et al. 2003: 267).

Equation (ii) presents the scoring function we propose for the classification task of a FE Evoking Text (noted T) consisting of several words. This function is based on the similarity of a term's vector t with a cluster vector

c_i with $W(c_i)$ terms in a given LSA space. The cluster belongs to the set $K_{cf}(fe)$ of clusters of the FE Representation *fe* built with *cf* as the clustering threshold. For each *fe* we know the number of terms $W(fe)$ and the average annotation length $avgLen(fe)$.

(ii) $$\alpha(T, fe) = \sum_{t \in T} \sum_{\substack{c_i \in K_{cf}(fe) \wedge \\ \cos(t, c_i) > s_{\min}}} \frac{\cos^k(t, c_i) W(c_i)}{avgLem(fe)}$$

We chose to add the similarities and not just select the pair (FE, term) with the highest similarity, because of the multiple terms that constitute a FE Evoking Text. This ensures that a candidate FE Evoking Text with terms that match with several important clusters of a FE Representation will have a higher score than a candidate FE Evoking Text with only one excellent term. The parameter k is used to increase the impact of the pure semantic similarity. The factor $W(c_i)$ gives more importance to big clusters (since they are, for a given FE Representation, reliably better clues than smaller clusters), while $avgLen(fe)$ corrects the inappropriate advantage it would confer to FEs for which annotations are longer (and thus have necessarily bigger clusters).

Apart from the pure semantic similarity, there is another feature available in our low-resource approach: the average length (in words) of FE annotations in English. More specifically, the correlation of text length between languages has been shown to be a very good predictor for bilingual text alignment (see, e.g., Church 1993). Equation (iii) defines a predictor based on the ratio of the length of a given FE Evoking Text, labeled $len(T)$, with the average length of the annotations of a particular FE *fe*, represented as $avgLen(fe)$. The parameter *lenFactor* is used for smoothing of the ratio function. This predictor is expected to decrease the score of FE Evoking Texts whose length drastically differs from the average FE's annotation length. The final combination of equations is illustrated in (iv), where the semantic scoring function is added an ε arbitrarily set at 10^{-5}. This serves as a minimal similarity when no semantic information is available (i.e. when the terms of the FE Evoking Text being processed are not in the LSA space).

(iii) $$lr(T, fe) = \left(\frac{\min(len(T), avgLem(fe))}{\max(len(T), avgLen(fe))} \right)^{lenFactor}$$

(iv) $$score(T, fe) = (\varepsilon + \alpha(T, fe)) \times lr(T, fe)$$

Considering the small number of samples in the gold standard corpus and the unbalanced distribution of frames and FEs, the choice of the learning method fell back to the simplest one, namely expectation maximization (McLachlan and Thriyambakan 1997). This method uses a small number of features in order to avoid over-fitting, which occurs when one uses too powerful a classification approach on a small set of examples. In such cases, the classifier performs perfectly on the training sample, but fails to generalize over the test set. As noted by an anonymous reviewer, it would have been perfectly possible to use a more powerful learning method, provided the learning would have been performed on the English FrameNet dataset. Since our model is almost completely language-independent, it is indeed a viable alternative that should be evaluated in the next experiments. However, learning the parameters for a monolingual set-up may cause an overestimation of the *k* parameter because of a higher accuracy of LSA similarity between terms of the same language. This is the main reason for choosing to learn on a dataset in the target language. We now turn to the problem of FT Evoking Text classification, which is closely related to FE Evoking Text classification, but presents different problems.

4.3.2. Frame target classification

Even with a complete FrameNet lexicon, the lexical ambiguity would require classification to be performed to find the frame evoked by a word in a sentence. We consequently worked on an adaptation of the FE Evoking Text cross-language classification method to FT Evoking Texts. The method presented here is intended for lexicon-free use, i.e., the possible frames are taken from the complete FrameNet frame set. Future versions intended for a disambiguation task between a restricted set of frames would more likely be based on a global optimization of FE assignments.

Unlike classification of FE Evoking Texts, classification of FT Evoking Texts does not benefit from the length of annotated segments. Consequently, the score representing the adequacy of a frame relative to a FT Evoking Text only relies on the semantic similarity and the weight of the relative cluster. The score is described in equation (v). The notation used is the same as for FE Evoking Text classification. Equation (v) defines a function that takes a list T of terms and a frame target representation *f*. This function returns the highest similarity between T and the clusters of *f*. The similarity itself is based on the cosine between the vector representing T and a cluster of *f*. The parameters of the function that have to be learned are *k, cr* and *fr*. The classification consists of finding *f* such that $\beta(T, f)$ is maximized.

(v) $$\beta(T, f) = \max\left(\left\{\cos^k(T, c_i)\left(\frac{W(c_i)^{cr}}{W(f)}\right)^{fr} : c_i \in K_{cf}(f)\right\}\right)$$

We now turn to the results of our classification methods for FEs and frame targets. We start with a description of the French gold standard corpus we created for these purposes.

4.4. Experimental setup and results

In this section we present the experimental setup used to evaluate the methods presented above. We first present the French gold standard annotation created for this evaluation and compare it to its English and German counterparts. We then present the results of the Frame Target classification task followed by the results of the FE classification task.

4.4.1. French FrameNet gold standard annotation

We created a French corpus corresponding to the English/German EuroParl sub-corpus used by Padó and Lapata (2005b) and annotated it to obtain a gold standard annotation. The annotation of 1,076 sentences was performed with the SALTO tool (Burchardt et al. 2006b), which allows assigning FEs to phrases in a graphical interface. Two annotators, native speakers of French, performed the annotation. The two annotators independently annotated each occurrence of 740 sentences, the rest being annotated by only one of them.

The annotators were given an annotation guide which contained for each sentence the probable target word and a set of possible semantic frames. The list of possible frames was established from the French target, using the automatically inferred lexicon by Padó and Lapata (2005a). This guide was mandatory because the annotated French corpus was primarily intended to be used for the evaluation of the approach of Padó and Lapata (2005b) on the French/English language pair. The annotators also had access to the syntactic parse of the corpus from the Syntex parser (Bourigault 2005), as well as to French/English dictionaries and the FrameNet database. Finally, when they observed major discrepancies between the corpus and the guide, the annotators had access to the English version of the sentence.

The French annotation utilizes 121 different frames, while the English and German sides counted 83 and 73 different frames, respectively. In French, 957 out of the 1,076 sentences were actually linked to a frame, the remaining sentences were considered as evoking frames that were not available in the FrameNet 1.2 dataset. Note that some sentences were marked as being related to frames from the 1.3 version, but not annotated.

Adjudication was performed after the annotators finished their work. Adjudication (see, e.g., Strassel 2000) determines the choice of the annotation that will go into the final gold standard corpus, whenever the annotations for a sentence are dissimilar. In the ideal case, the adjudicator should be a third person, but due to lack of participants in the project, the two annotators cooperated on this task. Table 5 compares the inter-annotator agreements (before adjudication) on frames, FEs and FE spans for the three languages. Data for English and German come from Padó and Lapata (2005b) on a calibration set of 100 sentences. The French data come from a calibration set of 500 sentences. The table shows a slight difference for the French annotation on FE agreement and span. The low score on span agreement is probably due to a problem with the span measure relying on syntactic nodes, since the French syntactic analysis was taken directly from an uncorrected automatic analysis.

The other results for the cross-language matching are quite close to those obtained by Padó and Lapata for German and English (2005b: 861), as shown in Table 6. This is particularly interesting since the subset of the Europarl corpus is also the subset used in our own work. It was initially

Table 5. Monolingual inter-annotator agreements

Measure	English	German	French
Frame Agr.	0.9	0.87	0.87
FE Agr.	0.95	0.95	0.89
Span Agr.	0.85	0.83	0.72

Table 6. F-measures of cross-lingual annotations matching between French, English and German sub-corpora

Measure	French/English	German/English
Frame Match	0.69	0.71
FE Match	0.88	0.91

selected using the following criteria for sentence pairs: (1) Having at least one pair of aligned terms listed as LUs in the English FrameNet and in SALSA, and (2) having these target terms evoke at least one common frame.

These results illustrate the problems described in section 2.2 and show that the methods developed to serve as workarounds turn out not to perform as expected. In Table 5, inter-annotator agreements at the frame level for each of the three languages are equivalent: 87% for French and German; 90% for English. Table 6 shows that the inter-lingual agreement at the frame level varies from 69% (French/English) to 71% (German/English). This may demonstrate that translation-caused frame loss for these language pairs is about 21 $\pm$ 2% for the sample used in the experiment.

Table 7 presents evidence for a different distribution of frames in the annotations for the three languages. For instance, in French the number of frames with less than 10 annotations and the total number of their annotations are about twice as many as the equivalent in both English and German. Conversely, frames with 10 to 50 annotations represent only 44% of all annotations in French, compared to 66% in German and 63% in English. This observation is best explained by the rules that drove the selection of the original sub-corpus for English and German. Indeed, selecting only sentences with probable parallel frame-evoking terms avoids many translational divergences. Consequently, several French translations made use of new frames that occurred only a few times in the corpus. These results clearly support our hypothesis that many translations are not frame-conserving.

Table 7. Distribution of frames in the three gold corpora. Each row counts the number of frames with the number of annotations in a given range, and (in parentheses) the sum of annotations for all of these frames

Annot./Frame	French	German	English
100 +	1 (144)	1 (154)	1 (142)
50–99	2 (130)	1 (78)	1 (68)
25–49	5 (144)	11 (346)	7 (237)
10–24	20 (315)	14 (228)	25 (389)
5–9	19 (118)	7 (51)	12 (77)
0–4	74 (115)	38 (82)	37 (74)
Total	121 (966)	73 (987)	83 (987)

4.4.2. Frame target classification results

We now turn to our experiment evaluating the automatic frame target classification approach. We show how our method compares when used with a monolingual English corpus for training the LSA space in comparison with a bilingual French/English space. In a real manual annotation task, the automatic Frame Target classification would provide one or more potentially evoked frames given a particular word. This would be especially useful for a continuous text annotation task in a new language. In that situation, the annotator is forced to first translate the target word into English, and then search in the English FrameNet database for the frames evoked by all the translations.

The frame target projection was initialized for the whole set of available frames for the latest two versions of FrameNet (data releases 1.2 and 1.3). The 1.2 version contains 415 frames with annotations for the target LUs, while the 1.3 version contains 500 such frames.[9] Considering the high number of potential frames, the best baseline is based on the systematic assignment of the most probable frame (`Statement`), which leads to a baseline of only 14.9% (for both English and French). Another baseline should be taken into account if a lexicon was available for the new language, but then the classification method would be different, too.

Recall that our goal here is to identify the frame that can be evoked by a French fragment of text, using only the English data from FrameNet in combination with a bilingual parallel corpus that is used for training the LSA space. There is a cross-lingual transition of knowledge about frame targets and FEs. Considering the noise introduced by the bilingual corpus and the LSA training, we evaluated the performance of the frame target classification. In addition, we evaluated the difference in the annotation of English with a monolingual approach as well as with bilingual data to check the impact of the noise of the alignment. We used an LSA space trained on pure English data from the BNC, and the bilingual French-English LSA space trained on the Europarl (EP) corpus.

Each evaluation was conducted with a set of parameters for the scoring functions that were obtained from expectation-maximization on a training sub-corpus containing 100 sentences. The optimal functions parameters are $k = 14$, $fr = 0.2$, and $cr = 0.9$. Results are stable across a wide range

9. The total number of defined frames for FrameNet 1.2 and 1.3 are 609 and 795, respectively. Some of them have no or too few annotations to be used in the experiment, and thus we finally use only 415 (1.2) and 500 (1.3) frames.

Table 8. Results of the frame target classification task on the English gold annotation

Parameters	Prec.	Recall	F-measure
BNC(FN1.2)	0.735	0.735	0.735
EP1(FN1.2)	0.73	0.727	0.728
BNC(FN1.3)	0.718	0.717	0.718
EP1(FN1.3)	0.724	0.721	0.722

of thresholds for clustering and parameters for the LSA spaces. In the following tables, we use these labels: BNC is the LSA space trained on the British National Corpus in the simplified POS + lemma format, clustered with a threshold of 0.9, with SVD (Singular Values Decomposition) parameters: 50,000 rows, 1,000 columns, and 60 terms window (30 left, 30 right); EP1 is the LSA space trained from the interleaved corpus EuroParl French + English, same format and parameters as BNC except for the number of columns: 2,000; EP2 is the same as EP1 except: 120,000 rows, 5,000 columns, and 20 terms window (10 left, 10 right).

Table 8 shows the results for the annotation of the English gold standard corpus. It clearly demonstrates that the results for English are quite satisfying despite the small amount of data used in this approach. Moreover, using the monolingual corpus (BNC) or the bilingual corpus (EP1) does not significantly alter the results, even when they cover different domains (politics for EP) and genres (spoken language for EP). Changing the monolingual to the bilingual space does not alter the results significantly, which is a very interesting result since it proves that the bilingual space represents at least one of the languages with the same quality as the monolingual space.

Table 9 shows the results for French: the performance falls by about 14% F-score. The impact of the cross-lingual transition is clearly important in the case of the frame target classification. Recall, however, that the inter-annotator agreement for frames on the English gold standard corpus is 90% for English and 87% for French. The real impact of the cross-lingual transition in this case thus might be closer to an F-score of 11% rather than 16%. Another point shown in Table 9 is the impact of the parameters of the LSA training on the results of the classification. In the case of frame target classification, using an LSA space trained with a bigger matrix and a smaller window leads to a performance drop of about

Table 9. Results of the frame target classification task on the French gold annotation

Parameters	Prec.	Recall	F-measure
EP1(FN1.2)	0.589	0.58	0.584
EP2(FN1.2)	0.528	0.521	0.524
EP1(FN1.3)	0.58	0.571	0.576
EP2(FN1.3)	0.526	0.519	0.522

5–6% F-score (significant with the χ^2 test for $p = 0.01$). Finally, both Table 8 and Table 9 show that there is almost no difference in performance between FrameNet 1.2 and 1.3, which is quite interesting since version 1.3 describes 20% more frames than version 1.2.

4.4.3. *Frame element classification results*

We now present the results of the FE classification task. Considering the objective of the research, which is to provide robust help for manual annotation, the task consisted of selecting the right FE (from all the potential FEs, core and non-core) for a given frame. The FE annotation task has been conducted using clusters computed from the FrameNet annotations on 2,835 FEs (FrameNet 1.2) or 4,034 FEs (FrameNet 1.3), using different LSA spaces as references for the clustering and for the similarity measure. Considering the task, we define as our baseline the selection of the FE with the highest probability from all the FEs of the frame, producing a score with an F-measure as high as 41% (average distribution of the most probable FE of each frame). For instance, identifying the FE of the `Awareness` frame consists of selecting the correct FE from the 9 FEs in Table 10. The baseline we chose is equivalent to the systematic choice of the most probable FE, which in this case is the FE COGNIZER.

Using the clustering with very high thresholds (>0.97) is strictly equivalent to a term-by-term comparison. With a slightly lower threshold (0.9), there is a strong gain in terms of speed, and no loss in performance. As a consequence we chose this latter threshold for our experiments. Other parameters have been found to produce an optimum result for $k = 5$, $s_{min} = 0.2$, and $lenFactor = 0.535$.

The impact of the kind of data preparation applied to the corpus (raw text, pos + lemma, simplified pos + lemma) and the types of corpora used for bilingual training (Europarl, Europarl + BNC, Europarl + Hansard)

Table 10. Distribution of FE annotations in FrameNet 1.3 for the `Awareness` frame

Frame element	# of annotations	%
COGNIZER	789	40%
CONTENT	788	40%
DEGREE	47	2%
EVIDENCE	40	2%
MANNER	6	0.3%
PARADIGM	5	0.25%
ROLE	1	0%
TIME	1	0%
TOPIC	283	14%

Table 11. Average impact of data preparation and corpus choice on the resulting f-measure compared to the optimum choice

Version	Average impact
Raw text	– 0.19
POS + lemma	– 0.02
Simp. POS + lemma	0.0
Europarl	0.0
Europarl + BNC	– 0.03
Europarl + Hansard	– 0.11

are summarized in Table 11. It shows that the best choice for the FE classification task is the simplified version using only the Europarl corpus.

Table 12 shows the results of the classification of FEs in the English gold standard annotation. Our results can be directly compared with the results of the Senseval-3 non-restricted task (Litkowski 2004), with the notable difference that we performed our experiment on data that are not in the BNC corpus. In this task of the Senseval evaluation, the best system achieved 94.6% precision and 94.6% recall, the lowest score being 72.8%/72.5%, and the average score being 80.3%/75.7%. Without any syntactic information available, our system performs slightly better on the English

Table 12. Results of FE classification on the English gold annotation

Parameters	Prec.	Recall	F-measure
BNC(FN1.2)	0.729	0.726	0.727
EP1(FN1.2)	0.737	0.734	0.735
BNC(FN1.3)	0.718	0.717	0.717
EP1(FN1.3)	0.727	0.71	0.718

Table 13. Results of FE classification on the French gold annotation

Parameters	Prec.	Recall	F-measure
EP1(FN1.2)	0.658	0.62	0.638
EP2(FN1.2)	0.665	0.627	0.645
EP1(FN1.3)	0.647	0.633	0.64
EP2(FN1.3)	0.665	0.651	0.658

gold standard annotation than the system with the lowest score evaluated in Senseval-3 for this task. This suggests that using LSA as a lexical generalization model is a good choice. Another interesting insight is that our approach performs better (+1%/+1% precision/recall improvement in EP1, statistically significant with the χ^2 test for $\rho = 0.01$) when using the 1.2 version of FrameNet, which has fewer frames and fewer annotations. The significance of this small difference is mainly caused by the difference in terms of uncovered FEs: 38 with version 1.3 and 105 with version 1.2. The higher ambiguity introduced by a richer FrameNet thus has a negative impact on our system, which is the tradeoff for a potentially higher coverage in terms of LUs and frames.

Comparing Table 12 with Table 13, we see that the impact of cross-lingual transition from English/EP1 to French/EP1 is on average −8% on precision and −9.5% on recall. Considering that inter-annotator agreement on FEs was 95% for the English gold standard corpus and 89% for French, the real impact of cross-lingual transition is about −4% on precision and −5% on recall, which appears promising. Table 13 and Table 14 both show that using EP2 instead of EP1 do not significantly alter the performance of classification.

Table 14. Results of FE classifications on the French gold annotation without the length ratio predictor

Parameters	Prec.	Recall	F-measure
EP1(FN1.2)	0.619	0.584	0.60
EP2(FN1.2)	0.622	0.586	0.60
EP1(FN1.3)	0.607	0.595	0.60
EP2(FN1.3)	0.618	0.605	0.611

4.5. Comparison with other approaches

Our approach is novel in that it only uses English FrameNet and a bilingual corpus in order to directly classify FT Evoking Texts and FE Evoking Texts based on French texts. Gildea and Jurasfky's (2002: 266–271) lexical-only classification approach is, in essence, rather similar to our own system, even though there are some important differences: (1) their test data was taken from the BNC, which is also the corpus used for training; (2) it was constructed using a FrameNet release containing only 67 frames related to 1,462 LUs; (3) they used some syntactic knowledge to focus on the heads of the NPs constituents. The first point is probably not a significant factor, since the BNC is a balanced corpus. Also, we tried our system only on NPs, and its performance dropped by a few percent, so point (3) is probably not a significant factor. We will thus focus on point (2) to see how it may explain the differences between their approach and ours.

We compare Gildea and Jurafsky's results with our results on the FE classification task performed on the English gold standard corpus. The Gildea and Jurafsky system achieves a precision of 79.7% and a coverage of 97.9% (2002: 269). In contrast, our system, using EP1 and FrameNet 1.2, achieves a precision of 73.7% and a coverage of 99.7%. Note that coverage must be considered with caution because in our case the test corpus is taken from the corpus used for learning the LSA space. Considering that (1) we have demonstrated in section 4.4.3 that using FrameNet version 1.2 instead of 1.3 improved the precision and recall by a statistically significant 1% and (2) that FrameNet 1.2 contains 415 annotated frames as opposed to 500 in the 1.3 version, we might try interpolation. This would lead to a 5% expected improvement from the version of FrameNet used by Gildea and Jurafsky (2002) over FrameNet version 1.2. Such a result is roughly equivalent to the difference in precision of 6% observed between our two systems.

Our direct cross-lingual classification approach presents a fundamental advantage over projection-based approaches. Indeed, in the projection paradigm, at least three steps are ultimately necessary: (1) training of a classifier for the automatic labeling of the source language side of the parallel corpus, (2) projection of the annotation from the source to the target side and (3) training of a classifier in the target language from the projected annotation. Each step requires effort and introduces noise. Comparing our results with the projection-based approach of Johansson and Nugues (2006) for argument classification is possible because they performed an annotation of Swedish text based on English FrameNet, while Padó and Lapata (2005b) only evaluate the projection quality. More specifically, Johansson and Nugues used an automatic role labeling system in order to annotate the English side of a bilingual corpus (EuroParl) and then projected these annotations to Swedish. They finally trained an automatic role labeling system on the Swedish annotated corpus, and used it to automatically annotate 150 Swedish sentences. These sentences were obtained by manually translating the 150 sentences from the English FrameNet database. These sentences were also manually annotated in order to serve as the gold standard annotation for evaluation. In the non-restrictive case (i.e., FE Evoking Text classification), their system achieved a high precision (0.75), which outperforms our system by 9%. However, their evaluation is highly questionable, because they manually chose appropriate sentences and then translated them. This probably means that no non-frame-conserving translation was performed, either because sentences that would require the use of another frame were not selected, or because translations were made in a conserving way. This is relatively easy to accomplish between closely related languages such as English and Swedish. While the choice of the manual translation and the choice of the number of sentences of the gold standard corpus may be questionable, we will nonetheless take for granted that this result accurately reflects the performance of their system. In our opinion, the main difference between our approaches is not only the projection phase, but also the use of a chunk parser in Johansson and Nugues' approach as opposed to no parsing in our approach. In order to show that simple syntactic information may greatly improve our system, we analyzed some of the errors our system produced.

An analysis of the incorrect classifications appearing in our first 100 sentences shows that about 45% of the errors could be avoided with the simple knowledge of what elements are subjects or objects. For instance, in *je vous donne un exemple* ('I give you an example'), *vous* is classified as the DONOR instead of as the RECIPIENT of `Giving`, because *vous* can be both a nominative and a dative form of "*you* + Plural". This shows that the use of very simple syntactic information should improve the precision of our automatic classification approach. Another significant amount of errors (33%) could be corrected by a global optimization by which our approach could quite easily reach a precision as high as 77%. This would be the case after 33% of the errors are corrected. Considering that our system currently has an error rate of 34%, it should be lowered down to 23%, giving it a precision of 77%. The global optimization of the sentence categorization requires making the assumption that each FE can occur at most once in a sentence. In the following sentence part: *[...] bien que* [*j*$_1$]*'apprécie* [*son travail*$_2$] (Europarl: 18994668), our system classifies both FE Evoking Texts as COGNIZER, while [$_2$] should be classified as an EVALUEE. Looking more deeply into the results of the classifier and considering the two best choices, we see that the score of [$_1$] is 14.7 for COGNIZER and 0.7 for EVALUEE, while the score assigned to [$_2$] is 14.4 for COGNIZER and 12.2 for EVALUEE. Making a global optimization on that result entails selecting the best distribution of classes, which is in this case: COGNIZER for [$_1$] and EVALUEE for [$_2$]. This improvement is the obvious next step of our research, since it does not require any new or language-specific knowledge. A generalized global optimization method is, e.g. proposed by Punyakanok et al. (2004: 1350–1352), who use Integer Linear Programming.

Even though our results are not directly comparable to the results obtained by Gildea and Jurafsky (2002) and Johansson and Nugues (2006), it is apparent that our approach is not yet ready to be used as a full automatic labeling system. It still requires some improvements such as the use of deep syntactic knowledge since finding the boundaries of FEs may not be possible without such information.

An important question is whether our approach in its current state is useful as an annotation aid for low-resource languages. Considering that it would require annotators to select frames and boundaries of FEs, it is possible that a 65% precision rate will not be sufficient to actually improve the annotation speed. In contrast, the frame target classification task is more difficult for human annotators, as the inter-annotator agreement for frame targets of about 3–5% is below the one of FEs, and takes significantly more time. Considering that our automatic method shows a maximum precision of 58% using FrameNet version 1.3, it is probably more compelling than the automatic FE classification. The usefulness of the latter will certainly be proven once the global optimization improves it as expected since a precision near 77% is in the domain of monolingual classification approaches.

5. Conclusion and future work

Starting FrameNets for new languages can be an uncertain undertaking in terms of time and resources. The Berkeley FrameNet is now ten years old and still covers only a part of the English language, a part whose evaluation itself is difficult. Existing FrameNets for other languages such as Spanish FrameNet (Subirats and Petruck 2003) or Japanese FrameNet (Ohara et al. 2006) that choose manual annotation as their primary method demonstrate that the creation of a new FrameNet is still a time-intensive effort despite the availability of pre-existing frames offered by the Berkeley FrameNet database (see also Boas 2005).

Considering these facts, it is tempting to consider the use of automatic methods, either for a pure automatic annotation, or as a guide for annotators. A method using automatic role projection in a parallel bilingual corpus has already been developed by Padó and Lapata (2005b) and Johansson and Nugues (2006). It relies heavily on syntactic information, and thus may not necessarily be applied to other languages where such resources do not exist. Moreover, it may show some limits in terms of coverage, since there is almost necessarily some loss of information at each of the three steps of the process: (1) automatic annotation in English, (2) projection into the new language, and (3) learning by an automatic labeling system for the new language from the projected data. In this paper we explored an alternative method that takes a simpler approach to role annotation, based only on lexical similarity. This method is based on a bilingual vector space built with the Latent Semantic Analysis generalization method. With results of around 65% precision, there is still room for further improvement. However, considering the simplicity of our method, it already provides a solid minimal baseline for future research on cross-lingual automatic role annotation systems.

Based on our results we are planning to investigate a set of methods that we believe may significantly improve the performance of our approach. The first step is to perform global optimization at the sentence level. Considering our observations of the system's errors, and the fact that about 33% of all errors could be corrected with global optimization, the system should be able to reach precision near 77%. The second step will be to use an SVM-based classifier for the whole FE Evoking Text. It will use the distance to each of the clusters we have computed as learning features. A second classifier will be employed for the frame target classification. The choice of SVM as the classifier is lead by the observation that it allows for an optimal separation even with mislabeled data, which often occur in our setup where lexical ambiguities make the data noisy for classification.

Another potential improvement of our system, as proposed by a reviewer, is to use our scoring function as a means to decide whether or not to make a choice in the classification. For instance, if the first and second best results of the classification differ only by a few percent, it may be interesting to refrain from choosing the first one, which will produce no result. It will be interesting to see if it really will improve the recall of our system.

Finally, we will complete our system by integrating bracketing information, either with a syntactic parser or a shallow parser. This will allow us to have a complete system that will be comparable in breadth and depth to automatic role labeling systems based on a projection-based approach.

Acknowledgments

This work has been largely made possible thanks to funding from the France-Berkeley fund for a project headed by Charles Fillmore (ICSI, Berkeley) and Laurent Romary (initially at the LORIA/INRIA, Nancy, now at the Max Planck Gesellschaft, Berlin).

Furthermore, I would like to thank the following people of the Berkeley FrameNet team for their warm welcome during my stay: Charles Fillmore, Collin Baker, Michael Ellsworth, Josef Ruppenhofer, Carlos Subirats, and Kyoko Ohara. I also would like to thank Sebastian Padó (Computerlinguistik, Universität des Saarlandes), Hung-Suk Ji (Sungkyunkwan University, Korea), Sabine Ploux (Institut des Sciences Cognitives, CNRS, Lyon) and Mike Kellogg (Wordreference.com) for their help, Laurent Romary and Susanne Alt (ATILF, Nancy) for helping me starting this project and Christiane Jadelot (ATILF, Nancy) for her involvement in the gold standard corpus creation.

For reviewing and invaluable comments on this chapter, many thanks go to Patrick Blackburn (LORIA, Nancy), Eric Kow (LORIA, Nancy), Katrin Erk (University of Texas at Austin), Hans C. Boas (University of

Texas at Austin) and an anonymous reviewer. And finally, thanks to the whole TALARIS team (previously known as LeD) at the LORIA/INRIA laboratory, where this work took place.

References

Atkins, Sue, Charles J. Fillmore, and Christopher R. Johnson
2003 Lexicographic relevance: Selecting information from corpus evidence. *International Journal of Lexicography* 16.3: 251–280.

Baldewein, Ulrike, Katrin Erk, Sebastian Padó, and Detlef Prescher
2004 Semantic role labeling with similarity-based generalization using EM-based clustering. In: *Proceedings of the 3rd International Workshop on the Evaluation of Systems for the Semantic Analysis of Text*, 64–68. Barcelona, Spain.

Boas, Hans C.
2005 Semantic frames as interlingual representations for multilingual lexical databases. *International Journal of Lexicography* 18.4: 445–478.

Bourigault, Didier, Cécile Fabre, Cécile Frérot, Marie-Paule Jacques, and Sylwia Ozdowska
2005 Syntex, analyseur syntaxique de corpus. In: *Actes des 12èmes journées sur le Traitement Automatique des Langues Naturelles*, 373–382. Dourdan, France.

Burchardt, Aljoscha, Katrin Erk, Annette Frank, Andrea Kowalski, Sebastian Padó, and Manfred Pinkal
2006a The SALSA corpus: A German corpus resource for lexical semantics. In: *Proceedings of Language Resources and Evaluation Conference 2006*, 969–974. Genoa, Italy.

Burchardt, Aljoscha, Katrin Erk, Annette Frank, Andrea Kowalski, and Sebastian Padó
2006b SALTO – A versatile multi-level annotation tool. In: *Proceedings of Language Resources and Evaluation Conference 2006*, 517–520. Genoa, Italy.

Church, Kenneth W.
1993 Char_align: A program for aligning parallel texts at the character level. In: *Proceedings of 31st Annual Meeting of the Association for Computational Linguistics*, 1–8. Columbus, Ohio.

Erk, Katrin and Sebastian Padó
2005 Analyzing models for semantic role assignment using confusability. In: *Proceedings of Human Language Technology Conference and Conference on Empirical Methods in Natural Language Processing 2005*, 668–675. Vancouver, Canada.

Fellbaum, Christiane D.
1998 *WordNet: An Electronic Lexical Database*. Cambridge: MIT Press.

Fillmore, Charles J., Christopher R. Johnson, and Miriam R. L. Petruck
2003a Background to FrameNet. *International Journal of Lexicography* 16.3: 235–250.

Fillmore, Charles J., Miriam R.L. Petruck, Josef Ruppenhofer, and Abby Wright
2003b FrameNet in action: The case of attaching. *International Journal of Lexicography* 16.3: 297–332.

Flournoy, Raymond, Hiroshi Masuichi, and Stanley Peters
1998 Cross-language information retrieval: Some methods and tools. In: Djoerd Hiemstra, Franciska de Jong, and Klaus Netter (eds.) *Language Technology in Multimedia Information Retrieval (14th Twente Workshop on Language Technology)*, 79–83. Universiteit Twente, Enschede.

Fontenelle, Thierry
2000 A bilingual lexical database for frame semantics. *International Journal of Lexicography* 13.4: 232–248.

Gildea, Daniel and Daniel Jurafsky
2002 Automatic labeling of semantic roles. *Computational Linguistics* 28.3: 245–288.

Hart, Michael
1992 The history and philosophy of project Gutenberg. http://www.gutenberg.org/about/history.

Johansson, Richard and Pierre Nugues
2006 A FrameNet-based semantic role labeler for Swedish. In: *Proceedings of joint conference of the International Committee on Computational Linguistics and the Association for Computational Linguistics 2006*, 436–443. Sydney, Australia.

Karlgren, Jussi and Magnus Sahlgren
2001 From words to understanding. In: Uesaka, Yoshinori, Pentti Kanerva, and Hideki Asoh, (eds.), *Foundations of Real-World Intelligence,* 294–308. Stanford: CSLI Publications.

Koehn, Philipp
2005 Europarl: A parallel corpus for statistical machine translation. In: *Proceedings of the 10th Machine Translation Summit*, 79–86. Phuket, Thailand.

Landauer, Thomas K. and Susan T. Dumais
1997 A solution to Plato's problem: The latent semantic analysis theory of acquisition, induction, and representation of knowledge. *Psychological Review* 104: 211–240.

Lee, Lillian
1999 Measures of distributional similarity. In: *37th Annual Meeting of the Association for Computational Linguistics*, 25–32. Maryland, Maryland.

Litkowski, Ken
2004 Senseval-3 task: automatic labeling of semantic roles. In: *Proceedings of the 3rd International Workshop on the Evaluation of*

Systems for the Semantic Analysis of Text, 9–12. Barcelona, Spain.

McLachlan, Geoffrey and Krishnan Thriyambakam
1997 *The EM Algorithm and Extensions.* Wiley series in probability and statistics. New York: John Wiley & Sons.

Ohara, Kyoko H., Seiko Fujii, Toshio Ohori, Ryoko Suzuki, Hiroaki Saito, and Shun Ishizaki
2004 The Japanese FrameNet project: An introduction. In: *Proceedings of the Fourth international conference on Language Resources and Evaluation*, 9–11 (Satellite Workshop "Building Lexical Resources from Semantically Annotated Corpora"). Lisbon, Portugal.

Padó, Sebastian and Gemma Boleda
2004 The influence of argument structure on semantic role assignment. In: *Proceedings of the conference on Empirical Methods in Natural Language Processing 2004*, 103–110. Barcelona, Spain.

Padó, Sebastian and Mirella Lapata
2005a Cross-lingual bootstrapping for semantic lexicons: The case of FrameNet. In: *Proceedings of the Twentieth National Conference on Artificial Intelligence*, 1087–1092. Pittsburgh, Pennsylvania.

Padó, Sebastian and Mirella Lapata
2005b Cross-lingual projection of role-semantic information. In: *Proceedings of Human Language Technology Conference and Conference on Empirical Methods in Natural Language Processing 2005*, 859–866. Vancouver, Canada.

Padó Sebastian, and Mirella Lapata
2006 Optimal constituent alignment with edge covers for semantic projection. In: *Proceedings of the joint conference of the International Committee on Computational Linguistics and the Association for Computational Linguistics 2006*, 1161–1168. Sydney, Australia.

Ploux, Sabine and Hyungsuk Ji
2003 A model for matching semantic maps between languages (French/English, English/French). *Computational Linguistics* 29.2: 155–178.

Punyakanok, Vasin, Dan Roth, Wen-tau Yih, and Dav Zimak
2004 Semantic role labeling via integer linear programming inference. In: *Proceedings of International Conference on Computational Linguistics*, 1346–1352. Geneva, Switzerland.

Resnik, Philip and Dan I. Melamed
1997 Semi-automatic acquisition of domain-specific translation lexicons. In: *Proceedings of the fifth Association for Computational Linguistics Conference on Applied Natural Language Processing*, 340–347. Washington, DC.

Roukos, Salim, David Graff, and Dan I. Melamed
1995 Hansard French/English. Philadelphia: *Linguistic Data Consortium.*
Ruppenhofer, Josef, Michael Ellsworth, Miriam R.L. Petruck, Christopher Johnson, and Jan Scheffczyk
2006 FrameNet II: extended theory and practice. ICSI website: http://framenet.icsi.berkeley.edu/book/book.pdf.
Schmid, Helmut
1994 Probabilistic part-of-speech tagging using decision trees. In *Proceedings of the Conference on New Methods in Language Processing*, 44–49. Manchester, UK.
Strassel, Stephanie, David Graff, Nii Martey, and Christopher Cieri
2000 Quality control in large annotation projects involving multiple Judges: The case of the TDT corpora. In: *Proceedings of the Second International Language Resources and Evaluation Conference.* Athens, Greece.
Subirats, Carlos and Miriam R. L. Petruck
2003 Surprise: Spanish FrameNet! In: *Proceedings of the Seventeenth International Congress of Linguists.* Workshop on Frame Semantics, Prague (Czech Republic).
Velldal, Erik
2003 *Modeling word senses with fuzzy clustering.* Cand. Phil. diss, University of Oslo.

Part IV. Integrating semantic information from other resources

10. Interlingual annotation of multilingual text corpora and FrameNet

David Farwell, Bonnie Dorr, Rebecca Green, Nizar Habash, Stephen Helmreich, Eduard Hovy, Lori Levin, Keith Miller, Teruko Mitamura, Owen Rambow, Florence Reeder and Advaith Siddharthan[1]

1. Introduction

This article raises an issue of common interest to those interested in Interlinguas and interlingual MT as well as to those interested in developing a multilingual FrameNet. Specifically, it addresses the problem of teasing apart the difference between meaning and interpretation, between semantics and pragmatics and between semantic representation and the representation of information conveyed. No translation (nor paraphrase) conveys the exactly same information as the original utterance. Rather, additional information may be conveyed and information may be lost, or information originally expressed explicitly may be conveyed implicitly and vice versa. The semantic representation of an utterance (the result of integrating the semantic representations of its subcomponents) does not capture what people intuitively feel is the meaning of that utterance. Instead, various pragmatic factors must be taken into account, including the time

1. David Farwell and Stephen Helmreich, Computing Research Laboratory, New Mexico State University; Bonnie Dorr and Rebecca Green, Institute for Advanced Computer Studies, University of Maryland; Nizar Habash and Owen Rambow, Dept. of Computer Science, Columbia University; Eduard Hovy, Information Sciences Institute, University of Southern California; Lori Levin and Teruko Mitamura, Languages Technologies Institute, Carnegie Mellon University; Keith Miller and Florence Reeder, Mitre Corporation; Advaith Siddharthan, Computer Laboratory, University of Cambridge.

and place of utterance and the speaker's motivation for uttering something. The focus of the discussion here is on describing the IAMTC project[2] (Interlingual Annotation of Multilingual Text Corpora), a multi-site NSF-supported project to annotate six sizable bilingual parallel corpora for interlingual content. After setting out the basic issues, we present the background and objectives of the IAMTC annotation effort, the dataset being annotated, the interlingual representation language used, the annotator's interface and annotation process itself, along with the evaluation methodology and results of an initial evaluation. Finally, we conclude by summarizing the current state of the project and presenting a number of issues yet to be resolved.

2. Translation, meaning, and interpretation

The importance of linguistically-annotated parallel corpora and multilingual annotation tools is now widely recognized (Véronis 2000), yet there are currently few cases of annotated parallel corpora, and those that do exist tend to be bilingual rather than multilingual (Garside et al. 1997). Moreover, much of the previous work on the linguistic annotation of corpora has focused on the annotation of sentences with syntactic information only, e.g., part-of-speech tags (Brown Corpus (Francis and Kucera 1982)) and syntactic trees (Penn Treebank (Marcus et al. 1994)). Even where the focus is on semantic representation as in the case of PropBank (Kingsbury and Palmer 2002), NomBank (Meyers et al. 2004) or the FrameNet example corpus (Baker et al. 1998), the corpus has generally been monolingual.

Two exceptions to this general state of affairs are the multilingual FrameNet (Boas 2005) and the IAMTC project. In the case of multilingual FrameNet, a large corpus of sentences exemplifying and annotated for semantic frames and the relevant frame elements is being translated and annotated in a number of other languages, in principle creating a large multilingual parallel annotated corpus. In the case of the IAMTC project, six different but comparable corpora, each consisting of a set of source language news articles along with two or three independently produced manual English translations, are being annotated for interlingual (IL) content. Viewing semantic frame representations as interlingual repre-

2. IAMTC has been supported by NSF ITR grant IIS-0325887.

sentations, it would appear that the two projects are essentially the same, annotating parallel corpora for interlingual content. This, however, is not precisely the case.

Interlingual approaches to machine translation are based on the assumption that there is a level of utterance representation at which all the relevant aspects of information needed for generating an equivalent utterance (i.e., a translation in a second language or a paraphrase in the same language) can be captured. Similarly, multilingual FrameNet developers assume that there is some level of representation, the semantic frame, at which all aspects of information relevant to the description of the lexical content of a set of related predicates can be captured both within and across languages. Thus, both efforts attempt to represent "aspects of information."

For instance, just as providing *atravesar el río nadando* as a translation of *to swim across the river* depends on both expressions sharing a common interlingual representation, which can be broadly represented as:

MOVE
  (MODE SWIM)
  (ULTERIOR-SURFACE-CONTACT RIVER),

Similarly, providing *to cross the river swimming* as a paraphrase of *to swim across the river* is based on both having the same frame representation, again loosely:

MOVE
  (MODE SWIM)
  (ULTERIOR-SURFACE-CONTACT RIVER).

To the degree that IL representations must represent semantic content, then, both efforts seek an abstract representation of event-types commonly referred to by predicates – or a lexical semantic description for related verbs (e.g., verbs of commercial transaction). They differ only in that, for translation, the criteria for motivating a given representation are based on cross language correspondences whereas, for paraphrasing, the criteria for selecting a given representation are based on maintaining semantic equivalence within the language.

But interlingual representations and semantic representations are not concerned with exactly the same "aspects of information." IL captures interpretations rather than simply denotational content. So, for instance, the IAMTC annotator is faced with deciding whether *earthquake predictions* and *predicted earthquakes* should be provided with the same representation and, if so, what representation, since they appear as alternative translations of *anuncios sismicos* (seismic warnings). Similar decisions must be made in regard to *assassin* and *murderer* as variant translations of *asesino* in reference to a policeman on trial for killing a union organizer while in the pay of a local landowner, to *third floor* or *fourth floor* as legitimate alternative translations of *tercer piso* (lit. third floor) in a European Spanish text translated for a US English speaking audience (because of different conventions for naming the levels of a building), or to *started its business* and *opened its doors to customers* as alternative translations of *empezaron el negocio*. This means that it must capture the intended meaning of non-literal language as well as literal meaning. In addition, it means that IL must capture pragmatic information concerning the organization of the speech act (topic/focus, and so on).

In regard specifically to the two annotation efforts, the original FrameNet dataset is in fact monolingual. It consists of isolated English sentences selected because they exemplify some aspect of some lexical item's frame structure. The resulting multilingual corpus consists of translations of that original dataset. For IAMTC, on the other hand, the dataset consists of two or three independently created translations in the same language (English) along side of the original source language text. The texts are news articles consisting of cohesive sequences of sentences and are generally 300 words long. The news articles are randomly selected and may not exemplify anything in particular. Annotation proceeds by comparing translations, categorizing any differences (as errors, paraphrases or meaningful variations, reflecting information loss or gain) and especially in the case of meaningful variations, identifying the inferences and knowledge needed to produce that variant.

The representations themselves differ as well. Originally, frame representations are motivated by morphosyntactic criteria related to non-meaning changing paraphrases. Less clear are the criteria that apply in deciding whether expressions bear some other potential lexical relation when they are associated with the same metaframe (e.g., conversives *buy* and *sell* to the "commercial transaction" metaframe). The IAMTC IL is the result of successive abstractions away from surface form. Its defining features are as follows:

- syntactic dependency structures (normalized for cross-linguistic consistency between Arabic, English, French, Hindi, Japanese, Korean, Spanish and across translations),

- semantically enriched with ontological predicates and semantic relations (normalized as above), and
- "abstracted" merged meaning representations.

This progression through increasing abstract levels of IL representation, coupled with the ability to manipulate the granularity of the representation through splitting and merging of representational elements, is what allows the annotator to deal with many of the more subtle meaning decisions reflected in the examples cited above. In some cases, such distinctions are glossed over by selecting more coarse grained representational elements. In other cases, the representation of such distinctions is postponed until later, when progressively more elaborate versions of IL will have been developed.

IL, then, captures the intended semantic structure along with the inferences (and knowledge) used to arrive at that representation. It is expected that a broader range of "paraphrases" will be represented similarly because analysis is at the clause, sentence and, in some cases, paragraph levels as opposed to the lexical level.

In what follows, we will focus on presenting a more detailed description of the IAMTC project without dedicating much discussion to the similarities and differences between our project and the multilingual FrameNet effort. We assume rather that the reader will be able to compare the two and determine how the efforts might inform one another. In Section 3, then, we introduce the objectives of the IAMTC project and provide some background. In Section 4, we describe the corpus and, in Section 5, we present the IL representation scheme and supporting resources. In Section 6, we describe the annotation methodology and tools. In Section 7, we present an evaluation methodology and the results of an initial evaluation. Finally, in Section 8, we conclude with a discussion of the achievements thus far and point out a number of issues that have arisen or have yet to be addressed.

3. The Interlingual Annotation of Multilingual Text Corpora (IAMTC) Project

With the recent shift toward deeper, corpus-based acquisition of language-independent representations (Hovy et al. 2003), the next step is to provide a significant foundation for more sophisticated language-processing techniques. The IAMTC project focuses on that next step: the creation of a system of text meaning (or interlingual) representation and the development of a number of sizeable semantically-annotated parallel corpora, for use in applications such as machine translation, question answering, text summarization, information extraction, and information retrieval.

The IAMTC project is a multi-site NSF ITR funded effort concerned with the annotation of six comparable bilingual parallel corpora for interlingual content. The project participants include the Computing Research Laboratory at New Mexico State University, the Language Technologies Institute at Carnegie Mellon University, the Information Science Institute at the University of Southern California, the Institute for Advanced Computer Studies at the University of Maryland, MITRE Corp., and Columbia University. The central goals of the project are:

- to produce a practical, commonly-shared system for representing the information conveyed by a text, or *interlingua*,
- to develop a methodology and tools for accurately and consistently assigning such representations to texts in different languages and by different annotators,
- to annotate for IL content a sizeable multilingual set of parallel corpora of source language texts and multiple translations into English,
- to design new metrics and undertake evaluations of the interlingual representations, ascertaining the degree of annotator agreement.

The intended impact of this research stems from the depth of the annotation and the evaluation metrics that delimit the annotation task. They enable research on both parallel-text processing methods and the modeling of language-independent meaning. To date, such research has been impossible, since corpora have for the most part been annotated at a relatively shallow (semantics-free) level, forcing NLP researchers to choose between shallow approaches and hand-crafted approaches, each having its own set of problems. We view our research as paving the way toward solutions to representational problems that would otherwise seriously hamper or invalidate later larger annotation efforts, especially if they are monolingual.

The corpus is expected to serve as a basis for improving meaning-based approaches to MT and a range of other natural language technologies. The tools (such as a tree editor and annotation interface) and annotation standards (described in annotation manuals) for use by the parallel text processing community will serve to facilitate more rapid annotation of texts in the future. They have enabled effective and relatively problem free annotation at six different sites with subsequent merging of results.

3.1. Related projects

On a broad scale, projects which might be seen as in some sense similar to the IAMTC annotation effort include Eurotra, EuroWordNet and the Universal Networking Language initiative (UNL). A crucial difference between our annotations and these projects is that our work is conceived of as an annotation project, while none of these projects included annotation. Eurotra (Allegranza et al. 1991) is similar to our effort in that it was a multi-site, multilingual effort but focused on developing a common framework for describing different natural languages on a range of levels: lexical, morphological, syntactic and semantic. However, Eurotra assumed a transfer-based approach to MT and so each language had its own syntactic and semantic processes and representations which were to be interconnected by pair-wise transfer rules. There was no concern with developing an Interlingua and the methodology was essentially a linguistic one, motivating the framework on the basis of counter-examples rather than by way of corpus analysis and annotation.

EuroWordNet (Vossen 1998), initially an effort to build WordNet resources for six European languages in parallel, is essentially lexical in nature. The central methodology was to translate the original Princeton WordNet (Fellbaum 1998) for English into the other languages, most importantly facing up to the problems of lexical mismatches or overlaps of the target language and filling in any lexical gaps in the original English resource. It was not concerned with sentence meaning or how it is represented. With the introduction of links between corresponding synsets in the different languages, i.e., the so called Inter-Lingual-Indexes, an effort was made to establish cross-language equivalences at the lexical level but, again, the developers did not follow a corpus based methodology and there was no related annotation effort.

Universal Networking Language (UNL) is a formal language designed for rendering automatic multilingual information exchange (Martins et al. 2000). It is intended to be a cross-linguistic semantic representation of sentence meaning consisting of concepts (e.g., 'cat', 'sit', 'on', or 'mat'), concept relations (e.g., 'agent', 'place', or 'object'), and concept predicates (e.g., 'past' or 'definite'). UNL syntax supports the representation of a hypergraph whose nodes represent "universal words" and whose arcs represent "relation labels." Several semantic relationships may hold between universal words including synonymy, antonymy, hyponymy, hypernymy, meronymy, etc. Like the IAMTC effort, the UNL consortium is looking to create a practical IL by comparing translations across multiple languages at multiple sites and the results of both efforts may prove to be mutually informative both methodologically (multilingual, multi-site annotation) and at the level of formal representation.

Our goals are in some way similar to the goals of the ParGram project (Butt et al. 2002), in which grammars for several languages are developed in close consultation and in parallel; however, the ParGram project is motivated by the theoretical assumption that grammars of different languages are in fact similar (Universal Grammar), an issue about which we are agnostic. Furthermore, ParGram is a grammar development project, while our project is a text annotation project.

Other similar semantic annotation projects include the Semeval data (Moore 1994), PropBank and VerbNet (Kingsbury and Palmer 2002; Kipper et al. 2002) and FrameNet (Baker et al. 1998). The corpora resulting from these efforts have allowed for the use of machine learning techniques which have proven much better than hand-written rules at accounting for the wide variety of idiosyncratic constructions and expressions provided by natural language. However, machine learning approaches have in the past been restricted to fairly superficial phenomena. The work described below constitutes the first effort of any kind to provide parallel corpora annotated with detailed deep semantic information.[3] The resulting annotated, multilingual, parallel corpora will be useful as an empirical basis for a wide range of research, including the development and evaluation of interlingual NLP systems as well as a host of other research and development efforts in theoretical and applied linguistics, foreign language pedagogy, translation studies, and other related disciplines.

4. The corpora

The target data set is modeled on, and extends the DARPA MT Evaluation data set (White and O'Connell 1994). It consists of 6 bilingual parallel

3. The broader impact of this research lies in the critical mono- and multilingual resources it will provide, and in the annotation procedures and agreement evaluation metrics developed. Downloadable versions of results are freely available at: http://aitc.aitcnet.org/nsf/iamtc/.

corpora. Each corpus is made up of 125 source language news articles along with up to three independently produced translations into English. However, the source news articles for each individual language corpus are different from those in the other language corpora. Thus, the 6 corpora themselves are comparable to each other rather than parallel. The source languages are Arabic, French, Hindi, Japanese, Korean and Spanish. The Japanese, French and Spanish corpora are extensions of the DARPA MT data set. The Arabic corpus includes data from the Linguistic Data Consortium's Multiple Translation Arabic, Part 1 (Walker et al. 2003). Typically, each article is between 300 and 400 words long (or the equivalent) and each corpus has between 150,000 and 200,000 words. Consequently, the size of the entire data set is around 1,000,000 words. For any given corpus, then, the annotation effort is to assign interlingual content to a set of as many as 4 parallel texts, up to 3 of which are in the same language, English, and all of which theoretically communicate the same information. The following is an example set of parallel sentences from the Spanish corpus:

S: *Atribuyó esto en gran parte a una política que durante muchos años tuvo un "sesgo concentrador" y representó desventajas para las clases menos favorecidas.*

T1: *He attributed this in great part to a type of politics that throughout many years possessed a "concentrated bias" and represented disadvantages for the less favored classes.*

T2: *To a large extent, he attributed that fact to a policy which had for many years had a "bias toward concentration" and represented disadvantages for the less favored classes.*

T3: *He attributed this in great part to a policy that had a "centrist slant" for many years and represented disadvantages for the less-favored classes.*

The annotation process, among other challenges, involves identifying the variations between translations and assessing whether these differences are significant. For instance, *una política* is translated as *a policy* in T2 and T3, but as *a type of politics* in T1. The question arises as to whether T1 is an error, a paraphrase, or an alternative interpretation of the source language text. If it is a paraphrase then it should be assigned the same representation as the other examples (keep in mind that this sentence is translated in the context of a news article and so there is prior context to influence the translator's and the annotator's choices). If it is an (intelligible) error or an alternative interpretation (and most likely it is the former), then the annotations should reflect the different interpretations.

A more limited problem is related to the degree of specification. For instance, where *this* appears as the translation of *esto* in T1 and T3, *that fact* appears in T2. The translator's choice in T2 potentially represents an elaboration on the semantic content of the source language expression and the question arises as to whether the difference should be reflected in the annotation. If not, an additional question arises as to whether the more specific or the less specific interpretation should serve as the basis for the annotation of all three texts.

More striking, perhaps, is the variation between *concentrated bias*, *bias toward concentration*, and *centrist slant* as translations for *sesgo concentrador*. Here, T3 offers a clear interpretation of the source text author's intent. The first two attempt to carry over the vagueness of the source language expression into the translation (quite possibly because they are themselves unsure of what the author of the source text wished to say). They assume that the reader of the translation will be able to figure it out. But even here, the two translators appear to differ as to what the author of the source language text actually intended, the former referring to bias of a certain degree of strength and the second to a bias in favor of a certain state of affairs. Seemingly, then, the annotation of each of these expressions should differ, reflecting these differences.

More generally, however, the point here is that a multilingual parallel data set of source language texts and multiple English translations offers a unique perspective and represents an alternative set of problems for annotating texts for meaning.

5. The interlingua

Due to the complexity of an interlingual annotation as indicated by the differences described in the previous section, the IAMTC representation schema has been developed through three levels thus far, progressively enriching the information represented using knowledge from sources such as the Omega ontology (cf. Section 5.4) and theta grids. Since this is an evolving standard, we first present the three levels in order as building on one another and then turn to a description of the knowledge resources.

The three levels of representation are referred to as *IL0*, *IL1* and *IL2*. The aim is to perform the annotation process incrementally, with each level of representation incorporating additional semantic features and removing existing syntactic ones. *IL2* is intended as the initial Interlingua, the level that most abstracts away from the surface idiosyncrasies of particular languages. *IL0* and *IL1* are intermediate representations, each a useful starting point for annotating at the next level.

5.1. *IL0*

IL0 is an unordered deep syntactic dependency representation, constructed by hand-correcting the output of a dependency parser (see Section 6.1 below for details of the parsers), which produces a variant intermediate between the analytical and tectogrammatical levels of the Prague School (Hajič et al. 2001). The aim is to provide a representation that highlights meaning-bearing (autosemantic) lexemes and reduces cross-linguistic differences. Thus, only content words are represented. *IL0* includes part-of-speech tags and citation forms for inflected words and a parse tree that makes explicit the syntactic complement structure of verbs. The parse tree is labeled with syntactic categories such as *subject* or *object*, which here refer to deep-syntactic grammatical functions (e.g., normalized for voice alternations). It does not necessarily reflect surface syntactic relations (such as case marking or agreement). Apart from prepositions, *IL0* does not contain function words (determiners, auxiliaries, etc.), but rather encodes their contributions as features. Missing arguments (such as embedded subjects in control constructions) are added as lexically empty co-indexed nodes. Semantically void punctuation is removed. Though this representation is purely syntactic, various disambiguation decisions are made (e.g., relative clause and PP attachment) and it abstracts as much as possible from surface-syntactic phenomena. As a simple example, Figure 1 shows a common syntactic representation for the Spanish and English equivalents of *Juan will arrive late* even though the former is a 3-word sentence while the latter is a 4-word sentence.

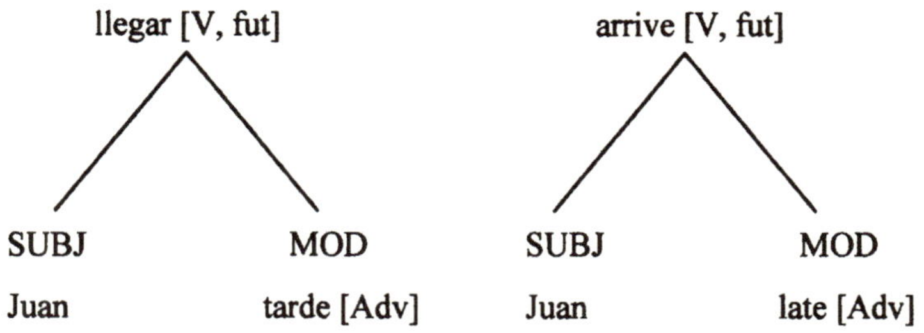

Figure 1. IL0 for *Juan llegerá tarde* and *Juan will arrive late*

By allowing annotators to see how textual units relate syntactically when making semantic judgments, *IL0* is a useful starting point for semantic annotation at *IL1*.

5.2. *IL1*

IL1 is an intermediate semantic representation. It associates semantic concepts drawn from an ontology of semantic concepts with lexical units like nouns, adjectives, adverbs and verbs (details of the ontology are presented in Section 5.4). It also replaces the syntactic relations like *subject* and *object* in *ILO* with thematic roles like *agent, theme* and *goal* (details are presented below in Section 5.5). Thus, like PropBank (Kingsbury and Palmer 2002), *IL1* neutralizes different alternations for argument realization. However, *IL1* is not an Interlingua; it does not normalize over different linguistic realizations with the same semantics. In particular, it does not address how the meanings of individual lexical units combine to form the meaning of a phrase or clause. It also does not address idioms, metaphors and other non-literal uses of language. Further, *IL1* does not assign semantic features to prepositions; these continue to be encoded as syntactic features of their objects.

Though some aspects of *IL1* remain to be fleshed out, we did create complete *IL1* annotations for our test corpus. The *IL1* representation corresponding to the sentence

> *The study led them to ask the Czech government to recapitalize CSA at this level.*

is shown in Figure 2:

```
[3,led,V,lead,Root,LEAD<GET,GUIDE]
  [2,study,N,study,AGENT,SURVEY<WORK,REPORT]
  [4,them,N,they,THEME,---,---]
  [6,ask,V,ask,PROPOSITION,---,---]
    [9,government,N,government,GOAL,AUTHORITIES,GOV-ORGAN]
      [8,Czech,Adj,Czech,MOD,CZECH~CZECHOSLOVAKIA,---]
    [11,recapitalize,V,recapitalize,PROP,CAPITALIZE<SUPPLY,INVEST]
      [12,CSA,PN,CSA,THEME,AIRLINE<LINE,---]
      [16,at,P,value_at,GOAL,---,---]
        [15,level,N,level,---,DEGREE,MEASURE]
          [14,this,Det,this,---,---,---]
```

Figure 2. Example IL1 annotation

Here, each bracketed expression represents a node label in the dependency tree. In order to simplify the presentation, indentation is the only indication of embedding; less indented expressions are parent node labels and equally indented expressions are sibling node labels. The surface form appears in the second position of the node label, the part of speech in the third position, the citation form in the fourth, the thematic relation in the fifth, and the ontological concept label in the sixth. The initial index corresponds to the position of the form in the sentence string. The annotators have added the information in capital letters; some nodes (e.g., government) have been assigned multiple concepts. As we discuss below, the annotation interface displays the information above in a more palatable form for annotators, who can also consult the tree using TrEd (Pajas 1998).

5.3. *IL2*

IL2, which is in its design stage, is intended to be an Interlingua, albeit a relatively simple one. As a representation of meaning that is (reasonably) independent of language, *IL2* captures similarities in meaning across languages and across different lexical/syntactic realizations within a language. For example, *IL2* normalizes over conversives (e.g., X *bought a book from* Y vs. Y *sold a book to* X) as does FrameNet (Baker et al. 1998) and certain fixed non-literal language usage (e.g. X *started its business* vs. X *opened its doors to customers*).

The *IL2* annotation of the corpus allows us to easily trace the different surface realizations of a given meaning pattern, as in the case of conversives, such as *Mary bought the book from John* vs. *John sold the book to Mary*, which are shown in Figure 3.

IL2: GO BOOK FROM JOHN TO MARY VIA PURCHASE ->
  IL1 candidate #1: buy MARY[agent] JOHN[source] BOOK[theme] ->
    IL0 candidate #1: Mary bought the book from John
  IL1 candidate #2: sell JOHN[agent] MARY[goal] BOOK[theme] ->
    IL0 candidate #2: John sold the book to Mary

Figure 3. Multiple Surface Realizations for a Given Meaning Pattern

In addition, *IL2* is instrumental in elucidating cases where different sentence plans express the same information through different realizations. Consider the following example:

Its network of eighteen independent organizations in Latin America has lent. . . .

The English *IL1* representation for this sentence is:[4]

lend
  AGENT: network
    MOD: comprise
    PART: 18 independent organizations
  THEME: ...

On the other hand, the French translational equivalent is:

Le réseau	*regroupe*	*dix-huit*	*organisations*	*indépendantes*	*qui*	*ont*	*déboursé...*
the network	comprises	eighteen	independent	organizations	which	have	disbursed...

In this case, the comprising event, which is subordinate in English, is superordinate while the lending event, which is superordinate in English, is subordinate. This is reflected in the corresponding French *IL1* representation:

comprise
  WHOLE: network
  PART: 18 organizations
    RECL-CL: disburse
      AGENT: network
      THEME: ...

The mapping between *IL1* and *IL2* is from *of* or *regroupe* to the COMPRISE concept and from *lend* or *déboursé* to the TRANSFER-MONEY concept, as shown here:

of/regroupe ↔ COMPRISE
lend/déboursé ↔ TRANSFER-MONEY

Thus, we arrive at the following *IL2* representation of the sentence fragment which consists of two independent event representations linked by a common argument, network:

COMPRISE:
  WHOLE: network
  PART: 18 independent organizations

4. The corresponding concepts for the predicates and arguments along with several other details are not expressed here in order to simplify the presentation.

TRANSFER-MONEY
  AGENT: network
  THEME:...

The exact definition of *IL2*, as well as annotation manuals and associated resources, has yet to be completed but they would constitute a major research contribution. Even so *IL2* is not a complete Interlingua by any means. It does not, for instance, include more complex phenomena such as discourse structure, pragmatic readings (of words such as *unfortunately* and *hello*), speech acts, or cross-event semantic relationships such as time, location, cause, or modality. These remain for *IL3* and beyond, to be developed in subsequent projects.

5.4. The Omega ontology

In progressing from *IL0* to *IL1*, annotators must select semantic terms (concepts) to represent the nouns, verbs, adjectives, and adverbs present in each sentence. These terms are represented in ISI's 110,000-node Omega ontology (Philpot et al. 2003). Omega is the result of semi-automatically combining a variety of resources, including Princeton's WordNet (Fellbaum 1998), New Mexico State University's Mikrokosmos (Mahesh and Nirenburg 1995), ISI's Upper Model (Bateman et al. 1989) and ISI's SENSUS (Knight and Luk 1994). Once the uppermost region of Omega was created by hand, the contents of these various resources were incorporated and, to some extent, reconciled. After that, several million instances of people, locations, and other facts were added (Fleischman et al., 2003). The ontology, which has been used in several projects in recent years (Hovy et al. 2001), can be browsed using the DINO browser which is a part of the IAMTC annotation environment.[5]

5.5. The theta grids

Each verb in Omega is assigned one or more theta grids specifying the arguments associated with the verb and its theta roles (or thematic roles). Theta roles are abstractions of deep semantic relations that generalize over verb classes. They are by far the most common approach for representing predicate-argument structure. However, there are numerous variations with little agreement even on terminology (Fillmore 1968; Stowell 1981; Jackendoff 1972; Levin and Rappaport-Hovav 1998).

5. Available at: http://blombos.isi.edu:8000/dino.

The theta grids used in our project were extracted from the Lexical Conceptual Structure Verb Database (LVD) (Dorr et al. 2001). The WordNet senses assigned to each entry in the LVD were then used to link the theta grids to the verbs in the Omega ontology. In addition to the theta roles, the theta grids specify syntactic realization information, such as Subject, Object or Prepositional Phrase, and the Obligatory/Optional nature of the argument. For example, one of the theta grids for the verb "load" is shown in Table 1 below.

The complete set of theta roles used for this project, although based on research in LCS-based (Lexical Conceptual Structure) machine translation (Dorr 1993; Habash et al. 2002), was in fact limited to 15 relations (described below in Table 4 in the Appendix). In devising this set, several different schemes at different levels of granularity were chosen. For example, the notion of agency – based on Dowty's (1991) *highest proto-agent* – served as the core of our definition of Agent, i.e., that an agent should have the features of volition, sentience, causation, and independent existence. The work of several other researchers was also taken into consideration, most notably, the works of Gruber (1965), Jackendoff (1972), and Gildea and Jurafsky (2002). The final set of relations selected for this project was intended to be comprehensive in its coverage, yet small enough to be manageable by our annotators. It is also the same set of theta roles that was used in the interlingua annotation experiment described in (Habash and Dorr 2002).[6]

Table 1. Theta grid for the verb *load*

Role	Description	Syntax	Type
Agent	entity doing the action	SUBJ	OBLIGATORY
Theme	entity worked on	OBJ	OBLIGATORY
Possessed	entity controlled or owned	PP	OPTIONAL

6. Incremental annotation

Throughout, we have made as much use of automated procedures as possible. Here we present the tools and resources for the interlingual annotation process and then describe our annotation methodology.

6. Other contributors to this list are Dan Gildea and Karin Kipper Schuler.

6.1. The annotation tools

We have assembled a suite of tools to be used in the annotation process, some of which were previously existing resources that were gathered for use in the project, while others were developed specifically with the annotation goals of this project in mind. Since we are gathering our corpora from disparate sources, we need to standardize the text before presenting it to automated procedures. For English, this involves splitting the text into sentences, but for other languages, it may involve segmentation, chunking of text, or similar language-specific operations. The text is then processed by a dependency parser. For English, we have two parsers, one from Prague (Hajič et al. 2001) and the other Connexor (Tapanainen and Jarvinen 1997). Their output is converted to a standard form and then viewed by the researchers in TrED (Pajas 1998), a graphically-based tree editing program.[7] The revised deep dependency structure produced by this process is the *IL0* representation for that sentence. At this stage, some of the lexical items are replaced by features (e.g., tense), morphological forms are replaced by features on the citation form, and certain constructions are regularized (e.g., passive) with empty arguments inserted.

In order to derive *IL1* from the *IL0* representation, annotators use Tiamat, a tool developed specifically for this project. This tool enables annotators to view the current sentence and corresponding *IL0* tree and provides them with easy access to all of the IL resources described above (i.e., the ontology and the theta grids). Using a simple point-and-click selection of words, concepts, and theta-roles, an annotator may select a lexical item (an *IL0* leaf node) to be annotated; this word is highlighted and the relevant options of the Omega ontology are displayed. In addition, if this word has dependents, they are automatically underlined in red. Thus, annotators can view all information pertinent to the process of deciding on appropriate ontological concepts. They can save decisions, undo them later, and flag problematic cases for later inspection. Following the procedures described below, annotators select the concepts, theta grids and roles appropriate for the particular use of the lexical item in question.

6.2. The annotation manuals

Annotation instructions are contained in three manuals: a user's guide for Tiamat (including procedural instructions), a definitional guide to semantic roles, and a manual for creating a dependency structure (i.e., *IL0*).

7. See: http://quest.ms.mff.cuni.cz/pdt/Tools/Tree_Editors/Tred/.

Together these manuals allow the annotator to (1) understand the intention behind aspects of the dependency structure; (2) how to use Tiamat to mark up texts; and (3) how to determine appropriate semantic roles and ontological concepts. In choosing a set of appropriate ontological concepts, annotators were encouraged to look at the name of the concept and its definition, the name and definition of the parent node, example sentences, lexical synonyms attached to the same node, and sub- and super-classes of the node. All these manuals are available on the IAMTC website: http://aitc.aitcnet.org/nsf/iamtc/.

6.3. The annotation process

The annotation process was identical for each text. For the initial testing period, only English texts were annotated, and the process described here is for English text. The process for non-English texts is, *mutatis mutandis*, the same. Each sentence of the text was parsed automatically into a dependency tree structure, and then corrected by one of the team PIs to produce an *IL0* representation. For the initial testing period, annotators were not permitted to alter these structures. This dependency structure was then loaded into the annotation tool for mark up.

The annotator was instructed to annotate all nouns, verbs, adjectives, and adverbs. In order to determine an appropriate level of representational specificity in the ontology, annotators were instructed to annotate each word twice – once with one or more concepts from WordNet synsets, as incorporated into Omega, and once with Mikrokosmos concepts. These two units of information were merged, or at least intertwined, in Omega as one of the goals of the annotation process is to facilitate a closer union between the concepts in both ontologies. Problem cases were automatically tagged and assembled for inspection by one of the PIs. Annotators were also instructed to provide a thematic role for each dependent of a verb. In many cases this was "NONE," since adverbs and conjunctions were dependents of verbs in the dependency tree. If an LCS verb was identified with the WordNet synset selected, the LCS grid for that verb was presented to the annotator. Where necessary, annotators determined the set of roles or altered them to suit the text. In either case, the revised or new set of case roles was recorded and sent to a PI for evaluation and possible permanent inclusion. Thus the set of event concepts supplied with roles grew through the course of the project.

For the initial testing phase of the project, all the annotators, regardless of site, worked on the same texts. Every week, over a three month period, two translations each of two different (non-English) texts were provided by each site. These texts were annotated by two annotators at each site, resulting in a total of 144 annotated texts. Each text annotation took about 3 hours. To minimize for any effects of coding two texts that were semantically close, i.e., translations of the same source document, the order in which the texts were annotated differed from site to site, with half the sites marking up one translation first, and the other half marking up the second translation first. In addition, a second variation was introduced by which half the sites marked up full texts, one translation after the other, while half the sites interleaved the two translations, marking up the two texts at the same time, consecutively annotating corresponding sentences.

For the production phase, a more complex schedule has been set up. We designed a round-robin annotation schedule in which two annotators at each site annotate two English translations from their own site, one annotator annotates the corresponding source language text, and the other annotates a translated text from some other site. This workflow is illustrated schematically in Figure 4.

Using this methodology, we can compare across a source text and its translations, across translations alone, across a site's annotators, across different sites' annotators, and (when everyone annotates the same text)

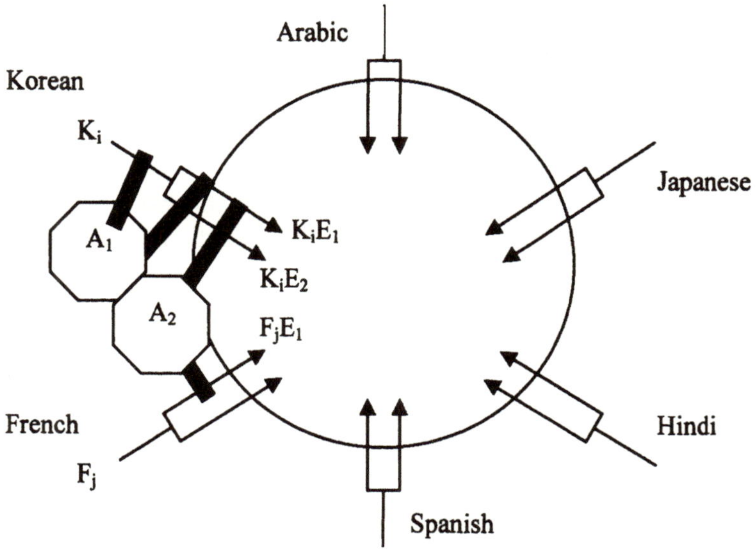

Figure 4. Annotator rotation

across all the annotators. This helps to ensure continued inter-annotator reliability.

7. Evaluation

Evaluation is a complex undertaking. Here we describe our evaluation methodology and the results of an initial evaluation. It should be noted that the evaluation criteria and metrics continue to evolve. Several potential approaches to evaluating the annotations and resulting structures might be taken and in the future we would expect to look at more than one.

7.1. Methodology

We developed several procedures and tools to compare annotations and to generate a series of evaluation measures that are described below. The reports generated by the evaluation tools allow the researchers to look at both gross-level phenomena, such as inter-annotator agreement, and at more detailed aspects of annotation such as lexical items on which agreement was particularly low, possibly indicating gaps or other inconsistencies in the ontology being used. The procedures and tools have been applied to:

- **Inter-translator consistency**: Two (or more) translations of a given text were compared and the different choices for nouns, verbs, etc. were listed. We classified these for how they affected the semantic term choices of the annotators.
- **Inter-annotation agreement**: The annotation decisions for each word and each theta role were recorded and agreement was calculated based on the number of annotators that selected a particular role or sense.
- **Inter-annotation reconciliation**: Each annotator reviewed the selections made by the other annotators, and voted as to whether they found them acceptable or not. The annotators then discussed the results and, finally, voted a second time.

We developed two general approaches to evaluation, one internal and one external. For internal evaluation, we measured inter-annotator agreement. After collecting data about the annotations, the Omega nodes selected and the theta roles described, inter-annotator agreement was measured in a profile that included a Kappa measure (Carletta 1996) and a

"Wood Standard" similarity (Habash and Dorr 2002). Multiple measures were used because, with respect to IL annotation, it is important to have a mechanism for evaluating inter-annotator consistency that does not depend on the assumption that there is a single correct annotation of a given text.

Calculating agreement and expected agreement when a number of annotators can assign zero or more senses per word was not straightforward. Also, because of multiple annotators, we calculated an average of pair-wise agreement per word for all pairs of annotators. Because multiple categories (senses) could be assigned for each word, we were faced with a decision: (a) to count explicit agreement, i.e. the annotators selected the same sense; or (b) to count implicit agreement, when the two annotators did not select the same sense. Also, we needed to account for cases when no concept was provided in Omega.[8] In the end, we opted for two different approaches.

For a specific word and pair of annotators who have made one or more selections of semantic tags, agreement was measured as the ratio of the number of agreeing selections to the number of all selections. This measure was based on positive selections only, i.e., when the two annotators selected the same semantic tag. For a word W, with a set of n possible semantic tags S_i, the function $N(S_i)$ is defined as the sum of the selections made by the two annotators A_1 and A_2. Pair-wise agreement for a specific word was defined using the following formula:

$$\text{Agreement}_{\text{word}} = \frac{\sum_i^n N(S_i) \cdot (N(S_i) - 1)}{\sum_i^n N(S_i)}$$

Pair-wise agreement was measured as the average of agreement over all the words in a document. The overall inter-annotator agreement was measured as the average of pair-wise inter-annotator agreement of every pair of annotators.

To calculate Kappa, we estimated chance agreement by a random 100-fold simulation where the number of concepts selected and concepts selected were randomly assigned, restricted by the number of concepts per word in Omega. If Omega had no concepts associated with the word, the

8. We are aware of the option of applying weighting to Kappa using Omega's hierarchical structure to compute similarity amongst options which can be explored later.

chance agreement was computed as the inverse of the size of all of Omega (1/110,000). Then chance agreement was calculated in exactly the same way as the overall agreement was calculated.

An alternative approach was to calculate the implicit agreement by looking at each sense on which a decision could be made as a separate test case. Here, implicit agreement for a word was calculated for each pair of annotators and word agreement was the average of the pair-wise agreement. Calculating Kappa then involved constructing a 3 by 3 matrix S where $S[0,0]$ was the number of times both annotators picked no sense; $S[1,1]$ was the number of times both annotators picked some sense. $S[0,1]$ and $S[1,0]$ contained mismatched selections. The proportion of agreement was $S[0,0] + S[1,1]$ divided by the number of senses. Each row and column of S was then summed, so that $S[0,2]$ was the number of times A1 did not select a sense and $S[1,2]$ was the number of times A1 selected a sense. In this case, Kappa was calculated as:

$$\text{Kappa} = \frac{2 * ((S[0,0] * S[1,1]) - (S[0,1] * S[1,0]))}{(S[0,2] * S[2,1] + S[2,0] * S[1,2])}$$

In addition to inter-annotator agreement, we are also designing and implementing an external measure of the quality of the IL annotations. Given the project goal of generating an IL representation useful for MT (among other NLP tasks), we measure the ability to generate accurate surface texts corresponding to input IL representations. At this stage, we are using an available generator, Halogen (Langkilde-Geary 2002). A tool to convert IL representations to meet Halogen input requirements is under construction. Following the conversion, surface forms will be generated and then compared with the originals through a variety of standard MT metrics (ISLE 2003; King et al. 2003). This will serve to determine whether the elements of the representation language are sufficiently well-defined and whether they can serve as a basis for inferring interpretations from semantic representations or (target) semantic representations from interpretations.

7.2. Results

For the evaluation of inter-annotator agreement, the data set consisted of six pairs of English translations (about 350 words apiece) from each of the six source languages. The ten annotators were asked to annotate the nouns, verbs, adjectives and adverbs with Omega concepts. The annotators selected one or more concepts from both WordNet and Mikrokosmos-derived nodes. The arguments of annotated verbs were also assigned thematic roles. An important issue in the data set was the problem of incomplete annotations which might stem from: (1) lack of annotator awareness of missing annotations; (2) inability to finish annotations; and (3) ontology omissions for words for which annotators selected *Dummy-Concept* or no annotation at all. For 1,268 annotated words, 368 (29%) have no Omega WordNet entry and 575 (45%) do not have an Omega Mikrokosmos entry.

To address incomplete annotations, we calculated agreement in two different ways that exclude annotations (1) by annotator and (2) by word. In the first calculation, we excluded all annotations by an annotator if the annotations were incomplete by more than a certain threshold. Table 2 shows the average number of included annotators over all documents (A#), the Average Pair-wise Agreement (APA) and Kappa for the Mikrokosmos portion of Omega, the WordNet portion of Omega and theta roles. The table is broken down by different thresholds for exclusion.

Table 2. Scores for explicit sense marking

	5% A#	APA	Kappa	10% A#	APA	Kappa
Mikrokosmos	3.50	0.745	0.743	4.42	0.731	0.730
WordNet	6.08	0.660	0.657	7.00	0.654	0.650
Theta Roles	5.75	0.538	0.509	6.58	0.549	0.521
	50%			100%		
Mikrokosmos	6.33	0.611	0.609	9.42	0.455	0.454
WordNet	8.33	0.598	0.594	9.42	0.517	0.513
Theta Roles	8.00	0.485	0.452	9.42	0.392	0.354

Again, since annotators did not annotate some texts or failed to choose an Omega entry, two types of agreement are reported here. The first is agreement based on counting cases where all senses were marked with zero as perfect agreement with a Kappa of 1; the second excludes zero cases entirely (see Table 3). In eliminating zero pairs, agreement does not change significantly.

Table 3. Implicit agreement numbers

		All cases		Exclude zero-pairs	
	Zero-Pairs	Agree	Kappa	Agree	Kappa
Theta Roles	78.58	0.945	0.418	0.943	0.392
WordNet	112.16	0.886	0.564	0.879	0.534
Mikrokosmos	258.5	0.811	0.522	0.784	0.433

8. Conclusions

8.1. Accomplishments

In a short period of time, we constructed corpora for six languages along with appropriate multiple parallel translations into English. We defined two levels of representation corresponding to syntactic dependency structure (*IL0*) and gross semantic predicate-argument structure (*IL1*), and initiated the process of designing the next level of interlingual representation (*IL2*). More importantly, we gained an understanding of how the component elements from these different levels of representation fit together. In addition, we designed an annotation methodology and supporting materials (e.g., manuals) as well as developing, testing and putting into use an annotator's toolkit (Tiamat). In short, an infrastructure now exists for carrying out a multi-site text meaning annotation project. Finally, we developed procedures for evaluating the accuracy of an annotation and measuring inter-annotator consistency, and we carried out a multi-site evaluation and reported the results to the NLP community. A growing corpus of annotated texts is now available at the project website: http://aitc.aitcnet.org/nsf/iamtc/.

8.2. Remaining issues

Not surprisingly, we have encountered a number of difficult issues for which we have only interim solutions. Principal among these is the granularity of the IL terms to be used. Omega's WordNet symbols, numbering over 100,000, afford too many alternatives with too little clear semantic distinction, resulting in large inter-annotator disagreement. On the other hand, Omega-Mikrokosmos, containing only 6,000 concepts, is too limited to capture many of the distinctions people deem relevant. We plan to manually prune out the extraneous terms from Omega. Similarly, the theta roles in some cases appear hard to understand. While we have considered following the example of FrameNet and defining idiosyncratic roles for almost every process, the resulting proliferation does not bode well for later large-scale machine learning. Additional issues to be addressed include: (1) personal name, temporal and spatial annotation (Ferro et al. 2001); (2) causality, co-reference, aspectual content, modality, speech acts, etc; (3) reducing vagueness and redundancy in the annotation language; (4) inter-event relations such as entity reference, time reference, place reference, causal relationships, associative relationships, etc; and finally (5) cross-sentence phenomena remain a challenge.

From an MT perspective, issues include evaluating the consistency in the use of an annotation language given that any source text can result in multiple, different, legitimate translations (see Farwell and Helmreich 2003 for discussion of evaluation in this light). Along these lines, there is the additional problem of annotating texts for interpretation without including inferences from the source text.

8.3. Concluding remarks

IAMTC is a radically different annotation project from those that have focused on morphology, syntax or even certain types of semantic content (e.g., for word sense disambiguation evaluation exercises). It is most similar to PropBank (Kingsbury and Palmer 2002) and FrameNet (Baker et al. 1998). However, our project is novel in its emphasis on: (1) a more abstract level of annotation (i.e., that of interpretation); (2) the assignment of a well-defined meaning representation to concrete texts; and (3) issues of a multi-site, community-wide consistent and accurate annotation of meaning.

Because of the unique annotation processes in which each stage (*IL0*, *IL1* and *IL2*) provides a different level of linguistic and semantic information, different types of natural language processing can take advantage of the information provided at the different stages. For example, *IL1* may be useful for information extraction in question answering, whereas *IL2* might be the level that is of most benefit to machine translation. These topics exemplify the research investigations that we can conduct in the future, based on the results of the annotation.

By providing an essential, and heretofore non-existent, data set for training and evaluating knowledge-based natural language processing systems, the resultant annotated multilingual corpus of translations is expected to lead to significant research and development opportunities for

Machine Translation and a host of other Natural Language Processing technologies. Not only will this lead to improved translation and language technologies but, just as importantly, it will increase our understanding of human cognitive processing.

References

Allegranza, V., P. Bennett, J. Durand, F. Van Eynde, L. Humphreys, P. Schmidt, and E. Steiner
1991 Linguistics for machine translation: The Eurotra linguistic specifications. In: C. Copeland, J. Durand, S. Krauwer, and Maegaard, B. (eds.), *The Eurotra Linguistic Specifications*, 15–124. CEC, Luxembourg.

Baker, C.F., C.J. Fillmore, and J.B. Lowe
1998 The Berkeley FrameNet project. In: C. Boitet and P. Whitelock (eds.), *Proceedings of the Thirty-Sixth Annual Meeting of the Association for Computational Linguistics and Seventeenth International Conference on Computational Linguistics*, 86–90. San Francisco, CA: Morgan Kaufmann Publishers.

Bateman, J.A., R.T. Kasper, J.D. Moore, J.D., and R.A. Whitney
1989 *A general organization of knowledge for natural language processing: The Penman upper model.* Unpublished research report. Marina del Rey, CA: USC/Information Sciences Institute.

Boas, H.C.
2005 Semantic frames as interlingual representations for multilingual lexical databases. *International Journal of Lexicography* 18.4: 445–478.

Butt, M., H. Dyvik, T. Holloway King, H. Masuichi, and C. Rohrer
2002 The parallel grammar project. In: *Proceedings of COLING-2002 Workshop on Grammar Engineering and Evaluation*, 1–7, Taipei, Taiwan.

Carletta, J.C.
1996 Assessing agreement on classification tasks: the kappa statistic. *Computational Linguistics* 22.2: 249–254.

Dorr, B., M. Olsen, N. Habash, and S. Thomas
2001 *LCS verb database. Online Software Database of Lexical Conceptual Structures and Documentation.* University of Maryland, College Park, MD. http://www.umiacs.umd.edu/~bonnie/LCS_Database_Documentation.html.

Dorr, B.
1993 *Machine translation: A view from the lexicon.* Cambridge, MA: MIT Press.

Dowty, D.
1991 Thematic proto-roles and argument selection. *Language* 67.3: 547–619.

Farwell, D. and S. Helmreich
2003 Pragmatics-based translation and MT evaluation. In: *Proceedings of the Workshop on Systematizing MT Evaluation*. AMTA-2003, New Orleans, LA.

Fellbaum, C.
1998 *WordNet: An electronic lexical database*. Cambridge, MA: MIT Press.

Ferro, L., I. Mani, B. Sundheim, and G, Wilson
2001 TIDES temporal annotation guidelines. Version 1.0.2 *MITRE Technical Report*, MTR 01W0000041.

Fillmore, C.J.
1968 The case for case. In: E. Bach and R. Harms (eds.), *Universals in Linguistic Theory*, 1–88. Holt, Rinehart, and Winston.

Fleischman, M., A. Echihabi, and E.H. Hovy
2003 Offline strategies for online question answering: Answering questions before they are asked. In: *Proceedings of the ACL Conference*. Sapporo, Japan.

Francis, W.N. and H. Kucera
1982 *Frequency analysis of English usage*. Boston, MA: Houghton Mifflin.

Garside, R., G. Leech, and A.M. McEnery
1997 *Corpus Annotation: Linguistic Information from Computer Text Corpora*. London: Addison Wesley Longman.

Gildea, D. and D. Jurafsky
2002 Automatic labeling of semantic roles. *Computational Linguistics*. 28.3: 245–288.

Gruber, J.
1965 *Studies in lexical relations*. Doctoral Dissertation. MIT, Cambridge, MA.

Habash, N. and B. Dorr
2002 Interlingua annotation experiment results. In: *AMTA-2002 Interlingua Reliability Workshop*. Tiburon, California, USA.

Habash, N., B. Dorr, and D. Traum
2003 Hybrid natural language generation from Lexical Conceptual Structure. *Machine Translation* 18.2: 81–128.

Hajič, J., B. Vidová-Hladká, and P. Pajas
2001 The Prague dependency treebank: Annotation structure and support. In: *Proceeding of the IRCS Workshop on Linguistic Databases*, 105–114. University of Pennsylvania, Philadelphia.

Hovy, E., M. Marcus, and R. Weischedel
2003 *Presentation at the DARPA PI Meeting*. Arden House, Harriman, New York.

Hovy, E.H., A. Philpot, J.L. Ambite, Y. Arens, J. Klavans, W. Bourne, and D. Saroz
2001 Data acquisition and integration in the DGRC's Energy Data Collection Project. In: *Proceedings of the NSF's dg.o 2001*. Los Angeles, CA.

ISLE
2003 Towards systematizing MT evaluation. In: *Proceedings of MT Summit IX Evaluation Workshop*. New Orleans, Louisiana.

Jackendoff, R.
1972 *Semantic interpretation in generative grammar*. Cambridge, MA: MIT Press.

King, M., A. Popescu-Belis, and E. Hovy
2003 FEMTI: Creating and using a framework for MT evaluation. In: *Proceedings of Machine Translation Summit IX*, 224–231. New Orleans, Louisiana.

Kingsbury, P. and M. Palmer
2002 From Treebank to PropBank. In: *Proceedings of the 3rd International Conference on Language Resources and Evaluation* (LREC-2002). Las Palmas, Spain.

Kipper, K., M. Palmer, and O. Rambow
2002 Extending PropBank with VerbNet semantic predicates. In: *Proceeding of the Workshop on Applied Interlinguas* (AMTA-2002). Tiburon, CA.

Knight, K. and I. Langkilde
2000 Preserving ambiguities in generation via automata intersection. In: *Proceedings of the American Association for Artificial Intelligence Conference* (AAAI).

Knight, K. and S.K. Luk
1994 Building a large-scale knowledge base for machine translation. In: *Proceedings of the American Association for Artificial Intelligence Conference* (AAAI). Seattle, WA.

Langkilde-Geary, I.
2002 An empirical verification of coverage and correctness for a general-purpose sentence generator. In: *Proceedings of the International Natural Language Generation Conference* (INLG). New York.

Levin, B. and M. Rappaport-Hovav
1998 From lexical semantics to argument realization. Borer, H. (ed.) *Handbook of Morphosyntax and Argument Structure*. Dordrecht: Kluwer Academic Publishers.

Mahesh, K. and S. Nirenberg
1995 A situated ontology for practical NLP. In: *Proceedings on the Workshop on Basic Ontological Issues in Knowledge Sharing* at IJCAI-95. Montreal, Canada.

Marcus, M., B. Santorini, and M.A. Marcinkiewicz
1994 Building a large annotated corpus of English: The Penn Treebank. *Computational Linguistics* 19.2: 313–330.
Martins, T., L.H. Machado Rino, M.G. Volpe Nunes, G. Montilha, and O. Osvaldo Novais
2000 An interlingua aiming at communication on the web: How language-independent can it be? In: *Proceedings of Workshop on Applied Interlinguas*, ANLP-NAACL 2000.
Meyers, A., R. Reeves, C. Macleod, R. Szekely, V. Zielinska, B. Young, and R. Grishman
2004 Annotating noun argument structure for NomBank. In: *Proceedings of LREC-2004.*
Moore, R.C.
1994 Semantic evaluation for spoken-language systems. In: *Proceedings of the 1994 ARPA Human Language Technology Workshop*, Princeton, New Jersey.
Pajas, P.
1998 *Tree Editor Manual.* CLSP Summer Workshop, Johns Hopkins University, Baltimore, MD.
Philpot, A., M. Fleischman, E.H. Hovy
2003 Semi-automatic construction of a general purpose ontology. In: *Proceedings of the International Lisp Conference.* New York, NY.
Stowell, T.
1981 *Origins of phrase structure.* PhD thesis, MIT, Cambridge, MA.
Tapanainen, P. and T Jarvinen
1997 A non-projective dependency parser. In: *Proceedings of the 5th Conference on Applied Natural Language Processing/Association for Computational Linguistics*, Washington, DC.
Véronis, J.
2000 From the Rosetta Stone to the information society: A survey of parallel text processing. In: J. Véronis (ed.), *Parallel Text Processing: Alignment and Use of Translation Corpora*, Chapter 1. London: Kluwer Academic Publishers.
Vossen, P.
1998 *EuroWordNet: A multilingual database with lexical semantic networks.* Dordrecht: Kluwer Academic Publishers.
White, J. and T. O'Connell
1994 The ARPA MT evaluation methodologies: evolution, lessons, and future approaches. In: *Proceedings of the 1994 Conference, Association for Machine Translation in the Americas.*
Walker, K., M. Bamba, D. Miller, X-Y. Ma, C. Cieri, and G. Doddington
2003 *Multiple-translation arabic corpus*, Part 1. Linguistic Data Consortium (LDC) catalog number LDC2003T18 and ISBN 1-58563-276-7.

Appendix

Table 4. List of Theta Roles

Role and Definition	Examples
Agent: An agent has the features of volition, sentience, causation and independent existence.	• **Henry** *pushed/broke* the vase.
Instrument: An instrument should have causation but no volition. Its sentience and existence are not relevant.	• **The Hammer** *broke* the vase. • She *hit him* **with a baseball bat**.
Experiencer: An experiencer has no causation but is sentient and exists independently. Typically an experiencer is the subject of verbs like *feel*, *hear*, *see*, *sense*, *smell*, *notice*, *detect*, etc.	• **John** *heard* the vase shatter. • **John** *shivered*.
Theme: The theme is typically causally affected or experiences a movement and/or change in state. The theme can appear as the information in verbs like *acquire*, *learn*, *memorize*, *read*, *study*, etc. It can also be a thing, event or state (clausal complement).	• **John** *went* to school. • John *broke* **the vase**. • John *memorized* **his lines**. • She *buttered* the bread **with margarine**.
Perceived: A perceived entity is not required by the verb but further characterizes the situation. The perceived is neither causally affected nor causative. It does not experience a movement or change in state. Its volition and sentience are irrelevant. Its existence is independent of an experiencer.	• He *saw* **the play**. • He *looked* **into the room**. • The cat's fur *feels* good **to John**. • She *imagined* **the movie to be loud**.
Predicate: A predicate indicates new modifying information about other thematic roles.	• We *considered* him a **fool**. • She *acted* **happy**.
Source: A source indicates the original state of the theme, or its original (possibly abstract) location/time.	• John left **the house**.
Goal: A goal indicates what its final state of the theme is, or where/when its final (possibly abstract) location/time is. It also can indicate the thing/event resulting from the verb's occurrence (the result).	• John *ran* **home**. • John *ran* **to the store**. • John *gave* a book **to Mary**. • John *gave* **Mary** a book.
Location: A location indicates static position – as opposed to a source or goal, i.e., the (possibly abstract) location of the theme or event.	• He *lived* **in France**. • The water *fills* **the box**. • **This cabin** *sleeps* five people.
Time: A time indicates time.	• John *sleeps* **for five hours**. • Mary *ate* **during the meeting**.

Beneficiary: A beneficiary indicates the thing that receives the benefit/result of the event/state.	• John *baked* the cake **for Mary**. • John *baked* **Mary** a cake. • An accident *happened* **to him**.
Purpose: A purpose indicates the purpose/reason behind an event/state.	• He *studied* **for the exam**. • He *searched* **for rabbits**.
Possessed: A possessed entity is the object of verbs such as *own*, *have*, *possess*, *buy*, and *carry*.	• John *has* **five bucks**. • He *loaded* the cart **with hay**. • He *bought* it **for five dollars**.
Proposition: A proposition is a secondary event/state	• He *wanted* **to <u>study</u> for the exam.**
Modifier: A modifier is a property of a thing such as *color*, *taste*, *size*, etc.	• The **red** book **sitting on the table** is old.
Null: This indicates no thematic contribution. Typical examples are impersonal *it* and *there*.	• **It** was raining all morning in Miami.

11. Universals and idiosyncrasies in multilingual WordNets

Piek Vossen and Christiane Fellbaum

1. Introduction

The structure of WordNet provides an excellent vantage point for investigating the relations among words and concepts. Concepts in WordNet are represented as independent structures, so-called synsets, which express word meanings. The lexicon of a language is represented as a list of forms that map to one or more of these synsets, such that distinct word forms with the same meaning – synonyms – map to the same synset, and word forms with multiple meanings – polysemous words – map onto different synsets. The question 'what is a concept and what is a word' becomes more challenging from a multilingual perspective. A concept expressed by a word in one language may not be lexicalized in another language.

As in EuroWordNet (Vossen 1998), concepts expressed in WordNets for different languages can be connected through a universal index, making it possible to compare lexicalizations across languages. We propose an extension of the EuroWordNet model to a large number of languages, including lesser known ones, which we call the "Global WordNet Grid" (GWG). The GWG will include an ontology as the basis for a universal concept index. Moreover, the GWG will allow the large-scale empirical investigation of fundamental theoretical questions that will reveal which lexicalizations are universal or idiosyncratic and how they can be linked to the universal concept index.

The idea for a Global WordNet Grid was born during the Third Global WordNet Conference in Korea (January 2006), where the need for interlinked WordNets was articulated by the community. The grid will be built around a set of concepts encoded as WordNet synsets in as many languages as possible and mapped to definitions in the SUMO ontology (Niles and Pease 2001).

We envision speakers from many diverse language communities creating and contributing synsets in their language. We initially solicit encodings for the nearly 5,000 Common Base Concepts used in many current WordNet projects. Base Concepts are expressed by synsets that occupy central positions in the WordNet structures. Below are a few illustrative examples of Base Concepts ranging over different semantic classes:

{body 3; organic structure 1; physical structure 1}
{human 1; individual 1; mortal 1; person 1; someone 1; soul 1}
{artefact 1; artifact 1}
{possession 1}
{cognitive content 1; content 2; mental object 1}
{event 1}
{change 1}
{create 2; make 13}
{change of location 1; motion 1; move 4; movement 1}
{change of position 1; motion 2; move 5; movement 2}
{act 1; human action 1; human activity 1}
{communicate 1; intercommunicate 1; transmit feelings 1; transmit thoughts 1}
{experience 7; get 18; have 11; receive 8; undergo 2}
{time 1}
{be 4; have the quality of being 1}
{be 9; occupy a certain area 1; occupy a certain position 1}
{attribute 1}
{form 1; shape 1}
{ability 2; power 3}
{relation 1}
{have 12; have got 1; hold 19}
{path 3; route 2}

The specific criteria for selecting these concepts varied across WordNets, due to the differences in available data and resources. Typical criteria are high frequency in corpora and high frequency in definitions of other words. In general they are found high up in the hierarchies and they are densely interconnected with other concepts. They reflect a certain level of abstraction or semantic generalization and are therefore usually more abstract than the basic level concepts familiar from psychology (see Vossen (1998) for a more extensive discussion).

A comparison of different WordNets led to a selection of English WordNet synsets that represent these concepts across a number of European languages, known as the Common Base Concepts (Vossen 1998). We anticipate cases of many-to-many mappings, where a given language will have more than one concept that covers the semantic space of a single Base Concept and vice versa. Eventually, the Grid will represent the core lexicons of many languages in a form that allows further study of lexical and semantic similarities as well as disparities. Both research and applications will benefit from the Grid.[1] In this paper, we will present the structure of the Grid and discuss a number of lexicalization issues from the multilingual perspective of the Grid.

2. WordNet, EuroWordNet, and Global WordNet

The Global Grid is a natural extension of the WordNets that have been built over the past decade. At the same time, developing the Grid has shown that we need to examine some fundamental assumptions that have guided past WordNets. We begin with a brief review of the major WordNets as well as a brief introduction to ontologies.

2.1. WordNet

The Princeton WordNet is the first manually constructed large-scale lexical database that was widely embraced by the natural language processing (NLP) community (Miller 1990, Fellbaum 1990, Fellbaum 1998). WordNet was originally intended to test the feasibility of a model of human semantic memory that sought to explain economic principles of storage and retrieval of words and concepts. This model was based on the hierarchical organization of concepts expressed by nouns and the inheritance of properties (expressed by adjectives) and events (encoded by verbs) associated with these concepts.

WordNet consists of four different semantic networks (one for each of the major parts of speech) that interrelate groups of cognitively synonymous words ("synsets") via lexical and conceptual-semantic relations. For details see Miller (1990) and Fellbaum (1998). When WordNet was initially constructed, its builders did not have NLP applications in mind, and density of the network was not a design criterion. WordNet's original motivation was to test theories of human semantic memory which claim that knowledge about a concept includes that of both its superordinate concepts and its parts. As a result, the standard Aristotelian relations, hyponymy and meronymy, were used to build the large network of nouns (Miller 1990). For adjectives, the proposed organization into direct and indirect antonyms was based on an experiment with a relatively small

1. The Grid will be publicly and freely available and we expect no proprietary claims to be made by the contributors.

number of adjectives (Gross, Fischer, and Miller 1989). For the bulk of the adjective lexicon, the neat divisions into antonym pairs and semantically related adjectives was often difficult to implement.

No model was available that could have guided the organization of verbs. A relation dubbed "troponymy" that was based on hyponymy was adopted. A troponym encodes a manner component that is not present in its superordinate. For examples *amble* and *whisper* are troponyms of *walk* and *speak*, respectively (Fellbaum 1990, 1998).

While these relations sufficed to build WordNet, they do not discriminate sufficiently among the concepts expressed by synsets. For example, Role nouns such as *hunting dog* and *food* are treated as Types, on par with *poodle* and *apples*.[2] Fellbaum (1990, 1998, 2002) notes that troponymy is in fact highly polysemous and subsumes a number of semantically diverse relations. For example, among the verbs of motion, "manner" troponyms encode different modes of locomotion (*fly, walk, swim*), locomotion by means of different conveyances (*train, bus, bike*), speed (*amble, race*), etc. Among verbs of communication, troponymy encodes different modalities (*speak, gesture*), volume (*whisper, scream*), etc.

The Princeton WordNet was designed and constructed with the goal of exploring the English lexicon, without a crosslinguistic perspective. Although it was not motivated by NLP needs, the WordNet model turned out to be useful for language processing. Consequently, WordNets started to be built for other languages.

2.2. EuroWordNet

Vossen (1998) presents the first expansion of WordNet into other languages. Lexical databases were constructed for eight European languages using the EuroWordNet design, which deviates from that of the Princeton WordNet. The Euro WordNet design contributed several fundamental innovations that have since been adopted by dozens of additional WordNets.

First, a number of new relations – cross-part-of-speech relations in particular – were defined to increase the connectivity among synsets. Furthermore, all relations were marked with features indicating the combination types of relations (conjunctive or disjunctive) and their directionality. The most important difference, however, was the multilingual nature of the

2. Instances, such as *Malta* and *Mohammed*, were separated from Types (Miller and Hristea 2006).

database. Within Euro WordNet, each individual WordNet was modeled after the Princeton WordNet, having its own separate inventory of synsets and relations. The synsets of each language are then linked via an "equivalence relation" to the InterLingualIndex, or ILI. By means of the ILI, a synset in a given language can be mapped to a synset in any other language connected to the ILI. This design allowed the straightforward comparison of the lexicons of different languages both in terms of coverage, relations, and lexicalization patterns.

Initially, the EuroWordNet ILI was populated with the concepts (synsets) from Princeton WordNet. The reasons for this were mostly pragmatic – WordNet had a large coverage and was freely available. Furthermore, English was the language that was most familiar to all of the European partners, making it feasible to judge equivalence. But several modifications and extensions of the ILI had to be considered. As the English WordNet was not designed as an ILI, establishing proper equivalence relations to it from the different languages was often difficult. This was true even for languages that are closely related to English (like Dutch and German), and despite the fact that most European lexicons contain words and concepts borrowed from contemporary Anglo-American culture.

Compatibility between the EuroWordNet languages and the ILI with respect to lexical coverage and relations varied moreover depending on which of the two basic methods for building the European WordNets was followed:

- **Expand**: English synsets are translated into the target language and the relations are copied
- **Merge**: synsets are independently created for the target language, interlinked with relations, and subsequently translated to English for mapping with ILI entries

The Expand approach results in WordNets that are very close to the Princeton original, while the Merge approach creates WordNets that often have a very different structure in cases where target language synsets do not straightforwardly match English language synsets.

2.3. Global WordNet

EuroWordNet was the first step towards the globalization of WordNets. Linguists and computer scientists in many countries then started to develop WordNets for other languages. In addition to individual efforts, there are also WordNets for entire geographic regions, such as BalkaNet (Tufis 2004) and the Indian WordNets (e.g., Sinha, Reddy, and Bhattacharyya 2006). Currently, WordNets exist for some 40 languages, including dead languages such as Latin and Sanskrit.[3]

The founding of the Global WordNet Association (GWA) was motivated by the desire to establish and maintain community consensus concerning a common framework for the structure and design of WordNets. Another goal is to encourage the development of WordNets for all languages and to link them such that appropriate concepts are mapped across languages. The multilingual WordNets allow comparison of the lexicons of different languages on a large scale, beyond the selected few lexemes that are often considered in the investigation of particular linguistic topics. Furthermore, the availability of global WordNets opens up exciting possibilities for crosslinguistic NLP applications.

3. The Global WordNet Grid

The addition of new and less familiar languages to the WordNet family has led to the idea of a Global WordNet Grid. In this Grid, the WordNets of many languages will not be interconnected via the lexicon of a particular language, as was the case in EuroWordNet, where each of the eight WordNets related their synsets to a list of unstructured concepts derived from English WordNet. Instead, the Grid languages will relate to a language-independent index of concepts based on a formal ontology. Important features of the ontology include the following:

(a) The list of primitive concepts is primarily based on ontological observations and not just on the lexicalized words of a particular language;
(b) The concepts are related in a type hierarchy and defined with axioms;
(c) It is possible to define additional complex concepts using primitive elements and expressions in a standard knowledge representation format (the Knowledge Interchange Format, KIF, based on first order predicate calculus).

A central question addressed in this paper is, which concepts should be included in the ontology? The ontology must be able to encode all concepts that can be expressed in any of the Grid languages. However, the

3. For information see www.globalwordnet.org.

ILI-ontology need not provide a linguistic encoding – a label – for all words and expressions found in the Grid languages. The source for the primitive concepts may very well be based on the vocabulary of the languages (preferably as many languages as possible) but lexicalization in *a language* can never be sufficient to include a concept in the Grid ontology. Reasons to include it must be based on ontological observations and/or on cross-linguistic evidence. As we will explain below, many lexicalizations are transparent and systematic while others are non-compositional or seemingly ad-hoc.

We assume a reductionist view and require the ontology to contain the minimal list of concepts necessary to express equivalence across languages and to support inferencing. Following the OntoClean method (Guarino and Welty 2002a, 2002b), identity criteria can be used to determine the minimal set of concepts in all cultures where the Grid languages are used. These identity criteria determine three essential properties of entities that are instances of these concepts:

- **Rigidity**: to what extent are properties of an entity true in all or most worlds? E.g., a *man* is always a *person* but may bear a Role like *student* only temporarily. Thus, manhood is a rigid property while studenthood is anti-rigid.[4]
- **Essence**: which properties of entities are essential? For example, "shape" is an essential property of "vase" but not an essential property of the clay it is made of.
- **Unicity**: which entities represent a whole and which entities are parts of these wholes? An "ocean" or "river" represents a whole but the "water" it contains does not.

The identity criteria are based on certain fundamental requirements. These include that the ontology is descriptive and reflects human cognition, perception, cultural imprints and social conventions (Masolo, Borgo, Gangemi, Guarino, and Oltramari 2003). One of the major research questions for the Grid is to what extent these criteria are indeed valid across different cultures.

The work of Guarino and Welty (2002a, 2002b) has demonstrated that the WordNet hierarchy, when viewed as an ontology, can be improved and reduced. For example, roles such as AGENTS of processes are anti-

4. See also Carlson's (1980) discussion of individual vs. stage level predicates and Pustejovsky's (1995) discussion of Roles. Note that the ontological notion of Role is different from Semantic Roles and theta-roles.

rigid. They do not represent disjunct types in the ontology, and they complicate the hierarchy. As an example, consider the hyponyms of *dog* in WordNet, which include both types (races) like *poodle*, *Newfoundland*, and *German shepherd,* but also roles like *lapdog, watchdog*, and *herding dog*. "Germanshepherdhood" is a rigid property, and a German shepherd will never be a Newfoundland or a poodle. But German shepherds may be herding dogs. The ontology would only list the **rigid** types of dogs (dog races): Canine ⇒ PoodleDog; NewfoundlandDog; GermanShepherdDog, etc.

The lexicon of a language then may contain some words that are simply names for these rigid types and other words that do not represent new types but represent roles (and other conceptualizations of types). For example, English *poodle*, Dutch *poedel* and Japanse *pudoru* will become simple names for the ontology type: ⇔ ((instance x PoodleDog). On the other hand, English *watchdog*, the Dutch word *waakhond* and the Japanese word *banken* will be related through a KIF expression that does not involve new ontological types: ⇔ ((instance x Canine) and (role x GuardingProcess)), where we assume that GuardingProcess is defined as a process in the hierarchy as well.[5] The fact that the same KIF expression can be used for all the three words indicates equivalence across the three languages.

In a similar way, we can use the notions of **Essence** and **Unicity** to determine which concepts are justifiably included in the type hierarchy and which ones are dependent on such types. If a language has a word to denote a lump of clay (e.g. in Dutch *kleibrok* denotes an irregularly shaped chunk of clay), this word will not be represented by a type in the ontology because the concept it expresses does not satisfy the Essence criterion. Similarly a word like *river water* (Dutch *rivierwater*) is not represented by a type in the onotology as it does not satisfy Unicity; such words are dependent on valid types. Satisfying the rigidity criteria, for example, is a condition for type status.

The type/non-type distinction will clear up many cases where we find mismatches or partial matches between English words and words from other languages. Previous evaluations of mismatches in EuroWordNet (Vossen, Peters, and Gonzalo 1999) suggest that most mismatches can be

5. This approach is compatible with the practice in FrameNet 1.3, in which agentive nouns are included with the frame which denotes the activity but marked with a semantic type to indicate that they refer to the agent rather than the activity.

resolved by using KIF-like expressions and thus avoiding extension of the type hierarchy with new categories. As we discuss below, gender lexicalizations, differences in perspective, aspectual variants, and other phenomena do not need to represent new types of concepts but can be defined with KIF expressions as well.

When words in the Grid languages suggest new types, the ontological criteria can decide on extensions of the type hierarchy. This is the case not only for culture-specific concepts but also for other kinds of lexicalization differences. We will discuss some of these cases in more detail below. In summary, the proposed ontology has the following characteristics:

(a) It is **minimal** so that terms are distinguished by essential properties only (reductionist);
(b) It is **comprehensive** and includes all distinct concept types of all Grid languages;
(c) It allows the definition of all lexicalizations that express non-essential properties of types, using KIF expressions;
(d) It is **logically valid** and allows reasoning and inferencing.

In EuroWordNet, equivalence relations from synsets to the concepts in the ILI as represented by WordNet currently vary considerably. Some WordNets only have "exact" equivalence, while others also allow "near equivalence" and have many-to-many relations among synsets and the corresponding concepts in the ILI. This variation severely complicates the cross-lingual comparison and usage of WordNets.

The ontology we propose here will be more explicit about the meaning of the equivalence relation. Because the ontology is minimal, it will be easier to establish precise and direct equivalences from Grid languages to the ontology and likewise across languages. The multilingual Grid database will thus consist of WordNets with synsets that are either simple names for ontology types in the type hierarchy or words that relate to these types in a complex way, made explicit in a KIF expression. These expressions allow for a more precise explication of the subtle meaning differences of words (if they apply). Note that if two Grid language WordNets create the same KIF expression, this still constitutes a statement of equivalence without an extended type hierarchy.

3.1. Toward the realization of the Global Grid

There are many ontologies that can be used for a universal index. We propose to take the Suggested Upper Merged Ontology (SUMO) (Niles and

Pease 2001) as a starting point for our ontology. The choice was motivated by three reasons:

(a) It is consistent with many ontologies and with ontological practice;
(b) It is has been fully mapped onto WordNet;
(c) Like WordNet, it is freely and publicly available.

SUMO is additionally desirable because it supports data interoperability, information search and retrieval, automated inferencing, and various NLP applications. SUMO has been translated into various representation formats, but the language of development is a variant of KIF.

SUMO consists of a set of concepts, relations, and axioms that formalize a field of interest. As an upper ontology, it is limited to concepts that are generic, abstract or philosophical and hence general enough to address a wide range of domains at a high level. SUMO provides a structure upon which ontologies for specific domains such as medicine and finance can be built; the mid-level ontology MILO (Niles and Terry 2004) bridges SUMO's high-level abstractions and the low-level detail of domain-specific ontologies.

The 1000 terms and 4000 definitional statements (formalized in SUO-KIF (Standard Upper Ontology Knowledge Interchange Format)) have been fully mapped to the English WordNet and to WordNets in many other languages as well (Niles and Pease (2003), Black, Elkateb, Rodriguez, Alkhalifa, Vossen, Pease, Bertran, and Fellbaum (2006), inter alia). WordNet synsets map to a general SUMO term or to a term that is directly equivalent to a given synset. New formal terms are defined to cover a greater number of equivalence mappings, and the definitions of the new terms depend in turn on existing fundamental concepts in SUMO.

Though SUMO is extensive, it is far from being large enough or rich enough to replace the Princeton WordNet as an ontology. The current mapping of SUMO to WordNet will be taken as a starting point; most of these mappings are subsumption relations to general SUMO types. The first step is therefore to extend the SUMO type hierarchy to be as rich as WordNet with respect to disjoint types.

Note that not all synsets from WordNet are necessary. In fact, all WordNet synsets must be reviewed with respect to the OntoClean methodology (Guarino and Welty 2002a, 2002b) so that only rigid (and semi-rigid) concepts, like *PoodleDog*, are preserved in the ILI. All remaining synsets need to be defined using KIF expressions as described earlier. In the case of the previous example of *watchdog* in the English WordNet, the relation to the ontology will be through a KIF expression that relates it to the types Canine and GuardingProcess. Similarly, we will relate female dogs, male dogs, baby dogs etc. with expressions.

Once SUMO has been extended as described, other languages that have already established equivalence relations with WordNet can replace these with the improved mappings to SUMO, which can be copied from WordNet. In practice, this means that if the Dutch word *waakhond* and the Japanese word *banken* have a direct equivalence relation to *watchdog* in the English WordNet, they can import the KIF expression to their language. In some cases, these imported KIF expressions may need to be revised in so far as the synsets were only globally mapped to WordNet and can now be related more precisely.

Finally, the synsets of Grid languages that cannot be mapped to WordNet need to be checked for adherence to OntoClean. This step will result in extensions to the type hierarchy in some cases; in other cases, the WordNet builders need to write a KIF expression clarifying the particular concept's relation to the ontology.

The Global WordNet Grid as envisioned can only be realized in a collaborative framework among builders of WordNets from many diverse linguistic and cultural backgrounds. Its development will undoubtedly involve several steps and many rounds of refinement processes. Throughout the development of the Global WordNet Grid, we expect discussion and the need for revisions as more languages join and the coverage for each language increases. Mapping the lexicons of many diverse languages, and the cultural notions they encode, is bound to be a long and painstaking process, but also a worthwhile one. The result will be a unique database that allows for a better understanding among people from different linguistic and cultural backgrounds and opens up new possibilities for research and applications.

3.2. Challenges

The goal of mapping the lexicons of genetically and typologically unrelated languages raises the question of whether there exists a universal lexicon, an inventory of concepts that are lexically encoded (or potentially encodable) in all languages. Second, what kinds of concepts does such a universal lexicon cover and how large is the common core of lexicalized concepts for most or all languages? How do language-specific lexicalizations radiate out from the core?

Conversely, we ask what the differences among the lexicons of diverse languages are, whether such differences are regular and systematic, and in which areas of the lexicon they are concentrated. For the cases where individual languages show lexical gaps, we ask whether these are attributable to grammatical and structural properties or to linguistic-cultural differences.

This second set of questions inevitably leads to another, more fundamental question. What constitutes a lexeme deserving of a legitimate entry in the databases? While even linguistically naive speakers have a notion of a "word," there is no hard definition of a word. One possible orthographic definition would state that strings of letters with an empty space on either side are words. While this would cover words such as *bank*, *sleep*, and *red*, it would wrongly leave out multiword expressions – like *lightning rod, find out, word of mouth*, and *spill the beans* – that constitute semantic and lexical units.[6] A clearer, more promising definition might say that a lexical unit will merit inclusion in a database when it serves to denote an identifiable concept. But as we shall see, this criterion is less than straightforward.

Assuming at least a working definition of word, the challenge is to arrange the words of a language into a structured lexicon. Although our starting point is the WordNet model, where lexically encoded concepts are interrelated to form a semantic network, we do not take it for granted that the WordNet relations are the most suitable to represent the structure of lexicons of English or other languages. More broadly speaking, we need to ask what constitutes a valid relation among words and concepts both in a given language and cross-linguistically.

Finally, we explore the differences and commonalities of semantic networks and ontologies. Given the notion of an ontology as a formal knowledge representation system, we ask how the lexicons of many diverse languages can be linked to an ontology such that reasoning and inferencing are enabled. Which relations should be encoded in the upper ontology and which ones are specific to one or more individual WordNets? Since each WordNet is also an (informal) ontology, incompatibilities between the WordNets and the formal ontology may arise. What do such mismatches tell us, and what are the practical consequences for the use of WordNets for reasoning and inferencing in NLP?

4. What belongs in a universal lexical database?

Adding the lexicons of many languages to the Global Grid will reveal which concepts are truly language-specific and which are also lexicalized

6. Note that the writing systems of many languages do not separate lexical units; clearly, this does not mean that these languages do not have words.

in other languages. Both formal, linguistic and informal, cultural criteria determine inclusion in the Global Grid; both turn out to be difficult to define.

4.1. Culture-specific words and concepts

In building a new WordNet and connecting it to the English WordNet, one comes across cases where a lexicalized concept in the language of interest has no corresponding lexicalization in English. An example from the Dutch WordNet is the verb *klunen*, which refers to walking on skates over land to get from one frozen body of water to another. Because of different climatic, geographic, and cultural settings, this concept is specific to Dutch and not shared by many other languages (although it can be explained to, and understood by, non-Dutch speakers). Another example is *citroenjenever*, which is a special kind of gin made with lemon skin. Unlike *klunen*, *citroenjenever* might more easily be adopted by inhabitants of English-speaking countries and become a familiar concept. Culture-specific concepts must be included in the ontology, although there may not be equivalence relations to any languages other than the one that lexicalizes such concepts.

4.2. Availability and salience

Words and phrases that express available concepts must be included in each language-specific WordNet but do not necessarily need to be present in the ontology of the Grid as a separate concept. Availability is the extent to which a word or phrase is **current** and **salient** within a language community. It affects the topics speakers talk about and the words they use to discuss these topics; it may well affect the way speakers view matters. While frequency and shared cultural background determine the degree of availability of a word or phrase, the **authority** of a speaker or a subgroup of speakers within a language community may have an effect on availability as well. For example, media have a significant influence on the words that are current; frequency counts for a given lexeme vary over time, as the newsworthiness of stories and topics grows and diminishes. Social groups determine availability and linguistic change, as studies of youth language have shown (e.g., Labov 1972).

Such usage-based criteria may conflict with purely linguistic criteria for including words in a lexical database. Compound nouns present a case in point. Standard lexical resources (e.g., the American Heritage Dictionary) tend to follow the rule that compositional phrases like *dinner table* and *vegetable truck* need not be listed. But non-compositional compounds whose meanings is not the sum of the meanings of their components and where the entire compound is a semantic unit (*horseplay, ice luge*) must be included, as their meaning cannot be easily be guessed even by competent speakers that are unfamiliar with these words or concepts. Non-compositionality is only one criterion for inclusion in a lexical database. Even seemingly transparent compounds like *table tennis* and *heart attack* are included in standard dictionaries (e.g., American Heritage), presumably because they encode frequent and salient concepts. Hence, these compounds are available to the language community, as ready-made expressions.

Some new compounds become established in a language community when they are frequent or salient and when their creators have a social standing that lends them what might be called "linguistic authority." This phenomenon can be seen in the areas of science and technology, popular entertainment and commercial branding, where people introduce new terms often with the explicit intention of adding them, along with a new concept, to the lexicon. An example is Dutch *arbeidstijdverkorting*. Although its members, *arbeid* ("work"), *tijd* ("time"), and *verkorting* ("reduction") suggest a straightforward compositional meaning, this compound is non-compositional. It denotes a special social arrangement invented in the 1980s to create jobs, whereby people's working hours were reduced in exchange for a reduced salary; this measure was intended to allow the employment of more workers and decrease unemployment.

Conversely, some compounds found in today's news headlines are not to be found in any dictionary: *ministry hostages*, *celibacy ruling*, and *banana duty*. Such compounds are created on the fly, and in the context of current news stories they are readily interpretable, yet their lifespan is limited by their newsworthiness; and only few such ad-hoc compounds will enter the lexicon on a long-term basis.

Whether or not such compounds also need to be added to the ontology is however an ontological issue. Availability does not play a role here and compositional concepts can very well be expressed through KIF-expressions that relate involved concepts such as *table* and *tennis* in a well-defined way. The ontology should therefore include primarily non-compositional concepts, incorporating compositional concepts only when they represent types that are rigid across all the involved cultures.

5. Lexical mismatches as evidence for concepts

Mapping the lexicons of different languages to a common ontology quickly reveals cases where one language encodes a given concept and others do not. A more subtle type of mismatch can show up in the different ways languages may encode a concept, raising the question of what constitutes a word. We illustrate this point below with a few specific cases of semantically complex verbs.

Like nouns, new verbs are regularly formed by productive processes. Different languages have different rules for conflating meaning components. Some components are free morphemes, others are bound affixes. A concept denoted by a compound or phrasal verb in one language, such as English *tear up* may be expressed by a simplex morpheme in other languages (*déchirer* in French). While one may not want to include complex verbs in one's lexicon based on the argument that they are productive and compositional, the existence of corresponding mono-morphemic lexemes in other languages argues for the conceptual status of complex verbs and hence their crosslinguistic inclusion in a multilingual resource.

5.1. Accidental gaps

Languages differ in the extent to which higher-level concepts are lexicalized, sometimes causing "gaps" in the mapping between lexicon and ontology. Consider Fellbaum and Kegl (1989), who examine the English verb lexicon in terms of WordNet hierarchies. They argue that English has a non-lexicalized concept "eat a meal", with its own subordinates (*dine*, *lunch*, *snack*, ...). This concept is said to be distinct from the sense of *eat* that denotes the consumption of food and has a number of manner subordinates (*nibble*, *munch*, *gulp*, ...). Here, the gap – namely, lexicalization of the "eat a meal" concept – is postulated on the basis of the two semantically distinct verb groups specifying manners of eating. We assume that such gaps are language-specific and that other languages may well have distinct lexicalizations for the two superordinate "eat" concepts.

In fact, a comparison of English and Dutch verbs of cutting reveals a similar crosslinguistic asymmetry. The English verb *cut* does not specify the instrument for cutting something. Only its troponyms do: *snip* and *clip* imply scissors, *chop* and *hack* a large knife or an axe, etc. Dutch does not have a verb that is underspecified for the instrument, and speakers select the appropriate verb based on the default instrument, which also expresses the manner of cutting (*knippen* "clip, snip, cut with scissors or a scissor-like tool", *snijden* "cut with a knife or knife-like tool", *hakken* "chop, hack, to cut with an axe, or similar tool").

The specific manners of cutting lexicalized in both English and Dutch are distinct rigid types of processes. From an ontological viewpoint it seems preferable to represent the specific processes in the ontology rather than the more abstract "cut", especially if lexicalizations in other languages confirm this pattern. Universality of lexicalization thus may become the source for the extension of event types.

5.2. Argument structure alternations

In some languages, verbal affixes change both the meaning and the argument structure of the base verb. For example, German *be-* is a locative suffix that allows the Location argument to be the direct object. Thus, verbs like *malen* ('paint') and *sprühen* ('spray') when prefixed with *be-* obligatorily take the entity that is being painted or sprayed (the "Location") as their direct object (see Anderson 1971, Michaelis and Ruppenhofer 2001, *inter alia*).

(1) Sie bemalte/besprühte die Wand (mit Farbe).

(2) She painted/sprayed/the wall (with paint).

When the material (the "Locatum") is the direct object, the verb is in its base form:

(3) Sie malte/sprühte Farbe an die Wand.

(4) She painted/sprayed paint on the wall.

The structure of the English WordNet forces one to encode the differences between these readings (e.g. between (1) and (3)) by assuming two distinct senses that are members of two different superordinates and that correlate with two different syntactic frames. The Location variants (e.g. (1)) are manners of *cover*, and the Locatum variants (e.g. (3)) are manners of *apply*.[7] On the other hand, both variants (e.g. (1) and (3)) can refer to one and the same event, and hence do not grant the distinction of two concepts in the ontology. A better way of representing the close semantic relation between such verb pairs would be by means of a "Perspective" relation. See Baker and Ruppenhofer (2002) and Iwata (2005) for additional discussions of this type of alternation.

---

7. It has been suggested that the Location/Locatum alternation in English is accompanied by a subtle semantic difference; Anderson (1971) states that the Location alternant implies a "holistic" reading whereby the Location is completely affected. In the first sentence, this would mean that the wall is completely covered with paint. However, this claim has been challenged (see Levin 1993).

6. Perspective

To illustrate what we mean by perspective, we give another example, this one involving two lexically distinct verbs. Converse pairs like the English verbs *buy* and *sell* (that are encoded as kinds of semantic opposition (converse) in the Princeton WordNet) express the actions of different participants in the same event, a sale in this case. While the verbs and the corresponding nouns each merit their own lexical entries in English WordNet, for the Grid we want to be able to represent them as encodings of different perspectives on the same event. We propose to do this in the ontology.

Currently, SUMO distinguishes the two processes with entries for the concepts of "Buying" and "Selling". As in FrameNet (Baker et al. 1998), both events are subclasses of "Financial Transaction" and have the same axiom that expresses a dual perspective. The SUO-KIF representation (Niles and Pease 2001, 2003) of the axiom expresses a mutual relation between two statements; one statement in which the Agent of Buying (entity *x*) obtains something from someone (entity *y*) that bears the role ORIGIN, and another statement where entity *y* is the Agent of the Selling process and where the entity *x* bears the role of DESTINATION.

The ontology thus encodes both entities as agents. A more compact encoding would be one where the two verbs *buy* and *sell* are linked to the same process and the argument structure of each verb can be co-indexed with the entities in the axiom (somewhat similar, in FrameNet (Fontenelle 2003, Ruppenhofer, Ellsworth, Petruck, and Johnson 2005), *buy* and *sell* are linked to the abstract event Commercial_transaction via a Perspective relation).

Converse and reciprocal events may be encoded very differently across languages. For example, Russian has two different verbs corresponding to English *marry*, depending on whether the Agent is the bride or the groom. And whereas English encodes the difference between the activities of a teacher and a student in two different verbs, *teach* and *learn*, French uses the same verb, *apprendre*, and encodes the distinction syntactically. Referring to the event (sale, marriage, etc.) in the ontology allows equivalence mappings to the different languages; the encoding of distinct verbs and roles is then confined to the lexicons of each language.

7. Relations in the Global Grid

We anticipate that some lexical and semantic relations will reside in the ontology while others will be restricted to the lexicons of individual languages. Which relations will be encoded, and where they will be encoded, is an open question, subject to the investigation of a sufficiently large number of lexicons. We cite here a few specific cases that must be considered.

7.1. Capturing semantic differences across languages via language-internal relations

Some languages regularly encode semantic distinctions by means of morphology. For example, languages have different means of encoding aspect. Slavic languages systematically distinguish between two members of a verb pair; one verb denotes an ongoing event and the other a completed event. English can mark perfectivity with particles, as in the phrasal verbs *eat up* and *read through*. By contrast, Romance languages tend to mark aspect with different conjugations of the same lexical verb.

In Dutch, verbs with marked aspect can be created by prefixing a verb with *door*: *doorademen*, *dooreten*, *doorfietsen*, *doorlezen*, *doorpraten* (continue to breathe/eat/bike/read/talk). These verbs can only be used with a progressive reading, whereas their base forms can have any aspectual interpretation.[8]

For such cases, an aspectual relation could be introduced to the ontology via formulation in KIF. This relation would link verb synsets expressing different aspects of a given event.[9] Aspectual variants are then considered to be language-specific realizations of more generic events listed in the ontology. The ontology lists a single general process that can have any duration in time and any phase as a component. Aspectual restrictions from the various lexicalizations in languages are thus nothing but phase operators or phase functions that are applied to the same process. They can be formulated in KIF as specific conditions on the generic process.

Other examples are words marked for biological gender. While *teacher* in English is neutral and underspecified with respect to gender, many such

8. Many of these verbs often have an additional specialized aspect of meaning. For example *doorademen* typically means *breathe deeply* as well.
9. Note that these cases cannot be accommodated with the classical WordNet relations, such as troponymy. The aspectually marked verbs do not encode manners of either the activity verbs (*eat*, *read*) or of aspectual verbs like *finish* or *complete*. Currently, these verbs are linked to both activity verbs and aspectual verbs through hyponymy relations, an unsatisfactory solution.

profession nouns in German, Dutch, and the Romance languages are not. In Dutch, "teacher" is expressed both by a morphologically unmarked form *leraar* for the masculine while the marked form *lerares* is feminine. While masculine and feminine nouns map to the corresponding nouns in languages that draw this distinction, both map onto a single noun in languages like English. In this case, the ontology will offer professional roles that are neutral in terms of gender but that can be combined with gender specific relations if the language requires morphological marking of gender.

Both the verbal aspect case and the biological gender case are governed by the same principle: systematic incorporations of semantic relations in lexical choice or morphological marking do not warrant new ontological types. Only if the concept is a type (rigid, essential or obeying unicity) will it be added to the ontology, irrespective of its linguistic encoding. For example, the fact that English and Dutch nouns such as *bos* ('wood') can be used both as group nouns (as in *veel bossen*, ('many woods')) and as mass nouns (as in *veel bos* ('much wood')), does not entail that we need two separate types in the ontology for a group and a mass conceptualization (Vossen 1995). The linguistic encodings of semantic relations can either be expressed through specialized lexicalization relations or through individual KIF expressions involving basic types.

It is an empirical question as to how many and which kinds of relations are optimal for constructing WordNets in the many different Grid languages. Only extensive work on the lexicons of diverse languages will reveal which relations need to be added to the existing ones and which coarse-grained ones should be split into semantically more specific relations.

7.2. Extending relations in WordNets for NLP

WordNet's success as an NLP tool is attributable to its large coverage, free availability, and above all its structure, which carries great potential for applications such as automatic Word Sense Disambiguation (WSD). The interconnection of semantically-related words in a hyper dimensional structure represents a great improvement over the alphabetically organized "flat" word lists in traditional dictionaries. However, the present network is too sparse to do WSD at a satisfactory level of accuracy. For example, there are no cross-part-of-speech (cross-POS) links, so nouns, verbs, adjectives, and adverbs each form their own separate networks within WordNet. Thus, syntagmatic relations, which are arguably as important as WordNet's paradigmatic ones, are not represented.[10] In EuroWordNet, these relations were foreseen but have only been marginally encoded. In comparison, the design of FrameNet was cross-POS from the beginning and is intended to capture exactly these syntagmatic relations.

Boyd-Graber, Fellbaum, Osherson, and Schapire (2006) discuss an effort to improve WordNet's internal connectivity. Students were asked to rate the strength with which one synset "evokes" or "brings to mind" another. Evocation deliberately avoids the common measures of semantic similarity, such as paradigmatic and syntagmatic relatedness, co-occurrence, etc. In fact, when the ratings were compared with the results that such measures give for the same concept pairs, it became clear that evocation captured additional levels of semantic relatedness (see Boyd-Graber, Fellbaum, Osherson, and Schapire 2006 for details). This work suggests that additional semantic relations remain to be explicated and encoded.

7.3. Relations expressed through the ontology or through a WordNet

Another question that must be addressed is that of the relation between the lexicon (the WordNet) and an ontology. The study of ontology goes back at least to Aristotle's "Metaphysics," and, as the name implies, is concerned with what exists, i.e., what concepts and categories there are in the world and what the relations among them are. Under this definition, WordNet is an ontology, in that it records both the concepts and categories that a language encodes and the relations among them, including the hyponymy and meronymy relations proposed by Aristotle. For this reason, WordNet is often called a "lexical ontology".[11]

Ontology has another meaning in the context of AI and Knowledge Engineering, where it is the formal statement of a logical theory. For AI systems, what "exists" is that which can be represented. A formal ontology contains definitions that associate the names of entities in the universe of discourse (e.g., classes, relations, functions, or other objects) with human-readable text describing what the names mean, and formal axioms that constrain the interpretation and well-formed use of these terms (see e.g., Gruber 1993).

---

10. The so-called morpho-semantic links that were recently added to WordNet (Fellbaum and Miller 2003) link morphologically and semantically related words from all four POS; however, they do not capture important co-occurrence phenomena like selectional restrictions.
11. See also, for example, the Ontolinguistic research program at the University of Munich (Schalley and Zaefferer 2007).

The design we have in mind for the Global WordNet Grid is that some relations will be found only in specific WordNets while others reside in the ontology. For example, a morphological-semantic relation that links male and female agents (*actor-actress*) is language-specific rather than universal. On the other hand, hyponymy is probably a universal relation that organizes the lexicon of all languages and that should therefore be part of the ontology.

WordNet's design is driven by at least two motivations. One is to better understand the structure of the lexicon and the way in which concepts are lexicalized according to systematic patterns. Second, WordNets are tools for a range of NLP applications.[12] WordNet can be used for reasoning, as its relations lend themselves to inferencing. For example, given a car, its parts – tires, brakes, etc. – can be inferred.

If WordNet synsets are linked to a formal ontology with First Order Logic statements, reasoning and inferencing would be enabled (Pease and Fellbaum in press). More strongly, reasoning based on logic and a shared ontology could be supported for all Grid languages.

8. Related work

Linguists have been wondering about the universality of concepts and their lexical encoding for a long time. We review two major approaches here that present alternatives to the Global WordNet Grid.

8.1. Natural Semantic Metalanguage

Wierzbicka (1991, 1992, 1996a,b) and Wierzbicka and Goddard (2002) are perhaps the most prolific defenders of a universal inventory of primitive, atomic concepts from which more complex concepts and words can be composed. On the basis of the investigation of many languages, Wierzbicka has proposed a Natural Semantic Metalanguage (NSM). The claim is that all words can be paraphrased by means of a limited number of primitives shared by all languages. The specific inventory of primitives is still subject to research, but currently includes sixty-one primitives.

While Wierzbicka and Goddard's work seems to aim at identifying commonalities among the world's languages and the concepts they encode, the Global WordNet Grid attempts to go further and additionally

12. See the WordNet bibliography at http://lit.csci.unt.edu/~WordNet.

capture language- and culture-specific words and concepts. We doubt that such words as *klunen* can be fully described in terms of a combination of universal semantic primitives.[13]

Another fundamental difference is that the Wierzbicka/Goddard approach starts from the examination of the lexicon of particular languages, based on the assumption that the way speakers label concepts reflects to some extent their view of the world. In the Global WordNet Grid, we are mindful of crosslinguistic differences in lexicalization while maintaining a universal conceptual inventory. This point was addressed by Vossen (1995) who drew a distinction between a conceptual level and a linguistic level of semantics. The ontology represents a language-independent representation of concepts that can be shared across languages. By making this representation explicit, we can determine where the linguistic lexicalization coincides with the independent representation and thus is redundant. Variation within and across languages can be more clearly specified, and an explicit differentiation between the linguistic information that is stored in a lexicon or WordNet and the shared world knowledge is possible. The latter enables logical reasoning that is not language-specific.

8.2. FrameNet, multilingual FrameNets, and SUMO

The FrameNet project (Baker et al. 1998, Fontenelle 2003, Ruppenhofer, Ellsworth, Petruck, and Johnson 2005) is constructing a corpus-based lexicon that can be seen as complementary to the WordNet effort in that it focuses on the syntagmatic properties of words. Word senses, or lexical units, are defined in FrameNet as pairings of word forms with semantic frames. A frame represents a schema or scenario and the roles of its participants, which are called frame elements. Semantic frames may be fundamental (e.g., Being_located) or complex (e.g., Revenge). Frames and frame elements are connected via frame-to-frame relations including Inheritance, Perspective, Using, Precedes, Causative of, and Inchoative of.

FrameNets are being created for different languages. Boas (2005) discusses the use of frames for interlingual representation (see also Boas 2002, Heid and Krüger 1996). With the help of dictionaries and corpora,

13. For that matter, it seems doubtful that the NSM fully captures the meanings of many common concepts. For example, to paraphrase *plant* as "living things/these things can't feel something/these things can't do something," while expressing essential properties of plants, insufficiently reflects the meaning of *plant*.

corresponding semantic frames, lexical units, and their syntagmatic behavior are identified in the target languages, and correspondence links can be established.

One might argue that, like Euro WordNet's ILI, semantic frames are not a true language-independent interlingua, as they are based on English corpus data, and the frame and frame element labels are assigned somewhat intuitively by the builders of FrameNet. However, Boas (2005) argues that frames are language-independent conceptual schemas and that their universality will become clearer as more languages are linked. Already, language- and culture-specific frames have been identified and specifically exempted from the claim to universality made for many other frames (Petruck and Boas 2003).

Scheffczyk, Pease, and Ellsworth (2006) have linked FrameNet Semantic Types like "Manner," "Sentient," and "Location" to SUMO classes. This both allows the formal expression of such Semantic Types and constrains the filler types for frame elements for specific domains when such mapping is done semi-automatically. Moreover, this linking facilitates mapping to WordNet senses.

Frames and frame elements are inspired by the vocabularies of natural language, and FrameNet does not attempt to draw a distinction between linguistic meaning and world knowledge. There are no knowledge constructs independent of the linguistic evidence. By contrast, an ontology may contain concepts not directly motivated by linguistics. Universality in the FrameNet approach follows only from the shared frames across languages, with no independent criteria. It may very well be that the frame encoding of other languages will be influenced by the English FrameNet database, or other languages that preceded the encoding. It is also possible that the implicit interpretation of the corpus occurrences varies across encoders of frames within and across languages, or that criteria are understood differently. Such problems also apply to the EuroWordNet model, where encoders had different interpretations of relations or different interpretations of the target concepts in the WordNet based on the ILI. For these reasons, we advocate a strict independent definition of objects to anchor the meaning of words.

The FrameNet databases will be excellent knowledge sources for mining universal concepts that can be added to the ILI-ontology. Furthermore, FrameNets are valuable linguistic resources to capture the syntagmatic behavior of languages, which is complementary to the information encoded in WordNets and in language-independent ontologies.

9. Conclusion

We discussed a proposal for the development of the GlobalWordNet Grid, an extension of the EuroWordNet model, where the universal index is based on an ontology rather than a language-specific WordNet. We argued that such a database provides a unique opportunity to study words and expressions in languages from a multilingual perspective and relative to an independent notion of what defines a concept.

We are aware of the formidable challenges in realizing the ideas put forth here; much time and effort will be required to build the Grid and to resolve the many complex questions we touched upon. But the result – a unique database for fundamental (cross-)linguistic research and NLP applications – is a goal worth striving for.

Note

Fellbaum's work is supported by the National Science Foundation and the Office of Disruptive Technology.

References

Anderson, Stephen
1971 On the role of deep structure in semantic interpretation. *Foundations of Language* 7 (1982): 387–396.

Apresyan, Yurij
1973 Regular polysemy. *Linguistics* 142: 5–32.

Baker, Collin and Josef Ruppenhofer
2002 FrameNet's Frames vs. Levin's Verb Classes. In: J. Larson and M. Paster (eds.), *Proceedings of the 28th Annual Meeting of the Berkeley Linguistics Society*, 27–38.

Baker, Collin, Charles Fillmore, and John Lowe
1998 The Berkeley FrameNet. In: *Proceedings of the COLING-ACL.* Montreal, Canada.

Black, William, Sabri Elkateb, Horacio Rodriguez, Musa Alkhalifa, Piek Vossen, Adam Pease, Manu Bertran, and Christane Fellbaum
2006 The Arabic WordNet Project. In: *Proceedings of the Conference on Lexical Resources in the European Community*. Genoa, Italy.

Boas, Hans C.
2002 Bilingual FrameNet dictionaries for machine translation. In: M.G. and Araujo, C.P.S. (eds.), *Proceedings of the Third International Conference on Language Resources and Evaluation*, Vol. IV, 1364–1371. Las Palmas (Spain).

Boas, Hans C.
2005 Semantic frames as interlingual representations. *International Journal of Lexicography* 18.4: 445–478.

Boyd-Graber, Jordan, Christiane Fellbaum, Daniel Osherson, and Robert Schapire
2006 Adding dense, weighted, connections to WordNet. In: *Proceedings of the Third Global WordNet Meeting*. Jeju Island, Korea.

Carlson, Gregory
1980 *Reference to kinds in English*. New York: Garland Press.

Fellbaum, Christiane
1990 The English Verb Lexicon as a Semantic Net. *International Journal of Lexicography* 3: 278–301.

Fellbaum, C. (ed.)
1998 *WordNet: An electronic lexical database*. Cambridge, MA: MIT Press.

Fellbaum, Christiane
2002 The semantics of troponymy. In: R. Green, S.H. Myang, and C. Bean (eds.), *The Semantics of Relationships: an Interdisciplinary Perspective*, 23–34. Dordrecht: Kluwer.

Fellbaum, Christiane and Judy Kegl
1989 Taxonomic structure and object deletion in the English verbal system. In: K. de Jong, and Y. No (eds.), *Proceedings of the Sixth Eastern States Conference on Linguistics*, 94–103. Columbus, Ohio: Ohio State University.

Fellbaum, Christiane, and George A. Miller
2003 Morphosemantic links in WordNet. *Traitement Automatique des Langues* 44.2: 69–80.

Fontenelle, Thierry (ed.)
2003 *International Journal of Lexicography*, Vol. 28. Special issue devoted to FrameNet.

Gross, Derek, Ute Fischer, and George A. Miller
1989 The organization of adjectival meanings. *Journal of Memory and Language* 28: 92–106.

Gruber, Thomas
1993 A translation approach to portable ontologies. *Knowledge Acquisition* 5: 199–220.

Guarino, Nicola and Christopher Welty
2002a Identity and subsumption. In: R. Green, S.H. Myang, and C. Bean (eds.), *The Semantics of Relationships: an Interdisciplinary Perspective*. Dordrecht: Kluwer.

Guarino, Nicola and Christopher Welty
2002b Evaluating ontological decisions with OntoClean. *Communications of the ACM* 45.2: 61–65.

Heid, Ulrich and Katja Krüger
1996 Multilingual lexicons based on Frame Semantics. In: *Proceedings of the AISB Workshop on Multilinguality in the Lexicon*. Brighton, UK.

Iwata, Seizi
2005 Locative alternation and two levels of verb meaning. *Cognitive Linguistics* 16.2: 355–407.
Labov, William
1972 *Language in the Inner City*. Philadelphia: University of Pennsylvania Press.
Levin, Beth
1993 *English Verb Classes and Alternations*. Chicago: University of Chicago Press.
Masolo, Claudio, Stefano Borgo, Aldo Gangemi, Nicola Guarino, and Alessandro Oltramari
2003 *WonderWeb Deliverable D18 Ontology Library*. Laboratory for Applied Ontology – IST-CNR. Trento, Italy.
Michaelis, Laura and Josef Ruppenhofer
2001 *Beyond alternations*. Stanford: CSLI Publications.
Miller, George A. (ed.)
1990 WordNet. *Special Issue of the International Journal of Lexicography* 3.
Miller, George A. and Florentian Hristea
2006 WordNet Nouns: classes and instances. *Computational Linguistics* 32.1: 1–3.
Niles, Ian and Adam Pease
2001 Towards a standard upper ontology. In: *Proceedings of the 2nd International Conference on Formal Ontology in Information Systems*. Ogunquit, Maine.
Niles, Ian and Adam Pease
2003 Linking lexicons and ontologies: mapping WordNet to the Suggested Upper Merged Ontology. In: *Proceedings of the International Conference on Information and Knowledge Engineering*. Las Vegas, Nevada.
Niles, Ian and Allan Terry
2004 The MILO: A general-purpose, mid-level ontology. In: *Proceedings of the International Conference on Information and Knowledge Engineering*, 15–19. Las Vegas, Nevada.
Pease, Adam and Christiane Fellbaum
(in press) Formal ontology as interlingua. In: C.-R. Huang and Laurent Prevot (eds.), *Ontologies and Lexical Resources*. Cambridge: Cambridge University Press.
Petruck, M.R.L. and H.C. Boas
2003 All in a day's week. In: E. Hajičová, A. Kotěšovcová, and J. Mírovský (eds.), *Proceedings of the 17th International Congress of Linguists*, CD-ROM. Prague: Matfyzpress.
Pustejovsky, James
1995 *The Generative Lexicon*. Cambridge, MA: MIT Press.

Ruppenhofer, Josef, Michael Ellsworth, Miriam Petruck, and Christopher Johnson
2005 *FrameNet: Theory and Practice*. ICSI Berkeley. http://framenet.isci.berkeley.edu

Schalley, Andrea and Dietmar Zaefferer (eds.)
2007 *Ontolinguistics*. Berlin: Mouton de Gruyter.

Scheffczyk, Jan, Adam Pease, and Michael Ellsworth
2006 Linking FrameNet to the Suggested Upper Merged Ontology. In: Brandon Bennett and Christiane Fellbaum (eds.), *Proceedings of Formal Ontology in Information Systems (FOIS-2006)*, 289–300. IOS Press.

Sinha, Manish, Mahesh Reddy, and Pushpak Bhattacharyya
2006 An approach towards construction and application of multilingual Indo-WordNet. In: *Proceedings of the Third Global WordNet Conference*, 259–264. Jeju Island, Korea.

Tufis, Dan (ed.)
2004 The BalkaNet Project. *Special Issue of the Romanian Journal of Information Science and Technology*, 1–248.

Vossen, Piek
1995 *Grammatical and conceptual individuation in the lexicon*. Ph.D. Thesis, Universiteit van Amsterdam.

Vossen, Piek (ed.)
1998 *EuroWordNet: a multilingual database with lexical semantic networks for European Languages*. Kluwer, Dordrecht.

Vossen, Piek, Wim Peters, and Julio Gonzalo
1999 Towards a universal index of meaning. In: *Proceedings of ACL-99 Workshop, Siglex-99, Standardizing Lexical Resources*, 81–90. University of Maryland, College Park, MD.

Wierzbicka, Anna
1991 *Cross-cultural pragmatics*. Berlin: Mouton de Gruyter.

Wierzbicka, Anna
1992 *Semantics, culture and cognition*. Oxford: Oxford University Press.

Wierzbicka, Anna
1996a *Semantics, primes and universals*. Oxford: Oxford University Press.

Wierzbicka, Anna
1996b *Understanding cultures through their key words*. Oxford: Oxford University Press.

Wierzbicka, Anna and Cliff Goddard (eds.)
2002 *Meaning and Universal Grammar*. Amsterdam: John Benjamins.

Subject index

Author index

Frame index

Bei Fragen zur Produktsicherheit wenden Sie sich bitte an:
If you have any questions regarding product safety,
please contact:

Walter de Gruyter GmbH
Genthiner Straße 13
10785 Berlin
productsafety@degruyterbrill.com